Scientific Discovery

W9-CKF-374

Scientific Discovery
Computational Explorations of the Creative Processes

Pat Langley
Herbert A. Simon
Gary L. Bradshaw
Jan M. Zytkow

The MIT Press
Cambridge, Massachusetts
London, England

© 1987 by The Massachusetts Institute of Technology

All rights reserved. No part of this book may be reproduced in any form by any electronic or mechanical means (including photocopying, recording, or information storage and retrieval) without permission in writing from the publisher.

This book was set in Times New Roman by Asco Trade Typesetting Ltd., Hong Kong, and printed and bound by Halliday Lithograph in the United States of America.

Library of Congress Cataloging-in-Publication Data

Langley, Pat.
  Scientific discovery.

  Bibliography: p.
  Includes index.
  1. Science—Methodology. 2. Science—Philosophy. 3. Science—History.
  4. Creative ability in science. I. Title.
Q175.L2443 1987   502.8   86-10258
ISBN 0-262-12116-6
ISBN 0-262-62052-9 (pbk.)

Contents

I abhor your pretentious "insight." I respect conscious guessing, because it comes from the best human qualities: courage and modesty.

Imre Lakatos, *Proofs and Refutations* (p. 30)

Preface

This book, like all works of science, is a progress report. Science is a seamless web: each idea spins out to a new research task, and each research finding suggests a repair or an elaboration of the network of theory. Most of the links connecting the nodes are short, each attaching to its predecessors. Weaving our way through the web, we stop from time to time to rest and survey the view—and to write a paper or a book.

This book could have been written a year earlier, with a few omissions; it could have waited until next year, when perhaps some of the problems it leaves unsolved will have their answers. The very strategy that underlies it makes stopping points almost arbitrary; our ultimate goal is to provide a comprehensive theory of the processes that scientists employ in making scientific discoveries, and there is not a single such process but a great many. Hence, we have adopted the strategy of divide and conquer. After constructing a rough taxonomy of the processes of discovery, we examine those processes one by one, taking up a new candidate whenever we think we have given a fairly satisfactory explanation of the previous one.

The table of contents indicates how far this strategy had carried us when we paused to make this report. The book is divided into four parts. Part I introduces the subject of discovery, defines the scope of our work, and discusses some of the issues that have surrounded and still surround our topic. Parts II and III contain the main body of our results, largely in the form of accounts of the performance of computer programs that simulate human thought processes to make scientific discoveries. Part II is devoted largely to the processes for inducing quantitative theories from data. Part III is devoted mainly to the processes for inducing qualitative descriptive and structural theories from data. In part IV, on the basis of our experience, we discuss at a lower level of precision how the programs described in the preceding chapters could be combined into a single, more general discovery system, and we describe a wide range of the other component processes that enter into scientific discovery.

Throughout the book, but especially in chapters 1, 2, 10, and 11, we address some of the central issues in the philosophy and history of science. Do data lead and theories follow (as is the case in most of our discovery programs), or is theory the driving force? What is the evidence for "paradigms" and "paradigm shifts," in the Kuhnian sense? Can there be such a thing as a theory of scientific discovery (as distinguished from a theory of verification)? Can the magic and mystery be removed from such terms as "creativity" and "insight," and can an empirical account be given of the processes to which those terms are applied? We do not think that we have arrived at definitive answers to all of these questions. We do believe that our findings, derived mainly from the evidence provided by our computer programs, cast new light on them.

Does this book represent "data-driven" science, as do many of the discovery processes that we examine? Not entirely. Our starting point and "paradigm" is contemporary information-processing psychology, or cognitive science. Currently accepted theory in this domain suggests that the processes of scientific discovery may be describable and explainable simply as special classes of problem-solving processes, closely akin to the processes that have been identified in other domains of problem solving. This possibility provides the central heuristics that guided us in constructing our theory and embodying it in computer programs. The book itself provides the evidence of how well these heuristics served us and how powerful the paradigm has proved to be.

In conducting the research and in writing the book, we have incurred the usual number of intellectual debts. Most of these are acknowledged in the references and the footnotes, but we should like to mention here the friends who have read and commented upon drafts of our manuscript—Saul Amarel, Clark Glymour, Frederic L. Holmes, Elaine Kant, Allen Newell, and Paul Thagard—and The MIT Press's anonymous readers. Their advice, suggestions, and words of support and disagreement have enabled us to improve the book in innumerable ways. If it still does not meet the high standards they set for it, only we are to blame. We are grateful also to Elaine Atkinson and to Dorothea P. Simon, who assisted with the references and the bibliography and helped put the manuscript into shape. Finally, we thank The MIT Press and its editors for their cheerful and effective aid in the final stages of the long journey from our initial glimpse of the possibilities of explaining scientific discovery to the publication of this book.

The research reported in this book received generous support from a number of foundations and funding agencies. Grants for various parts of the work were made over the past decade by the National Institute of Mental Health (MH-07722), the National Science Foundation (HES75-22021, SPI-7914852, and IST-7918266), the Office of Naval Research (N00014-82-K-0168), the Advanced Research Projects Agency of the Department of Defense (F33615-78-C-1551 and F44620-73-C0074), and the Alfred P. Sloan Foundation. We are grateful to all of them for their aid, but our findings and conclusions are, of course, our own.

When we were carrying out the research described in this book, all four of us were associated with Carnegie-Mellon University. We are deeply indebted to the university, and especially its Psychology and Computer Science departments, for lavish provision of computing resources, intellectual stimulation, and the friendship of colleagues. As the book goes to press, our academic affiliations are as follows. Langley: Department of Computer Science, University of California, Irvine. Simon: Departments of Computer Science and Psychology, Carnegie-Mellon University. Bradshaw: Department of Psychology, University of Colorado, Boulder. Zytkow: Department of Computer Science, Wichita State University, and Institute of Philosophy, University of Warsaw.

I INTRODUCTION TO THE THEORY OF SCIENTIFIC DISCOVERY

In this part we define scientific discovery and its many facets and discuss the relation between the processes of discovering theories and the processes of verifying them.

1 What Is Scientific Discovery?

In the scientist's house are many mansions. Not only does science divide into innumerable disciplines and subdisciplines, but within any single discipline the progress of science calls for the most diverse repertoire of activities—activities so numerous and diverse that it would seem that any person could find one to his or her taste. Outsiders often regard science as a sober enterprise, but we who are inside see it as the most romantic of all callings. Both views are right. The romance adheres to the processes of scientific discovery, the sobriety to the responsibility for verification.

Histories of science put the spotlight on discovery. Everyone knows by what accident Fleming discovered penicillin, but only specialists can tell us much about how that discovery was subsequently put to the test. Everyone knows of Kekule's dream of the benzene ring, but only chemists can tell us why the structure of that molecule was problematic, and how and when it was finally decided that the problem had been solved. The story of scientific progress reaches its periodic climaxes at the moments of discovery; verification is the essential but not very glamorous aftermath—the sorting out of facts that comes after the tale's denouement and tells us that matters worked out all right (if only for a while, as in the story of phlogiston).

The philosophy of science has taken a very different tack than the discipline of the history of science. In the philosophy of science, all the emphasis is on verification, on how we can tell the true gold of scientific law from the fool's gold of untested fantasy. In fact, it is still the majority view among philosophers of science that only verification is a proper subject of inquiry, that nothing of philosophical interest can be said about the process of discovery.

In one respect the philosophers are right. What distinguishes science from the other works of the human imagination is precisely the insistence on testing, on subjecting hypotheses to the most intense scrutiny with the help of empirical evidence. If we are to distinguish science from poetry, we must have a theory of verification or confirmation that tells us exactly how to make that distinction.

But we believe that science is also poetry, and—perhaps even more heretical—that discovery has its reasons, as poetry does. However romantic and heroic we find the moment of discovery, we cannot believe either that the events leading up to that moment are entirely random and chaotic or that they require genius that can be understood only by congenial minds. We believe that finding order in the world must itself be a process impregnated with purpose and reason. We believe that the process of discovery can be described and modeled, and that there are better and worse routes to discovery—more and less efficient paths.

With that claim, we open ourselves to attack from the other flank. Do we think it is possible to write books of advice to poets? Are we not aware that writing poems (and making scientific discoveries) is a creative process, sometimes even calling for genius? But we can avoid dangerous terms like "genius" by asking more modest questions. We can at least inquire into the *sufficient* conditions for making a poem (or a discovery). If writing poetry calls for creativity, it also calls for craft. A poet becomes a craftsman (if not a creative poet) by long study and practice. We might aspire to distill and write down what a poet learns in this arduous apprenticeship. If we did that, we would have a book on the writing of poetry (there are some such on the library shelves). Perhaps its advice would take us merely to the level of superior doggerel, but we could determine that only after we had tested the advice by experiment—by writing poetry on its principles. Thus, the question of how poetry is written (or can or should be written) becomes a researchable question, one that can be approached with the standard methods of scientific inquiry.

This is no less true of scientific discovery than it is of poetry. Whether there is method in discovery is a question whose answer is open to scientific study. We may fail to find methods that account for discovery, or for the greater success of some would-be discoverers than of others, but we are free to look for them. And if we arrive at some hypotheses about them, then we must test these just as we test any other hypotheses in science.

The aims of this book are to give an account of some methods of scientific discovery and to demonstrate the efficacy of these methods by using them to make a number of discoveries (more accurate, rediscoveries). The methods we propose are embedded in a set of computer programs, and they are tested by providing the programs with data that they can explore in search of regularities.

The work has several motivations, which have already been hinted at in our introductory remarks.

First, it seeks to investigate the psychology of the discovery process, and to provide an empirically tested theory of the information-processing mechanisms that are implicated in that process. (However, it is mainly limited to finding a set of mechanisms that is sufficient to account for discovery. It will provide little in the way of detailed comparison with human performance.)

Second, it undertakes to provide some foundations for a normative theory of discovery—for the "how to make discoveries" book. Specifically, it proposes and evaluates a substantial number of heuristics that are designed to facilitate the discovery process and raise its efficiency over chance or blind trial-and-error search.

Third, it reexamines the relations between the processes of discovery and the processes of verification, finding that these two classes of processes are far more intimately connected than is generally suggested in the literature of philosophy of science.

Fourth, since most of the examples we use to test our hypotheses are drawn from the history of science, it suggests a methodology for examining the history of discoveries that may prove to be a useful addition to the repertoire of the historians of science.

Thus, this book enters a number of science's mansions, including cognitive psychology, artificial intelligence, the philosophy of science, and the history of science. We hope that it will excite the interest (and elicit the corrections) of practitioners in all these fields and of scientists working in other fields who are curious about their own cognitive processes. If it does that, it will have served its purpose: to contribute to the understanding of discovery in science.

Discovery as Problem Solving

A hypothesis that will be central to our inquiry is that the mechanisms of scientific discovery are not peculiar to that activity but can be subsumed as special cases of the general mechanisms of problem solving. The question whether this hypothesis is true, and to what extent, is properly postponed until we have reached the end of our exploration, for as we go along we shall be collecting just the materials that are needed to test it.

Our method of inquiry will be to build a computer program (actually a succession of programs) that is capable of making nontrivial scientific discoveries and whose method of operation is based on our knowledge of human methods of solving problems—in particular, the method of heuristic selective search.

The attractiveness of our approach lies precisely in the fact that it allows us to draw on a large body of knowledge that has been accumulated by research on human problem solving. We do not have to make our theories of discovery from whole cloth; rather, we can derive them from theories of problem solving that have already been tested extensively in the laboratory. Of course, if our hypothesis is wrong—if scientific discovery is something quite different from ordinary problem solving—our labor will be lost. But we have already peeked at the end of the book and know that matters did not work out too badly.

There is a second attraction in the hypothesis that scientific discovery is a species of normal problem solving: It meets our desire for parsimony. It minimizes the degree to which the work of discovery must be treated as the exercise of a special human faculty. It preserves a framework in which all forms of serious human thought—in science, in the arts, in the professions, in school, in personal life—may reveal their commonalities.

The thesis that scientific discovery is problem solving writ large, and that it can be simulated by computer, is not completely novel. It goes back at least as far as a paper delivered in 1958 by Newell, Shaw, and Simon (see Newell et al. 1962), and it was carried forward in additional investigations by Simon (1966, 1973a) and Buchanan (1966) and in the construction of such computer programs as meta-DENDRAL (Buchanan and Mitchell 1978), AM (Lenat 1977), and EURISKO (Lenat 1983). Huesmann and Cheng (1973) described a program that induced numerical laws from data, and Gerwin (1974) described another such program. A decade earlier, Simon and Kotovsky (1963) had constructed a program that could find the pattern in letter sequences and extrapolate them. The research on BACON, the first of the simulation programs to be discussed in this book, began in the mid 1970s (see Langley 1978).

Of course, there are several respects in which scientific discovery is obviously different from other instances of problem solving. First, scientific inquiry is a social process, often involving many scientists and often extending over long periods of time. Much human problem solving, especially the sort that has been studied in psychology laboratories, involves a single individual working for a few hours. A second way in which scientific inquiry differs from much other problem solving is in the apparent indefiniteness of its goals. Consider the missionaries-and-cannibals puzzle: Three missionaries and three cannibals are trying to cross a river in a boat that holds no more than two persons. Everyone knows how to row. Missionaries may never be left on either bank with a larger number of cannibals, because the missionaries will then be eaten. How can the party cross the river? Here we know exactly what we want to achieve as a solution: We want a plan for transporting the missionaries and the cannibals across the river in the available small boat without any casualties from drowning or dining.

Some scientific discovery is like that. The mathematicians who found a proof for the four-color theorem knew exactly what they were seeking; so did Adams and Leverrier when they detected Neptune while searching for a celestial object that would explain anomalies in the orbits of the other planets. However, in much scientific inquiry—including some of the most important and challenging—the targets are less sharp. Initially, what were Darwin and his predecessors seeking more definite than a way of bringing order to the complex, confusing data of biology and fossil geology? Toward the end of the eighteenth century, just before the work of Lavoisier, exactly how would one have defined the "problem of combustion," and what would have been accepted as a satisfactory account of the phenomena to which that term was applied? Indeed, finding problems and formulating them is as integral a part of the inquiry process as is solving them, once they have been found. And setting criteria of goal satisfaction, so that indefinite goals become definite, is an essential part of formulating problems.

In spite of these differences between scientific inquiry and other problem solving, it is quite possible that the component processes of scientific discovery are not qualitatively distinct from the processes that have been observed in simpler problem-solving situations. Solving complex problems generally involves decomposing them into sets of simpler problems and attacking those. It could well be the case (and we will argue that it is) that the component problem solving involved in scientific discovery has no special properties to distinguish it from other problem solving.

In this book we will be concerned more with describing and explaining scientific discovery than with providing a normative theory of the process. Indeed, as we shall discuss more fully in chapter 2, the very possibility of a normative theory has been challenged by many philosophers of science. However, if we succeed in producing a credible explanation of discovery, that explanation will itself constitute a first approximation to a normative theory. This is especially true if the explanation is constructive—if it exhibits a set of processes that, when executed, actually make scientific discoveries. The explanation we shall propose is of this constructive kind.

Problem Spaces and Search

Since in this book scientific discovery is to be treated as a special case of human problem solving, we must begin with an account of the problem-solving process as it is currently described in cognitive psychology. In the broadest terms, the account is this (see Anderson 1983; Newell and Simon 1972; Simon 1979):

• The human brain is an information-processing system whose memories hold interrelated symbol structures and whose sensory and motor connections receive encoded symbols from the outside via sensory organs and send encoded symbols to motor organs. It accomplishes its thinking by copying and reorganizing symbols in memory, receiving and outputting symbols, and comparing symbol structures for identity or difference.

• The brain solves problems by creating a symbolic representation of the problem (called the *problem space*) that is capable of expressing initial, intermediate, and final problem situations as well as the whole range of concepts employed in the solution process, and using the *operators* that are contained in the definition of the problem space to modify the symbol structures that describe the problem situation (thereby conducting a mental *search* for a solution through the problem space).

• The search for a problem solution is not carried on by random trial and error, but is selective. It is guided in the direction of a *goal situation* (or symbolic expressions describing a goal) by rules of thumb, called *heuristics*. Heuristics make use of information extracted from the problem definitions and the states already explored in the problem space to identify promising paths for search.

Thus, for problem solving we postulate an information-processing system that creates problem representations and searches selectively through trees of intermediate situations, seeking the goal situation and using heuristics to guide its search.

The missionaries-and-cannibals puzzle provides a classical example of this problem-solving paradigm. The problem space allows the system to represent the various possible distributions of missionaries, cannibals, and the boat on the two sides of the river—illegal as well as legal combinations. A "move" operator changes the distribution, carrying various boatloads of passengers from one side of the river to the other. Test processes determine whether the boat has been overloaded, or whether the resulting redistribution is a legal one. The process that chooses moves compares them and selects one that seems to carry the system closer to its goal. It may employ a heuristic to consider first the move that carries the greatest number of passengers to the far side of the river, or the move that brings back the smallest number.

Dozens of computer programs have been written to represent and solve the missionaries-and-cannibals problem, and many other puzzle-like problems, within the framework of the heuristic-search paradigm. A mountain of empirical evidence has shown that human subjects solve these and other kinds of problems using the same general paradigm (but, of course, with innumerable variations in the precise structure of the problem space, the move operators, the tests, and the selective heuristics embedded in the operators and the tests). The heuristic-search paradigm has become the core of a theory of human problem solving that is now widely accepted.

The search space in the missionaries-and-cannibals problem is trivially small—there are only sixteen possible legal distributions. (The difficulty of that problem for people lies not in the size of the space to be searched but in the counterintuitive direction of a crucial move that violates the heuristic rules of selection by calling for more than the minimum number of passengers to be taken back to the starting point.) In most problems that people encounter, however, the problem space is far larger than could be searched in any acceptable amount of time. The search can be expected to grow exponentially with its length. If B is the number of alternative moves at each choice point and L is the length of the path to the goal (measured in number of choice points), than a random search would require, on average, $\frac{1}{2}B^L$ moves. Heuristics that can reduce the "branchiness" (B) of the search tree, or its length (L), may diminish the search time by many orders of magnitude. Solution time may also be reduced dramatically by the discovery of a problem representation, and a corresponding problem space, that calls for less search.

In any problem situation where the solver has a large amount of substantive knowledge to bring to bear, the theory of problem solving must be enlarged to show how that knowledge is used to facilitate the solution of problems. One strongly supported hypothesis is that the knowledgeable person (the "expert") holds in memory specific information about steps to take in any one of a large number of eventualities. Further, this information is "indexed" by features of situations to which the information is relevant, so that the expert, on noticing the feature in the current problem situation, will retrieve and apply the information. These cue-action pairs are usually called *productions*; it is thought that in typical domains of human professional expertise they may number 50,000 or more (Chase and Simon 1973). Most of the expert systems now burgeoning in artificial intelligence are built around systems of productions of this kind, although the size of the production set usually falls far short of 50,000. In such production systems, then, artificial or human, the productions contain most of the heuristic information that guides search. The flexibility of such systems, their sensitivity to situational cues, is limited only by the number and the discriminating power of the productions that are stored.

Many details of the human problem-solving process remain to be nailed down. There is not full agreement on the structure of memories, although in broad terms there is some consensus that part of the human cognitive system serves as a large store of indefinite duration (long-term memory) and another part as a very small working memory (short-term memory). Short-term memory, where the arguments of operators must be held, constitutes a bottleneck that, at the macro level, requires the system to operate in serial fashion. There is much disagreement and debate as to the respective roles of serial and parallel processes in finer descriptions of the system. These undetermined features of system architecture will not, in general, concern us in this volume, although we will have occasion to comment on them from time to time. The "hardware" we have employed in all our computer simulations is a standard von Neumann computer, essentially a wholly serial machine. However, the computer is capable of simulating processes that may be parallel in the human brain—for example, the discrimination of cues, which could be argued on the basis of evidence available at the present time to be either serial or parallel (Feigenbaum and Simon 1984).

The preceding paragraphs describe as much of the general structure of human problem solving as we shall need to draw upon. There remain the tasks of characterizing more specifically the heuristics that make search selective and the peculiar characteristics of the search for laws (inductive search).

Heuristics

The selectivity of heuristics is based on information, and that information must come from the structure of the task. If a task has no structure other than a random one, then there is no pattern to be detected and incorporated in the problem solver's problem space. And if there is no pattern in the problem space, then there is no basis for the construction of selective heuristics. Then, search will necessarily proceed randomly, by trial and error.

The safecracker's problem provides a simple example of how problem structure is translated into selective heuristics. Consider a safe that, for security, has been provided with ten dials, each numbered from 0 to 99. One must set all ten dials to the correct numbers in order to open the safe. If that is all the information one has about the safe, one can expect to take, on average, $\frac{1}{2} \times 100^{10}$ (that is, 50 billion billion) trials to open it. If, however, each dial emits a faint click when it is turned to the correct setting (and if one knows that), one can open the safe with only 50×10 (that is, 500) trials. A little information here—ten small clicks—goes a long way.

The ordinary algorithm for solving linear equations provides an example of a heuristic so powerful that it eliminates search entirely. Consider the equation

$$AX + B = CX + D.$$

The test defines a solution as any expression of the form $X = E$ such that $AE + B = CE + D$. A stupid search, not requiring any special information, would simply substitute arbitrary numbers for X until a solution was found. However, the algorithm tells us exactly what to do in order to arrive directly at the answer: First, get rid of B on the left-hand side of the equation by subtracting it from both sides. Then, eliminate CX in exactly the same way. Finally, divide both sides of the resulting expression by $(A - C)$; this yields the answer. (We will have something to say later about where the knowledge of this method came from—that is, how we knew it to be an efficient procedure. For the moment, we can just agree that we learned it in algebra class and that it works.)

Now, the powerful algorithm for our algebra problem seemed to derive from very special knowledge of algebra. Do all heuristics call for such special knowledge, or are some of them more general? The answer is that there are more general heuristics, but that these, in contrast with the algebra algorithm (a *strong method*) are properly denoted *weak methods*. We can picture a hierarchy of heuristics, with the top levels consisting of very general algorithms that require little information about the task domain to which they are applied and are correspondingly applicable to a great many domains. As we proceed downward in the hierarchy of heuristics, we make more and more demands on information about the task domain, and there are correspondingly fewer domains to which the heuristics apply—they become more and more task specific as we descend through the hierarchy. Since the more general heuristics operate on the basis of less information, we may expect them to be less selective, and hence less powerful, than heuristics that make more use of information about the task structure. Hence, general heuristics are weak methods, while task-specific heuristics, such as our procedure for solving algebra equations, may be strong methods. The less structured a problem-solving task is, the less information one can draw upon to construct strong heuristics.

The following is a rough description of some of the weak methods that have emerged from the study of problem solving by humans and computers. The first method is very general; the other two are specializations of it.

- The most basic method is *generate and test*. One operator generates moves in the problem space; a second operator tests the after-move situations to determine if the goal has been reached. Whether the generate-and-test heuristic produces completely random search or whether it searches selectively depends on the structure of the generator. If the generator is itself selective, trying only certain moves and trying them in an efficient order, then problem solutions may be found relatively rapidly. Thus, to evaluate such a system we must know something about the knowledge that is built into the generator.
- A slight modification of a generate-and-test procedure brings us to *hill climbing*, in which the evaluation of progress provided by the test is used to select the next branch from which to search. The effectiveness of this heuristic depends upon the accuracy with which the evaluative test estimates the distance of the current situation from the goal.
- An important weak method that has been observed to be widely used in human problem solving in domains where more specialized heuristics are not available is *means-ends analysis*, in which a test heuristic detects specific differences between the current situation and the goal and evokes specific move operators that are relevant to removing just those kinds of differences that have been detected. the algorithm we used to solve the algebraic equation could be redescribed as an application of means-ends analysis: Differences are noted between the current equation and the form of the goal ("$X = E$"). Thus, at the beginning, there is a constant on the left side of the equality, which is absent from the goal expression. When that difference has been removed, there is a term on the right containing X, which is absent from the goal expression. Finally, when that has been removed, the X on the left has a coefficient, $(A - C)$, which has to be removed to match the goal expression.

Corresponding to each of these differences, the skilled problem solver has available an action for removing the difference. If there is a constant on the left, it is removed by subtracting it from both sides; and so on. In fact, the whole system of heuristics can be organized as a very simple production system in which the cues or "conditions" are the differences noted between current and goal expressions, while the action associated with each condition is an action that removes that difference. This production system (containing only three productions!) can be regarded as an expert system for solving these simple equations in algebra.

It should not be supposed that means-ends analysis will always, or even often, provide such a powerful and efficient problem-solving engine as it does in this particular case. Again, all depends on the content of the productions that connect differences with actions for removing them. And the productions depend, in turn, on what structure the problem has, and what the problem solver knows about that structure.

Some systems of heuristics guarantee the production of solutions to problems in a particular domain.[1] Most do not. Some systems of heuristics even guarantee to find the solution without false leads or backtracking. Generally, however, for most of the difficult problems of everyday life and of science, we have no guarantee that our heuristics will lead us to a solution, or that the path that gets there (if one does) will be the shortest path. Most often, we have to settle for heuristics that provide a relatively good chance of success without extraordinary effort. (Of course, both chances and effort are defined relative to other heuristics that may be available for the problem domain.)

There are other weak methods besides the three mentioned above, but a complete list is not needed. When we describe BACON and our other simulation programs, we will introduce the specific heuristics (many of them clearly weak methods) that the program employs.

Inductive Search

If scientific discovery is problem solving, as we claim, then it is problem solving of a special kind. The starting point for the discoveries with which

---

1. Programs that offer such guarantees are often called "algorithms," in distinction from "heuristic programs" that do not. But outside the discipline of artificial intelligence the term "algorithm" is usually applied to any computer program that is guaranteed to terminate, with or without a solution of the problem posed. For precision, it is better to follow the general usage and to say "algorithms that guarantee solution" when that is intended.

we shall be concerned is a body of data and/or some scientific laws that are presumed to be already known. The goal is a new law, or pattern, that describes the data (and, possibly, explains them). In the extreme case in which the set of previously known laws is empty, we call the discovery process *data driven*. At the other extreme, the data set may be empty, in which case we will call the discovery process *theory driven*. We will consider data-driven discovery first; later, we will consider discovery in which both data and prior theory play a role.

Induction—the process of going from a finite set of facts (a body of data) to a universally quantified generalization (a law)—has been the subject of an enormous literature. That literature is concerned with both discovery (how to make the induction) and verification (how to justify the induction once it has been made). In early discussions of induction, such as those of Francis Bacon (1620), the questions of discovery and verification are not sharply distinguished; what is wanted is a law that fits the data and can be defended as a proper description of them. Since Hume, however, the great weight of emphasis has been put on the process of justifying inductions. After two centuries of vigorous discussion, there is no consensus among philosophers about the correct answer to the problem of justification, or even as to whether there is something that might properly be called a "correct answer."

Since the 1930s it has often been denied that the process of discovery is a proper topic for philosophy. Karl Popper (1961), and others, banished it from the philosophy of science. Only since the mid 1970s has there been a renewal of interest in the nature of the discovery process and the logic underlying it. We will have a great deal more to say on this topic in the next chapter, but here we will simply assume that the discovery process is describable and that there are ways of talking about better and worse methods of discovery.

Problems may be categorized on the basis of how *well structured* they are. Problems are called well structured to the extent that they meet the following conditions:[2]

• There is a definite criterion for testing any proposed solution, and there is a mechanizable process for applying the criterion.
• There is at least one problem space in which can be represented the initial

2. See Simon 1973b, pp. 305–306.

problem state, the goal state, and all other states that may be reached or considered in the course of attempting a solution of the problem.

- Attainable state changes (legal moves) can be represented in a problem space as transitions from given states to the states directly attainable from them. Considerable moves, whether legal or not, can also be represented.
- Any knowledge that the problem solver can acquire about the problem can be represented in one or more problem spaces.
- All these conditions hold in the strong sense that the basic processes postulated require only practicable amounts of computation, and the information postulated is effectively available to the processes (that is, available with the help of only practicable amounts of search).

To the extent that these conditions are not met, the problem is called *ill structured*. Clearly, "well structured" and "ill structured" define a continuum of problem types and not a dichotomy. Moreover, such phrases as "practicable amounts of computation" are defined only relative to the computational power of a problem-solving system. Finally, as problems are attacked, they acquire new structure progressively, especially in the form of well-structured subproblems. At first blush, it might seem that problems of scientific discovery will all be far toward the ill-structured end of this continuum. That is not necessarily so. For the most part, the problems we shall pose to our programs in later chapters, although they are important scientific problems, are relatively well structured. It will be convenient to postpone most discussion of this point until we see what those problems are, and how they are presented to the programs. But we will anticipate that discussion with a few comments.

First, what is the criterion for testing the proposed solution to a discovery problem? In our programs the criterion simply is that the law that is discovered should fit the data set well enough. In turn, "well enough" is defined in terms of criteria of approximation that are incorporated in the programs as parameters. For example, it may be required that no observation depart from its theoretically predicted value by more than 3 percent. In later chapters we will consider what constitutes an acceptable approximation and how inexact data can be handled in a discovery program.

Second, the distinction made here between well-structured and ill-structured problems of discovery is reminiscent of Kuhn's (1970b) distinction between normal and revolutionary science, for the Kuhnian notion of paradigm shift would seem to imply a change in problem representation.

Perhaps a discovery system that handles only relatively well-structured problems, operating within a stable problem space, is engaged only in normal science. Revolutionary science may require capabilities for handling ill-structured problems. However, the boundaries between well-structured and ill-structured, on the one hand, and normal and revolutionary, on the other, cannot be quite the same; if we understand Kuhn correctly, normal science does not involve finding any fundamental new laws at all, but simply applying laws that are already known or developing subsidiary laws that fill in the dominant paradigm. Normal science may discover anomalies within the current paradigm, and failure to resolve them calls for revolutionary activity that, at least at the outset, is sufficiently ill structured to admit changes in representation. But it would appear that an effective discovery system, no matter what its restriction to well-structured problems, must be revolutionary by one of Kuhn's criteria, for such a system does discover new laws that are not consequences of an existing paradigm but derive directly from data. Of course, the system may be capable only of producing little, nonviolent revolutions, not those of a more earthshaking kind after which one would say that a new paradigm had emerged. Our final evaluation of these questions must await our examination of the simulation programs and their performance.

Third, a brief comment on the justification of induction. It is well known that no universally quantified generalization can be verified decisively by a finite set of observations. Not only may subsequent observations overthrow the verification, but it will never be the case that the generalization that has been found to fit the observations is unique. Other generalizations, known or not, will describe or explain the data just as well as the one being considered. It is our claim that, in the discovery phase of its work, science solves these problems of certainty and uniqueness largely by ignoring them. The problem of discovery is precisely to find some generalization that is parsimonious and consistent with all the given data (within some criterion of accuracy). At the point of discovery, no claim is made that the generalization will survive the test of additional evidence, or that another generalization will not be found that is equally adequate for describing the original data. Where there are two or more explanations for a given set of phenomena, investigations must be undertaken to choose among them. But, as in the recipe for rabbit stew, one must first catch the rabbit; the first task is to find one or more laws, as simple and general as possible, that explain the data. If even one generalization or explanation can be found to fit a body of data reasonably well, it will usually be accepted, at least until a competitive law or explanation comes along or until new important data are found that do not fit at all. When two or more explanations for the same data or for overlapping data are discovered, there arise the new tasks of evaluating them relative to one another and (usually) discovering new laws that reconcile the discrepancies. In all these circumstances, the first and vital task is to discover laws. While that is going on, the existence of competitors, actual or potential, is simply irrelevant. The concern that the philosophy of science has had for the certainty and uniqueness of inductions stems from a misconception of the nature of science. Science initates life more closely than has been admitted. As with the rest of life, uncertainty is intrinsic to it, and every situation may be viewed from multiple perspectives. The scientist is a lighthearted gambler, making no greater demands on the world for insurance than the world is willing to supply. Laws, or supposed laws, will often be discovered (a happy moment). They will often be refuted by later evidence (a sad moment), and they will sometimes have to contend with rival laws that explain the same data (a perplexing moment). We do not wholly dismiss the problem of induction—of prediction and uniqueness. Rather, we redefine it. The function of verification procedures is not to provide scientists with unattainable certainty or uniqueness for discoveries, but to inform them about the risks they are running in committing themselves to hypotheses that have been discovered and to provide guidance that may enhance their chances of making relatively durable discoveries. Even Newton and Einstein were vouchsafed no more certainty than that.

Returning now to the structure of discovery problems, we need to say a word about the problem spaces that such problems call for. An example from Simon and Kotovsky 1963 will make the matter clear.

Suppose we are presented with the sequence of symbols

A B M C D M . . .

and asked to extrapolate it—to find the "law" that generated it. If we respond to this challenge as most takers of intelligence tests do, we will reply: . . . E F M. . . . If asked to describe the generating pattern on which our extrapolation is based, we might reply: The sequence consists of the Roman alphabet, interrupted at every third place by an M. Now, these answers suffer from all the inadequacies of induction that we have just been discussing. We have no guarantee that the correct continuation is not

...A B M C D M A B....

(There are, of course, an infinity of such alternatives.) We have neither certainty nor uniqueness in our answer. But we do not wish to return to such issues. Rather, we wish to ask about the nature of the problem space used in finding an answer.

One space that clearly has to be represented by the problem solver is the space of possible sequences of Roman letters or other symbols. (Let us call it the space of *instances*.) However, the rules that generate these sequences lie in some quite different space: a space of generative programs, perhaps represented by systems of productions. Let us call this the space of *rules* (Simon and Lea 1974). Now, the induction problem may be represented as a search of the space of rules to find a rule that will generate the given partial sequence. The test of whether a solution has been found is to compare, in the space of instances, the actual sequence with the sequence generated by the rule.

If selective heuristics are used to guide the search for a rule, the information for these heuristics must also be extracted from the space of instances. For example, if the induction system can notice that, in the original partial sequence, B is the successor to A in the Roman alphabet, then it can hypothesize that the rule incorporates an alphabetic sequence, and it can pass this information on from the instance space to the rule generator that is searching in the space of rules. The information that the letter M appears to be repeated at regular intervals can be passed on in the same way.

In inductive problem solving, then, the data (in the instance space) not only provide the information that is used to test the adequacy of a proposed solution; they may also provide guidance for the search of the rule generator (in the space of rules), enabling that search to be vastly more efficient than it could be without that information. Effective inductive search involves a continuous interaction between the information in the instance space and the search through the rule space.

Processes of Discovery

The scientific enterprise is dedicated to the extension of knowledge about the external world. It is usually conceived as being made up of four main kinds of interrelated activities: gathering data, finding parsimonious descriptions of the data, formulating explanatory theories, and testing the theories. Sometimes the second category (description) and third (explanation) are merged. Usually these activities are conceived as occurring in cyclical fashion. Theories are formulated, predictions are made from them, data are gathered, and the theories are tested by confronting their predictions with the data. Failure of data to support theories leads, in turn, to the formulation of new theories. It is generally agreed, however, that the actual sequences of events are less regular. Data may be gathered without clear theoretical preconceptions, and theories may be retained, especially in the absence of viable alternatives, even after some of their predictions have been disconfirmed.

Taxonomy of Scientific Theories

Whether or not data gathering, description, explanation, and theory testing are strictly cyclical, each of these activities can be subdivided further. Data may be gathered by the observation of natural events or by the "production" of phenomena through experimentation. If the data are to be obtained by experimentation, the experiments must be designed; in either case (experiment or observation), data-gathering instruments must be invented and improved.

Data are seldom reported in wholly raw form. They must usually be digested and summarized. Summarizing requires the detection of regularities and invariants—that is, the development of *descriptive generalizations*, which may or may not be dignified by the label "theory."

Descriptive generalizations or theories may, in turn, be derivable from *explanatory theories*. We will have more to say later in this chapter about how a line might be drawn between these two categories of theories. Whether or not there is indeed such a boundary, science includes a number of "theoretical" activities, among them inventing theories, deriving theorems from them (including predictions and derivations of descriptive from explanatory theories), and directly predicting observations.

Another collection of activities comes under the general heading of *testing theories*, which subsumes all statistical techniques for comparing theoretical statements with data and making judgments of "significance."

The *diffusion* of scientific discoveries, and expository writing about them, are usually regarded as meta-activities of science. Yet we must remember that Mendeleev discovered the periodic table while planning the arrangement of topics for an elementary chemistry textbook.

On one occasion or another, virtually every one of the species of activities mentioned above (except for diffusion) has been judged worthy of the Nobel Prize. Since this book is going to be concerned mainly with just one subset of them, the induction of descriptive and explanatory theories from data, perhaps it is worth emphasizing that this is not the whole of science. In particular, we would call attention to the invention of new instruments (the CAT scanner is a rather recent example) that make possible the production of new kinds of data. Later, we will see how Ohm arrived at his law of electrical resistance, and Black at his law of temperature equilibrium. In each of these cases, the story does not begin with the induction of the law from data; it goes back to the invention of the instruments (Seebeck's battery and Ampère's ammeter employed by Ohm; Fahrenheit's thermometer employed by Black) that virtually created new variables for scientific study.

More generally, the discovery of a pattern in data must be preceded by discovery of the phenomena from which the data emerge. New phenomena—the x ray, the effect of penicillin on bacteria, the Mossbauer Effect, the synchrony between the pulsations of the heart and the arteries, Brownian movement—must be counted among the most important discoveries of science. Only in the final chapter will we have much to say about how the prepared mind (to use Pasteur's phrase) notices such phenomena when they occur, cultivates them, and draws them into the body of science. In time, the theory of scientific discovery will have to be expanded to provide a fuller treatment of these processes of finding new phenomena. In this volume we will be able only to provide a sketch of the nature of such processes.

It is often said that a problem that is well represented is nearly solved, and, hence, that creativity lies in finding good representations of problems rather than in solving them. This claim, while correct in emphasizing the significance of representation, is grossly exaggerated. In the pages of this book we will have occasion to refer to many important scientific discoveries that did not require the discovery of new representations, but rather made use of problem representations already available and being used by others working in the same problem domain. In our final chapter, we will explore the hypothesis that problem-formulation processes, like the processes for finding and solving problems, are simply a particular variety of problem-*solving* processes—that problem discovery and representation is problem solving. Although we cannot give conclusive evidence for this hypothesis (that will require the empirical work of constructing and testing new computer programs), we will try, in chapter 10, to indicate what the general structure of such programs would look like.

Closely related to the discovery of new phenomena and new representations is the discovery of what have been called "laws of qualitative structure" (Newell and Simon 1976). Not all important scientific laws have the quantitative precision of Newton's Three Laws of Motion. Pasteur formulated and tested the germ theory of disease. Initially, what was that theory? It could hardly be stated more precisely than "If an organism is suffering from a disease that appears to be contagious, look for infestation by a microorganism that may be causing it." Subsequently, Koch's postulates for assigning a connection between particular bacteria and a particular infective disease made the claim of the germ theory more precise, without, however, changing its qualitative nature. Of a similar character is the cell theory, "Complex organisms are made up of (usually large numbers of) tiny cellular units," where the definition of "cellular units" gradually changed with the accumulation of observations and the refinement of the theory. "Evolution by natural selection" is an equally vague but fecund concept.

The concepts of germ, cell, and evolution are important precisely because each of them provides a focal point around which whole congeries of scientific research activities and findings can be organized. A complete theory of scientific discovery would have to explain both how such concepts originate and how they serve as seeds around which great bodies of data and theory crystallize.

When we look at some of the later versions of our discovery program, BACON, we will see that certain of the search heuristics and presuppositions the program draws upon have a kinship with what we have been calling here "laws of qualitative structure." In addition, the newer programs, auxiliary to BACON, that we call STAHL and GLAUBER are specifically designed to discover qualitative rather than quantitative laws.

Hence, although they will not be our main themes, laws of qualitative structure and the phenomena from which they usually derive will not be absent from our considerations.

Strong and Weak Methods in Discovery

By and large, it is characteristic of all these activities of scientific inquiry (with the partial exception of hypothesis testing) that they are usually carried out in a rather tentative and inefficient way. There is no powerful factory method—no assembly line—for the manufacture of scientific truth. In fact, indications in any domain of science that problem solving can be accomplished systematically and routinely causes that activity to be classified as mere development or application rather than basic scientific inquiry. Even if the activity falls far short of complete systematization and routinization, if its "doability" and its outcome are nearly predictable it falls under Kuhn's rubric of "normal" rather than "revolutionary" science. In fact, methodologists of science sometimes hint that the fundamentality of a piece of scientific work is inversely proportional to the clarity with which its outcome can be anticipated.

In our discussion of heuristics, we saw that similar gradations and distinctions in degree of systematization are made in theories of problem solving. Expert problem solving in any domain is characterized by the systematic application of powerful methods, each adapted to a recognizable subdomain. Experts do not have to seek and search; they recognize and calculate. Problem solving by novices, on the other hand, is characterized by tentativeness and uncertainty. Novices often do not know what to do next; they search and test, and they use crude and cumbersome weak methods because they are not familiar with the powerful tools of the expert.[3]

It is understandable, if ironic, that "normal" science fits pretty well the description of problem solving by experts and "revolutionary" science the description of problem solving by novices. It is understandable because scientific activity, particularly at the revolutionary end of the continuum, is concerned with the discovery of new truths, not with the application of truths that are already well known. While it may incorporate many expert techniques in the manipulation of instruments and laboratory procedures, such activity is basically a journey into unmapped terrain. Consequently, at the level of overall strategy, it is mainly characterized, as is novice problem solving, by trial-and-error search and the extensive use of weak methods. The search may be highly selective (the selectivity depending on how much is already known about the domain), but it generally reaches its goal only after many halts, turnings, and backtrackings.[4]

Weak methods exploit as little or as much knowledge about the structure

3. For a general view of this contrast in problem solving between experts and novices, see Larkin et al. 1980 and Chi et al. 1981.
4. As a fascinating example, see the detailed account by Holmes 1980 of Hans Krebs's discovery of the ornithine cycle for urea synthesis.

of the problem space as is available to them. When little knowledge is available, they are about equivalent to, and as inefficient as, random search through the problem space. If a great deal of knowledge is available, especially to the means-ends method, they may home in on solutions with little extraneous search.

Research in artificial intelligence and cognitive simulation has shown that weak methods can solve problems in domains that are regarded as difficult for intelligent human problem solvers, and can do so without intolerable amounts of search. (See Newell and Simon 1972; Nilsson 1980.) The programs for scientific discovery on which we shall comment, and specifically our own discovery programs, employ heuristic search and other weak methods as their problem-solving tools.

Data-Driven and Theory-Driven Science

Since theories encourage the acquisition of new data, and data the generation of theories—as surely as hens engender eggs, and eggs hens—scientific discovery can enter the cycle of scientific activity at any point. In the contemporary literature of the philosophy of science, with its mistaken emphasis on theory testing as the quintessential scientific activity, the tale usually begins with a theory. The theory, emanating from the brain of Zeus or some other unexamined source, calls for testing, which demands, in turn, that appropriate data be obtained through observation or experiment. In this scheme of things, the discovery process is what we earlier described as theory driven.

Especially when a theory is expressed in mathematical form, theory-driven discovery may make extensive use of strong methods associated with the mathematics or with the subject matter of the theory itself. In this case, the discovery procedures will not be general; rather, they will be tailored to the problem domain.

The converse view (often called Baconian induction) takes a body of data as its starting point[5] and searches for a set of generalizations, or a theory, to describe the data parsimoniously or to explain them. Usually such a theory takes the form of a precise mathematical statement of the relations among the data. This is the kind of discovery process we described earlier as data driven. Data-driven discovery will perforce make use of weak methods, but

---

5. It is well known that data are impregnated by theories to various degrees, but consideration of that fact just takes us one step back in the chicken-egg cycle.

with the compensating advantage that the methods are quite general in their domain of application. Moreover, we must remember that "weak methods" will still usually be far more powerful than blind trial-and-error search.

The very strength of the methods available in theory-driven discovery sometimes produces the danger that theories will be created that rationalize rather than explain the empirical data. In discussing the many attempts that were being made at the turn of the century to accommodate the avaiable data about ether drift (or its absence), the apparent dependence of mass upon velocity, and other "anomalies" relating to relativity, Poincaré had this to say: "Experiments have been made that should have disclosed the terms of the first order; the results were nugatory. . . . a general explanation was sought and Lorentz found it. He showed that the terms of the first order should cancel each other, but not the terms of the second order. Then more exact experiments were made, which were also negative. . . . An explanation was necessary, and was forthcoming; they always are; hypotheses are what we lack the least." (quoted in Miller 1984, p. 65)   Perhaps the conclusion is too cynical, but we shall see a little later, in discussing Planck's discovery of the law of blackbody radiation, that he found a theory to explain Wien's erroneous law; then, a year later, patched up the theory to reconcile it with the new empirical data.[6]

Both data-driven and theory-driven processes give partial views of the scientific enterprise. It is easy to find in the history of science examples of very important discoveries that fit each view. Published accounts usually cut the cycle so as to emphasize theory as the first mover—for example, by suggesting that Lavoisier's experiments on mercuric oxide were motivated by his concern with the phlogiston theory, the experiments of Michelson and Morley by the classical theory of the ether, and the observations of the solar eclipse of 1919 by the goal of testing general relativity.

On the other hand, the historical records of Mendeleev's discovery of the periodic table (Kedrov 1966–67) and Balmer's discovery of the formula for the hydrogen spectrum (Banet 1966) reveal both of these discoveries to have been clear-cut cases of data-driven Baconian induction. They could not have been otherwise, since the regularities discovered were, at the time of discovery, purely descriptive generalizations from the data, lacking any theoretical motivation.

6. The patch has held up.

Francis Bacon wrote in the *Novum Organum*: "Those who have treated the sciences were either empirics or rationalists. The empirics, like ants, lay up stores, and use them; the rationalists, like spiders, spin webs out of themselves; but the bee takes a middle course, gathering up her matter from the flowers of the field and garden, and digesting and preparing it by her native powers." There is no question, then, of choosing between data-driven and theory-driven discovery. Rather, what is needed is an understanding of how each of these processes can occur. In the third chapter of this book, we will address one part of the task: We will describe the computer program BACON.1, which as its name implies is a system capable of making scientific discoveries by induction on bodies of data. In later chapters, we will discuss more sophisticated versions of BACON, and some additional programs, that can be described, at least to a modest degree, as driven by theory as well as by data.

Finding and Representing Problems

The view is sometimes advanced that the truly creative part of the discovery process lies not in solving problems once the problems have been identified and formulated, but in finding and defining them. The real discovery, in this view, consists in finding the problem and in discriminating the specific data that are relevant to solving it.

An immediate objection to this view is that it would reverse the verdict of history on many prominent scientific discoveries and require a radical reassignment of credit. For example, in 1900, when Max Planck arrived at the equation for blackbody radiation and the physical explanation of that formula, the problem of searching for the formula had been defined at least a generation ago. There was also no question as to what data were the relevant ones. If finding the problem and the relevant data are the real test of creativity, then Planck's discovery of the law named after him was not creative.

The case of Planck is in no way unusual. Johann Jakob Balmer (who was not a physicist) took up the search for the formula that would describe the frequencies of the known lines in the hydrogen spectrum when the data were called to his attention at a physics lecture. The problem and the data had already been identified by the physics community as important. Likewise, the problem of finding new ways of describing the regular movements of the planets and their satellites was not invented by Isaac Newton, and the data he used to explore this problem were provided by his predecessors. The problem of characterizing planetary forces was of wide interest in Newton's time; thus, if the real creativity lay in formulating the problem of gravitation, Newton would have to share credit for the discovery with Kepler, Hooke, Wren, Halley, and perhaps others.

Among Louis Pasteur's great accomplishments was his discovery that liquids would not ferment if kept under sterile conditions. The problem he was addressing when he made this discovery—the spontaneous generation of organisms—had been addressed by many of his contemporaries and predecessors; Pasteur did not invent or formulate it. The anomalies in classical physics that presumably led Albert Einstein to take up the problem of special relativity were of great concern to his contemporaries, and the problem had already been formulated by Fitzgerald, Lorentz, Abraham, and others. James Clerk Maxwell's problem—formulating equations to describe electrial and magnetic fields and their interaction—was provided to him by the work of Michael Faraday; no new problem formulation was required of him. Both the problem representation (in terms of force fields) and the goal (to explain the known phenomena without invoking action at a distance) were inherited by Maxwell from Faraday.

It is clear that credit for discovery is awarded to a scientist who finds an important law, whether or not he or she was the first to formulate the problem of looking for a law in the phenomena under consideration. To assert this is not to claim that problem finding and problem formulation may not also be creative activities, important for discovery. There is no reason why we must exclude the one species of creativity in order to recognize the other. In the case of Ohm's law, it may be argued that Ohm's genius lay not only in finding the law but also in conceiving of the experiment in which he placed wires of varying length in a circuit and measured the corresponding currents. Or we might find the "real" creativity to lie in Ohm's ingenuity in assembling the components of his circuit (Seebeck's battery; Ampère's ammeter), for constructing novel experimental systems is also an important scientific activity.

But seeking to identify a unique "real" act of creativity is an illusory task. We have already characterized discovery as a sequence of steps, each of which represents a small advance from an initial state of knowledge to a new state knowledge, and all, some, or none of which, taken individually, might seem creative. The process, like any process that can be described by differential or difference equations, has neither beginning nor end. To explain the process is simply to provide an explanation for each of the individual steps, whether they be steps of problem formulation, of problem solving, of constructing new experimental objects, or of some other kind. In this book, the steps we shall undertake to explain are mainly the problem-solving steps. We will usually begin each of our examples with a scientific problem that has already been formulated, and with the data (not necessarily excluding irrelevant data) already provided.

Since the main body of our results will not bear upon problem-finding processes, we should like to say a few words about these at this point, postponing a fuller discussion to chapter 10. We agree that these processes are often creative, but not that they are the locus of the only real creativity. We should like to advance the hypothesis that problem-finding and problem-formulating processes are simply a particular variety of problem-*solving* processes—that problem discovery is problem solving. We cannot give conclusive evidence for this hypothesis—that would require the construction and testing of new computer programs—but we can provide some of our general reasons for believing it. In chapter 10 we will give hypothetical but quite plausible accounts of the processes that are involved in problem finding and problem representation. In the present state of the art, that is about as far as we can go.

Description, Explanation, Cause

Scientific laws are sometimes classified as descriptive or explanatory, and explanatory laws often take the form of statements of causal relation. Here we shall comment on the distinction between description and explanation, and then discuss briefly the role of causal language in explanation.

Description and Explanation

This distinction that is commonly made between *descriptions* and *explanations* is a matter of degree rather than a dichotomy. Generalizations are viewed as "mere" descriptions to the extent that they stick close to the data, stating one or more relations among the observable variables. Thus, Kepler's laws, which are expressed entirely in terms of the shapes of the planetary orbits, the areas over which they sweep, their radii, and their times, are regarded today (though they were not by Kepler) as descriptions rather than explanations of the planetary motions. On the other hand, Newton's law of universal gravitation, $M_1 a_1 = g M_1 M_2 / d^2$, from which

Kepler's laws can be derived, is regarded as an explanation of the latter and, by transitivity, of the phenomena they describe. In the law of gravitation, the acceleration, a_1, and the distance between the objects, d, are observables, but the masses, M_1 and M_2, are theoretical terms whose values must be inferred indirectly from those of the observables.[7]

Newton's law, then, is regarded as an explanation both because it contains theoretical terms and because Kepler's descriptive laws can be deduced from it. The presence of theoretical terms and the derivability of more specialized, descriptive consequences seem to be two of the criteria that underlie our intuitions of the distinction between explanatory and descriptive theories.

Although this distinction is intuitively plausible, it does not hold up terribly well under critical examination. For example, Kepler's third law can be stated in the forms $S = K$, where K is a constant and where $S = P^2/d^3$ (P being the period of the orbit and d the distance of the planet from the sun). However, S is then a theoretical term, for it is not observed directly but is computed via the equation given above from the values of P and d, which are observed. Consequently, if we take the presence of a theoretical terms in a law as the test for its being explanatory, we have to classify Kepler's third law as explanatory—a classification that does not match our intuitions very well.

Without trying to arrive at an immediate judgment, let us carry the story a step farther. If we connect two blocks, X and Y, with a spring, stretch the spring to various lengths and then release it, and measure the initial accelerations of the blocks, we can discover the invariant relation $a_X/a_Y = -K_{XY}$, where the a's are accelerations, as before, and K is a theoretical term that is constant. With a new pair of blocks, W and Z, a similar invariance will be found, possibly with a new constant, K_{WZ}. Now we might seek to state the invariance in another way by attributing to each block, X, an invariant property, M_X, and asserting the law $M_X a_X = -M_Y a_Y$, or its equivalent, $M_Y/M_X = K_{XY}$. Expressing the ratios of the accelerations in terms of the postulated masses yields a stronger law than the first form of the invariance, for it implies transitivity of these ratios over the whole set of blocks—that is, $K_{XZ} = K_{XY}K_{YZ}$. The first form of the invariance is expressed in terms of the ratio of the accelerations; the second is

---

7. For a thorough discussion of the notion of "theoretical term" and references to the literature on the topic see Tuomela 1973.

expressed as a relation between these accelerations and the inertial masses of the individual blocks. Yet there are theoretical terms in both forms of the law: the K's in the first and the M's in the second. As a matter of fact, the number of different values of the theoretical terms (constants) in the first form of the law is n^2 for a set of n blocks, but for the second form of the law it is only n.

There is a difference, however, between the ratios of accelerations, K_{XY}, and the masses, M_X. The former can be computed directly as ratios of observables, whereas the latter cannot. The *existence* of the mass numbers must be postulated, and the mass of one of the blocks taken as the standard; then the values of the remaining masses can be computed from the ratios of the accelerations. The same distinction between two kinds of theoretical terms can be found by comparing the directly computable constant in Kepler's third law with the mass numbers that appear in Newton's gravitational law. In both examples, the explanatory law is slightly more parsimonious than the descriptive law; it also makes use of a more sophisticated kind of theoretical term, introducing into the picture a new property that is not obtainable by taking simple functions of the observables. We will call invariants that are introduced in this way *intrinsic properties*. From the two examples we have examined, we can conjecture that the introduction of intrinsic properties gives a generalization an explanatory rather than a merely descriptive flavor.

These remarks fall far short of providing a formal basis for a distinction between explanations and descriptions, but they provide a background for understanding the fact that the BACON programs employ different mechanisms to introduce the two different kinds of theoretical terms that we have distinguished here. All these mechanisms remain in the category of weak methods, so they do not reduce the generality of BACON or introduce any great element of complexity. Before we leave the subject of explanation, however, we should comment on a third viewpoint on this topic that has not yet been mentioned.

Explanation and Causation

We have said that explanatory power may be attributed to a law if it leads deductively to the derivation of previously known descriptive laws, or if it postulates intrinsic properties. Sometimes, on the other hand, laws are said to be explanatory if they give *causal* accounts of phenomena. Since the correct explication of the notions of causality and explanation are still topics of discussion and dispute in philosophy,[8] we will again proceed informally. Fortunately, most of the difficulties relate to the attribution of causes in nonexperimental situations, whereas most of our data and our theories (except Kepler's laws) are derived not from observations but from experiments, in which matters are relatively straightforward.

If the value of a dependent variable changes when the value of an independent variable is altered, we say that the latter change causes the former. When we replace one of the blocks in the conservation-of-momentum experiment with a heavier one, the corresponding acceleration decreases. Hence, we say that inertial mass is a deterrent (i.e., a negative cause) to acceleration. We do *not* make the converse inference: that decreasing the acceleration will cause the mass to increase. The asymmetry between the variables appears to arise from the fact that we have a way of intervening directly in the situation to change the masses but no way of directly intervening to change the ratio of the accelerations. In any event, if we associate explanation with causality, we can regard the law of conservation of momentum as a causal law.

Ohm's law provides a similar example. In a circuit with a battery and a resistance wire, we can replace one battery with another and one resistance wire with another and measure the current (the dependent variable) each time. In the theory we derive from these data, the voltage of the battery and the resistance of the wire are the causes that determine the amount of current that flows. The asymmetry is genuine, since we have no physical way of causing the battery or the wire to change by varying the current directly. Ohm's law, by this criterion, is not merely descriptive; it is an explanatory law.

What shall we say about Kepler's third law and the law of universal gravitation? In the former, there seems to be a perfect symmetry between distance and period of orbit; neither seems to take precedence in causing the other. Of course, in our age of Sputniks, we can turn the situation into an experimental one. Say we launch a satellite with sufficient energy to put it in orbit at a specified height above the earth. At that altitude, it will orbit with a period given by Kepler's law. Does the law now provide a causal explanation of the period?

In the case of Newton's law of universal gravitation, we instinctively feel an asymmetry. We read $M_1 a_1 = g M_1 M_2 / d^2$ from right to left and not from

---

8. See Simon 1977, section 2: "Causes and Possible Worlds."

left to right. We think of the masses and their distances as causing the acceleration (via the force field caused by the gravitation mass), and not vice versa. This reaction may be related to the fact that the acceleration contains an implicit reference to future velocity and position; hence, if we read the equation from right to left the causal arrow will agree with the arrow of forward movement through time, whereas if we read it in the other direction it will reverse that arrow.

We will not try to resolve here the philosophical issues raised by these examples. Our purpose in mentioning them is to point out that if we take the assertion of causality to be the criterion for a law's being explanatory, then all laws derived from experimental manipulations as well as laws that involve termporal asymmetry can be given explanatory interpretations. Nor do we claim that we have explicated, in this section and the preceding one, all the criteria that might be advanced for distinguishing explanatory from descriptive laws. In particular, we have said nothing about laws that *reduce* a description at one level of aggregation to a description at a lower level (as the laws of thermodynamics can be reduced to the laws of statistical mechanics, or the laws of chemistry to those of quantum mechanics and atomic physics). There would be general agreement that all such laws are explanatory, but not that *only* such laws are explanatory.

Computer Simulation

At some point in the course of their lives, many people undertake to explore their family trees. After searching back a number of generations, they often find themselves at a blank wall—or, more aptly, in a dense, impenetrable fog. The search has come to an end, but the question of origins has not been answered. As they now realize, it can never be answered; it can only be carried back to some arbitrary point.

The account of every historical process is like that. Each beginning is the end of an earlier beginning. It would appear that we cannot explain historical events with finality. We will continue to wonder what events preceded the Big Bang, the initial act of creation. Physics, with Newton, found a clever and profound partial escape from the dilemma: The search for final causes, for the unmoved mover, was replaced by a search for *efficient causes*. An efficient cause is a mechanism, described by a law, that predicts the behavior of a system during a brief interval of time from its condition, or state, at the beginning of that interval. A historical sequence is explained, in this paradigm, by the repeated operation of the invariant law (usually in the form of a system of differential or difference equations) upon the gradually evolving states of the system. Of course, the explanation leaves open the determination of the initial conditions (the starting point) as well as the boundary conditions (continuing inputs into the system).

Programs as Theories of Dynamic Systems

Systems of differential equations (and their close relatives, difference equations) have for three centuries provided a powerful and highly successful representation for mathematical theories in the natural and the social sciences. They are applicable, at least in principle, whenever the behavior of a system at a given moment is determined by the state it is in at that moment. Hence, they incorporate an assumption of local causation with respect to time; the past influences the future only through the present situation it has created.

If a set of relations can be found (the differential equations) that give an invariant time-independent relation between system behavior and system state, this set of relations provides a highly parsimonious description of the behavior of the system through time. Time paths are calculated by integrating the differential equations symbolically, or integrating them by numerical computation if the symbolic integrals cannot be found in closed form.

Now, a computer program is, formally, a set of difference equations, for it determines the behavior of the computer during its current operation cycle on the basis of the state of its memories and its input at the beginning of that cycle. The action taken in each cycle determines a new state of the machine, and hence, in combination with new input, the next cycle's action. Therefore, it is possible to use a computer program as a theory of a system in the same way that it is possible to use any other set of difference equations.

Most computer programs are so complex that integration in symbolic form to determine the general properties of the paths is impossible. However, it is possible to perform an integration in each particular case (the equivalent of numerical integration) simply by allowing the program to run from one or more initial states.

Today it is commonly understood that a computer is a quite general symbol-processing system and that computer simulation of behavior is not limited to systems expressed in numbers. This is particularly convenient for the simulation of cognitive processes; the human mind is also a symbol-processing system, and it has never been easy to see how it can be described in terms of real numbers. How much more convenient it would be if theories of thinking, instead of employing conventional mathematics, could be expressed formally using the same kinds of symbolic representations as are used in thought itself! This is precisely the opportunity that the computer provides.

We can write in an information-processing language—a symbolic rather than numerical language—a computer program that describes, say, the processes that intelligent adults are hypothesized to use in solving some class of problems. We can then present the program and some human subjects with identical problems and compare their behaviors. From the computer we will obtain a trace, from the human subjects a verbal and written protocol of their behavior while they were solving the problems. We can then test the program—our theory of the behavior—by comparing the trace with the protocol, just as any theory is tested by comparing the system path it predicts with data showing the actual path.

Such a program can be tested at various levels of detail, down to the level of resolution of the data. In the case of human problem solving, behavior can usually be tracked from second to second, but detail cannot usually be resolved for shorter intervals of time. The parts of our theory that describe finer detail can be tested only indirectly, much as an electron microscope that can observe directly objects that are tens or hundreds of angstroms in diameter can provide only indirect evidence about smaller details.

Our simulation programs are theories of this kind, but the resolution of their present versions is rather coarse. Moreover, the materials of the history of science do not usually provide us with a basis for testing theories at a resolution of seconds, or hours, or even days. We have focused, in constructing our programs, on the level of heuristics, trying to incorporate in them the kinds of selective processes that we believe scientists use to guide their search for regularities in data.

In testing our simulations, we will usually have to be content with a sufficiency criterion: Can a program that contains only these selective heuristics to guide it actually discover significant scientific laws with only a modest amount of computing effort? If an affirmative answer can be given to this question, then we can claim to have driven the mystery out of these kinds of scientific discovery, at least. We will have shown how simple information processes, resembling those that have already been identified in other kinds of problem solving, can give an adequate account of the discovery process.

At the level of resolution of which we are speaking, our programs are fully compatible with the small number of other programs of discovery that have been constructed and tested, such as meta-DENDRAL, AM, and EURISKO. These programs differ in the tasks they address and in many of their processing details, but all of them are essentially based on the idea of selective search guided by heuristics. At present, there is no need to try to choose among them. Nor, at the present time, can we compare our programs with competing theories of scientific discovery that do not take the form of computer programs, for there are no such theories that can pass the same test of sufficiency—that are capable of giving constructive demonstrations of how discoveries could be made.

At the level of resolution we are interested in, it will not be hard to match initial conditions, equating the data and knowledge provided to our programs with the data and knowledge available to the scientists who made the historical discoveries under study. In some cases, the historical evidence may also provide us with (usually coarse) data on the path followed by the discoverer. All this information can be used to judge a simulation's veridicality.

The chief conclusions we shall be able draw from our experiments with our simulation programs concern the nature and the efficacy of search heuristics. We will be especially interested in finding out how general, over various problem domains, is the applicability of particular heuristics; and we will study how the effectiveness of a discovery program increases or decreases when particular heuristics are included in it or excluded from it. This is the level of resolution at which most of our analysis and discussion will be conducted, and this is the level at which the theory must receive serious consideration.

Design Issues

Chapters 3 through 8 will be devoted mainly to describing and discussing four computer programs—BACON, STAHL, GLAUBER, and DALTON—that we have constructed to simulate some of the processes of scientific discovery. In the general architecture of these programs we have followed the mainstream of artificial-intelligence research, so the resulting systems are quite similar in form to many other problem-solving programs that incorporate the principles of heuristic search.

Our programs make use of *list structures* (also known as schemas, frames, scripts, directed graphs, and relational data bases) as their basic representation for semantic information, and *productions* (condition-action pairs) as their basic representation for the processes that act on the information (Newell and Simon 1972, chapters 2 and 14). Information in schemas is represented, in turn, primarily by objects (nodes) with which are associated attribute-value pairs. For example, in GLAUBER a node may represent a particular chemical reaction, some of whose attributes are the inputs to the reaction and its outputs. The value of *inputs* is a list of chemical substances that are required for the reaction; the value of *outputs* is a list of the substances produced by the reaction.

Since the value of an attribute may itself be a node, with its own list of attributes and values, schemas of arbitrary complexity can be constructed within this representation. Thus, the substances that are values of an attribute of a chemical reaction may themselves have attributes whose values are the constituent elements.

In the set of productions that act upon the system, each production has a set of associated conditions. Whenever these conditions are all simultaneously satisfied by the data structures that are stored in working memory, that production is executed. (Conflict-resolution rules enforce priorities when the conditions of two or more productions are satisfied at the same time.) In the systems that are described in this book, no attempt has been made to segregate long-term memory from short-term memory or to restrict the testing of conditions in productions to limited subsets of the semantic information. A more microscopic account of the psychological processes of discovery would presumably have to take such restrictions into account, for we know that the small capacity of human short-term memory is a major factor in determining the difficulty of problems. We do not try to model explicitly the way that scientists make use of external memory (paper and pencil, reference books).

The programs have been, at one time or another, written in a variety of higher-level list-processing languages, but principally in PRISM (Langley and Neches 1981). At the level of description we have used, the choice between this language and such alternatives as ACT (Anderson 1976) and OPS (Forgy and McDermott 1977) is mostly a matter of programming convenience; it has no substantive importance for the content or the operation of these programs.

More details about production systems and the architecture of the individual programs will be given in the chapters devoted to them. However, we also give semiformal accounts of all data structures and productions, independent of particular programming languages. We hope these simplified descriptions are understandable as a form of somewhat awkward English, with a minimum of algebraic notation.

Conclusion

In this chapter we have set the general terms of our enterprise, specifying what we mean by scientific discovery, what aspects of the discovery process we will examine, and what part discovery plays in the whole scientific enterprise. In the last part of the chapter we have given an account of the computer-simulation methods that we will use as our main research tool for studying scientific discovery.

The next chapter is also introductory in character, for we feel that we must address questions that have been raised in the literature of the philosophy of science about the feasibility of constructing a theory of scientific discovery. If constructing such a theory were impossible, as has sometimes been claimed, then we would have to bring our project to a halt at the end of chapter 2. Since the book continues for nine chapters more, it should be obvious that we were not persuaded that our undertaking is futile. Nevertheless, the arguments against it deserve thoughtful attention.

2 On the Possibility of a Normative Theory of Discovery

In chapter 1 we undertook to put our project in perspective by providing a brief taxonomy or anatomy of the scientific enterprise, indicating the place of data-driven discovery in that anatomy, and enumerating the many other processes that combine with it to make up the full activity of science. In the present chapter we discuss the relation of that anatomy to other widely held views on scientific development, especially the views of Karl Popper, Thomas Kuhn, and Imre Lakatos. In particular, we shall be concerned with elaborating the ideas introduced in the first chapter on the relation between the processes for discovering theories and the processes for verifying them.

Verification versus Falsification

In chapter 1 we proposed that the course of the development of science be thought of as falling within the heuristic-search paradigm of cognitive science. In terms of this paradigm, scientists, collectively, are viewed as searching immense spaces of possible data, concepts, theories, representations, rules of reasoning, directions of further inquiry, and so on. The search is not random but selective, being guided by rules of thumb (heuristics)—some of them very complex—in directions that have some likelihood of being fruitful. New paths are continually being generated, and new points in the spaces being reached. Each successive discovery is tested or evaluated for its contributions to the enterprise and for its prospects as a launching spot for yet more searches. This description of the search process makes an important distinction between generation (taking new paths) and testing (evaluating the points reached—a distinction that corresponds to the distinction made in the literature between the context of discovery (generation) and the context of confirmation (testing).

Francis Bacon undertook to construct a theory of discovery that included advice and heuristics for effective discovery processes (Bacon 1620), and John Stuart Mill's famous rules of induction (Mill 1843) were intended to facilitate and systematize the process of generating hypotheses. However, in the late nineteenth century, philosophers of science began to express more and more doubt about the feasibility of providing "rules of discovery" and to turn their attention more and more toward the process of verification. As a result, until very recently, twentieth-century philosophy of science was focused amost exclusively on the context of confirmation; almost no attention was paid to the context of discovery. In fact, it was frequently claimed that there could be no logical method or theory of scientific discovery; that discovery was a matter of "creativity"—the free play of the human creative spirit. The task of building a theory of discovery was passed on to psychologists.

Nowhere has the denial of the possibility of rules of scientific discovery been stated more forcefully than in Popper's influential book *The Logic of Scientific Discovery* (1961):

> ... the work of the scientist consists in putting forward and testing theories.
>
> The initial stage, the act of conceiving or inventing a theory, seems to me neither to call for logical analysis nor to be susceptible of it. The question of how it happens that a new idea occurs to a man—whether it is a musical theme, a dramatic conflict, or a scientific theory—may be of great interest to empirical psychology; but it is irrelevant to the logical analysis of scientific knowledge. The latter is concerned not with *questions of fact* (Kant's *quid facti?*), but only with questions of *justification or validity* (Kant's *quid juris?*). ...
>
> Accordingly, I shall distinguish sharply between the process of conceiving a new idea, and the methods and results of examining it logically. As to the task of the logic of knowledge—in contradistinction to the psychology of knowledge—I shall proceed on the assumption that it consists solely in investigating the methods employed in those systematic tests to which every new idea must be subjected if it is to be seriously entertained. ...
>
> My view of the matter, for what it is worth, is that there is no such thing as a logical method of having new ideas, or a logical reconstruction of this process. My view may be expressed by saying that every discovery contains "an irrational elements," or "a creative intuition," in Bergson's sense. In a similar way, Einstein speaks of the "search for those highly universal laws ... from which a picture of the world can be obtained by pure deduction. There is no logical path," he says, "leading to these ... laws. They can only be reached by intuition, based upon something like an intellectual love (*Èinfühling*) of the objects of experience." (pp. 31–32)

A more recent statement of this same view can be found in Kuhn 1970a:

> But neither Sir Karl [Popper] nor I is an inductivist. We do not believe that there are rules for inducing correct theories from facts, or even that theories, correct or incorrect, are induced at all. Instead we view them as imaginative posits, invented in one piece for application to nature. (p. 12)

The position we shall take in this book is quite different. We shall argue, with Bacon and Mill, for the possibility of both a psychological (descriptive) and a normative theory of discovery. Whether "normative" is synonymous with "logical" is a matter of definition. However, we shall not find it necessary to postulate unanalyzed "inspiration" or "creative intuition," or even an "intellectual love of the objects of experience," to account for scientific discovery.[1] On the contrary, we shall see that the scientist has reasons for what he does when he is generating new theories as well as when he is testing those already found. The efficacy ("rationality," "logicality") of the discovery or generation process is as susceptible to evaluation and criticism as is the process of verification.

Verificationism

The problem of testing scientific theories for their validity is a natural descendant of the problem of induction. Scientific laws are not particularistic statements about specific facts or events; rather, they are universally quantified generalizations that are supposed to hold for all situations of a certain type, or at least for specified broad classes of conditions. The potential verifiers for scientific laws or theories, however, are usually thought to be statements of particular empirical observations. If by "verifying" a scientific theory we mean deducing its laws from a set (however large) of observation sentences determined by experimenters, then the case is hopeless; where there is a possibility of further observations, no universally quantified sentence can be deduced rigorously from a finite set of sentences describing specific observations. No matter how many x's have been found for which $F(x)$ holds, there is no guarantee that it will hold for the next x that we observe. The notion that theories are to be validated by deriving them deductively from observations—usually called *naive verificationism*—is clearly invalid.

To surmount the difficulties of naive verificationism, some philosophers of science (Rudolf Carnap[2] is an important example) have proposed that theories can be validated only in a probabilistic sense. In the probabilistic version of verificationism, each observation that can be derived from a theory increases the probability that the theory is valid, and by constantly increasing the number of observations one can hope to increase the probability of the theory's validity to any desired level.

With the rise in popularity of Bayesian statistical theory, doctrines of probabilistic verification have gained new adherents. (Several examples will be found in Earman 1983.) Nevertheless, serious difficulties remain. Attempts to implement such proposals in concrete terms sometimes lead to

---

1. Our position is not that "intuition" and "inspiration" do not occur in the course of scientific discovery, but that the phenomena to which these labels are applied can be explained quite straightforwardly in terms of information processing. See Simon 1973a.
2. See Carnap 1952.

contradictions in the probabilities assigned, and always require arbitrary assumptions about prior probability distributions. Changing the assumptions can change radically the probability that any given theory is valid, and there has been no consensus as to what are the right assumptions. Moreover, the Bayesian calculations become intractable when one tries to apply them to complex problems. And if we are interested in describing the human discovery process, there is today a mass of evidence that humans do not behave like Bayesian statisticians (Kahneman et al. 1982).

It is striking that most statistical methods for testing hypotheses focus not on the theory whose effectiveness is ostensibly being tested but on the "null hypothesis" (the hypothesis that the observed data could have been produced by random processes). The "significance" of a statistic at some level of probability does not confirm a theory any more than the "insignificance" of the statistic invalidates it. These tests are best regarded not as indications of the truth or the falsity of theories but as measures of the precision with which the data have been measured.

Thus, the debates of scientists about competing theories do not generally center on the levels of probabilities, but on the range of data accounted for, or on questions of goodness of approximation, or on whether damaging observations can be explained by minor modifications or qualifications that save the theory.

Of course, many scientific papers contain statements about evidence "supporting," "strengthening," or "weakening" a theory. Moreover, a theory for which the evidence is slim may be put forward as a "suggestion" rather than a "proposal." But such statements fall far short of constituting quantitative claims of "degree of justifiable belief." There does not seem to be any essential requirement in science for such claims.

Falsificationism

Popper (1961) proposed to escape from the problems of induction by turning from the concept of verification to its converse, falsification. Since, Popper argued, theories can never be fully verified if true, what one should require of them is that they can be falsified if false. If there are potential observations that would falsify a theory but one finds the theory consistent with the observations that have been made so far, one is justified in retaining it until an observation comes along that is inconsistent with it. One is especially justified in retaining it if the theory was obtained by induction from the observations. Newton had made that point much earlier, and with great emphasis. In the opening pages of book III of his *Principia* he offers as his rule IV the following:

> In experimental philosophy we are to look upon propositions inferred by general induction from phenomena as accurately or very nearly true, notwithstanding any contrary hypotheses that may be imagined, till such time as other phenomena occur, by which they may either be made more accurate, or liable to exceptions.
>
> This rule we must follow, that the argument of induction may not be evaded by hypotheses.

The more vulnerable a theory is to falsification (i.e., the larger the number of potentially falsifying observations) the better, for that means that we are not likely to be long deceived into thinking the theory valid if it in fact is not. Moreover, highly falsifiable theories are strong theories; they are falsifiable precisely because they make strong predictions that are readily chekced agains observations.

As a particular (strict) form of falsifiability, Simon and Groen (1973; see also Simon 1983) have proposed the requirement of "FITness" (finite and irrevocable testability). According to this requirement, a theory should be admissible for consideration only if it can, in principle, be falsified by a finite set of observations, and if, once it has been falsified, additional observations cannot rehabilitate it. The FITness criterion formalizes Popper's requirement that admissible theories be falsifiable.

Application of the FITness test requires a clear distinction between observable quantities and theoretical terms (quantities that are not directly observable). In the work described in this book, the data provided to our programs constitute the observables; the programs themselves construct theoretical terms as constituents of the laws they develop. The theory-generating systems that we will describe will produce only FIT theories.

FIT theories have the interesting property that all their theoretical terms are eliminable—that is to say, the theories can be stated (although perhaps not parsimoniously) without them, solely in terms of the observables. We will see how this comes about when we consider some concrete examples of theories containing theoretical terms.

In the simplified form in which we have stated them here, Popper's doctrine and the FITness requirement can be called "naive falsification-ism." They are naive for at least two reasons. First, they postulate that there are wholly theory-free observation sentences, sentences whose truth or falsity can be determined by observation without any theoretical pre-suppositions whatsoever. But such sentences do not exist—among other reasons, because every observation requires instruments, including those complex instruments we call sensory organs, whose use embodies built-in theoretical presuppositions. If a sentence inferred from an observation contradicts a theory, it may be that the theory is wrong or it may be that the observer has a wrong notion of how sense organs and instruments operate. Any observation sentence based on a view through a microscope, a tele-scope, or a human eye, if interpreted as a statement about what is "out there," is already infected by at least a rudimentary (implicit or explicit) theory of light and lenses. A second reason why the simple form of falsificationism is naive is that it is far too strict to apply to any real theory. With Newton, we are usually prepared to admit that the theories we test provide only an approximate description of reality. We do not wish a theory to be falsified by "small" discrepancies between it and the obser-vations; we would prefer to attribute those discrepancies to second-order effects that can be removed by modest modification of the theory, avoided by limiting the theory's application to stated conditions, or ignored as deriving from more or less random errors of observation.

These considerations have led to proposals of weaker and more complex notions of falsification. Popper (1961) and Lakatos (1970) have been prominent in making such proposals. One restriction we may place on falsification is to allow "small" anomalies, at least as long as it is felt that ingenuity directed at removing them within the existing theoretical frame-work has not been exhausted. A related idea is to treat anomalies gently as long as there is no competing theory that explains both the anomaly and all the other observations already explained by the theory being tested. Ac-cording to Lakatos's notion of "progressive research programs," scientists are continually at work trying to modify and improve reigning theories in order to remove the anomalies that endanger them. As long as there continue to be successes, by reinterpretation of the observations or by modification of the theories, the research program associated with the theory is "progressive." If the anomalies persist, or if they can be removed only by the introduction of ad hoc assumptions that do not explain or predict new facts correctly, then the research program "degenerates." If an alternative progressive theory is available to replace it, the degenerate program is then likely to be abandoned.[3]

3. A statement of this position can be found in Lakatos 1970. See especially the distinction between progressive and degenerating problem shifts on page 108.

Lakatos's proposal has an aura of realism about it that is not shared by the simpler versions of the falsificationist doctrine. But this realism is achieved at the cost of vagueness. The proud verificationist criterion of regarding a theory as verified only if it can be deduced from observations has now been watered down to the criterion of abandoning a theory when it does not work "well enough."

Kuhn, in his well-known theory of scientific revolutions (1970b), is one step deeper into this vagueness or subjectivity. His position is that, most of the time, scientists are not testing their theories at all but are carrying on "normal science." But this he means that they are working out the observational implications of the reigning theory and applying it to new objects or systems. If observations fail to fit their expectations (the prediction of the reigning theory) they do not abandon the theory; instead they look for errors in their procedures or in the auxiliary assumptions embedded in the observational technique. Only as a last resort do they challenge the theory.

In Kuhn's view, as in those of Lakatos and Popper, a cumulation of anomalies may force an abandonment of an old theory in favor of a new one—a scientific revolution, in Kuhn's terminology. However, like political revolutions, scientific revolutions are not easy to predict simply from a knowledge of the objective situation. They are not just intellectual events, determined by laws of evidence and inference; they are social events as well, dependent on the dynamics of the scientific disciplines. Paul Feyerabend (1970) has carried this subjectivity even further, arguing that "anything goes" as far as discovery and the criteria of verification and falsification are concerned. In his view, there should be no formal limitations on the scientific method, either in the phase of verification or in the phase of discovery.

Bootstrapping

In his book *Theory and Evidence* (1980), Clark Glymour puts forth a new notion about the testing of theories, which he calls *bootstrapping*. Glymour is concerned with *confirmation*—that is to say, with the way in which evidence contributes to our warranted belief in a theory. Thus, Glymour shows some sympathy with the Bayesians in treating confirmation as a matter of degree rather than an all-or-none matter. Unlike the Bayesians. Glymour is not interested in assigning probabilities as numerical measures of degree of confirmation; indeed, he doubts the usefulness of expressing these matters in probabilistic terms.

The basic idea in the bootstrapping method is to use evidence in conjunction with theory to test hypotheses. The procedure is called bootstrapping because the hypotheses to be tested may be part of the theory employed in the test. At this point we will not try to make this idea more precise, or to evaluate it. We mention it because our later discussion of gravitation will show that bootstrapping has a close affinity to Newton's processes of discovery and can be viewed as a discovery method (specifically, a method of discovery by data-driven induction) as well as a method of confirmation.

Conclusion: Verification and Falsification

We do not need to take sides in this debate about how theories are tested, beyond acknowledging that the testing of scientific theories is far from a simple matter and that there may be, at a particular time, wide differences in opinon as to whether a particular theory has been verified or falsified, and to what degree. What is more germane here is that the entire debate is focused on the validation process. Not once is it asked where theories come from; they are simply *there*, born from the brow of Zeus and waiting to be tested. In fact, some of those who have developed these particular lines of thought in the philosophy of science have explicity denied that the process of theory generation can be discussed in rational terms.

Theory Generation

In recent years there have been several challenges to the idea that the process of theory generation is mysterious and inexplicable. One of the first contemporary philosophers of science to return to this topic and to propose a theory of discovery was Norwood Russell Hanson. In 1958 (the year in which Hanson's book *Patterns of Discovery* appeared), Newell, Shaw, and Simon, in "The processes of creative thinking" (published in 1962) argued that discovery could be modeled by garden-variety problem-solving processes, such as means-ends analysis. Simon elaborated this argument in "Scientific discovery and the psychology of problem solving" (1966), and in 1973 he undertook to give an affirmative answer to the question "Does scientific discovery have a logic?" More recent philosophic discussion of scientific discovery can be found in the two volumes of the Reno Conference (Nickles 1978a, 1978b).

There is not one issue at stake, but three. First, there is the question for psychology and sociology of how, in fact, scientific discoveries are made by scientists. Second, there is the task for philosophy of devising normative rules for scientific discovery, rules for the rational and efficient conduct of scientific activity. One might regard the former topic as a legitimate object of empirical research in psychology and, at the same time, question whether it is possible to devise a normative theory. Any claim, however, that the empirically observed processes of discovery are "rational," or that one approach to discovery is more efficacious than another, immediately raises the normative question. Even if the two kinds of questions are logically independent, it is still profitable to consider them together. Finally, if devising a normative theory of discovery is possible, a third question arises: What is the relation between the processes of discovery and the processes of confirmation? We shall address all three questions.

What is a Normative Theory of Discovery?

As we have already seen, a "normative theory of discovery" cannot mean a set of rules for deriving theories conclusively from observations. Instead, a normative theory of discovery would be a set of criteria for judging the efficacy and the efficiency of processes used to discovery scientific theories. Presumably the criteria can be derived from the goals of the scientific activity. That is to say, a normative theory rests on contingent propositions such as "If process X is to be efficacious for attaining goal Y, then it should have properties A, B, and C." (See Simon 1973a.) Given such norms, we would be justified in saying that a person who adhered to them would be a better scientist ("better" meaning "more likely to make discoveries").

The idea that there can be a normative theory of discovery is no more surprising than the idea that there can be a normative theory of surgery. Some surgeons do better work than others, presumably because they have better heuristics and techniques (some in the form of conscious principles and problem-solving methods, some in the form of abilities to recognize the critical features of situations, some in the form of tools and instruments, and some in the form of practiced motor skills). The combination of all these heuristics and techniques makes skill in surgery more than a matter of chance, but not a matter of certainty in any particular operation. Patients who might have been saved do die, even in the hands of the most skillful surgeons.

Some scientists, too, do better work than others and make more important discoveries. It seems reasonable to presume that the superior scientists have more effective methodological principles and problem-solving methods, are better able to recognize critical features in data and theoretical formulations, have better laboratory and computing instruments, and are more skillful in the laboratory than their less successful colleagues. Of course, even the finest scientists often fall to solve problems to which they have addressed themselves; Einstein's unsuccessful search for a unified field theory comes immediately to mind, as does the failure of Lorentz and Poincaré to find a wholly satisfactory theory of special relativity.

Skill in surgery may be specialized to particular classes of operations. The superiority of a brain surgeon may rest on heuristics specialized to the anatomy of the human head, and may provide him with no special ability with organ transplants. Similarly, the heuristics possessed by a particular scientist may provide him with a comparative advantage only in some relatively limited domain of science. It is even possible that there is no "scientific method" at all, but only special methods for doing research involving gene transplants, or experiments on nuclear magnetic resonance, or theoretical work in particle physics. The processes of experimentation and theory construction may be quite different in physics, geology, economics, and psychology.

The work reported in this book derives from the hypothesis that, if there is no single "scientific method," there are at least a number of scientific methods that are broadly applicable over many domains of science. This is not to deny that there are also special methods, some of them applicable to only very narrow realm, nor is it to claim that general methods are more important for carrying out scientific work successfully than are special ones. Our only claims are that relatively general methods do play (and have historically played) a significant role in scientific discovery, that such methods are numerous, that they can be identified, and that their effects can be studied.

Cognitive-science research on human problem solving has revealed that humans, in solving all kinds of problems, use both special and general methods. Methods adapted to a particular domain, when available, may be far more powerful than general methods that make no use of the knowledge and structure of the domain. However, general methods, which will usually be weak methods, may be the only ones at hand on the frontiers of knowledge, where few relevant special techniques are yet available. Thus, our task here is to elucidate the role of weak methods in scientific discovery, where they can be expected to play a major role in creative scientific work.

The standard against which weak methods must be judged is the limiting case of random search. Scientific discoveries seldom, if ever, emerge from random, trial-and-error search; the spaces to be searched are far too large for that. Rationality for a scientist consists in using the best means he has available—the best heuristics—for narrowing the search down to manageable proportions (sometimes at the cost of ruling out good solution candidates). If the scientist's tools are weak (perhaps because of the novelty of the problem), a great deal of residual search may still be required; but we must regard such a search process as rational if it employs all the heuristics that are known to be applicable to the domain. This is the concept of rationality that is relevant to the creative process and to problem solving in general, and it is with this kind of rationality that a normative theory of creativity and scientific discovery is concerned.

An Example: Blackbody Radiation

Our way of conceptualizing the discovery process can perhaps best be explained with the help of concrete examples. The two examples we shall employ lie beyond anything we have simulated with our computer programs. We chose them because they represent two of the most remarkable events in the history of physics, so that the encomium of "creativity" cannot be denied to them. If discoveries of the magnitude considered here can be explained in terms of understandable cognitive processes, even though they have not yet been simulated, they should give us some basis for approaching the modeling through simulation of other scientific discoveries of the first magnitude.

The first example is Max Planck's discovery of the law of blackbody radiation, a discovery that opened the way to the development of the quantum theory and provided the initial formulation of that theory. The example is really a whole set of examples, for a complex set of events was involved. At least one of these events can be explained with very good resolution in terms of steps each taking only a few hours; others require much more time.

In the case of blackbody radiation, the problem was to characterize the equilibrium distribution, by wavelength, of radiating energy inside a perfectly reflecting cavity. The goal was to find a function expressing the relative intensity of radiation at each wavelength as a function of that wavelength and the temperature of the cavity. The problem emerged in the middle of the nineteenth century and received considerable attention from

Gustav Kirchhoff and other leading physicists from that time until the first decades of the twentieth century. Steady advances in experimental instruments over the last quarter of the nineteenth century permitted increasingly accurate measurements of the intensity function over broader and broader ranges of temperatures and wavelengths. Thus, theorists concerned with the problem were confronted with increasingly stringent tests of their hypotheses, which culminated in 1899–1900 in the availability of data spanning a wide range of conditions.

Planck, a theoretical physicist, devoted a major part of his attention and activity to the blackbody problem over the years 1895–1900. Another German theoretical physicist, Wilhelm Wien, also played an important role in the events we shall describe. Of course, we cannot tell the whole story here; it has been the subject of several substantial books as well as a number of briefer accounts. The facts on which we shall draw are well established in this literature; see Klein 1962 and Kuhn 1978.

By the early 1890s, a good deal of theoretical work had been done on the blackbody problem, bringing to bear upon it the theories of electromagnetism, thermodynamics, and mechanics of that era. However, the theory had not developed to the point of yielding deductive derivations of a complete formula for blackbody radiation. Meanwhile, several empirical formulas ("curve-fitting exercises") had been proposed to account for the available empirical data. In particular, Wien had constructed (in 1896) an incomplete and not entirely satisfactory explanation of a formula first proposed on wholly empirical grounds by Friedrich Paschen. Wien's formula, as it was generally called, provided an excellent fit to the data then available. It was of the form

$$I(v) = \frac{A}{\exp(kv/T)}, \tag{2.1}$$

where $I(v)$ is the intensity of radiation of frequency v, T is the temperature of the cavity, and A and k are constants. Discrepancies between the formula and data for low temperatures and high frequencies (short wavelengths) were seldom more than a few percent. Data were unavailable for high temperatures and low frequencies. Wien's formula gained wide acceptance as a correct description of the phenomena and as the basis for a physical explanation of them.

In 1899, Planck succeeded, or thought he had succeeded, in deriving Wien's law deductively from the principles of classical physics. Planck believed that his demonstration showed that the law was unique—that no alternative law was compatible with classical principles. By "deriving the law from the principles of classical physics" we mean that Planck formulated a physical model to describe the black body and its cavity, and described the behavior of the model in classical terms.

Here we see already, in coarse grain, some of the kinds of developmental steps with which we shall be concerned throughout this book. In the period up to 1899 there were theoretical steps (by Kirchhoff, Wien, Planck, and others) connecting blackbody radiation to established physical theory; there were experimental steps, improving and extending the measurements; and there were curve-fitting steps, seeking to provide parsimonious descriptions of the data. As each step of whichever kind was taken, it provided a new set of initial conditions for the next act of theorizing, experimenting, or curve fitting. If there was an autonomous first mover in this system, it was the experimentation, which largely responded to new advances in instrumentation and which was not directly affected by theoretical progress. Nevertheless, the growing richness and interest of the theory undoubtedly contributed major motivation to the vigor of the experimental activities and the desire to extend the range of the empirical data. The theoretical work provided a rationale for the experimentation without much influencing its specifc course.

Neither Wien's law nor Planck's derivation of it, completed in 1899 and published early in 1900, survived very long the empirical tests provided by new experiments with higher temperatures and lower frequencies. By the summer of 1900, in the new range of observation, discrepancies had been discovered between data and formula that could not easily be explained away as errors of measurement. On the afternoon of Sunday, October 7, Heinrich Rubens (one of the experimentalists in Berlin working on blackbody radiation) and his wife called on the Plancks. Rubens described to Planck new findings that clearly violated Wien's law. In fact, he told Planck, these findings demonstrated that, for small values of v/T, I was linear in the reciprocal, T/v; that is, $I(v) = AT/kv$. Before he went to bed that night, Planck had conjectured a new formula to replace Wien's law, and had mailed a postcard to Rubens describing it. The new formula was closely similar to Wien's. Planck had simply replaced $\exp(kv/T)$ in the former by $\exp(kv/T) - 1$, to obtain

$$I(v) = \frac{A}{exp\,(kv/T) - 1}.$$

(2.2)

This is the law that has been known ever since as Planck's quantum-theoretical law of blackbody radiation. Planck announced it on October 19, explaining that he had arrived at it by constructing "completely arbitrary expressions for the entropy which although they are more complicated than Wien's expression [i.e., the expression consistent with Wien's formula] still seem to satisfy just as completely all requirements of the thermodynamic and electromagnetic theory" and pointing out, with some note of apology, that his earlier demonstration of the "necessity" of Wien's law had obviously been erroneous. He also identified the probable locus of the error in his reasoning: the expression for entropy, which he had postulated with very little physical motivation.

We will return to the crucial day of October 7, 1900, but before doing so we will sketch out the rest of the story. Planck was now faced with the task of providing a physical explanation for the new law. He was able to construct and announce one by December. The explanation rested on the nonclassical quantization of energy; however, as Klein (1962), Kuhn (1978), and others have shown, the derivation was sufficiently complex and difficult that neither Planck nor other physicists were aware of its deadly consequences for classical physics until about 1905 or 1906, when these were pointed out by Albert Einstein and Paul Ehrenfest.

Notice that in this last phase, the final months of 1900, Planck was working backward from a known result, a formula induced directly from the data, and was aiming at providing a physical "story" that would explain why the formula was just so and not otherwise. This was exactly what he had done in 1899 for Wien's law. By the verdict of history, the 1899 story was invalid, the 1900 story valid (or essentially so; we do not tell it today in exactly the same way). The history of events would seem to imply that, whatever the facts (or whatever they were thought to be at a given moment of time), a physicist of sufficient expertise and ingenuity (but perhaps only one at Planck's level) might find a rationalization that would fit these facts to theory. We are reminded again of Poincaré's dictum that "hypotheses are what we lack the least." There is no reason to believe, and no evidence, that the reasoning processes Planck applied to his task of 1899 were any different from those he applied in 1900. The goal was different, however—a different formula to which he had to build a bridge from classical theory.

A crucial step in Planck's 1900 derivation employed probabilities. The particular probability model he selected (involving indistinguishable electrons) had no special physical motivation except that it led to the right, and already known, formula. In fact, had Planck used the standard (and more defensible) Boltzmann statistics, he would have been led to the "classical" Rayleigh-Jeans law of blackbody radiation, with $I(v)$ linear in T/v, which, like Wien's law, holds only asymptotically for one range of v/T. (The correct law, given by Planck's formula, is in fact an interpolation between Wien's formula, which fits large values of v/T, and that of Rayleigh and Jeans, which fits small values.)

Planck's theoretical derivation, therefore, was in considerable measure driven by the data (or, more exact, by a formula obtained inductively from the data). The solution to the problem that Planck posed for himself had to satisfy constraints imposed by the data as well as constraints imposed by classical theory. The latter were sufficiently ill defined that it was possible to violate them inadvertently and thereby find a solution under the driving force of the given empirical formula.

We go back now to October 7, 1900. What happened during the hours in which Planck was seeking an alternative, consistent with the data, to Wien's formula? There are two possible answers to this question, but they both lead to the same conclusion: The problem was solved by finding a formula that interpolated smoothly between the two known limiting functions, Wien's formula for high values of the v/T ratio and the linear (in T/v) formula communicated to Planck by Rubens for low values of v/T. In his October 19 paper, Planck describes one path toward this interpolation without asserting quite explicitly that it was the actual path of his discovery. There was also a second path, and it seems even simpler and more obvious.

First, consider the path mentioned by Planck (see Kangro 1972). From the radiation formula (either Wien's or the linear one), and with the help of the then-accepted physical theory of the phenomena, it is easy to calculate the second derivative, d^2S/dU^2, where S is the entropy of the system and U is its energy. S and U are connected with T by the relation $dS/dU = 1/T$. Planck was already familiar with this derivation in connection with Wien's law, and the same derivation can be carried through directly for the linear formula. We obtain

$$\frac{d^2S}{dU^2} = \frac{A}{U}$$

(2.3)

for Wien's law and

$$\frac{d^2S}{dU^2} = \frac{A}{U^2} \tag{2.4}$$

for the linear intensity law.

Now, Planck goes on to say in his October 19 paper (Kangro 1970, p. 36):

> I finally started to construct completely arbitrary expressions for the entropy which although they are more complicated than Wien's expression still seem to satisfy just as completely all requirements of the thermodynamic and electromagnetic theory.
>
> I was especially attracted by one of the expressions thus constructed which is nearly as simple as Wien's expression and which would deserve to be investigated since Wien's expression is not sufficient to cover all observations. We get this expression by putting
>
> $d^2S/dU^2 = \alpha/[U(\beta + U)]$.
>
> It is by far the simplest of all expressions which lead to S as a logarithmic function of U. . . .

If we accept this account as an actual description of the process that Planck used to solve his problem, then we see that he searched among an undefined class of functions until he found a "simple" one that had the desired limiting properties. We do not have any very good measure of how hard or how easy a search this is, except that Planck completed it in a few hours.

There is an alternative path to the goal that makes use of the intensity laws without calculating the derivatives of the entropies. It consists in looking directly for a "simple" interpolating function between Wien's law, for high v/T, and the law that is linear in T/v, for low v/T. Consider Wien's law in the form $I = A/e^x$, where x is essentially v/T. To find the behavior of the function in the neighborhood of $x = 0$ (low v/T), we expand e^x into a Taylor series, obtaining the familiar expression

$$e^x = 1 + x + x^2/2! + \cdots, \tag{2.5}$$

whence, subtracting unity from both sides and neglecting higher-order terms, we obtain

$$e^x - 1 = x. \tag{2.6}$$

Hence, if we replace e^x in Wien's law by $(e^x - 1)$, we obtain a function that, by equation 2.6, is approximately linear in x for small x, but which goes asymptotically to e^x as x (that is, v/T) grows large. Thus, we have obtained a new function, $I = A/[\exp(v/T) - 1]$, which interpolates between Wien's law for large v/T and the linear law for small v/T and which is precisely Planck's law of radiation as stated in equation 2.2.

In the spirit of casual empiricism, we sought to assess just how difficult this derivation is, and whether it is likely to occur to a skilled applied mathematician within a moderate span of time. We gave the interpolation problem, without explaining its physical origins, to eight colleagues who are professional physical scientists and applied mathematicians. Five gave the same answer that Planck arrived at, each in under two minutes. Three of the five used exactly the process described above (expansion of e^x into series); the other two used different, but equally simple, procedures. None of them recognized the problem as related to blackbody radiation or thought of Planck's law until they had derived it.

Given this evidence, we must conclude that, for someone possessing the standard heuristics of an applied mathematician (all of which were known in 1900), even in the absence of the physical cues that were available to Planck, no extensive search is required to solve the problem. Planck's success in solving it within a few hours should occasion no surprise. We do not know, of course, whether Planck took the route just described, or the one he himself described, or some other route. We known only that no unusual processes, but only standard processes used by and generally available to theoreticians in the physical sciences, need be postulated in order to explain the actual discovery.

It would be hard to argue that either Planck's behavior or the behavior of our colleagues when they were presented with Planck's problem was a matter of chance or of pure "inspiration." Rather, they quite patently represent applications of these entirely sensible heuristic principles:

• Given two distinct functions that fit the data excellently in two different regions, look for an interpolating function that approximates the given functions in the limit in the appropriate regions.
• To examine the limiting behavior of a function, express it as a Taylor series around the limit point.

These procedures will not always work—they are weak methods, but scientists who apply them will more often be successful in finding laws that fit data well than scientists who do not. Why, then, didn't others discover Planck's law in 1900 or earlier? Planck was one of a small number of theoreticians interested in this problem, and one of an even smaller number who were conversant with the most recent data. Moreover, the refutation by these data of Planck's previous "explanation" of Wien's law gave him strong motivation to put the problem at the top of his agenda. The "accident" happened to a thoroughly prepared and motivated mind.

Planck's construction in December 1900 of a physical explanation or rationalization of the new formula also is attributable to something other than inspiration or intuition. His previous derivation of Wien's law told him at just what point his theory needed correction, and his new knowledge of the "correct" law provided a criterion that any new explanation must satisfy: It must lead to the new law. Planck applied the heuristic of working backward from a known result, generating subgoals as he went, and examined alternative probability models until he found one (a very unorthodox one, although he was not aware of that fact at the time) that yielded the desired result. Knowing what answer he had to reach greatly limited the size of his search space and informed him immediately when he had succeeded.

This example should make clear the sense in which we think normative statements can be made about the discovery process. Such statements will take the form of descriptions of good heuristics, or of evaluative statements about the relative merits of different heuristics or other methods. The evaluative statements can be generated, in turn, either by examining historical evidence of discovery or failure of discovery or by constructing computer programs that incorporate the heuristics and then testing the efficacy of the computer programs as machines for making discoveries.

A Second Example: Universal Gravitation

If one swallow does not make a summer, observing two of them may at least create the presumption that summer is on its way. Our second example of an efficacious discovery process, Newton's discovery of the law of universal gravitation, is as important to the history of science as our first. Although, as with the example of Planck's law, we have not written or run a simulation program that derives the gravitational law, we can account for the discovery process in reasonable and programmable detail.

Twice in the *Principia* Newton states his theory of scientific discovery, but his words have not usually been taken seriously as a description of the discovery process.[4] In his preface to the first edition, Newton says: "... the whole burden of philosophy seems to consist in this—from the phenomena

4. See, however, Glymour 1980.

of motions to investigate the forces of nature, and then from these forces to demonstrate the other phenomena...." (Newton 1636, pp. xvii–xviii) He is even clearer on the final page of book III: "In [experimental] philosophy particular propositions are to be inferred from the phenomena, and afterwards rendered general by induction. Thus it was that the impenetrability, the mobility, and the impulsive force of bodies, and the laws of motion and of gravitation, were discovered." (Newton 1636, p. 547)

The last assertion—"Thus it was that the... laws of motion and gravitation were discovered"—is especially deserving of attention, as it represents the firsthand testimony of the discoverer.[5] Such testimony should not be taken at face value; it must be subjected to scrutiny. In this case, however, Newton's assertions about his methods of discovery are fully supported by the historical record culled from his early papers (Westfall 1980, chapter 5) and by the logical structure of the *Principia*. Let us follow Glymour's (1980) analysis of this logic.

At the time of the discovery of the inverse-square law of gravitation, the three laws of motion were accepted as part of the known body of mechanical laws. Newton does not try to prove or support them in the *Principia*, but simply takes them, when appropriate, as premises in his arguments. In addition, Newton employs two geometrical theorems about circular motion (book I, proposition IV, p. 45):

- The velocity of a body rotating in a circle (with constant speed) is proportional to the diameter of the circle and inversely proportional to the period of rotation: $V = k_1 D/P$.
- The acceleration of the same body is proportional to the ratio of the square of its velocity to the diameter of the circle: $A = k_2 V^2/D$.

Finally, Newton employs an empirical law, Kepler's third law, induced from observations of the movements of the satellites of Jupiter and Saturn and of the primary planets about the Sun:

- These satellites and planets rotate in (approximately) circular orbits about their respective attracting bodies, with periods whose squares vary with the cubes of the diameters of the orbits: $P^2 = k_3 D^3$.

---

5. In a letter to Henry Oldenburg, Newton was even more explicit about the path of discovery: "You know the proper Method for inquiring after the properties of things is to deduce them from Experiments. And I told you that the Theory wch I propounded was evinced by me, not by inferring tis this because not otherwise, but by deriving it from Experiments concluding positively & directly." (cited on p. 179 of Laymon 1983)

Now, Newton deduces the inverse-square law of gravitation directly (book I, proposition IV and corollaries I, II, and VI, pp. 54–55) from these three relations by using the first to eliminate V from the second, and the third to eliminate P from the resulting equation, thus giving a as a function of D:

$$A = k_2 V^2/D$$
$$= k_2 k_1{}^2 D^2/(P^2 D)$$
$$= k_4 D/P^2$$
$$= k_4 D/k_3 D^3$$
$$= k_5/D^2.$$

The acceleration, A, is the force per unit mass (i.e., $A = F/m$), so the total force exerted on a planet or satellite is

$$F = mA = k_5 m/D^2.$$

(From other considerations, $k_5 = gM$, where M is the mass of the attracting body and g the universal gravitational constant, so we have the familiar form: $F = gmM/D^2$.)

The important point to notice here is that, in discovering the relation between acceleration and distance, the only step of *induction* is the inference of Kepler's third law from the observations—a data-driven induction.[6] Once this step has been taken and the goal of expressing A as a function of D has been set, the remaining steps are purely deductive and can be discovered by application of a heuristic in algebra that was well known in Newton's time: Given a set of n equations in $(n + 1)$ variables, $x_1, \ldots, x_{n+1}$, to express x_1 as a function of x_2, use $(n - 1)$ of the equations to eliminate the $(n - 1)$ other variables from the remaining equation. This heuristic (which, of course, cannot always be carried out in closed form) is usually executed by solving particular equations for particular unwanted variables in terms of the others, then inserting those values in the remaining equations. This is precisely what we have done above, and what Newton does in the *Principia*.

6. To carry out the induction, Newton initially had to make the counterfactual assumption that the orbits were circular. Only twenty years after his derivation of the law for circular orbits was he able to carry out the corresponding derivation for elliptical orbits.

Glymour regards this derivation as an example of bootstrap[7] *confirmation* of a theory. Our analysis shows that it also provides a plausible path to the *discovery* of the theory (as Newton claimed). An efficient problem-solving system, given Kepler's third law and the goal of finding a relation between gravitational force and distance, would be impelled by the heuristic just cited along this very path.

The Interaction of Discovery and Confirmation

The two examples just discussed should also make it evident that processes of discovery and processes of confirmation are not separate and distinct. In fact, they live in very close proximity and relation. When a search process is provided with heuristics, especially when those heuristics take the form of tests of progress, the partial results of a search receive confirmation or refutation, or some evaluative feedback, before a full-blown hypothesis is produced. Each step or group of steps of the search is evaluated in terms of the evidence of progress it has produced, and the continuing search process is modified on the basis of the outcome of these evaluations. The confirmations of partial results cumulate and make the confirmation of the final hypothesis coincide with its generation. In particular, an inductive generalization is confirmed in the very same way it is generated.

The alternation and intermingling of generation and test processes in the course of the search for a scientific law can be illustrated by means of the pattern-discovery process that was discussed in chapter 1. Consider again the alphabetic sequence

A B M C D M F E M. . . .

A person asked to extrapolate the sequence will notice that it consists of the Roman letters in alphabetic order, interrupted at every third position by repetition of the letter M. The pattern can be represented by a formula like A(nMn)*, where n stands for "next letter in the Roman alphabet," A and M stand for themselves, and the asterisk stands for indefinite repetition. Humans have easily understandable ways of finding the formula. Instead of depending on random search in the space of possible formulas, they examine the original letter sequences for repeating relations of "same" and "next" among the letters and construct a formula directly from the re-

---

7. Glymour regards it as bootstrap because a theoretical postulate—Newton's second law of motion—is required as a premise.

lations they discover (Simon and Kotovsky 1963; Kotovsky and Simon 1973). Each instance of the relation that is noticed becomes a partial confirmation of the formula that is being evolved. People of normal intelligence solve this particular problem in a few seconds, and require no "intuitive," "inspirational," or magical powers to do so—unless one wishes to employ the term *intuition* to refer to recognition of familiar relations that have long been stored in long-term memory.

Notice that in pattern finding, whether for letter series or for the kind of data involved in Planck's law, no leap of infinite induction is involved. A finite body of data is available for examination, and the task is to find a simple law that will fit *those* data. One hopes that as new data are found they will continue to satisfy the law, but the accuracy of such prediction need not be assumed in the discovery process itself. The criteria used to evaluate the progress or success of a discovery process have to do with the compatibility of a law with a finite set of given data, not with its predictive powers in the future.

Once a law has been discovered, we can, of course, continue to test it against any new data that may be generated. It is our faith in some kind of continuity and simplicity of nature that leads us often to expect that such prediction will be successful. But the efficacy of the discovery process does not rest on that faith.

That evaluative tests of progress are available during the successive stages of the process of discovery is a major source of the efficiency of discovery methods. In the case of the letter series, we do not have to discover the complete formula in a single step. As in the example of a clicking safe, we can discover particular relations, one by one, and gradually piece them together into a more complete hypothesis. In the same way, the discovery of Wien's law from data over a limited range of variation provided information that made the subsequent discovery of the interpolating formula relatively easy. Large discoveries take place by the cumulation of little steps, and it is the understanding of these steps and of the processes by which they are accomplished that strips the larger discovery of its aura of mystery.

Let us sum up the import of our discussion for the relation between discovery and confirmation. First, a new discovery is not usually taken out of the air. Instead, it is generally developed through a step-by-step search guided at each step by data. Second, at each step in this process, the developing hypothesis is guaranteed to be confirmed by the data examined thus far. Third, since only a finite body of data is in question, the verification can be complete (that is, compatibility with the data can be definitely confirmed), although uniqueness cannot be guaranteed. Fourth, because of the incremental character of the process, the discovery, once arrived at, has already achieved a considerable degree of confirmation, although it still may fail when tested against new data.

In the literature on Bayesian confirmation procedures, many different interpretations have been proposed for the concept of the prior probability of a hypothesis. When the discovery process is taken into account, a new[8] possibility for interpretation arises: We might think of the prior probability as the probability that a hypothesis selected at random from among those generated by this same discovery process is correct.

This interpretation of the Bayesian prior probability conforms with the fact that one's prior belief in a hypothesis rises with one's confidence in the competence of the scientist who has proposed it. Other things being equal, a theory proposed by an outstanding scientist (read "a scientist whose discovery process has made a large percentage of hits") has greater credibility, as soon as it is announced, than the same theory proposed by an unknown scientist or by one who has proposed hypotheses that subsequently have been disconfirmed. Of course, if we have access to the path of discovery and the evidence used by the heuristics to guide search, we can base our prior belief on that information instead of the reputation of the proposer.

Earlier Attempts at Modeling Discoveries

One of the earliest attempts to model scientific discovery was the simulation work of Donald Gerwin (1974).[9] Gerwin was interested in how humans infer numerical laws or functions from knowledge of specific data points. In order to understand this process, he gave his subjects several sets of data and asked them to find the relations that best summarized each data set. Using verbal protocols collected from this task, Gerwin built a working simulation of the subjects' behaviors. The model first attempted to identify a general pattern in the data, such as a periodic trend with increasing amplitudes or a monotonic decreasing trend. A class of functions was

8. Actually, this possibility is not entirely new; see Simon 1955.
9. Gerwin drew on the work of Huesmann and Cheng (1973), who had built a system for fitting mathematical functions to data but who were less concerned with human simulation than was Gerwin.

stored with each pattern the program could recognize; once a class was hypothesized, the system sought to determine what specific function in the class was responsible for the data. If unexplained variance remained, the program treated the differences between the observed and the predicted values as a new set of data. This procedure was used to elaborate the hypothesis until no pattern could be found in the residual data. The program also could backtrack if the latest addition to the rule failed to improve the predictions. One limitation of Gerwin's simulation was that the program incorporated specific knowledge about the shapes of functions within a specified range, and variable parameters could not be associated with these functions. Even though Gerwin's model could only solve a very restricted range of problems, it did reproduce some of the gross phenomena of human discovery, and it was an important step in understanding the discovery process.

DENDRAL (Buchanan et al. 1969; Lindsay et al. 1980), a problem-solving program that identifies organic molecules from mass spectrograms and nuclear magnetic resonances, can also be viewed as a discovery program. The system identifies chemical structures in three main stages: planning, generating plausible structures, and testing those structures. The first stage uses patterns in the data to infer that certain familiar molecules are present. Considering these molecules as units reduces drastically the number of structures produced during the generation stage. This second phase uses knowledge of valences, chemical stability, and user-specified constraints to generate all plausible chemical structures. In the final testing stage, the system predicts mass spectrograms for each of these structures, which are then ranked according to the closeness of their agreement with the data. DENDRAL relies on considerable domain-specific knowledge, acquired laboriously through interaction with human experts in organic chemistry.

In order to reduce dependence on human experts, the same researchers designed meta-DENDRAL (Buchanan and Mitchell 1978), a system that induces new rules of mass spectroscopy which can then be used by the DENDRAL Program. Meta-DENDRAL is provided with known organic compounds and their mass spectrograms, from which it formulates rules to explain those data.[10]

10. The designers of DENDRAL and meta-DENDRAL were strongly influenced by Carl Hempel's (1965) theories of explanation and confirmation, respectively, in shaping their inference strategies. Hence, these programs provide interesting illustrations of what is involved in operationalizing principles drawn from the philosophical literature on induction.

Two types of events are used to explain spectograms: cleavages in the bonds of a molecule and migrations of atoms from one site to another. Although plausible actions are determined using domain-specific chemical knowledge, the conditions on rules are found through a much more general technique. Meta-DENDRAL has successfully discovered new rules of mass spectroscopy for three related families of organic molecules.

AM (Lenat 1977) is a system that has rediscovered important concepts from number theory. In contrast with the programs discussed previously, AM's criterion of success is not that a concept be compatible with empirical data but that it be "interesting" in terms of its relations with other concepts, its capacity to generate examples, and so on. The program begins with about 100 basic concepts such as sets, lists, equality, and operations, and about 250 heuristics to direct the discovery process. The heuristics are responsible for filling out the descriptions of concepts, suggesting new tasks, and creating new concepts based on existing ones. New tasks are ordered according to their interestingness. (Tasks proposed by a number of different heuristics tend to be more interesting than those proposed by a single rule.) Using this measure to direct its search through the space of mathematical concepts, AM defined concepts for the integers, for multiplication, for divisors of, and for prime numbers, and proposed the unique-factorization theorem. Like meta-DENDRAL, Lenat's system incorporates some very general strategies and some domain-specific knowledge about the field of mathematics.

Lenat's AM was followed by EURISKO (Lenat 1983), which can discover not only new concepts but new heuristics as well. Automatic programming schemes (Amarel 1972; Simon 1972) and induction programs (see, e.g., Mitchell 1977) perform tasks that can be viewed as discovery. The vagueness of the boundary between discovery systems and other problem-solving systems is to be expected in light of our hypothesis that discovery is simply a form of problem solving, which uses the same basic processes as the other systems.

In our work on BACON and the other systems we will decribe, we have attempted to develop general-purpose, and mostly descriptive, discovery systems. Rather than rely on domain-dependent heuristics, as many of the earlier discovery systems have done, BACON incorporates weak yet general heuristics that can be applied to many different domains. The current version addresses only the descriptive component of scientific discovery. It does not attempt to construct explanations of phenomena, such as the atomic theory or the kinetic theory of gases. Neither is it meant to replicate the historical details of various scientific discoveries, though of course those details are interesting. Instead, it is intended as a model of how discoveries *might* occur in these domains.

Conclusion

In this chapter we have reviewed, briefly, the main lines of the discussion of confirmation and verification in the contemporary literature of the philosophy of science. We have seen that little or no justification has been given in that literature for the frequent claim that a normative theory of discovery, paralleling the theory of confirmation, is impossible. We have outlined the nature of such a theory, have provided several examples of historical episodes of discovery that fit the theory, and have shown that the processes of discovery and confirmation are, in fact, closely interwoven. Finally, we have outlined briefly the history of attempts to construct a theory of scientific discovery. We are now ready to set forth, in the next six chapters, our own models of the discovery process and the theory that is embodied in these models.

II THE Bacon PROGRAMS

In this part we construct, step by step, a system of considerable generality that is capable of significant scientific discovery. This system, BACON, makes use of a few powerful heuristics to search with relative efficiency through a space of possible laws, sometimes inventing useful concepts to state the laws more parsimoniously.

3 Discovering Quantitative Empirical Laws

Since there are advantages in translating theories about information processing into running computer programs, we have followed this route in our research on scientific discovery. Our first efforts along these lines led to a sequence of computer programs collectively called BACON. The BACON systems (versions 1 through 6) are named after Francis Bacon, because they incorporate many of his ideas on the nature of scientific reasoning. The successive versions of BACON share a common approach to discovery, as well as a common representation of data and laws. The differences among the various systems lie in the discovery heuristics that each uses in its search for empirical laws. In general, later versions of BACON retain the heuristics of earlier versions, but also incorporate additional ones.

BACON.1 is the simplest of the systems and thus the easiest to describe and to understand. In addition, since the BACON.1 heuristics are used by later incarnations of the system, their description here will provide a solid foundation for what is to come. Later in this chapter we will describe BACON.3 in terms of amendments and additions to BACON.1. We will follow the same strategy in discussing BACON.4 and BACON.5 in the next two chapters. In each case, we describe the systems in terms of their heuristics and provide numerous examples of those heuristics in action.

BACON.1 uses a general representation and a few heuristics to discover an impressive range of empirical laws. The system is general in the same sense that the General Problem Solver of Newell, Shaw, and Simon (see Newell and Simon 1963) was general. That is to say, the basic methods of BACON make no reference to the semantic meaning of the data on which they operate and make no special assumptions about the structure of the data. BACON.1 also has much in common with the General Rule Inducer proposed by Simon and Lea (1974), since it searches a space of data and a space of rules and attempts to relate one to the other.

We have striven for generality in BACON because we wish to explore the role in scientific discovery of heuristics that may be relevant over a wide range of scientific disciplines and hence may contribute to our basic understanding of discovery wherever it may occur. In adopting this strategy, it is not our intention to deny the important role that discipline-specific knowledge and heuristics play in the work of science; rather, we want to see how far we can go initially with data-driven, semantically impoverished processes. Having clarified our bias toward general mechanisms, let us consider an example of how one might employ such mechanisms to discover an empirical law.

A Sample Protocol

In 1618, Johannes Kepler discovered his third law of planetary motion: The cube of a planet's distance from the Sun is proportional to the square of its period. This law can be restated as $D^3/P^2 = c$, where D is the distance, P is the period, and c is a constant.

How might one discover such a law? Here is a sample protocol that draws on three very simple heuristics:

• If the values of a term are constant, then infer that the term always has that value.
• If the values of two numerical terms increase together, then consider their ratio.
• If the values of one term increase as those of another decrease, then consider their product.

The value of these heuristics can best be seen in their operation. The three planets considered below, A, B, and C, obey a version of Kepler's law where the constant is 1. The discoverer must begin by gathering some data, selecting different values for the nominal variable (planet), and obtaining the values of the numerical terms (D and P):

When planet is A
What is P?   Answer: 1.0
What is D?   Answer: 1.0

When planet is B
What is P?   Answer: 8.0
What is D?   Answer: 4.0

When planet is C
What is P?   Answer: 27.0
What is D?   Answer: 9.0

D increases with P
so I'll consider their ratio.
I'll define Term-1 as the ratio of D and P [D/P].

Here the second heuristic has been applied. The distance and the period have been observed to increase together, so the new concept Term-1 has been defined as their ratio. Next, the values of this new term are calculated.

When D is: 1.0   4.0   9.0
and P is: 1.0   8.0   27.0
Term-1 is: 1.0   0.5   0.333

D increases as Term-1 decreases
so I'll consider their product.
I'll define Term-2 as the product
of D and Term-1 $[D(D/P) = D^2/P]$.

When D is: 1.0   4.0   9.0
and P is: 1.0   8.0   27.0
Term-2 is: 1.0   2.0   3.0

Term-1 increases as Term-2 decreases
so I'll consider their product.
I'll define Term-3 as the product
of Term-1 and Term-2 $[(D/P)(D^2/P) = D^3/P^2]$.

By this point, the third heuristic has been applied twice. Two more concepts have been defined: Term-2 as D^2/P and Term-3 as D^3/P^2. Since the latter of these is the most recently formed, we next examine its values:

When D is: 1.0   4.0   9.0
and P is: 1.0   8.0   27.0
Term-3 is: 1.0   1.0   1.0

Term-3 has the constant value 1.0

Finally, the first heuristic applies, for the new concept Term-3 (defined as D^3/P^2) has the constant value 1.0 for all three planets. The statement that this term is constant across planets is equivalent to Kepler's third law of planetary motion, and the above protocol is a plausible trace of how one might discover this law. In this example we used idealized data for the sake of clarity, but later in the chapter we will reconsider Kepler's law in the context of the original data.

BACON.1's Representation

The above protocol was actually generated by the BACON.1 program. Of course, BACON.1 was not designed to produce fluent English; we gave it the ability to generate simple protocols only in order to be better able to trace the path it travels toward discovery. Here we attempt to clarify the nature of the program still further by considering the representations it uses for its data and for its heuristics.

The Representation of Data

BACON.1 represents its data in terms of *data clusters*. A data cluster is a set of attribute-value pairs linked to a common node; it represents a series of

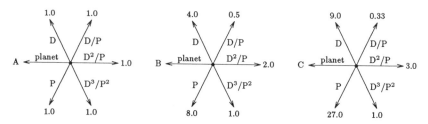

Figure 3.1

observations that have occurred together. The program knows about two types of terms or attributes: *independent* and *dependent*. It has control over independent attributes; it can vary their values and request the corresponding values of the dependent attributes (i.e., the values that the system is trying to explain). Independent terms may take on either numerical or nominal (symbolic) values, whereas the version of BACON.1 described here allows only numerical values for its dependent terms.[1] In the above example, the values of the independent term were the names of planets; the values of the dependent terms were the distances and periods of those planets.

Figure 3.1 shows three data clusters from the Keplerian example. In this case, there are three primitive (directly observable) attributes: the planet being observed, the planet's distance D from the sun, and the period P of the planet's orbit. However, much of BACON.1's power comes from its ability to define higher-level (theoretical) attributes in terms of more primitive ones. Thus, the clusters in figure 3.1 also show the values for three non-primitive attributes: Term-1 (defined as D/P), Term-2 (defined as D^2/P), and Term-3 (defined as D^3/P^2). Since these terms include dependent terms in their definitions and thus cannot be manipulated by experiment or observation, they are considered dependent.

When BACON.1 defines a new term, it generates a name for the variable (e.g., "Term-1") and treats it in the same way it treats directly observable terms. Defined terms can be used to define other new terms as well, so the process is recursive. The generation of higher-level attributes is useful mainly because it allows for parsimonious representation of the data; it permits complex laws to be stated as simple constancies. For instance, it is

1. See appendix A (pp. 115–120) for a discussion of the relation between this version and that described in Langley 1978 and in Langley 1979b.

Table 3.1
Data obeying Kepler's third law of planetary motion.

Planet	Distance (D)	Period (P)	Term-1 (D/P)	Term-2 (D^2/P)	Term-3 (D^3/P^2)
A	1.0	1.0	1.0	1.0	1.0
B	4.0	8.0	0.5	2.0	1.0
C	9.0	27.0	0.333	3.0	1.0

only because BACON.1 defines Term-3 as D^3/P^2 that it can state Kepler's third law in such a simple manner. As this example shows, BACON.1 can always restate the laws in terms of observables by replacing the theoretical terms with their definitions.

Although BACON.1's internal representation of data is much like the clusters shown in figure 3.1, it is more convenient to display these data in tabular form. Table 3.1 presents the same data as figure 3.1. Each column in the table lists the values for a given term, such as the planet, the distance D, and Term-1; each row corresponds to one of the data clusters shown in the figure. In the remainder of this book, we will use tabular rather than graphic notation for the data gathered by BACON. We will not mark higher-level terms explicitly to distinguish them from observables, but they will generally occur in the rightmost columns of tables.

The data used in this example were contrived to fit Kepler's law exactly. Except for rounding errors, BACON did not have to deal with any form of noise or imprecision in the numbers given to it. The BACON programs do have modest capabilities for handling imprecise data by ignoring small deviations from the predictions of the laws they hypothesize. The amount of noise that is accepted is controlled by parameters in the programs. We will have a little more to say later about the processing of inexact data, and about laws that are only approximate, but this will not be a main theme of our discussion.

The Representation of Heuristics

BACON.1 is implemented in the production-system language PRISM, described in Langley and Neches 1981 and in Langley and Ohlsson 1984. In turn, PRISM is implemented in LISP, a list-processing language widely used in artificial-intelligence research.

A production-system program (see also chapter 1) has two main components: a set of condition-action rules, or *productions*, and a dynamic *working memory*. A production system operates in cycles. On every cycle, the conditions of each production are matched against the current state of the working memory. From the rules that match successfully, one is selected for application. When a production is applied, its actions affect the state of the working memory, making new productions match. This process continues until no rules are matched or until a stop command is encountered.

BACON.1's discovery heuristics are stated as PRISM productions. Each rule contains a set of *conditions* describing the system's goals or specifying patterns that may occur in the data. In addition, each rule contains a set of *actions*, which are responsible for setting goals, formulating laws (e.g, that some term has a constant value), defining new terms, computing the values of these terms, and so forth. Conditions and actions can be written either directly in PRISM or as LISP functions. On each cycle, one of the matching rules is selected for application, and its associated actions are carried out. When two or more rules match, BACON.1 prefers the rule that matches against elements that have been added to memory most recently. This leads the system to pursue possibilities in a depth-first manner. That is, since the newest goals and data always receive the most attention, BACON continues each line of search until it is successful or until it peters out. In the latter case, the program returns to an earlier step and sets out on a new line of search in the same way.

Production systems were first proposed as a general framework for modeling human cognition by Newell and Simon (1972), who listed a number of advantages of these systems, some of which are particularly relevant to discovery systems. First, production systems carry out an essentially parallel search to determine which rules are applicable to the current situation. Thus, they seem well suited for searching a large set of data for constancies and trends. Second, production systems can be "data driven" in the sense that new data can strongly influence the course taken by a set of rules. At the same time, production rules can also incorporate information about the current goals of the system, so that a compromise between data-driven, bottom-up behavior and goal-driven, top-down behavior can be achieved. Finally, since each production is relatively independent of every other production, one can (with care) construct modular programs that continue to run after new rules have been inserted or old rules removed. This characteristic will allow us to add new heuristics to BACON without modifying the system in other ways.

The Processes of BACON.1

Now that we have discussed BACON.1's representation for data and the form of its heuristics, let us turn to some details of its processes. BACON.1 consists of sixteen productions, which can be divided into four main sets:[2]

- a set of five productions for running simple experiments and gathering data by requesting them from the user and recording them,
- a set of five productions that detect regularities in the data produced by the first and third sets,
- a set of three productions that actually define the higher-level terms proposed by the second set, and that compute the values of these terms, and
- a set of three productions that clean up the memory when certain elements stored there are no longer useful.

We discuss the first three components in more detail below.

During its discovery process, BACON.1 generates a number of goals and subgoals to focus its attention in useful directions. Figure 3.2 presents the main goals used in BACON.1, along with the relations among them (i.e., which goals call on which others). We will refer to these goals in our discussion of the details of the system.

Gathering Data

BACON.1's top-level goal is to incorporate the single independent term into one or more laws. In order to accomplish this goal, the system includes a number of rules that let it gather data systematically. These operate by setting subgoals which cause the other rules to match. The first rule to be applied is INITIALIZE-INDEPENDENT, which matches against the top-level *incorporate* goal, initializes the values of the independent term,

---

2. The initial version of BACON.1 (Langley 1978, 1979b) was considerably more complex than the version described below. The early version also contained heuristics for placing conditions on overly general laws and for noting periodic relations. As a result, that version of BACON.1 was also able to solve concept-attainment tasks and sequence-extrapolation problems. We have focused on the simpler, less general version of BACON.1 in this chapter for two reasons. First, our concern with scientific discovery has led us to concentrate on the BACON.1 heuristics that are relevant to this domain, rather than on methods necessary for rule-induction tasks such as concept attainment and sequence extrapolation. Second, later versions of the system (BACON.3 through BACON.6) abandoned these heuristics to focus on those relevant to the discovery of empirical laws. Thus, we simplify our presentation considerably by treating BACON.1's heuristics as a subset of those used by later systems, even though this was not the actual sequence of development. To indicate the generality of the original BACON.1, however, we have described some of its capabilities in appendix A.

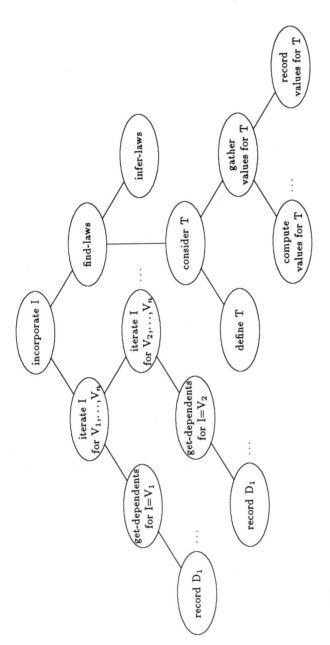

Figure 3.2

Table 3.2
BACON.1's rules for gathering data.

INITIALIZE-INDEPENDENT
If you want[a] to *incorporate* the independent term I into laws,
  and the suggested values of I are $V_1, V_2, \ldots, V_n$,
then *iterate* through these values of I,
  but retain the list $V_n, \ldots, V_2, V_1$ for later use.

UPDATE-INDEPENDENT
If you want to *iterate* through values $V_1, V_2, \ldots, V_n$ for term I,
then *get dependent* values for all dependent terms when $I = V_1$,
  and *iterate* through the values of $V_2, \ldots, V_n$ for term I.

RECORD
If you want to *get dependent* values for all dependent terms when $I = V$,
  and D is an observable dependent term,
then request the value for D under these conditions,
  and *record* the resulting value.

INITIALIZE-DEPENDENT
If you want to *get dependent* values for all dependent terms when $I = V$,
  and you have *recorded* the value V_k for D,
  but you do not have a list of values for D,
then create an initial list for the values of D.

UPDATE-DEPENDENT
If you want to *get dependent* values for all dependent terms when $I = V$,
  and you have *recorded* the value V_k for D,
  and you have a list of values $V_n, \ldots, V_1$ for D,
then update the list of values as $V_k, V_n, \ldots, V_1$.

---

a. "If you want" means "if there is a symbol denoting this goal in working memory."

and creates a goal to *iterate* through these values. A second production, UPDATE-INDEPENDENT, matches against this *iterate* goal and sets two subgoals: to *get dependent* values for the current value of the independent term and to *iterate* through the remaining values of the independent term.

BACON.1's recency-based conflict-resolution strategy ensures that the first of these goals (*get dependent*) receives priority, so that it will be satisfied before other independent values are examined. The rule RECORD matches against the *get dependent* goal, applying once for each dependent term known to the system. In each case, it requests the value of that dependent term from the user and *records* this value in working memory. Two more rules transform this information into a more useful form: INITIALIZE-DEPENDENT initializes the list of values to be stored for a given dependent term, and UPDATE-DEPENDENT updates this list for future values of the same term. These five rules are presented in table 3.2;

for the sake of clarity, we have paraphrased them in English and italicized the goal symbols.

Although these rules were designed to interact well with BACON.1's other heuristics, they can run perfectly well on their own, and it will be useful to consider their operation in the independent mode on our Keplerian example. In this case, we present the system with a single independent term—the planet under observation— and tell it to examine three values of this term: *A*, *B*, and *C*. Furthermore, we inform the system of two dependent terms: the distance *D* of the planet from the sun and the planet's period *P*. Finally, we include the top-level goal of *incorporating* the independent term into one or more laws.

Given this information, the first rule in table 3.2 (INITIALIZE-INDEPENDENT) applies, setting the subgoal to *iterate* through the known values of the term *planet*.[3] Given this goal, UPDATE-INDEPENDENT selects one of the known planets (says *A*) and sets the subgoal to *get dependent* values of all dependent terms under this condition. Matching off this goal, the RECORD production fires against one of the dependent terms (say *D*), asking for the value of the term and adding the result to memory. When it has recorded this value, INITIALIZE-DEPENDENT uses it to initialize a list of such values. Next, the RECORD rule applies a second time, collecting an initial value for the second dependent term (say *P*). This leads to a second firing of INITIALIZE-DEPENDENT, and thus to the beginnings of a second list of dependent values.

At this point, no more rules match against the goal of obtaining dependent values, so rules matching against the less recent goal of iterating through the values of the planet are considered. Thus, UPDATE-INDEPENDENT applies, setting the new subgoal to examine dependent values when the independent term has the value *B*. Again the RECORD rule applies for both *D* and *P*; however, since an initial list of values already exists for each dependent term, the rule UPDATE-DEPENDENT is executed for each instead of the rule INITIALIZE-DEPENDENT. The UPDATE-DEPENDENT production adds the newly recorded values of *D* and *P* to their respective lists, and again control returns to the higher-level goal of iterating through the list of planets.

This time around, UPDATE-INDEPENDENT sets a goal to examine

---

3. We could combine the first two rules into a single production, but the present division of labor will prove useful in later versions of BACON.

dependent values when the planet is C, leading RECORD to request and record a final pair of values for D and P. After these are added to the lists for each term by UPDATE-DEPENDENT, the system has generated a complete list of values for D and P, which can be compared with each other (or with the list of independent values if they had been numerical). At this point, since none of the rules in table 3.2 match any of the goals in memory, any system composed of only these productions would stop with the generation of the data set. However, BACON.1 contains additional rules that match in this situation, so the actual system continues to operate. Now let us examine these additional rules and the role they play in BACON's discovery process.

Discovering Regularities

The second set of five productions (table 3.3) is responsible for noting regularities in the data collected by the first set of rules. The first production (FIND-LAWS) simply notes when BACON.1 has completed its iteration through the list of independent values and adds to working memory a goal to *find laws* summarizing the dependent values it has gathered. The remaining rules in table 3.3 match only after the goal to find laws has been set by this first production.

The second rule (CONSTANT) notes when the list of values associated with a dependent term are constant and forms a simple law based on this regularity. This is simply a restatement of a traditional inductive inference rule (Mill's Rule of Agreement); however, when combined with the ability to define higher-level attributes, it gains considerable power. Although this rule is stated as a PRISM production, the test for constancy is implemented as a LISP function that is called in the condition side of CONSTANT. (We will discuss the details of this constancy test in a later section, when we consider the issue of noise.)

The other three regularity detectors in table 3.3 also match against the lists of values constructed by the data-gathering productions and note relations between the values of two different terms. For example, the first of these (LINEAR) notes when two sets of values are related linearly. The test for linearity is also implemented as a LISP function that is called in the condition side of the rule. This function computes the slope and the intercept of the line and passes these to the action side of LINEAR, where this information is added to memory.

By themselves, the rules CONSTANT and LINEAR will note relations

Table 3.3
BACON.1's rules for noting regularities.

FIND-LAWS
If you want to *iterate* through the values of independent term I,
  and you have iterated through all the values of I,
then try to *find laws* for the dependent values you have recorded.

CONSTANT
If you want to *find laws*,
  and the dependent term D has value V in all data clusters,
then *infer* that D always has value V.

LINEAR
If you want to *find laws*,
  and you have recorded a set of values for the term X,
  and you have recorded a set of values for the term Y,
  and the values of X and Y are linearly related
      with slope M and intercept B,
then *infer* that a linear relation exists between X and Y
  with slope M and intercept B.

INCREASING
If you want to *find laws*,
  and you have recorded a set of values for the term X,
  and you have recorded a set of values for the term Y,
  and the absolute values of X increase,
      as the absolute values of Y increase,
  and these values are not linearly related,
then *consider* the ratio of X and Y.

DECREASING
If you want to *find laws*,
  and you have recorded a set of values for the term X,
  and you have recorded a set of values for the term Y,
  and the absolute values of X increase
      as the absolute values of Y decrease,
  and these values are not linearly related,
then *consider* the product of X and Y.

---

between directly observable terms and record the slope and intercept parameters, but nothing more. However, BACON.1 also has two rules that let it define new terms that may prove useful. The first of these (INCREASING) applies when two sets of values are related monotonically but not linearly. We saw this rule in operation in the Keplerian example when BACON.1 noted that the distance D increased with the period P. As a result, the program defined the ratio D/P and examined its values. We will consider the rules responsible for definition and calculation shortly, but first let us examine BACON's final regularity detector.

DECREASING applies when the values for one term increase as those of another term decrease. This production also came into play during the Keplerian example, both when BACON noted that D/P increased as D decreased (leading it to compute the product D^2/P) and when the system noted that D^2/P increased as D/P decreased (leading to the product D^3/P^2). The INCREASING and DECREASING rules are especially important to BACON.1's operation, since they enable the system to move beyond directly observable variables into the realm of theoretical terms. this enables the CONSTANT rule to apply in cases where it would otherwise see only confusion, and (as we shall see in a later example) it allows the LINEAR rule to do the same.

Actually, both INCREASING and DECREASING examine the *absolute* values of the two terms rather than their signed values. This enables the rules to respond correctly to values located in different quadrants of the $(X\,Y)$ coordinate system. Consider the idealized curves shown in figure 3.3. The upper right quadrant represents cases in which the values of X and Y are both positive. If X and Y were related by the law $XY = c$ (shown by the hyperbolic curve in the quadrant), then the values of X would increase as the values of Y decrease. Thus, we want the heuristic DECREASING to apply in this situation, proposing the product XY. The same inverse relation holds for data in the lower left quadrant that obey the law $XY = c$, and we would want DECREASING to apply in this case as well.

Now consider the lower right quadrant, in which the values of X are positive but the values of Y are negative. In this case, if X and Y were related by the law $XY = c$ (see the hyperbolic curve in the quadrant), then the values of X and Y would increase together. However, we would still like BACON to propose the product XY, since this law would predict the observed relation. Of course, we could insert another rule (DECREASING') with the same action as DECREASING and different conditions, but this

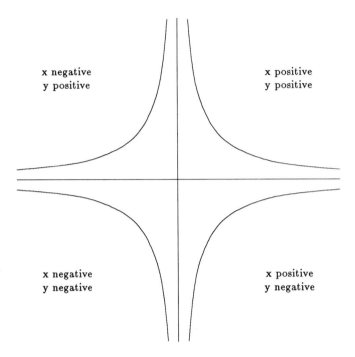

x negative
y positive

x positive
y positive

x negative
y negative

x positive
y negative

Figure 3.3

would not be very elegant. Instead, note that for the lower right hyperbola the *absolute* values of X increase as the *absolute* values of Y decrease. The same relation holds for points on hyperbolas in all four quadrants. Thus, we need simply to have DECREASING (and its analog INCREASING) examine absolute values rather than the original signed values. This strategy allows a simple yet general statement of BACON's regularity detectors.

Once a theoretical term such as XY or X/Y has been proposed, it must still be defined and its values computed, so that these values can be examined for regularities. Thus, unlike the rules for noting constants and linear relations, INCREASING and DECREASING require additional rules to follow up on their proposals. We now turn to the component of BACON that has this responsibility.

Defining Terms and Computing Values

BACON.1's third set of productions is responsible for defining new terms and for computing the values of terms once they have been defined. For example, the rule DEFINE-RATIO-OR-PRODUCT applies immediately after one of the rules INCREASING or DECREASING has applied, matching against the *consider* goal that these rules add to working memory. This production retrieves the definitions of the two related terms X and Y, generates a new term T, and computes T's definition in terms of X and Y. All definitions are specified as the products of directly observable terms taken to some power. In the Keplerian example, the ratio D/P was defined in terms of D and P and its definition was found to be $(D^1)(P^{-1})$. Later in the same run, the term D^3/P^2 was defined as the product of D^2/P and D/P; since the definition of D^2/P was known to be $(D^2)(P^{-1})$ and that for D/P was known to be $(D^1)/(P^{-1})$, the definition of the new term was found to be $(D^3)/(P^{-2})$.

In some cases, the definition of a new term is equivalent to that of an existing term. For instance, in the Keplerian run, BACON.1 noted that the values of D/P increased as those of P decreased, leading the system to consider the product (D/P) P. However, since the definition of this term would have been equivalent to D (a term already present), the rule DEFINE-RATIO-OR-PRODUCT did not apply, and the *consider* goal (with the product term it proposed) was discarded.

Once a new product or ratio has been given a name and a definition, its values can be computed. BACON.1 includes two rules to compute these values, MULTIPLY-VALUES and RECORD-VALUES, both of which match against the *gather values* goal added to memory by DEFINE-RATIO-OR-PRODUCT. MULTIPLY-VALUES applies a number of times, each time incorporating the values of one of the observable terms involved in the definition of the higher-level term. In each case, it multiplies the current values (initialized to a vector of ones by DEFINE-RATIO-OR-PRODUCT) for the new term by the values of the component term raised to the power specified in the definition.

In computing the values for $T = D^3/P^2$, MULTIPLY-VALUES would apply twice: once to incorporate the values of D and again to incorporate the values of P. Assume that three data clusters have been recorded, with $P = \{1, 8, 27\}$ and $D = \{1, 4, 9\}$, and that the rule DEFINE-RATIO-OR-PRODUCT has initialized the values of T to $\{1, 1, 1\}$. Upon matching against the component term D, MULTIPLY-VALUES multiplies the values of $D^3 = \{1, 64, 729\}$ by $\{1, 1, 1\}$. The resulting values $\{1, 64, 729\}$ are stored as the current values of T. Next MULTIPLY-VALUES matches against the component term P, multiplying the values of $P^{-2} = \{1/1, 1/64, 1/729\}$ by $\{1, 64, 729\}$. This gives $\{1, 1, 1\}$ as the current (and final) values of the term T.

Table 3.4
BACON.1's rules for defining terms and computing their values.

DEFINE-RATIO-OR-PRODUCT
If you want to *consider* the product (or ratio) of X and Y,
   and the definition of X is D_X,
   and the definition of Y is D_Y,
   and there does not already exist a term
      with definition equivalent to XY (or Y/X),
then *define* the term T as $D_X D_Y$ (or D_X/D_Y)
   and *gather values* for the term T (initializing them to 1).

MULTIPLY-VALUES
If you want to *gather values* for the term T,
   and the definition of T is D_T,
   and A^p is one of the components of D_T,
   and the recorded values of A are $a_1, \ldots, a_k$,
then *multiply* the current values of T by $a_1{}^p, \ldots, A_k{}^p$.

RECORD-VALUES
If you want to *gather values* for the term T,
then *record* the current values for T.

Once all relevant values have been incorporated, the rule RECORD-VALUES applies by default. (Its conditions are a subset of those in MULTIPLY-VALUES.) This rule simply stores the current values of the new term in a form where they can be accessed by other productions. Once these values have been recorded, BACON.1's regularity detectors can look for constant values and relations to other terms. In other words, the program's discovery methods make no distinction between directly observable terms and computed ones.

New terms are defined only when the INCREASING and DECREASING rules come into play. Since both the CONSTANT and LINEAR rules apply in situations where the data can be summarized successfully, there is no need for additional terms in these cases. However, we will see that linear relations do permit the introduction of new terms (the slopes and intercepts) in later versions of BACON.

Testing Laws

In chapter 2, in discussing the relations between discovering laws and testing them, we argued that these two processes are wholly intermingled. A law is not first discovered, in full and final form, and then tested for its validity. Usually the discovery process itself involves search, where each step that is taken is evaluated for progress. By the time the search has been

completed and the discovery accomplished, the consistency of the proposed law with the data from which it has been induced has already been
guaranteed by the generation process.

Thus, BACON.1, which is conservative in not announcing invariants until it
has examined all the relevant evidence, does not require separate productions for testing the laws it has found. Other versions of BACON (such as
BACON.1A, described in appendix A) announce laws on the basis of partial
evidence, but they are capable of revising their conclusions after examining
new evidence and of qualifying their generalizations by specifying the
conditions under which they hold.

The Discoveries of BACON.1

Here we shall trace BACON.1's steps in rediscovering three additional laws
from the history of science: Boyle's law, Galileo's law of uniform acceleration, and Ohm's law. We shall also reconsider the discovery of Kepler's
third law from noisy data. The derivation of Ohm's law follows a somewhat
different path than the other derivations. The repetition of the Keplerian
example illustrates BACON.1's methods for noting constants when noise is
present.

Boyle's Law

Around 1660, Robert Boyle discovered that the pressure exerted by a given
amount of gas varies inversely with its volume. This relation can be stated
mathematically via the equation $PV = c$, where P is the pressure, V is the
volume occupied by the gas, and c is a constant. As we shall see later in the
chapter, the value of this constant is a function of other variables, such as
the temperature of the gas; however, Boyle's discovery was limited to
pressure and volume.

Table 3.5 presents the volume and pressure data from Boyle's 1662 book,
converted to decimals from the fractional form that was commonly used in
Boyle's time.[4] The data we have used may be found in Magie 1935 (p. 187,

---

4. We have not found it possible to be wholly consistent throughout this volume in the
number of significant (or insignificant!) figures we display in our tables. In cases like the
present one, we have retained the full decimal equivalents of the published fractions, although
the accuracy of the measurements may not go beyond two or three figures. In other tables
too, unless the clutter became excessive, we have retained figures to facilitate the checking of
our computations, even when the final digits are surely not significant.

Table 3.5
Boyle's original gas data.

Volume (V)	Pressure (P)	PV
1.0	29.750	29.750
1.5	19.125	28.688
2.0	14.375	28.750
3.0	9.500	28.500
4.0	7.125	28.500
5.0	5.625	28.125
6.0	4.875	29.250
7.0	4.250	29.750
8.0	3.750	30.000
9.0	3.375	30.375
10.0	3.000	30.000
12.0	2.625	31.500
14.0	2.250	31.500
16.0	2.000	32.000
18.0	1.875	33.750
20.0	1.750	35.000
24.0	1.500	36.000
28.0	1.375	38.500
32.0	1.250	40.000

columns A and D). Despite the roughness of Boyle's data, BACON.1 has no difficulty discovering the law. Upon examining the data, the system notes that the volume increases as the pressure decreases, and so considers the product, PV, which has a mean value of 31.6.

BACON's crude way of determining what deviations from constancy are acceptable is to incorporate a maximum percentage deviation around the mean, Δ, and require all observations to fall in the interval $[M(1 - \Delta),\ M(1 + \Delta)]$. In this case, if Δ is set to 0.3, the values of PV will be judged to be constant. We hold no particular brief for this method (or for the specific value of Δ used here). It might be thought preferable, for example, to place a limit on the ratio of the standard deviation σ to the mean M, and to accept a value as constant if the absolute value of σ/M falls below Δ. (In Boyle's data, two-thirds of the observations of PV lie within about 10 percent of the mean.)

Of course, whether a particular degree of constancy is acceptable lies in the eye of the beholder. During the nineteenth century, there was great

Table 3.6
Idealized data obeying the law of uniform acceleration.

Time (T)	Distance (D)	D/T	D/T^2
0.1	0.098	0.98	9.8
0.2	0.392	1.96	9.8
0.3	0.882	2.94	9.8
0.4	1.568	3.92	9.8
0.5	2.450	4.90	9.8
0.6	3.528	5.88	9.8

dispute among chemists as to whether the data supported or refuted William Prout's hypothesis that all atomic weights were integral multiples of the atomic weight of hydrogen. This was (nearly) true for many elements, but there were gross anomalies (e.g. chlorine, with a weight of 35.5 in hydrogen units). Some chemists were impressed by how many elements conformed to Prout's hypothesis, others by how many exceptions there were. Not until Francis Aston discovered isotopes was the dispute settled and a much amended and reinterpreted form of Prout's hypothesis generally accepted.

The Law of Uniform Acceleration

In his studies of motion, Galileo Galilei performed experiments with inclined planes and rolling balls to determine the laws governing velocity and acceleration. (See Magie 1935, p. 11.) The result of these experiments was the law of uniform acceleration, which relates the distance D an object has fallen to the time T since it was dropped. The law may be stated as $D/T^2 = k$, where k is a constant and the ratio D/T^2 is the acceleration of the object at each point in its downward path. In finding this law, BACON.1 varied the time T at which it obtained data on the position of the object, and recorded the distance D provided to it for each time. Table 3.6 presents some contrived (noise-free) values for observations in such an experiment.

Upon gathering the values for various times, BACON's trend detectors noticed that the values of D increased with the values of T. Since these quantities were not linearly related, the system defined the ratio D/T and computed its values. Although these were not constant, they increased with increases in the values of D. However, since the resulting ratio D/TD would have beeen equivalent to $1/T$, the system abandoned this path and focused

Table 3.7
Ohm's original data for electrical circuits.

Length (L)	Current (I)	LI	Slope(Li, I)	Inter(Li, I)
2.0	326.75	653.5	−0.049	358.5
4.0	300.75	1,203.0	−0.049	358.5
6.0	277.75	1,666.5	−0.049	358.5
10.0	238.25	2,382.5	−0.049	358.5
18.0	190.75	3,433.5	−0.049	358.5
34.0	134.50	4,573.0	−0.049	358.5
66.0	83.25	5,494.5	−0.049	358.5
130.0	48.50	6,305.0	−0.049	358.5

on a second regularity: that the values of D/T increased with those of the time T. On the basis of this relation, BACON.1 defined a second ratio, D/T^2, and computed a new set of values. These values appeared to have the constant value 9.8, leading BACON to infer that D/T^2 always has this value. This statement is equivalent to the inverse-square law described above.

Ohm's Law

In 1826, Georg Simon Ohm began a series of experiments on currents and batteries. (See Magie 1935, pp. 456–472.) Finding the voltaic pile too unstable for his work, he built a version of the thermoelectric battery (invented by Seebeck only four years earlier). In this type of battery, the ends of a copper wire are attached to opposite ends of a bar of metal. If the two ends of the bar are kept at different temperatures, a current flows through the wire. Ohm found that the current I, as measured by the twist of a galvanometer needle, and the length of the wire L fit the equation $I = v/(r_i + L)$, where v and r_i are constants associated with a given experiment.

In order to let it discover this law, we gave BACON.1 experimental control over the length L of the wire in an electrical circuit and told it to examine the values of the current I for the same circuit. Table 3.7 presents some of Ohm's original data, converted to decimals, along with BACON's transformation of these data. (The data are given in Magie 1935, p. 469, first line of table.) The system began by noting that the values of I increased as those of L decreased. This led it to define the product LI. Although the values of this new term were not constant, they were linearly related to the values of I (assuming a relative noise limit of 0.15 above or below the mean). As a

Table 3.8
Borelli's data for Jupiter's satellites.

Moon	Distance (D)	Period (P)	Term-1 (D/P)	Term-2 (D^2/P)	Term-3 (D^3/P^2)
A	5.67	1.769	3.203	18.153	58.15
B	8.67	3.571	2.427	21.036	51.06
C	14.00	7.155	1.957	27.395	53.61
D	24.67	16.689	1.478	36.459	53.89

result, BACON.1 summarized the data with a line of the form $LI = aI + b$, with $a = -0.049$ and $b = 358.5$. Subtracting aI from both sides, factoring out I, and dividing both sides by $(L - a)$ yielded the expression $I = b/(L - a)$, which had the same form as Ohm's original law. (Ohm interpreted the constant b as measuring the voltage of the battery and interpreted the constant a as its internal resistance.)

Kepler's Law Revisited

Let us now return to a less idealized set of data for Kepler's third law. Table 3.8 presents data on the Galilean satellites of Jupiter. These data, originally reported by Giovanni Borelli, were used by Newton in the *Principia* as one basis for his empirical verification of Kepler's third law. The periods were originally given in days, hours, minutes, and seconds, and the distances in fractions, but we converted them to decimals for BACON's convenience. The distances are expressed as multiples of the radius of Jupiter.

As before, BACON noted that the distance D and the period P increased together, and defined the ratio D/P. This term decreased as the distance increased, leading BACON to define the product D^2/P. That term increased as D/P decreased, and so the product D^3/P^2 was examined. This term had a mean value of 54.17. With Δ/M set at 0.075, BACON decided that all values were sufficiently close to the mean to be considered constant. (The data on the distances from the Sun and the periods of revolution of the planets that Kepler himself used to verify his third law were more precise; the maximum deviations from constancy of D^3/P^2 were less than 2 percent of the mean value. See Gingerich 1975.)

Laws Discovered by BACON.1

To summarize: The BACON.1 system has rediscovered a number of empirical laws involving two numerical terms, in several cases using actual data.

Table 3.9
Physical laws discovered by BACON.1.

Boyle's law	$PV = c$
Kepler's third law	$D^3 P^2 = k$
Galileo's law	$D/T^2 = g$
Ohm's law	$IL = -rI + v$

Table 3.9 lists the names of these laws, along with their forms. As the table shows, the system's heuristics lead it to quite different laws, depending on the regularities they find in the data. In this sense, BACON.1 is a data-driven discovery system. The program has many limitations (some of which will be addressed in the following section), but its accomplishments are quite impressive in view of the small set of heuristics it employs. Although later versions of BACON inevitably increase in complexity as they gain in power, our concern with retaining simple, general models of the discovery process will remain.

The BACON.3 System

The methods described in the previous section can discover numerical relations between two variables; however, more complex relations are largely beyond their scope. For instance, one would like to have methods for discovering functions involving many terms, such as the ideal-gas law and Coulomb's law of electric attraction. In cases where one has experimental control over the independent terms, the traditional method of "varying one term at a time" can be used to separate the effects of each independent term on the dependent variables. We have implemented this basic approach in BACON.3, an extension of BACON.1 that can discover much more complex laws than its predecessor.[5] In our discussion of BACON.3 we will restrict ourselves to the naive version of this data-gathering method, in

5. The second incarnation of the system, BACON.2, employed somewhat different discovery methods than BACON.1. For example, it found empirical laws using a differencing method that searched for constant derivatives rather than considering products and ratios. The system could also solve sequence-extrapolation tasks, but it employed heuristics for noting recurring chunks rather than the periodicity detector of BACON.1A. We have chosen to bypass the BACON.2 system for the same two reasons that we presented a simplified version of BACON.1: our concern with scientific discovery and our desire for continuity in our description of the BACON systems. A fuller description of BACON.2 is given in appendix B, and additional details can be found in Langley 1979b. BACON.3 was first described in Langley 1979c.

which all possible combinations of the independent terms are examined in turn so that a complete factorial design is generated. In chapters 4 and 5 we will examine more sophisticated forms of the method that employ knowledge of symmetry to reduce this search through the space of data.

The distinction between experimental science (in which one has experimental control over most terms) and observational science (in which one is only able to observe co-occurring values) is certainly an important one. Since BACON.3 is designed to work in experimental domains, we will concentrate on experimental science in this and the following chapters. Much later, we will return to the issue of observational discovery and outline one approach to this task that is based on a generalization of the heuristics used in BACON.1; for now, let us turn to BACON.3.

Levels of Description

The BACON.1 system made a sharp distinction between the data it had "observed" and the laws that summarized those data. As a result, the program could summarize the relation between two terms, but it could not apply its discovery heuristics recursively to those summaries as if they were data. In contrast, BACON.3 blurs the distinction between data and laws by allowing various *levels of description*. In the new system, regularities in one level of *descriptive clusters* lead to the creation of a descriptive cluster at the next higher level. In turn, this new cluster and its neighbors can lead to a yet higher level of description. A descriptive cluster is simply a conjunction of attribute-value pairs. (In the examples that will follow shortly, each row in a table corresponds to a single descriptive cluster.)

In order to take advantage of this new ability, BACON.3 also requires the ability to systematically gather data involving many independent terms. The system's approach to gathering data is straightforward. It begins by holding all but one of the terms constant and attempting to discover a specific law in that context. The constant values found in this situation are stored, along with the independent values for which they occurred. Different constants are found for different contexts. When enough constant values have been found, the system treats them as dependent values at a higher level of description and attempts to find a higher-level relation between independent terms and the newly defined dependent terms. The system employs the same method to find the second-level law that it used at the lower level. After a law at the second level has been found, the program recurses to still higher levels until all the independent terms have been incorporated into a unified law and all the data have been summarized. In short: BACON.3's search for laws is embedded within its search through the data space. An example should clarify the basic approach further, so let us examine its application to the discovery of the ideal-gas law.

An Example: The Ideal-Gas Law

BACON.3 can be viewed as searching two distinct problem spaces: the space of data and the space of laws. These searches interact in a complex manner. Before we examine this interaction, let us examine each of the search schemes independently, starting with search through the data space.

As already noted, BACON.3 is provided with a set of independent terms and with possible values for each term. Using these values, the system generates a complete factorial design involving all combinations of independent values and then examines the values of the known dependent terms for each combination. BACON.3's generation of all independent combinations can be viewed in terms of search through a space of states containing partially specified experimental combinations. The initial state has no independent values specified; the goal states include values for all the independent terms. The operator for moving through this space inputs a partially specified experimental combination and decides on the value for one of the unspecified terms. Search control is depth-first; however, since many combinations must be generated, the system must backtrack and explore many different paths.

Suppose that BACON.3 is given three independent terms—the pressure P on a gas, the temperature T of that gas in degrees Celsius, and the quantity N of the gas—and the single dependent term V, the volume of the gas. Suppose further that BACON.3 is told to examine N with values 1, 2, and 3, T with values 10, 20, and 30, and P with values 1,000, 2,000, and 3,000. In order to generate an experimental combination, the system begins with an initial state in which no values have been specified, which we may represent as [ ]. Next, BACON generates a new state in which the value of N is determined, say [$N = 1$]. In its next step, the system generates a third state in which the value of T is given, say [$N = 1$, $T = 10$]. On its third step through the data space, BACON.3 generates the complete experimental combination [$N = 1$, $T = 10$, $P = 1,000$], and the program can report and record the volume associated with this combination.

However, if BACON.3 is to gather sufficient data on which to base its laws, it must continue the search. Accordingly, the system backs up to the

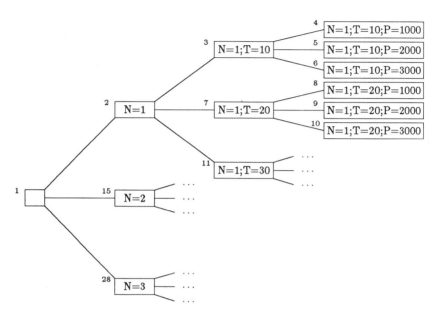

Figure 3.4

previous state, [$N = 1$, $T = 10$], and generates a second goal combination, [$N = 1$, $T = 10$, $P = 2,000$]. This allows data for a second value of the volume to be recorded and associated with an experimental combination. At this point, the system again backtracks to [$N = 1$, $T = 10$] and then generates a third goal state, [$N = 1$, $T = 10$, $P = 3,000$], thus gathering a third observation of the volume. Having exhausted the potential values of P, BACON.3 then backs up two steps to [$N = 1$]. From there it generates the states [$N = 1$, $T = 20$] and, finally, [$N = 1$, $T = 20$, $P = 1,000$]—another complete experimental combination. BACON.3 continues in this fashion until it has generated all the experimental combinations of the independent values it was given and recorded the volumes associated with each combination. Figure 3.4 shows the tree that results from this search through the space of data; the numbers on the states represent the order in which the states are generated.

In directing its search through the space of laws and theoretical terms, BACON.3 employs the same heuristics as BACON.1, but now these have been generalized to operate at any level of description. Thus, the system looks for constant values and linear relations, and, failing this, considers monotonically increasing and decreasing relations. In each case, BACON attempts to relate the values of an independent term to those of some dependent term, though if multiple dependent terms are involved these may be related to one another as well.

Unlike BACON.1, however, the current system considers laws at each level in its search through the data space. Basically, BACON.3's search for laws is embedded within its search through data. To understand this statement, let us return to figure 3.4, which presents the order in which BACON.3 gathers its data. Consider the topmost terminal nodes, $[N = 1, T = 10, P = 1,000]$, $[N = 1, T = 10, P = 2,000]$, and $[N = 1, T = 10, P = 3,000]$. For each of these combinations, the system records some value of the dependent volume V. When all three values have been noted, BACON.3 attempts to find a law relating them to the three values of the pressure P, using the regularity detectors from BACON.1. The results of this search are one or more theoretical terms and their constant values, which are stored at the next higher state in the data-search tree. For instance, for $P = 1,000, 2,000$, and $3,000$, the recorded values for V would be 2.354, 1.177, and 0.785. Given these data, BACON notes that V decreases as P increases, considers the product $a = PV$, and notes that this term has the constant value 2,354.0. The value for a is stored with the state $[N = 1, T = 10]$ for future use.

Upon requesting and recording a second set of values, BACON.3 attempts to find a second law. For the experimental combinations $[N = 1, T = 20, P = 1,000]$, $[N = 1, T = 20, P = 2,000]$, and $[N = 1, T = 20, P = 3,000]$, the system finds the values 2.438, 1.218, and 0.813 for the volume. Again the term $A = PV$ proves useful, this time with the value 2,438.0, and again this value is stored at a higher state, in this case $[N = 1, T = 20]$. Very similar events occur when the value of T is 30, giving the parameter value $a = 2,521.0$, which is stored with $[N = 1, T = 30]$. At this point (see table 3.10), BACON.3 has three sets of values for the higher-level dependent term a. Moreover, these values are stored with the abstracted combinations $[N = 1, T = 10], [N = 1, T = 20]$, and $[N = 1, T = 30]$. Given the values 10, 20, and 30 for T and the values 2,354.0, 2,438.0, and 2,521.0 for a, the program attempts to find a law relating these two terms. In this case, it finds the linear relation $a = bT + c$, with slope $b = 8.32$ and intercept $c = 2,271.4$. These values are stored with the next higher state in the data tree, $[N = 1]$, for future use (table 3.11).

This process is continued as more data are gathered. First, BACON.3 finds three additional laws relating the variables P and V. Then, on the basis of the resulting parameter values, analogous linear relations are found

Table 3.10
Simulated data obeying the ideal-gas law.

Moles (N)	Temperature (T)	Pressure (P)	Volume (V)	$a = PV$
1	10	1,000	2.354	2,354
1	10	2,000	1.177	2,354
1	10	3,000	0.785	2,354
1	20	1,000	2.438	2,438
1	20	2,000	1.218	2,438
1	20	3,000	0.813	2,438
1	30	1,000	2.521	2,521
1	30	2,000	1.265	2,521
1	30	3,000	0.840	2,521

Table 3.11
Second-level summary of the gas-law data.

Moles (N)	Temperature (T)	$a = PV$	b	c
1	10	2,354	8.32	2,271.4
1	20	2,438	8.32	2,271.4
1	30	2,521	8.32	2,271.4
2	10	4,709	16.64	4,542.7
2	20	4,876	16.64	4,542.7
2	30	5,042	16.64	4,542.7
3	10	7,064	24.96	6,814.1
3	20	7,313	24.96	6,814.1
3	30	7,563	24.96	6,814.1

between a and T, this time with $b = 16.64$ and $c = 4,542.7$. These higher-level dependent values are stored with the state [$N = 2$]. Similar steps lead to three more laws involving the product $a = PV$, and then to a third law of the form $a = bT + c$. This time, BACON.3 finds the best fit with $b = 24.96$ and $c = 6,814.1$, and stores these values with [$N = 3$].

Now the system has three values of N, along with three associated values of b and three of c (table 3.12). For each of these dependent terms, BACON.3 searches for some law, arriving at the two linear relations with zero intercepts: $b = dN$ and $c = eN$, in which $d = 8.32$ and $e = 2,271.4$. These two parameter values, which are stored at the initial data state [   ], represent invariant parameters that do not depend on any independent terms.

Substituting these values into the forms found at each level in BACON.3's search, we arrive at the relation

Table 3.12
Third-level summary of the gas-law data.

Moles (N)	b	c	$d = b/N$	$e = c/N$
1	8.32	2,271.4	8.32	2,271.4
2	16.64	4,542.7	8.32	2,271.4
3	24.96	6,814.1	8.32	2,271.4

$PV = 8.32NT + 2,271.4N$.

By factoring out $8.32N$ on the right-hand side, we arrive at

$PV = 8.32N(T + 273)$,

which is the standard form of the ideal-gas law. Note that, in some way, BACON.3 has determined that the Celsius temperature scale is inconvenient for describing the relation among the four terms and has effectively introduced the Kelvin scale by adding 273 to the recorded Celsius values.

As this example shows, BACON.3 carries out as many searches through the law space as there are nonterminal states (figure 3.4) in the data space. Figure 3.5 summarizes the parameter values that result from each of these searches, along with the data states at which they are stored. The numbers next to the states represent the order in which the laws were discovered. Note that this order is different from the order in which the data space itself was searched. In an important sense, the search for data provides structure to BACON.3's search for laws, since it provides both direct observations and a place to store parameters so that they can be used as data at later stages. Thus, BACON.3's search through the data space can be viewed as providing top-down constraints on the types of laws that will be discovered (e.g., which variables are related). The system must still search (bottom up) through the resulting law space to determine the particular laws that best summarize the data.

Once BACON.3 discovers that a particular form of law is useful in one context, it uses that information to constrain search in similar contexts. For instance, when the system finds that the form $PV = a$ is useful when $[N = 1, T = 10]$, it considers only this form when $[N = 1, T = 20]$, $[N = 1, T = 30]$, and so forth. In other words, BACON.3 redefines its problem space in the light of its previous experience, so that considerably less search is required.

Table 3.13 summarizes the steps taken in rediscovering the ideal-gas law,

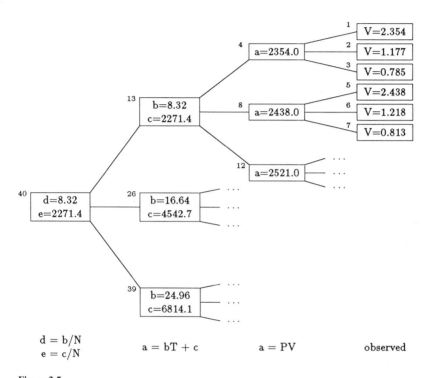

$$d = b/N$$
$$e = c/N$$
$$a = bT + c \qquad a = PV \qquad \text{observed}$$

Figure 3.5

Table 3.13
Summary of discovery of ideal-gas law.

Bacon's version	Standard version	Constant terms
$PV = a$	$PV = k$	T, N
$PV = bT + c$	$PV = k(T - 273)$	N
$PV = dNT + eN$	$PV = 8.32N(T - 273)$	

comparing BACON's version of the law with the standard version, and showing the independent terms held constant at each level of description.

The Heuristics of BACON.3

Now that we have examined BACON.3's basic approach to discovering empirical laws, let us examine the heuristics that implement this approach. BACON.3's heuristics are very similar to those used by BACON.1. In fact, its rules for detecting constancies and trends are identical to those of BACON.1, except that they have been generalized to deal with multiple levels of description. Like BACON.1, the new system defines theoretical terms such as PV, PV/T, and PV/NT to describe its data parsimoniously. Each term is tied to a particular level, so that its values are calculated only if the necessary regularities are found at lower levels. Table 3.14 summarizes the new and significantly modified rules used in BACON.3.

The most significant differences occur in the data-gathering productions. Rather than simply *iterate* through values of the current independent term, the rule UPDATE-INDEPENDENT also sets a goal to *incorporate* the remaining independent terms into laws. In addition, the production INITIALIZE-INDEPENDENT must be generalized slightly to deal with a list of independent terms rather than a single term. These small changes lead to an entirely new goal structure for BACON.3, as shown in figure 3.6. For instance, given the two independent terms X (with values X_1, X_2, and X_3) and Y (with values Y_1, Y_2, Y_3), the system first sets X to X_1 and then iterates through the values of Y, observing dependent values for each X-Y combination. When this is done, BACON.3 sets X to X_2 and iterates through the values of Y a second time. Finally, X is set to X_3 and the values of Y are used a third time. These changes in INITIALIZE-INDEPENDENT and UPDATE-INDEPENDENT lead BACON to generate a complete factorial design and to gather observations for each cell in that design.

In addition to the generalized heuristics from BACON.1, the new system requires three rules to handle multiple levels of description. First, BACON.3 must assign names to the slopes and the intercepts of lines, since these may be related to other terms at higher levels of description. The rule DEFINE-LINEAR is responsible for generating names for the slope and intercept terms when a linear relation between two variables is first found. If analogous relations are later found under different conditions, the same names are used. In addition, the values of these terms must be added to memory so that BACON.3 can attempt to relate them to other terms at the next higher

Table 3.14
Additional rules for BACON.3.

INITIALIZE-INDEPENDENT'
If you want to *incorporate* the independent terms I_1, I_2, ..., I_n into laws,
 and the suggested values of I_1 are V_1, V_2, ..., V_n,
then *iterate* through these values of I_1,
 but retain the list V_n, ..., V_2, V_1 for later use.

UPDATE-INDEPENDENT'
If you want to *iterate* through values V_1, V_2, ..., V_n for term I_1,
 and you want to *incorporate* the independent terms I_1, I_2, ..., I_n into laws,
then *incorporate* the independent terms I_2, ..., I_n into laws when $I_1 = V_1$,
 and *get dependent* values for all dependent terms when $I_1 = V_1$,
 and *iterate* through the values of V_2, ..., V_n for term I_1.

DEFINE-LINEAR
If you have discovered a linear relation between X and Y at level L
 with slope S and intercept I,
 and you do not have a linear relation between X and Y at level L,
then *define* a new term for the slope(X, Y) at level L
 and *define* another term for the intercept(X, Y) at level L.

UPDATE-LINEAR
If you have discovered a linear relation between X and Y at level L
 with slope S and intercept I,
 and you have *defined* T_1 as the slope(X, Y) at level L,
 and you have *defined* T_2 as the intercept(X, Y) at level L,
then *record* the value of T_1 as S,
 and *record* the value of T_2 as I.

FIND-LAWS'
If you want to *iterate* through the values of independent term I at level L,
 and you have iterated through all the values of I,
then *check your expectations* for level L,
 and try to find laws at level L for the dependent values you have recorded.

CONSTANT'
If you want to *find laws* at level L,
 and the dependent term D has value V in all data clusters,
then *infer* that D always has value V at level L,
 and expect D to have a constant value in other contexts.

CHECK-EXPECTATIONS
If you want to *check your expectations* at level L,
 and you have a nonprimitive term T defined at level L,
 and you expect T to have a constant value,
then *gather values* for T at level I.

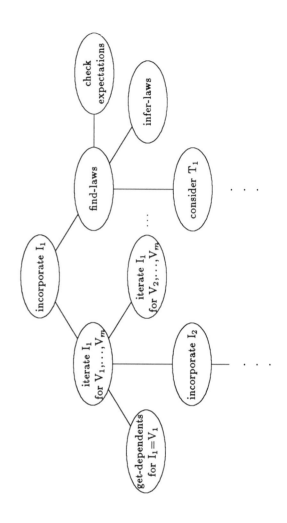

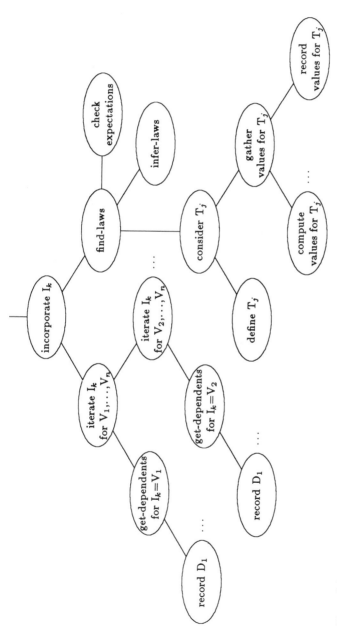

Figure 3.6

level. Thus, the second new rule, UPDATE-LINEAR combines the name of a slope or intercept term with its computed value, so that INITIALIZE-DEPENDENT or UPDATE-DEPENDENT can incorporate this value into the appropriate list.

Finally, since BACON.3 must often rediscover laws with identical forms under slightly different conditions, it is useful for the system to recall which terms have been directly involved in the laws it has found. For instance, if X^2/Y was constant when $A = 1$ and $B = 1$, then there are good reasons to expect that X^2/Y will be constant (though with a different value) when $A = 1$ and $B = 2$, or even when $A = 2$ and $B = 2$. With this expectation, there is no reason for BACON.3 to retrace its previous steps—noting that X and Y increase together, defining the ratio X/Y, and so forth. Instead, it should compute the values of X^2/Y immediately and check for constancy.

Accordingly, BACON.3 includes a modified version of the rule CONSTANT that, in addition to noting that the term T has a constant value and forming a law, notes that the system should expect T to have constant values in other contexts. An analogous variant of the LINEAR rule performs a similar function for terms involved in linear relations. To keep these expectations under control, each one is tied to a particular level of description, and a modified version of FIND-LAWS adds the goal to *check expectations* at the current level whenever it applies. Finally, the third new rule CHECK-EXPECTATIONS matches whenever it has both a goal to *check expectations* at the current level and some term T which it expects to have a constant value (or to be involved in a linear relation). Upon firing, this rule adds the goal to *gather values* for T immediately, bypassing any lower-level regularities that might obscure the system's search for laws. This expectation-based method considerably simplifies BACON.3's discovery process after it has found a set of initial laws.

The Discoveries of BACON.3

The extensions described above enable BACON.3 to rediscover a number of the laws of physics. We have already seen the manner in which BACON.3 arrived at the ideal-gas law. Here we summarize the program's behavior while rediscovering Coulomb's law, as well as versions of Kepler's third law and a form of Ohm's law more complex than BACON.1 could discover. In each case, we review briefly the law and its history and then summarize the major steps BACON.3 follows in its rediscovery of the law. We begin with the new version of Kepler's third laws.

Kepler's Third Law

Johannes Kepler established three laws of astronomy that were later fundamental to the Newtonian revolution. The first of these laws states that the
planets move in ellipses, with the Sun at one focus. The second states that
the line joining a planet with the Sun sweeps out equal areas in equal times.
We are already familiar with the third law (published nine years after the
other two, in 1618); it states that the periods of the planets about the Sun
are as the $\frac{3}{2}$ power of their distances from the Sun.

Kepler's third law, then, can be stated as $D^3/P^2 = c$, where D is the
distance from the central body, P is the period, and c is a constant.
However, BACON.3's ability to deal with multiple independent terms suggests a more complex version of the law that subsumes a simplified version
of the second law as well.

Let us assume a simplified solar system in which all orbits are circular.
The assumption of circular orbits has two important implications. First,
the distance between a satellite and the body it orbits is a constant over
time. Second, equal angles of a satellite's orbit are covered in equal times.
This second point obviously follows from the second law.

In order to discover these relations, BACON.3 must be given control over
three observational variables: a primary body, a satellite of that body, and
the time T at which these two objects are observed. Two dependent variables are used. One of these is the distance D between the primary body and
the satellite. The second assumes a fixed coordinate, such as a star, that is
distant enough that motions within the system can be effectively ignored in
computing angles with respect to it.[6] BACON.3 is given data on the angle A
found by using the fixed star and the planet as the two endpoints and the
primary body (the Sun) as the pivot point. The system begins by collecting
values of these last two attributes for various pairs of solar objects at
various times. Table 3.15 shows some of the data gathered in this manner.
Given these data, BACON notes that the distance D has the constant value
0.387 when the primary object is the Sun and the satellite is Mercury. In
addition, BACON.3 notices that the time T and the angle A are related
linearly, with slope 4.09 and intercept -151.6.[7]

Similar relations are found to hold when the satellites are Venus and

6. This is true of even the closest stars. Astronomers attempted to use the method of parallax
to estimate stellar distances for many centuries before Copernicus and three centuries after
his time, before their instruments were made sensitive enough to detect any motion.
7. This assumes knowledge that A's values are periodic, e.g., that $30° - 90° = 300°$.

Table 3.15
First-level data for the solar system.

Primary body	Satellite	T	D	A	$\text{Slope}_{A,T} = s$
Sun	Mercury	50	0.387	52.9	4.09
Sun	Mercury	60	0.387	93.8	4.09
Sun	Mercury	70	0.387	134.7	4.09
Sun	Venus	50	0.724	49.0	1.60
Sun	Venus	60	0.724	65.0	1.60
Sun	Venus	70	0.724	81.0	1.60
Sun	Earth	50	1.000	185.8	0.99
Sun	Earth	60	1.000	195.7	0.99
Sun	Earth	70	1.000	205.5	0.99

Table 3.16
Second-level description of the solar system.

Origin	Planet	D	s	Ds	$D^2 s$	$D^3 s^2$
Sun	Mercury	0.387	4.091	1.584	0.613	0.971
Sun	Venus	0.724	1.600	1.158	0.839	0.971
Sun	Earth	1.000	0.986	0.986	0.986	0.971
Sun	Mars	1.524	0.524	0.798	1.217	0.971
Sun	Jupiter	5.199	0.083	0.432	2.247	0.971
Sun	Saturn	9.539	0.033	0.319	3.044	0.971

Earth, though different constants, slopes, and intercepts occur in these cases. The second-level values for the six inner planets are summarized in table 3.16. Upon examining these data (table 3.16, columns 3 and 4), BACON.3 finds an inverse relation between the distance D and the slope s. As a result, the new term Ds is defined and its values are computed. On the basis of these new values, the system notes an inverse relation between Ds and D. This leads to the product $D^2 s$; once its values have been calculated, yet another relation is found. Since the terms $D^2 s$ and Ds are also related inversely, their product, $D^3 s^2$, is also defined. This term is found to have the constant value 0.971, and this statistic is stored at a third level of description, where the only condition is that the Sun is the primary object. Since the slope s is related inversely to each planet's period, BACON has arrived at a more complex version of Kepler's third law, with a simplified (circular) version of the second law embedded therein.

Later, when BACON considers a different set of objects (Jupiter and its satellites), its previous experience is put to good use. Rather than repeat its search through the space of products, ratios, and linear relations, the system simply calculates the values of $s_{A,T}$, and using the results, computes the values for $D^3 s^2$. Again this term is found to be constant, but this time with a different value. This constant is also stored at the third level of description, with the condition that Jupiter be the primary object. In no case is any relation found involving the intercept of the line relating A and T, so A and its values never move beyond the second level of description.

Coulomb's Law

In 1785 Charles Coulomb began publishing the results of his studies on electrical forces. (On these experiments, see Magie 1935, pp. 408–420.) Coulomb invented a sensitive instrument, now called the torsion balance, which consisted of a rod balanced by equal spheres on each end and suspended by a fiber that allowed the rod to twist when force was applied. An opening allowed a charged sphere to be inserted at varying distances from one of the spheres on the end of the rod. The charge on either sphere could be halved by touching it to another conducting sphere of equal size. By varying the initial distances and the charges on the spheres, Coulomb arrived at a law relating these variables to the electrical force between the spheres; this force was measured by the angle at which the rod twisted. The law can be stated as

$$FD^2/Q_1 Q_2 = 8.99 \times 10^9,$$

where F is the electrical force, D is the distance initially separating the spheres, Q_1 is the charge on the balanced sphere, and Q_2 is the charge on the inserted sphere. The dimensions of the constant are newton-meters^2/coulombs^2.

In arriving at this law, BACON.3 is given control over three of these variables: the initial distance D, the first charge Q_1, and the second charge Q_2. As usual, the program begins by varying one of the variables (in this case Q_2) while holding the others constant. Once this is done, it varies Q_1, and so on. Table 3.17 shows the data that BACON gathers in this fashion when the distance D is 1.0.

The system's first discovery is that the dependent term F and the independent term Q_2 are related linearly (for the given values of D and Q). Analogous linear relations occur for different values of Q_1; table 3.18

Table 3.17
First-level data obeying Coulomb's law.

D	Q_1	Q_2	F	F/Q_2
1.0	2×10^{-5}	2×10^{-5}	3.6	1.8×10^5
1.0	2×10^{-5}	4×10^{-5}	7.2	1.8×10^5
1.0	2×10^{-5}	8×10^{-5}	1.4×10	1.8×10^5
1.0	4×10^{-5}	2×10^{-5}	7.2	3.6×10^5
1.0	4×10^{-5}	4×10^{-5}	1.4×10	3.6×10^5
1.0	4×10^{-5}	8×10^{-5}	2.9×10	3.6×10^5
1.0	8×10^{-5}	2×10^{-5}	1.4×10	7.2×10^5
1.0	8×10^{-5}	4×10^{-5}	2.9×10	7.2×10^5
1.0	8×10^{-5}	8×10^{-5}	5.8×10	7.2×10^5

Table 3.18
Second-level description for Coulomb's law.

D	Q_1	F/Q_2	$F/Q_1 Q_2$
1.0	2×10^{-5}	1.8×10^5	8.99×10^9
1.0	4×10^{-5}	3.6×10^5	8.99×10^9
1.0	8×10^{-5}	7.2×10^5	8.99×10^9
2.0	2×10^{-5}	4.5×10^4	2.25×10^9
2.0	4×10^{-5}	9.0×10^4	2.25×10^9
2.0	8×10^{-5}	1.8×10^5	2.25×10^9
4.0	2×10^{-5}	1.1×10^4	5.62×10^8
4.0	4×10^{-5}	2.2×10^4	5.62×10^8
4.0	8×10^{-5}	4.5×10^4	5.62×10^8

summarizes the second-level data that result. Since the intercept for these lines is always 0, we can rewrite the slope as F/Q_2 for convenience. (We will not discuss the intercept term further. BACON continues to note that this term is constant at higher and higher levels of description, eventually storing this law with no conditions.)

BACON.3 can now apply its discovery methods to this new level of description. Not only are fewer clusters invloved, but each cluster is simpler, since only three variables (D, Q_1, and F/Q_2) must be considered instead of the four used initially. This time, BACON.3 notices that the values of F/Q_2 are linear with the values of Q_1. Again the intercept is always 0, so again we refer to the slope term as a simple ratio, $F/Q_1 Q_2$. This term also has a

Table 3.19
Third-level description for Coulomb's law.

D	F/Q_1Q_2	FD/Q_1Q_2	FD^2/Q_1Q_2
1.0	8.99×10^9	8.99×10^9	8.99×10^9
2.0	2.25×10^9	4.50×10^9	8.99×10^9
4.0	5.62×10^8	2.25×10^9	8.99×10^9

number of recurring values, each associated with a different value of the distance D. The result is the third level of description shown in table 3.19.

Now that these higher-level descriptions are available, BACON.3 notes that the values of F/Q_1Q_2 decrease as those of the distance D increase. Hence, it defines the product FD/Q_1Q_2 and examines its values. These are not constant, but they are related to the other two terms represented at this level. BACON.3 initially tries defining the ratio of F/Q_1Q_2 and FD/Q_1Q_2, but this is the same as $1/D$ and thus it is rejected as redundant. After this, the system defines FD^2/Q_1Q_2. Since this has the constant value 8.99×10^9, a fourth level of description is added, with no conditions placed on its single cluster. Additional laws at this level concern the zero intercepts of the two types of linear relations that have arisen. At this point BACON halts, having varied all its independent terms and having summarized all its original data.

BACON arrives at the law expressed in the final column of table 3.19 by data-driven induction, uninfluenced by any theory. In contrast, Coulomb was prepared for the appearance of an inverse-square law by the analogies of electrical and magnetic forces to Newtonian gravitational force. Thus, whereas Coulomb needed only to test the hypothesis suggested by the analogy, BACON has to discover the law by searching through a space of functions. Of course, BACON's search is directed by its heuristics and is thus highly selective, but in this case it is clear that our system does not model the historical details of Coulomb's discovery.

Ohm's Law

G. S. Ohm's experiments with thermoelectric batteries, and the law he discovered relating the length of a wire to the current in an electrical circuit, were described above. However, the full story is somewhat more complex than our first account indicated. In addition to discovering the law $I = v/(r_i + L)$, Ohm found that if he changed the composition of the bar

Table 3.20
First-level data obeying Ohm's law.

Metal	T	D	L	I	LI	Slope$_{LI, I}$	Intercept$_{LI, I}$
Iron	100	0.01	0.5	0.1451	0.0726	-5.81×10^{-4}	7.27×10^{-2}
Iron	100	0.01	1.0	0.0726	0.0726	-5.81×10^{-4}	7.27×10^{-2}
Iron	100	0.01	1.5	0.0484	0.0726	-5.81×10^{-4}	7.27×10^{-2}
Iron	100	0.02	0.5	0.5787	0.2894	-2.33×10^{-3}	2.91×10^{-1}
Iron	100	0.02	1.0	0.2900	0.2900	-2.33×10^{-3}	2.91×10^{-1}
Iron	100	0.02	1.5	0.1935	0.2903	-2.33×10^{-3}	2.91×10^{-1}
Iron	100	0.03	0.5	1.2946	0.6473	-5.23×10^{-3}	6.54×10^{-1}
Iron	100	0.03	1.0	0.6507	0.6507	-5.23×10^{-3}	6.54×10^{-1}
Iron	100	0.03	1.5	0.4345	0.6518	-5.23×10^{-3}	6.54×10^{-1}

(e.g., if he used a bar made of a different metal) the constant r_i was changed but v was unaffected. The constant r_i is called the *internal resistance* of the battery. Similarly, if he changed the difference T in temperature between the ends of the bar, the constant v varied in direct proportion to this difference; this constant is known as the *voltage* of the battery. In addition, a more general version of Ohm's law takes into account the diameter D of the wire used. This expanded law may be stated as

$$I = v/(r_i + L/D^2).$$

Because it can handle multiple levels of description, BACON.3 can discover this more complete version of Ohm's law. To do so, the system must be given experimental control over the temperature difference T between the two ends of the bar, the metal the bar consists of, and the length L and diameter D of the connecting wire. Like the earlier program, it considers only one dependent variable: the current I flowing through the wire. As always, BACON.3 begins by systematically varying the variables under its control. Suppose it first varies the length of the wire, then the wire's diameter, then the temperature difference, and finally the metal making up the bar. Table 3.20 shows some (noise-free) data that might be gathered in this fashion using a battery consisting of an iron bar with a 100° difference in the temperature at its ends.

Given these data, the system first notes that the current I decreases as the length L of the wire increases. This leads it to define LI, the product of the current and the length. Upon examining its values, BACON.3 notices that LI is related linearly to the current, and defines new terms for the slope

Table 3.21
Second-level description of data obeying Ohm's law (for slopes).

Metal	T	D	Slope (s)	s/D	s/D^2
Iron	100	0.01	-5.8140×10^{-4}	-5.8140×10^{-2}	-5.8140
Iron	100	0.02	-23.2560×10^{-4}	-11.6280×10^{-2}	-5.8140
Iron	100	0.03	-52.3260×10^{-4}	-17.4420×10^{-2}	-5.8140
Iron	120	0.01	-5.8140×10^{-4}	-5.8140×10^{-2}	-5.8140
Iron	120	0.02	-23.2560×10^{-4}	-11.6280×10^{-2}	-5.8140
Iron	120	0.03	-52.3260×10^{-4}	-17.4420×10^{-2}	-5.8140
Iron	140	0.01	-5.8140×10^{-4}	-5.8140×10^{-2}	-5.8140
Iron	140	0.02	-23.2560×10^{-4}	-11.6280×10^{-2}	-5.8140
Iron	140	0.03	-52.3260×10^{-4}	-17.4420×10^{-2}	-5.8140
Silver	100	0.01	-0.9477×10^{-4}	-0.9477×10^{-2}	-0.9477
Silver	100	0.02	-3.7907×10^{-4}	-1.8953×10^{-2}	-0.9477
Silver	100	0.03	-8.5291×10^{-4}	-2.8430×10^{-2}	-0.9477
Silver	120	0.01	-0.9477×10^{-4}	-0.9477×10^{-2}	-0.9477
Silver	120	0.02	-3.7907×10^{-4}	-1.8953×10^{-2}	-0.9477
Silver	120	0.03	-8.5291×10^{-4}	-2.8430×10^{-2}	-0.9477
Silver	140	0.01	-0.9477×10^{-4}	-0.9477×10^{-2}	-0.9477
Silver	140	0.02	-3.7907×10^{-4}	-1.8953×10^{-2}	-0.9477
Silver	140	0.03	-8.5291×10^{-4}	-2.8430×10^{-2}	-0.9477

(call it s) and intercept (call it i) of this line. When analogous linear relations between these two variables are found for different diameters, these lines have different slopes and intercepts. The slopes are given in table 3.21; the intercepts are summarized in table 3.22. Both these tables are second-level descriptions of the original data.

Examining the summaries in table 3.21, BACON notes that the absolute value of the slope increases as the diameter D increases; hence, the system defines the ratio of the two, s/D. When this term's absolute values are calculated, they are also found to decrease as D's values increase, so the ratio s/D^2 is specified. This term has the constant value -5.814 when the metal is iron and the temperature difference T is 100, and this value and analogous ones are stored at the third level of description shown in table 3.23. The theoretical term s/D^2 corresponds to the internal resistance first proposed by Ohm.

Examining the second-level values for intercepts (table 3.22), BACON.3 discovers that the values of the intercepts increase with the diameter D of the wire. Thus, the new ratio term i/D is defined, where the values of i are the intercepts of the lines relating the current, I, and the length times the

Table 3.22
Second-level description of data obeying Ohm's law (for intercepts).

Metal	T	D	Intercept (i)	i/D	i/D^2
Iron	100	0.01	0.072674	7.267	726.2
Iron	100	0.02	0.290700	14.535	726.2
Iron	100	0.03	0.654070	21.802	726.2
Iron	120	0.01	0.087209	8.721	872.1
Iron	120	0.02	0.348840	17.442	872.1
Iron	120	0.03	0.784880	26.163	872.1
Iron	140	0.01	0.101740	10.174	1017.4
Iron	140	0.02	0.406980	20.349	1017.4
Iron	140	0.03	0.915700	30.523	1017.4
Silver	100	0.01	0.072674	7.267	726.2
Silver	100	0.02	0.290700	14.535	726.2
Silver	100	0.03	0.654070	21.802	726.2
Silver	120	0.01	0.087209	8.721	872.1
Silver	120	0.02	0.348840	17.442	872.1
Silver	120	0.03	0.784880	26.163	872.1
Silver	140	0.01	0.101740	10.174	1017.4
Silver	140	0.02	0.406980	20.349	1017.4
Silver	140	0.03	0.915700	30.523	1017.4

Table 3.23
Third-level description of data obeying Ohm's law.

Metal	T	s/D^2	i/D^2	TD^2/i
Iron	100	-5.8140	726.7	0.1376
Iron	120	-5.8140	872.1	0.1376
Iron	140	-5.8140	1017.4	0.1376
Silver	100	-0.9477	726.2	0.1376
Silver	120	-0.9477	872.1	0.1376
Silver	140	-0.9477	1017.4	0.1376

Table 3.24
Fourth-level description of data obeying Ohm's law.

Metal	TD^2/i	s/D^2
Iron	0.1376	-5.814
Silver	0.1376	-0.9477

current, LI. After the values of i/D are computed, BACON.3 notes that i/D also goes up with the diameter D. Another ratio, i/D^2, is defined, and its values are gathered. The values of this term have the constant value 726.74 when the metal is iron and the temperature difference is $100°$, and have different constants for other combinations. The theoretical term i/D^2 corresponds to Ohm's concept of voltage; the values for this term are also presented in table 3.23, along with the analogous values for s/D^2.

When BACON.3 treats this new level of clusters as data, it finds a linear relation between the temperature differential T and the term i/D^2. Since the intercept is 0, the new slope is equivalent to TD^2/i. This term has the value 0.1376 when the metal is iron, and it has the same value when the metal is silver. These values are stored at the fourth level of description (shown in table 3.24), where the recurring value of 0.1376 is noted, and the final law is stored at a fifth level, with no conditions placed upon its applicability. In addition, during its examination of the third-level data, BACON.3 notes that the term s/D^2 has the constant value -5.814 when the metal is iron, and the value -0.9477 when the metal is silver. Both values are stored at the fourth level, along with the intercept regularities; since the term's values differ for the two metals, no fifth-level law can be formulated here. At this point, BACON.3 stops its cycle of definition and discovery, since it has varied all its independent terms and formulated as many laws as the data justify.

The final laws arrived at in this case deserve some discussion. In the other four discovery tasks, a single descriptive cluster or set of clusters is used to describe all the original data.[8] In rediscovering Ohm's law, BACON.3 arrives at two independent sets of descriptive clusters. One of these sets relates to the concept of internal resistance, the other to the voltage.

8. This statement requires a minor qualification. When linear relations are found, the main law is usually formulated in terms of the slope; however, the intercepts of the various lines are often found to be equal. The important point is that in other cases these intercepts are not used in defining any more complex theoretical terms, as they are in the present case.

Table 3.25
Laws discovered by BACON.3.

Ideal-gas law	$PV = aNT + bN$
Kepler's third law	$D^3[(A - k)/t]^2 = j$
Coulomb's law	$FD^2/Q_1Q_2 = c$
Ohm's law	$TD^2/(LI - rI) = v$

Both sets describe all the original observations, but they are complementary in that they describe different aspects of the same data.

Evaluating BACON.3

In the preceding section we saw the manner in which BACON.3 rediscovered a number of physical laws. Before closing the chapter, we evaluate this performance in terms of its complexity and generality. We begin by considering the diversity of the laws discovered. After this, we discuss the relative complexity of the four laws for BACON.3, and the reasons for this complexity. Finally, we examine the generality of the program along a number of dimensions.

Diversity of the BACON.3 Tasks

Each of the laws discovered by BACON.3 can be stated as a straightforward mathematical equation. Table 3.25 does not do justice to BACON.3's discoveries; only one equation is shown in each case, whereas for some tasks a number of equations were formulated. However, the table does suggest the diversity of the laws the program generated from its data. The ability to define ratios and products led not only to simple combinations like those found for the gas law, but also to terms taken to a power, as in the case of Coulomb's law. The ability to note linear relations interacted with these two heuristics in the case of Kepler's third law (where the square of a slope played an important role) as well as in the case of Ohm's Law. Combined with the ability to recurse to higher levels of description, these methods were able to discover an impressive range of empirical laws.

Relative Complexity of Laws

Although BACON.3 discovered the four laws listed above using the same small set of heuristics, those discoveries were by no means of equal difficulty

Table 3.26
Relative complexity of the discovery tasks.

	Gas law	Kepler's law	Coulomb's law	Ohm's law
Productions fired	348	316	303	956
CPU time (seconds)	87	101	73	327
Number of variables	4	5	4	5
Number of initial clusters	27	18	27	54
Number of levels	3	3	3	4
Number of defined terms	5	6	4	8

for the program. Table 3.26 presents statistics on the relative complexity of the tasks. Two measures are included: the number of productions fired and the central processing unit (CPU) time measured in seconds. Although the first three tasks are comparable on both dimensions, Ohm's law scores noticeably higher than the others. The relatively great difficulty of this discovery task should not be surprising. Table 3.26 also presents some characteristics of the problem spaces for the four laws. Of the five measures presented there, Ohm's law ties on the first and wins (is more complex) on the remainder. Of course, these measures are interrelated. The Ohm case generates more complex clusters and requires more levels of description because it involves more independent terms than the other discovery tasks. Moreover, two completely independent sets of laws were discovered in this run: one relating the temperature differential T and the distance D to the intercept term, and one associating D with the slope term. (This also occurred with the gas law, but only at the final level.) The multiple laws required a large number of theoretical terms, producing complex clusters even at high levels of description.

Other tasks approached Ohm's law in complexity on some of these measures, but mitigating factors simplified the search in each case. For example, in the rediscovery of Kepler's law, slope and intercept terms were defined at the lowest level to relate the angle and the time of observation. As in the Ohm's-law run, there was the potential for two independent laws, one predicting the slopes and one predicting the intercepts. However, in this case only the slope was incorporated into a higher-level law; no regularities were found in the values of the intercepts, and much computation was avoided.

Generality of System

The most obvious test of a system's generality is whether it succeeds at a variety of tasks. Although BACON.3's discoveries all lie within the realm of numerically based empirical laws, we have found considerable variety in the forms of these laws, and we can conclude that BACON has passed the initial test. However, more stringent tests of generality are desirable, since one could design a system that handled multiple tasks by using components handcrafted for each special case. Thus, we should also examine the heuristics of BACON.3, in order to determine the generality of its components.

Upon inspection, we see that the system fares well along this dimension. BACON.3's main heuristics were used in each of the four discovery tasks we have considered. For instance, constancies were noted in arriving at the ideal-gas law, Kepler's law, Coulomb's law, and Ohm's law. Similarly, at least one of the monotonic-trend detectors (and sometimes both) was used in discovering each of the laws, and of course the method for recursing to higher levels of description was required in each case. Even the linear-relation heuristic was applied in each run, despite the fact that some laws (such as Coulomb's) can be stated entirely as products and ratios. As a result, we can safely conclude that BACON's heuristics meet our generality criterion.

Another test of the generality of a discovery system relates to the order in which data were observed. If the system can discover the same or equivalent laws regardless of the order of observation, then this suggests considerable generality. We have already seen an example where the order in which BACON.1 examined dependent terms affected the form of the law it found. The same occurs with BACON.3. However, since BACON.3 has the ability to run more complex experiments than its predecessor, the order in which independent terms are varied can also affect its behavior. In a second run on the ideal-gas law, BACON varied the number of moles (N) first, then the temperature (T), and then the pressure (P). In the run we reported earlier, five major theoretical terms were generated: $a = PV$ at level 1, the slope b and the intercept c at level 2, and the ratios $d = b/N$ and $e = c/N$ at level 3. In the second run, a different path was taken to the same conclusion: $f = V/N$ was defined at the first level, the slope$_{V/N, T} = g$ and the intercept$_{V/N, T} = h$ at the second level, and the products $j = gP$ and $k = hP$ at the third level. In this case, 287 productions fired, and 69 CPU seconds were required. Table 3.27 summarizes the laws found at each level

Table 3.27
Summary of ideal-gas-law discoveries.

First run	Second run	Level
$PV = a$	$V/N = f$	1
$a = bT + c$	$f = gT + h$	2
$d = b/N, e = c/N$	$gP = j, hP = k$	3

in the two runs. Although different terms are defined in each case, the final laws are mathematically equivalent.

Time Required for Discoveries

Before proceeding to the subsequent versions of BACON, we must comment on a phenomenon that may have struck the reader as rather surprising: that the program requires only a few minutes to recreate such major discoveries as Kepler's third law, Ohm's law, the gas laws, and Coulomb's law. The biographies of the original discoverers show that in most cases they concerned themselves with these matters over periods of months or years. A scientist's working month may contain more than 20,000 minutes, and his year nearly a quarter million. How do we account for the fact that BACON is speedier than human scientists by a factor of 10^4 or 10^5? The sense of puzzlement must be especially strong for those who began their examination of BACON with some doubts as to whether a computer program could discover anything. Now it appears that such discovery is not only possible but lightning swift. How do we reconcile our feeling, based on the experience of human scientific work, that discovery is very difficult, with our observation that BACON accomplishes it rapidly and apparently almost effortlessly?

We may not argue that BACON is faster because it describes the discovery process only at a coarse level, omitting much of the detail through which the human scientist must plod. Since BACON actually makes the discoveries we are discussing, it must carry out, at whatever level of detail is required, all the processes that are essential to a successful search for the solutions. There is no shortcut that would allow it simply to sketch out the solution paths without handling this detail. The "grain size" of BACON's processes must be comparable to that of the human who solves the same problem.

Our explanation of BACON's celerity rests not upon a single factor but upon several that operate jointly. The first, and most obvious, is that humans do not generally address their attention to a single problem over periods of years and months, or even days and hours. Sleeping time and time for ordinary daily chores will reduce the time devoted to discovery by at least a factor of 2 for almost anyone. Furthermore, any particular problem usually shares time—especially if we are talking about intervals of months and years—with a number of others. Combining these factors, we would have to reduce our estimate of the time devoted to a particular discovery by a human by at least a factor of 10 from the calendar time, and in many cases by much more.

Second, as we have emphasized several times, BACON is concerned with only one stage in the entire process of discovery: the induction of laws from data. Scientists are also usually engaged in inventing, improving, and building instruments, in carrying out experiments, and in interpreting and writing up their results—to say nothing of studying and digesting the work of their predecessors and contemporaries. The amounts of time required for the building of instruments and the actual carrying out of experiments are likely to be especially great, and the inductive part of the task has to await the production of noteworthy data.

The fraction of time spent in activities other than data analysis varies from scientist to scientist, but in most cases it is quite large. Although we have no quantitative data on which to build an estimate, it is reasonable to suppose that the induction of laws from data might typically occupy only from 1 to 10 percent of a scientist's time. Hence, combining the factors we have mentioned thus far, we would have to reduce the total time of the human scientist by perhaps three orders of magnitude before comparing it with BACON's time.

Third, the human nervous system that carries out the processes of inducing laws from data is probably substantially slower (say, by one or two orders of magnitude) than the hardware of the electronic computers on which BACON was implemented. This is a controversial claim, for their is great uncertainty as to how the nervous system accomplishes its processing. We do know that the brain uses electro-chemical processes that seem to be measured in milliseconds or tens of milliseconds, rather than the microseconds and nanoseconds we are now accustomed to in computers.

It is often claimed that the nervous system is much faster than has just been suggested because it performs many of its processes in parallel and hence simultaneously. However, for the main processes in any task requiring conscious attention, short-term memory serves as a severe bottleneck that forces processes to be executed serially. In other task domains where human problem solving has been simulated (see, for example, Newell and Simon 1972) the human processes also seem very slow in comparison with the computer simulations of those processes.

In inducing laws from data, BACON carries out a great many arithmetic calculations that would require one or two orders of magnitude more time for a human (particularly one unaided by modern calculating devices) than for a computer. For example, using Kepler's original data, it took one of the authors 18 minutes simply to check, without a calculator, the fit to the data of Kepler's third law, even though no search was required to find the correct law. The same task would take a fraction of a second on a computer. We have few data that would allow us to estimate how long human scientists take to induce laws from data, but in some cases the time may be quite short. From the case of Planck (discussed in chapter 2) we know that a major discovery of this kind may take less than half a day, and from our own informal experiments with Planck's data we know that it may take only a minute or two; however, where extensive calculations are involved one would not expect the process to be so speedy.

We now have a few studies of scientific discoveries that are based on detailed examination of laboratory logs and notebooks. For example, Holmes (1980) reports that H. A. Krebs devoted about 9 months to the discovery of the urea cycle but spent most of that time designing and running experiments, or awaiting their results. Substantial time was also spent in searching the literature for clues as to what chemical reactions might be involved. The speed of the discovery was paced by these activities rather than by induction of the chemical reactions from the experimental data.

Putting all these factors together, we see that it is not too hard to account for times of human discovery that are five or even six orders of magnitude longer than the times spent by BACON. At the same time, since the time for the induction itself is brief, the frequent reports of sudden human discovery during a "flash of creativity" need not surprise us. These reports refer to the final step or steps of a process whose total duration may be substantial. A great deal more work must be done before we can be sure that BACON does not leave major segments of time unaccounted for, but we cannot emphasize too often that the present system accounts only for time used in the induction of laws from data, not for time used in formulating the problem or obtaining the data.

Finally, let us recall the fundamental principle of explanation on which the BACON simulations rest. To explain human information-processing means to account for each step in the search for a problem solution in terms of the state of the system at the moment the step is taken, including its knowledge, its processes, and its goals. The discovery processes that BACON handles are relatively brief sequences that begin with a set of data and some heuristics for examining the data and end with a law that describes the data. Our hypothesis is that the other processes of scientific discovery, taken one by one, have this same character, so that programs for discovering research problems, for designing experiments, for designing instruments, and for representing problems will be describable by means of the same kinds of elementary information processes that are used in BACON.

Conclusion

In this chapter we introduced BACON, a sequence of artificial-intelligence systems concerned with discovering empirical laws. We focused initially on BACON.1, examining its discovery heuristics and their application to the discovery of some simple laws from the history of science. In response to BACON.1's inability to discover laws involving multiple independent variables, we moved on to its successor, BACON.3. This system was capable of representing information at multiple levels of description, which enables it to discover complex laws involving many terms. We applied BACON.3 to the discovery of four laws from the history of physics, some of them quite complex.

Although we have argued for BACON.3's generality, certain limitations of the system are apparent. As described, BACON is useful only for discovering quantitative empirical laws. Though such laws abound in physics, other domains involve more qualitative relations. Another issue is that, although BACON.3 (and BACON.1) introduces "theoretical terms," such as D^3/P^2, such terms are not always defined in such a straightforward manner. In the following chapter we will continue to focus on the BACON family, but we will also respond to these issues by adding to BACON's repertoire of discovery heuristics. In this incremental fashion, we hope to achieve a gradually deepening understanding of scientific discovery.

Appendix A
BACON.1: An Earlier Version

The version of BACON.1 described and analyzed in chapter 3 is somewhat simpler than the BACON.1 described in earlier publications (Langley 1978, 1979b) and somewhat more limited in its capabilities. We chose the simpler version to emphasize the continuity in the sequence of BACON models and to provide a concrete and detailed, yet readable, introduction to the representations and mechanisms used by these systems. In this appendix, we will describe the additional features of the original BACON.1 systems and provide examples of the additional kinds of tasks they were able to handle. For convenience, we will continue to call the version of BACON described in chapter 3 BACON.1, and we will call the version we discuss here BACON.1A.

Heuristics of BACON.1A

There are two principal differences between BACON.1 and BACON.1A. First, although each of them can discover and state laws, only BACON.1A can include in its law statements specifications of a range of conditions under which a law is valid. Second, only BACON.1A can discover laws governing nominal, rather than quantitative, dependent variables and laws encompassing periodic relations.

Since data and heuristics are represented in BACON.1A in essentially the same way as in BACON.1, representation does not require new discussion here. We can proceed immediately to consider the productions of BACON.1A that are not present in BACON.1, classifying them under the same categories that were used in chapter 3.

Generating Data

There are no essential differences between BACON.1A and BACON.1 with respect to the processes for generating data, except that the former program, but not the latter, can assign nominal values to the dependent variable.

Discovering Regularities

In BACON.1A, the constancy-detecting production could handle either nominal or numerical data. The program's heuristic for finding the conditions under which laws are valid may be regarded as an application of Mill's rule of agreement and differences. It may be paraphrased as

If you are looking for a condition on a generalization,
and the generalization is true in a number of data clusters,
and attribute *a* **has value** *b* **in those same data clusters,**
and the generalization is false in a number of other data clusters,
and attribute *a* **does not have value** *b* **in those data clusters,**
then propose the attribute-value pair *a*, *b* **as a condition on the generalization.**

In BACON.1A, one set of the trend detectors looks for periodic relations
in the data when the system needs a condition. These lead to the construction of modulus attributes. The major production that accomplishes this
may be paraphrased

If you are looking for a condition on a generalization,
and the generalization is true in a number of data clusters,
and there is an equal interval *p* **between those data clusters along attribute** *a*,
then propose that a new attribute, *a modulo p*, **be defined.**

A similar rule can lead to the construction of linear combinations of independent attributes. Once such attributes are defined and their values examined, the condition detector can discover their relation to a generalization.

Sometimes a qualified generalization is confirmed, but it fails to explain
all instances of the generalization, because they do not satisfy all the
conditions. In this case, a new hypothesis is added that makes the same
prediction, and a set of disjunctive conditions is searched for. Once this
hypothesis is confirmed, if there remain other leftover tirples, yet another
hypothesis is added, and so on until all triples with this attribute-value pair
have been explained.

Defining Terms and Computing Values

BACON.1A defines new theoretical terms and computes their values in essentially the same way that BACON.1 does.

Testing Hypotheses

BACON.1 does not, as we have seen, test hypotheses explicitly, but BACON.1A
has specific productions to perform this function. When a generalization
is first made, a counter is initialized. A set of preexisting text productions
then compare the known data with the generalization. For each agreement
they find, they increment the counter by 1 and the data triple is marked as
explained; if the counter reaches 4, the hypothesis is accepted and the
system moves on to other matters. However, if a data triple is found that

disagrees with the generalization, the counter is reset to 0 and a goal is set up to qualify the generalization. This gives control back to the regularity detectors, which, if successful, will discover a condition on the generalization.

When a condition has been found, one of the test productions creates a new set of test productions that incorporate knowledge of the new condition. These mask the old productions (through the conflict-resolution rules that are bulit into the production system) with respect to the current hypothesis; the more general productions never have anything to say about this generalization again. The new productions test the revised hypothesis in much the same way that the initial ones did, except that they consider only those data clusters that satisfy the new condition. If the qualified hypothesis fits enough data, it is confirmed; if another counterexample is reached, a new condition is found, a new set of test productions that mask the last set is added, and the cycle begins again. This continues until the hypothesis is confirmed or until no useful conditions can be found to qualify a faulty generalization.

Some Examples

Below we trace BACON.1A's discovery path in two environments that exercise the additional productions we have just described. The first is a concept-attainment task in which the *feedback* is "yes" if the color is *red* and "no" if the color is *blue*. The second is sequence extrapolation, which involves discovering laws that will continue sequences like 1 3 10 5 7 10 9 . . . .

The first task draws on BACON.1A's condition detectors, the second on the trend detectors for direct, inverse, and periodic relations. Both tasks draw on the core of BACON.1A, the constancy detector.

Concept Attainment

In the concept-attainment task, BACON.1A is told about three nominal independent attributes, *size*, *color*, and *shape*, and the values each can take. It is also informed of the single dependent attribute, the *feedback*. The system begins by systematically examining combinations of the three attributes. Since it was given *size* as the first attribute, it initially considers a *large blue square* and then a *small blue square*. The data clusters for these may be seen in diagram a of figure A.1. Since the *feedback* for both of these is "no," the system generalizes by building the data cluster shown in diagram b (i.e., the system infers that the value of the dependent attribute is always "no").

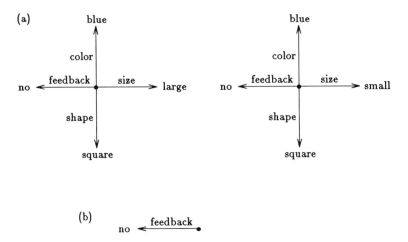

Figure A.1

BACON.1A next considers a *large red square* and a *small red square*; the data clusters for these are shown in diagram a of figure A.2. This time the *feedback* is "yes." This causes the program to set up a goal to qualify its first hypothesis, and this goal is almost immediately satisfied. The condition-finding production proposes that the *feedback* is "no" if the *color* is *blue*. BACON.1A also sees that the *feedback* is sometimes "yes," and finds that the *color* being *red* is a good condition for this generalization. Both hypothesis clusters are illustrated in diagram b of figure A.2.

So far, all values of the *feedback* have been explained. However, BACON.1A is not yet ready to accept its hypotheses. Two more data clusters must be found that agree with each rule before it will be confident. The combinations *large blue circle* and *small blue circle* do this for the first hypothesis, and the combinations *large red circle* and *small red circle* do it for the second. Both hypotheses are accepted, and productions are added to the system's permanent memory which will let it make predictions in the future. The program continues to gather data, making predictions and verifying them along the way, until its factorial design is completed.

Periodic Discovery Tasks

One of the periodic tasks BACON.1A can handle is an analog of the letter-sequence extrapolation tasks found on intelligence tests that use sequences like T E T F T G.... BACON.1A must represent this sequence as 20 5 20 6 20 7...; it must replace the letters with their positions in the alphabet

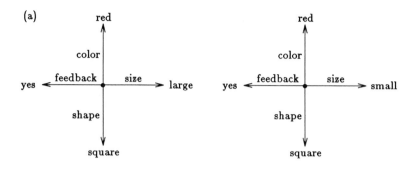

(a)

(b)

Figure A.2

because it has not been provided with the *next* relation between adjacent letters.

A second periodic task is the class of sequences studied by Klahr and Wallace (1976), such as *blue square, red circle, red square, blue circle, red square, red circle, blue square,* .... In this example, there are two dependent attributes, *color* and *shape*, whose values are nominal; also, the periodicities for each attribute are different.

BACON.1A can also handle sequences in which the periodicity is longer and some of the values are repeated within the period. An example of this is the sequence of pegs on which the smallest disk rests in the Tower of Hanoi puzzle. There are three pegs: the initial peg, the goal peg, and the other peg. A set of disks, ordered by size, form a pyramid on the initial peg. The goal is to move all the disks to the goal peg, with the constraints that only one disk may be moved at a time and that a larger disk may never be placed on a smaller one. The correct sequence of positions, on successive moves from the initial position, of the smallest disk for a five-disk problem is initial, goal, goal, other, other, initial, initial, goal, goal, and so on. In each of these tasks the program represents the position in the sequence as the single independent attribute.

Finally, Gardner (1969) has discussed a class of discovery tasks called Patterns. In these tasks there are two independent variables, the row and the column, each of which can vary from 1 to 6. The goal is to find some rule to predict the numerical symbol associated with each combination of row and column, and the rule is often periodic in nature. BACON.1A can solve a number of Patterns tasks.

Conclusion

Our description of BACON.1A in this appendix shows how, with rather modest additions, BACON.1 can be expanded to handle a much wider range of tasks, including tasks involving nominal dependent variables, tasks involving conditional laws, and tasks involving periodic relations. This extension of the system shows its close kinship with earlier law-finding systems, like those of Simon and Kotovsky (1963), that also handled sequence-extrapolation tasks, and thus it contributes to our confidence that the general structure of BACON does not limit it to discovering a narrow and specialized range of lawful regularities.

Appendix B
BACON.2 and Sequential Regularity

For historical and other purposes, it will be useful to describe briefly BACON.2 (Langley 1979b), the immediate successor to BACON.1. Although later versions of BACON build upon BACON.1 rather than BACON.2, the latter has a number of interesting features. It employs the same representation of data as its predecessor, but its representation of laws and the heuristics it uses to discover those laws are quite different. The new heuristics revolve around two notions involving sequential regularities: chunking and finding differences.

The Chunking Method

Consider the sequence-extrapolation task A B C A B C A B.... BACON.1A would summarize this sequence using three separate rules: one for the first position in the period, one for the second, and one for the third. However, there exists another representation of sequentual regularity that involves the notion of *chunks*. In this case, if we define the chunk X = A B C, the sequence can be rewritten as X X X and the missing component of the third X can be used to predict the letter C. The chunk can be viewed as a class of theoretical constructs that was absent in the BACON.1 system.

The theoretical terms we examined in chapter 3 were new variables defined in terms of other variables. In contrast, a chunk is a new *value* that is defined in terms of other values. In the example above, the independent

Table B.1
Chunking rules for BACON.2.

If X is a sequential independent variable,
    and Y is a nominal dependent variable,
    and Y has value A when X is P,
    and Y has value B when X is P + 1,
    and Y has value A when X is Q,
    and Y has value B when X is Q + 1,
then define C to be a new value of Y
    with A and B as its first two components.

If X is a sequential independent variable,
    and Y is a nominal dependent variable,
    and a new value C of Y is being defined,
    and the current values of X are P and Q,
    and Y has value D when X is P + 1,
    and Y has value D when X is Q + 1,
then add D to the definition of C.

If X is a sequential independent variable,
    and Y is a nominal dependent variable,
    and a new value C of Y is being defined,
then stop adding values and store the definition.

---

term is position in the sequence, and the dependent term is the letter found in a given position. For the dependent variable *letter*, one can define a new value *ABC* as the sequence A B C.

BACON.2 employs a modified form of constancy detection to discover chunks such as ABC. Table B.1 paraphrases the three rules the system uses to identify recurring sequences. The first rule notes when one value follows another in two cases, and defines a new chunk with the recurring values as its first two components. The second rule iterates through any remaining values that may be part of the recurring sequence, adding additional values to the chunk one at a time.

The final rule, which specifies when to end the definition of a new sequential chunk, applies in two situations. First, the values may stop repeating after a point. This will occur if a more complex chunk is needed to describe the sequence, or if only partial regularities exist. Second, the end of one instance of the chunk may be adjacent to the beginning of the next instance. This occurs in simple repetitive sequences like A B C A B C. The third rule in table B.1 will be selected in both situations, since neither of the first two rules is matched.

Just as BACON.1 could define new theoretical terms recursively, BACON.2

can define sequential chunks recursively. For instance, consider the sequence A T A A T B A T A A T B.... The rules in table B.1 would first note the recurring sequence A T and define the chunk X = A T. Using this definition, the system would rewrite the sequence as X A X B X A X B. This would lead it to define the second-level chunk Y = X A X B and to rewrite the sequence as Y Y. Describing the sequence in such a hierarchical manner seems much more natural than BACON.1's method, which would require six separate rules (one for each position in the sequence).

Although we devised the chunking method to deal with sequence-extrapolation tasks, the basic method is much more general. Indeed, one could imagine using a similar method to note regularities in speech, producing chunks corresponding to English words. Wolff (1978) has used a very similar method to model the acquisition of words and phrase-structure grammars. We discuss his approach in more detail in chapter 6, in the context of GLAUBER.

The Differencing Method

The second method employed by BACON.2 operates on sequences with numerical dependent values. For instance, consider the sequence 6 15 28 45 66 91 . . . . This set can be summarized by the function $N = 2P^2 + 3P + 1$, where P is the position in the sequence and N is the number found in that position. In order to discover this relation, we must return to theoretical terms defined as combinations of numerical variables but having a form different from those used in BACON.1. In this case, one might define the term $N - 2P^2$, having the values 4 7 10 13 16 19. Using this new term, one might then define the combination $N - 2P^2 - 3P$, having the constant value 1. As before, the difficulty lies in selecting theoretical terms that will lead to constant values.

BACON.2 relies on a differencing method to direct its search through the space of numerical combinations. Let us examine the method in action on the sequence 6 15 28 45 66 91..., considered above. The program first computes the differences between numbers in adjacent positions, giving the derived sequence 9 13 17 21 25. Since these are not constant, the system takes the differences of these differences, arriving at the values 4 4 4 4. These are constant, so BACON.2 knows at this point that the data can be summarized by a law. However, the final form of this law must still be determined.

The depth of the differencing tells BACON the power of the highest term,

Table B.2
Finding the law $N = P^4 + 2P^3 + 4P^2 + 3P + 2$.

P	1	2	3	4	5
N	12	56	182	462	992
$N - P^4$	11	40	101	206	367
$N - P^4 - 2P^3$	9	24	47	78	117
$N - P^4 - 2P^3 - 4P^2$	5	8	11	14	17
$N - P^4 - 2P^3 - 4P^2 - 3P$	2	2	2	2	2

which is 2 in this case. From this information and the constant difference, the system determines the coefficient of this term, which is 2 in this case. In general, if V is the constant value, N is the depth, and D is the difference between successive values of the independent term, then the coefficient C is equal to $V/DN!$. Since D was 1 in this example, we have $4/(2 \times 1) = 2$ as the coefficient. On the basis of these results, BACON.2 defines the new term $N - 2P^2$ and computes its values, which are 4 7 10 13 16 19. These are not constant, so more work remains to be done. Like the system's other discovery heuristics, this one can be applied recursively; thus, the differences of the new sequence are computed, and we get the constant sequence 3 3 3 3. This recurring value is divided by the depth of 1 and the increment of 1, which gives 3 as the coefficient of P^1. This leads to the new term $N - 2P^2 - 3P$, for which the values are computed. Since these have the constant value 1, BACON.2 halts, having found the law $N - 2P^2 - 3P = 1$. Table B.2 gives the values of terms generated while finding the law $N = P^4 + 2P^3 + 4P^2 + 3P + 2$.

The differencing technique can also be used to discover exponential laws of the form $N = a(b^P) + f(P)$, where $f(P)$ is a polynomial. In this variation, differences are computed as before, but at each level of differencing BACON.2 checks for constant ratios as well as for constant differences. Upon finding that, for the Nth difference, the successive terms have a constant ratio, the system defines the new term $N - c(b^P)$, where b is the constant ratio and where c equals $1/b$ times the first element in this sequence of differences. Since $c(b^P)$ has now been set equal to the Nth difference of the original sequence, if the successive terms of this Nth difference are now subtracted from that sequence, the remainder is $f(P)$, a polynomial. The form of this polynomial can now be found by the differencing method.

The history of astronomy provides an interesting set of data to which this method can be applied. The Bode-Titus law, set forth around 1800,

Table B.3
Finding the law $N = 3 \times 2^P + 2P^2 - P + 4$.

P	1	2	3	4	5
N	11	22	43	80	145
$N - 3 \times 2^P$	5	10	19	32	49
$N - 3 \times 2^P - 2P^2$	3	2	1	0	-1
$N - 3 \times 2^P - 2P^2 + P$	4	4	4	4	4

relates the positions of the planets to their distances from the Sun. The agreement of the law with the observations is, however, so approximate that the reality of the relation has often been doubted. Since our interest lies not in the validity of Bode's law but in the manner in which BACON.2 might extract it from data, we will use smoothed data that fit the law exactly. The sequence can be stated as 5.5 7 10 16 28 52 100 196, where distance is measured in tens of astronomical units. At the time the law was put forth, the value 28 had not been observed between the value for Mars (16) and that for Jupiter (52). Thus, Bode postulated that an unobserved planet existed at 2.8 astronomical units from the Sun. Only a few years later, the first asteroid was discovered at the predicted distance.

Let us examine the path BACON.2 follows to discover Bode's law. Applying the differencing method to the idealized planetary data, BACON.2 derives the first difference 1.5 3 6 12 24 48 96. Comparing successive ratios, it notes the constant ratio 2, which causes it to define the new term $N - 0.75 \times 2^P$. The base 2 is the observed ratio of the successive terms of the difference sequence; the coefficient 0.75 is half the first term of the difference sequence. Substracting the difference terms from the original sequence, we obtain the constant difference 4. Hence, the original sequence is written as $N = 0.75 \times 2^P + 4$, and the system halts. The statement that $N - 0.75 \times 2^P = 4$ is a restatement of the Bode-Titus law. More complicated laws, such as $3 \times 2^P + 2P^2 - P + 4$, can be found by the same method. Table B.3 summarizes the constancies found at various steps in the generation of the latter law.

Summary

BACON.2, the second in the line of BACON systems, shares many features with BACON.1. Both systems represent and gather data in the same way, both define theoretical terms, and both search for terms with constant values. However, BACON.2 specializes in constancies based on sequential regularities and relies on heuristics that match against sequential information. These include methods for noting recurring sequences, for finding constant differences, and for uncovering constant successive ratios.

In experiments with BACON.1 and BACON.2, we have generally found that the latter system performed better on discovery tasks that both could handle. For instance, the chunking method is a more efficient method for solving symbolic sequence-extrapolation problems than BACON.1's method. Similarly, BACON.2's differencing technique requires less search than BACON.1's trend detectors. However, BACON.2's reliance on sequential information makes it less general than BACON.1. This provides another instance of the well-known tradeoff between power and generality. In chapters 4 and 5 we examine versions of BACON that build mainly on BACON.1 rather than BACON.2, though one version of BACON.5 did employ a differencing method.

4 Intrinsic Properties and Common Divisors

Although the heuristics of BACON.3 are appropriate for finding relations between numerical variables, such as distance and current, they cannot by themselves provide a complete treatment of situations involving nominal or symbolic terms. A nominal or symbolic variable is a variable that takes on names or labels as its values. Thus, the nominal variable "material" may take on as values lead, water, and the like; the nominal variable "object" may take on such values as "object A" and "object B." Values of numerical properties may sometimes be associated with values of nominal variables, as in "the density of lead is 13.34 grams per cubic centimeter" and "the mass of object A is 3 grams." In many cases, the dependent variables may be numerical while the independent terms take on nominal values.

In this chapter, we describe BACON.4 (Bradshow et al. 1980) and its heuristics for discovering laws involving nominal variables. The approach involves postulating new terms, called *intrinsic properties*, associated with the nominal variables; inferring a set of numerical values for the intrinsic properties, each associated with one or more nominal values; and retrieving the numerical values when appropriate. For example, if "material" is an independent term, and "lead," "silver," and "iron" are its nominal values, then an intrinsic term "density" might be introduced, a property of materials whose values are the densities of lead, silver, and iron, respectively. Once BACON has associated numerical intrinsic values with a set of nominal values, it can apply its numerical heuristics to discover new laws involving these new variables. In some cases, the inferred values have a *common divisor*, in which case BACON.4 computes a set of integral numerical values to be associated with the original nominal values.

After beginning the chapter with a simple example in which intrinsic properties are required, we propose an initial strategy for storing and retrieving intrinsic values. After this, we describe a more conservative retrieval strategy that has some advantages over the simpler method. Finally, we describe a variant of this method that deals with situations involving common divisors, and demonstrate its use on laws from the early history of chemistry.

Postulating Intrinsic Properties

In the preceding chapter, we saw that BACON could rediscover Ohm's law when given numerical measures for external resistance (the length of

Table 4.1
Postulating the property of conductance.

Battery	Wire	Current (I)	Conductance (c)	Voltage (v)
A	X	3.4763	3.4763	1.0000
A	Y	4.8763	4.8763	1.0000
A	Z	3.0590	3.0590	1.0000
B	X	3.9781	3.4763	1.1444
B	Y	5.5803	4.8763	1.1444
B	Z	3.5007	3.0590	1.1444
C	X	5.5629	3.4763	1.6003
C	Y	7.8034	4.8763	1.6003
C	Z	4.8952	3.0590	1.6003

the wire) and current. However, suppose we assume a slightly different situation in which the dependent variable I (the current) is still numerical but the two independent terms (the battery and the wire used in the circuit) take on only nominal values. For instance, let us use three batteries, A, B, and C, and three wires, X, Y, and Z. These can be combined in circuits in different ways to generate different currents, but nothing is known directly about the batteries and wires except their identities.

In this case, BACON.3 could vary the battery and the wire and observe the resulting current; however, since the independent values are nominal, it would not be able to find a numerical law. Our solution is to let the system invent numerical terms (which we will name voltage and resistance) that are associated with the batteries and the wires, respectively. We call such terms "intrinsic properties," because their values are associated with particular objects or sets of objects.

Postulating Properties and Inferring Values

Let us examine the process of postulating intrinsic properties for our modified electrical experiment. Table 4.1 presents the currents for nine combinations of batteries and wires. These currents were computed by assuming the voltages $V_A = 4.613$, $V_B = 5.279$, and $V_C = 7.382$ for the batteries and the resistances $R_X = 1.327$, $R_Y = 0.946$, and $R_Z = 1.508$ for the wires. In addition, we assumed that the internal resistance for each battery was negligible.

Upon examining the first three rows of the table (where the battery is A), BACON notes that the current I varies from one wire to another. Since it cannot relate a numerical term to a nominal one, it postulates a new term (let us call it the conductance,c), and assigns it values equal to the corresponding currents.

Given the two sets of numerical values, for I and c, BACON applies the heuristics described in the previous chapter and notes that the two terms are related linearly with a slope of 1.0 and an intercept of 0. Of course, this is hardly surprising, since the values of c were defined to be those of the current I. However, the tautology disappears when BACON considers the next three rows, in which the battery is B. In this case, the system has already encountered the wires X, Y, and Z, so it retrieves their associated intrinsic values and compares them with the observed currents. This time, BACON's numerical method also finds a linear relation with a zero intercept, but here the slope is 1.1444 rather than 1.0. An analogous law is discovered when the final three rows are examined, this time with 1.6003 as the slope. Once these three relations have been found, BACON uses the slopes of these lines to search for a relation at the second level of description, where the battery is the independent variable. However, the system again finds that it cannot relate a nominal variable (the battery) to a numerical variable (the slope). Accordingly, a new, higher-level intrinsic property is created (let us call it the voltage, v), with its values equal to the slope values and associated with the different batteries.

Again a tautological linear relation is found; however, since there are no other independent terms to be varied, the system cannot move beyond this stage to discover additional empirically meaningful laws. At this point BACON halts, having arrived at two intrinsic properties and their values for different objects. The values of the conductance, c, are associated with individual wires, while the values of the voltage v are associated with particular batteries. In addition, these terms are related to the current by the law $I/vc = 1$ (since the intercepts in both cases are 0).

Since the conductance c is the reciprocal of the resistance r, we can re-state this relation as $I = v/r$, which is one form of Ohm's law for electrical circuits. Moreover, the values obtained for v and r differ only by a constant factor (4.613) from the values we used to compute the currents for this example. This means that BACON has effectively estimated these values using only nominal terms and their associated currents. The constant factor was introduced when BACON used the first set of currents as its values for the conductance, since introducing an intrinsic property involves selecting an arbitrary unit of measurement. (Introducing an intrinsic property is equivalent to what is called *fundamental measurement* in the literature of the philosophy of science.)

Intrinsic properties are useful only in cases involving at least two independent variables. This is because the first set of dependent values must be used in defining the intrinsic values. Unless one or more additional sets of dependent values are observed, the law incorporating the new property will be tautological and will have no predictive power.[1] Thus, this method differs from the numerical techniques we have considered, since the latter can be used to find simple laws relating two variables whereas the intrinsic-property method applies only to the discovery of complex laws involving three or more variables and multiple levels of description. Further, any law involving an intrinsic property that has predictive power can also make incorrect predictions. To reduce the possibility of this happening, we can employ a more conservative version of the method, which we shall describe shortly.

Intrinsic Terms and Existential Quantifiers

What we have been calling intrinsic terms figure prominently in the literature of the philosophy of science as a special class of what are there called *theoretical terms*. Philosophers of science have often emphasized the difference between numbers that can be assigned directly on the basis of observations (*observables*) and numbers that are assigned indirectly by means of computations that may be laden with explicit or implicit theoretical assumptions (*theoretical terms*).[2]

As has often been pointed out, the line between theoretical terms and observables is not a sharp one, for all observation requires instruments (the human senses, if no others). Hence, a certain degree of indirectness and entanglement with theory (the theory of the observing instrument) infects even the most "direct" observation—of length, say, or weight or time. Awareness of the ambiguity of the notion of "directly observable" has been heightened by the discovery, in our century, of relativity theory and quantum mechanics. The former taught us how theory laden are observations even of lengths and time intervals; the latter showed the impossibility of making observations without the observing instrument's having some effect on the system being observed.

---

1. An example involving Archimedes' law of displacement will later require us to qualify this statement slightly. However, as long as only a single dependent term is involved, intrinsic properties require multiple independent terms to achieve predictive power.
2. Theoretical terms may designate nonobservable entities as well as variables. We will see examples in the atoms and molecules postulated in the DALTON program, which will be discussed in chapter 8.

At a pragmatic level, however, the distinction between observables and theoretical terms has not lost its value. In any given inquiry, we can treat as observable any term whose values are obtained from an instrument that is not itself problematic in the context of that inquiry. Thus, in our treatments of Kepler's laws we consider observations of the distances and periods of the planets to be direct and unproblematic; hence, we regarded these quantities as observables. In the same way, electrical current (measured by Ampère's instrument) was treated as an observable in Ohm's experiment, and temperature (measured by Fahrenheit's thermometer) was so treated in the experiments of Joseph Black.

Identifiability

Relative to a given experimental or observational setting, it may be possible to compute unique values for certain theoretical terms from the values of the observables. We then say that these theoretical terms are *identifiable*.[3] Those theoretical terms for which unique values cannot be computed from the observations are called *unidentifiable*. Whether a theoretical term can or cannot be identified will depend on what observations can be made or (in an experiment) what independent variables can be manipulated.

Thus, in the experiment with Kepler's data, the variables D/P, D^2/P, and D^3/P are theoretical terms computable from—and hence identifiable on the basis of—the observables, D and P. Suppose, however, that we had N observations of a triple of observables, $\{x_1, y_1, z_1\}, \ldots, \{x_N, y_N, z_N\}$, and the following theory exactly satisfied by these observables:

$$ax_i + by_i + cz_i = d \quad (i = 1, \ldots, n), \tag{4.1}$$

$$a'x_i + b'y_i + c'z_i = d'. \tag{4.2}$$

Then, the theoretical terms—a, b, c, d, a', b', c', and d'—are not identifiable, for either one of these equations could be replaced by a linear combination of both:

$$a''x_i + b''y_i + c''z_i = d'', \tag{4.3}$$

where $a'' = \alpha a + \beta a'$, $b'' = \alpha b + \beta b'$, $c'' = \alpha c + \beta c'$, and $d'' = \alpha d + \beta d'$ for

---

3. Identifiability is closely akin to, but weaker than, the logician's concept of definability. A theoretical term may be (and often is) identifiable without being strictly definable in the sense of Tarski. For the precise relation between these two terms, see Simon 1977, chapters 6.4 and 6.5.

any α and β. Equations 4.1 and 4.3, or 4.2 and 4.3, will describe the observations just as well as equations 4.1 and 4.2; hence, there is no way of choosing the parameters of the theory unambiguously.

Intrinsic Terms

Theoretical terms such as D/P, which are expressible as explicit functions of the observables, require no additional discussion. However, the special class of theoretical terms we have called intrinsic terms require a little more comment.

Consider a simple formalization of Ohm's law for a particular battery, where current I and resistance R are taken as the observables. The core of the formalization (see Simon 1977, chapter 6.5) is the axiom

$$\exists a, b \ \forall i \ I_i = a/(b + R_i); \tag{4.4}$$

that is, there exist constants a and b such that equation 4.4 is satisfied for all pairs of observations, I_i and R_i, of I and R, respectively. The term a refers to what we call voltage, and b to what we call the internal resistance of the battery, but they are simply introduced as parameters of the equation that fits the data. If Ohm's law holds, these terms are identifiable from sets of observations of the current and the resistance. The constants a and b, if they exist, are intrinsic terms. In BACON, they are created and computed simultaneously with the creation of the equations that contain them. In this example, they are constant parameters.

A somewhat different kind of intrinsic term, generated explicitly in the course of assigning numerical properties to nominal variables, is illustrated by the concept of inertial mass that BACON creates (as we will see later in this chapter) to describe the mutual accelerations of pairs of bodies connected by springs. Here, the law of conservation of momentum that emerges from the observation of the accelerations may be formalized as:

$$\exists m_i m_j \ \forall t, i, j \ (m_i a_{it} + m_j a_{jt} = 0). \tag{4.5}$$

That is, there exist constants, $m_i, \ldots, m_N$, associated with the N bodies, such that equation 4.5 is satisfied for all observations of the mutual accelerations of all pairs of the bodies. In this example, the names or labels of the N bodies are observables, and the intrinsic terms, the masses, are intrinsic variables associated with the labels as properties of the bodies.

The more elaborate example of Ohm's law considered at the beginning of this chapter, where resistance was not an observable but the battery and the wire were nominal variables, involved intrinsic terms, the voltages and conductances, that were of the same kind as inertial mass in the case just discussed. We will soon encounter still other intrinsic variables of this kind, such as specific heat and index of refraction. As the latter two examples illustrate, an intrinsic property may not merely be constant for a specific object (as mass and voltage are) but must be constant over a whole class of objects made of the same substance.

The fundamental constants of physics (and other sciences) are intrinsic terms having the same logical status as those described by the above formalizations, and basic concepts such as mass and length are intrinsic variables that can be introduced by a BACON-like system through operations similar to those we used to introduce voltage and resistance.

Thus, BACON can introduce new basic units of measurement. We have already mentioned measuring the relative accelerations of two bodies connected by a spring. An experiment to be described presently allows BACON, taking the mass of one object as the standard and using the equivalent of equation 4.5, to assign masses to other objects. The same thing could be done with a balance, by noting the equilibration of various sets of objects on the two arms. In fact, any instrument that defines an equivalence relation between pairs of objects or systems can be used with BACON to introduce an intrinsic variable and to test that variable for properties of commutivity, associativity, and transitivity.

Finally, although the laws described by our simple axioms are universally quantified, the intrinsic terms themselves are existentially quantified. It has often been claimed that only universally quantified terms may be admitted into scientific laws, since laws with existential quantifiers cannot be falsified. (There is no way of falsifying "Unicorns exist.") However, our examples using Ohm's law and conservation of momentum show that the presence of existentially quantified intrinsic terms does not interfere with the empirical falsifiability of these laws. In spite of the intrinsic terms that have been introduced, it is easy to see that new observations could falsify the laws that BACON.4 has discovered. For a discussion of the conditions under which existentially quantified terms can be admitted into laws without destroying their falsifiability, see Simon 1985.

Generalizing Conditions for Retrieval

The strategy we used for Ohm's law works well for cases in which intrinsic properties are associated with single nominal variables, as conductance was associated with the wire and voltage with the battery. However, some situations require that intrinsic values be associated with sets of terms rather than single terms. BACON.4 employs a more conservative strategy in order to deal with these cases.

As an example, consider the friction between two surfaces. Here there are two independent nominal terms (the composition of the first surface and the composition of the second) and one dependent numerical term (the friction observed when the two surfaces are in contact). Since this arrangement is superficially similar to the battery-wire situation, one might expect to be able to postulate an intrinsic property associated with individual surfaces, and to use its values to predict the friction between two surfaces that are in contact. However, we know (but BACON would not) that the friction between two surfaces cannot simply be expressed as a product or other function of the "roughness" of each.

Stepping through the strategy described earlier, we find that it encounters difficulties in the friction example. As before, the system would begin by holding the first surface constant and varying the value of the second surface. Upon noting that the friction was different for each pair of surfaces, BACON would postulate an intrinsic term for the second surface (let us call it F) and base its values on the observed friction. The program would also discover the tautological relation between F and the friction, and would store this information for later use at a higher level of description. BACON would then consider the same values for the first surface, this time using a different value for the first independent term. After observing the friction values, the system would retrieve the intrinsic values it had associated with the three values of the second surface, and would attempt to relate these values of F to the observed frictions. However, in this case, no relation would be discovered, nor could one be found when the first surface was again varied. In this case, associating the intrinsic values with the second surface alone is inappropriate. Instead, these values should be retrieved only when a particular pair of surfaces is involved.

In order to deal effectively with situations in which intrinsic values should be associated with sets of terms, BACON employs a more conservative strategy for retrieving intrinsic values. When a property is first postulated, the system assumes that all independent nominal terms are relevant, and so associates the various intrinsic values with a *conjunction* of the nominal values. For instance, given the first three rows of table 4.1, BACON associates 3.4763 with wire X and battery A, 4.8763 with wire Y and battery A, and

3.0590 with wire Z and battery A. When the battery is varied and the wires are reexamined, the system does not immediately retrieve the various conductances. However, it does attempt to relate the newly observed currents to the original conductances. Upon finding a linear relation, BACON infers that the battery does not affect the conductance and removes it as a condition for retrieval. When the battery C is considered, the three conductances (now associated only with the wires) are immediately retrieved and related to the observed currents.

In the friction example, no linear relation is found when the second set of values is examined, so the values of the first surface are retained as conditions for retrieving the values of F. New conditions are associated with the second set of F values, and still another set with the third. More complex examples are possible in which some nominal terms are relevant while others are not, and BACON's intrinsic-property heuristics are general enough to deal with such cases.

The retrieval of intrinsic values under certain conditions can be viewed as a form of expectation-driven discovery, since the system uses knowledge it has gained in one context to aid discovery in a similar yet different context. The main difference from numerical expectation-driven techniques is that with the latter the *form* of some law is retrieved and used to reduce search, whereas in the intrinsic-property method a set of *values* are retrieved and used in the discovery process. Also, the numerical methods BACON employs do not require it to generalize the retrieval conditions on the forms before they are used. However, one can imagine a more conservative version of the system that requires a particular form of law to prove itself useful in a number of contexts before being used with confidence.

The Heuristics of BACON.4

Now that we have described BACON.4's heuristics informally, we can turn to their implementation as production rules. First we should note that the relation between BACON.4 and its predecessor, BACON.3, is similar to the relation between BACON.3 and BACON.1. BACON.4 is an extension of BACON.3 produced by adding another set of productions. Table 4.2 presents the five additional rules that the system uses in postulating and manipulating intrinsic properties. The first of these rules, CONSIDER-INTRINSIC, simply sets a subgoal to *consider intrinsic properties* for the independent

Table 4.2
BACON.4's rules for postulating intrinsic properties.

CONSIDER-INTRINSIC
If you want to *find laws* at level L,
  and you have observed a set of nominal values for X,
then *consider intrinsic properties* for X at level L.

DEFINE-INTRINSIC
If you want to *consider intrinsic properties* for X at level L,
  and Y is a numerical dependent term at level L,
  and there is no intrinsic property associated with X and based on Y,
  and the observed numerical values for Y are $Y_1, Y_2, \ldots, Y_n$,
  and the values of the terms held constant are $A = A_1, B = B_1, \ldots, N = N_1$,
then *postulate* the intrinsic property I associated with X at level L,
  record the values of I as $Y_1, Y_2, \ldots, Y_n$,
  and *store* them under the conditions $A = A_1, B = B_1, \ldots, N = N_1$.

GENERALIZE-INTRINSIC
If you want to *consider intrinsic properties* for X at level L,
  and I is an intrinsic variable associated with X and based on Y,
  and the values of I for $X = X_1, X_2, \ldots, X_n$
    under the conditions $A = A_1, B = B_1, \ldots, N = N_1$ are $I_1, I_2, \ldots, I_n$,
  and the newly recorded numerical values for Y are $Y_1, Y_2, \ldots, Y_n$,
  and the values of the terms held constant are $A = A_2, B = B_2, \ldots, N = N_2$,
  and $A_1, \ldots, N_1$ differs from $A_2, \ldots, N_2$ only on the value of one term T,
  and $I_1, I_2, \ldots, I_n$ and $Y_1, Y_2, \ldots, Y_n$ are linearly related,
then *remove term* T from the $A = A_1, \ldots, N = N_1$ conditions on the values of I,
  note that this term is irrelevant for future cases,
  and record the values of I as $I_1, I_2, \ldots, I_n$,

RETRIEVE-INTRINSIC
If you want to *consider intrinsic properties* for X at level L,
  and I is an intrinsic variable associated with X,
  and the values of I for $X = X_1, X_2, \ldots, X_n$
    under the conditions $A = A_1, B = B_1, \ldots, N = N_1$ are $I_1, I_2, \ldots, I_n$,
  and the current set of independent values contains $A = A_1, B = B_1, \ldots, N = N_1$,
then *retrieve* the values of I, recording them as $I_1, I_2, \ldots, I_n$.

STORE-INTRINSIC
If you want to *consider intrinsic properties* for X at level L,
  and I is an intrinsic variable associated with X and based on Y,
  and the newly recorded numerical values for Y are $Y_1, Y_2, \ldots, Y_n$,
  and the values of the terms held constant are $A = A_2, B = B_2, \ldots, N = N_2$,
  and the known irrelevant terms for I are $T_1, \ldots, T_k$,
  and no values of I are stored under conditions matching $A = A_2, B = B_2, \ldots, N = N_2$,
then record the values of I as $Y_1, Y_2, \ldots, Y_n$,
  and *store* them under the conditions $A = A_2, B = B_2, \ldots, N = N_2$,
  after removing the irrelevant terms $T_1, \ldots, T_k$.

---

term that has just been varied. This rule matches immediately after the goal to *find laws* has been added to memory, applying only in cases where the independent term takes on nominal or symbolic values. Thus, the *find laws* goal provides the context in which we have placed the intrinsic property rules.

The remaining rules deal with the four different cases that BACON can encounter when dealing with intrinsic properties. As its name implies, DEFINE-INTRINSIC is responsible for defining an intrinsic property for a nominal term, based on the values of one of the numerical dependent terms at the same level of description. This rule applies the first time the goal to consider an intrinsic property has been inserted for a given term. It associates a set of numerical values with the symbolic ones, but it stores these with the other independent values (the ones that have been held constant) as conditions for their retrieval. These conditions realize the conservative strategy we described earlier.

The third production is GENERALIZE-INTRINSIC. As its name suggests, this rule is responsible for generalizing the retrieval conditions that have been placed on a set of intrinsic values. If we let X be the nominal term and Y be the numeric term on which the intrinsic values are based, three constraints must hold for generalization to occur:

- One set of intrinsic values for X must have already been stored, with their associated retrieval conditions.
- The current context (the values of those terms that have been held constant) must differ from the retrieval conditions for only one term.
- The stored intrinsic values and the newly recorded values for Y must be related linearly.

When all these conditions are satisfied, the rule removes the differing term and its value from the retrieval conditions that have been placed on the intrinsic values, so that in the future they will be retrieved (see RETRIEVE-INTRINSIC below) regardless of this term's value. In addition, this term is marked as irrelevant, so that if future sets of values are stored for this intrinsic property, its value will not be included in the conditions. Finally, the values of the intrinsic property are added to working memory in a form that BACON's numeric heuristics can use in the discovery process.

The production RETRIEVE-INTRINSIC matches in situations where BACON.4 has the goal of considering intrinsic properties for some nominal term, where such a property has already been created by DEFINE-

INTRINSIC and the conditions on its values have been altered by GENERALIZE-INTRINSIC, and where the conditions placed on these values are met by the current set of independent values. In such cases, this rule retrieves the set of intrinsic values and adds them to memory, where BACON may use them in formulating numerical laws.[4]

The final rule is STORE-INTRINSIC, which applies in cases where an intrinsic property has been defined, where there exist stored values for this property but none of their conditions are matched by the current set of independent values, and where the linearity condition of GENERALIZE-INTRINSIC is not met. In such a situation, this rule simply stores away a new set of intrinsic values based on the values of the same numerical term that was employed earlier, using the current independent values as conditions. However, any independent terms that have previously been determined to be irrelevant are omitted from the set of retrieval conditions.

Let us consider briefly how these rules would be used in the example we discussed earlier: Ohm's law. In dealing with the nominal version of Ohm's data, BACON.4 would collect the observations in the first three rows of table 4.1, at which point it would apply CONSIDER-INTRINSIC to set the goal for proposing an intrinsic property for the nominal term "wire." Since no such property exists, DEFINE-INTRINSIC would fire, generating the term "conductance" and storing values for the newcomer based on the values of the current. After finding a tautological linear relation between these values, BACON would gather the data shown in the fourth through sixth rows of table 4.1. At this point, GENERALIZE-INTRINSIC would note that the stored intrinsic values for conductance were linearly related to the new values for the current, and would decide that values of the battery should not be constrained from being retrieved. After the old intrinsic values were added to memory, a second (expected but nontautological) linear relation would be found between conductance and current, this time with a different slope. Next, the last set of observations shown in table 4.1 (for battery C) would be collected, and since the battery condition had been removed from the stored intrinsic values, the values of the conductance would immediately be added to memory by RETRIEVE-INTRINSIC. On the basis of these values, a third linear relation with a still different slope would be found. The three slopes would

---

4. Actually, these values already reside in working memory, but they are in a conditionalized form that cannot be matched by BACON's other rules.

be gathered together at a higher level of description, each associated with a different battery. Since the battery takes on nominal values, CONSIDER-INTRINSIC and DEFINE-INTRINSIC would generate the property of voltage, and a tautological law would result. However, since no other independent terms would remain to be varied, the system would halt at this point.

To summarize: In cases, such as that of Ohm's law, where BACON.4 can justify generalizing the retrieval conditions on intrinsic values, the rule sequence is CONSIDER-INTRINSIC, DEFINE-INTRINSIC, GENERALIZE-INTRINSIC, RETRIEVE-INTRINSIC. This sequence is followed by more instances of RETRIEVE-INTRINSIC if additional values of the nominal term (e.g., a fourth battery) occur. This contrasts with the events that took place in the friction example. In this case, we find the sequence CONSIDER-INTRINSIC, DEFINE-INTRINSIC, STORE-INTRINSIC, and STORE-INTRINSIC, since there is no evidence that the system should generalize its retrieval conditions. As mentioned earlier, more complex situations can occur in which GENERALIZE-INTRINSIC and RETRIEVE-INTRINSIC would be used at one level of description and STORE-INTRINSIC at another. Like the BACON.3 heuristics for discovering numerical relations, the BACON.4 intrinsic-property heuristics are driven by the data they encounter in their search for lawful regularities.

Physical Discoveries of BACON.4

Now that we have summarized BACON.4's methods and examined their implementation in terms of production rules, let us apply the system to some additional situations from the history of science. As the initial example in physics, we will trace the program's discovery of Archimedes' law of displacement and its development of the concepts of volume and density.

Archimedes, Volume, and Density

When Archimedes was asked to determine whether his ruler's crown was composed of pure gold, he knew that, given the density of gold, the weight of the crown, and the volume of the crown, he could determine its purity. The first of these was already known, and the second could be easily determined. However, the volume of the crown could not be found without

Table 4.3
First-level data for the displacement law.

Composition	Object	V	C	$S_{C,V}$	$I_{C,V}$
Silver	A	100.0	105.326	1.00	5.326
Silver	A	200.0	205.326	1.00	5.326
Silver	A	300.0	305.326	1.00	5.326
Silver	B	100.0	107.115	1.00	7.115
Silver	B	200.0	207.115	1.00	7.115
Silver	B	300.0	307.115	1.00	7.115
Silver	C	100.0	109.482	1.00	9.482
Silver	C	200.0	209.482	1.00	9.482
Silver	C	300.0	309.482	1.00	9.482

melting the object and thus destroying it. Archimedes' insight occurred while he was bathing: One could determine the volume of any object (however irregular) by observing the amount of water it displaced. This discovery so delighted Archimedes (so the story goes) that he jumped from the bath and ran through the streets of Syracuse, crying "Eureka." The result was a new means of measurement: defining an irregular volume in terms of the difference between regular volumes.

Archimedes' law of displacement provides us with another instance of intrinsic properties. Given the same variables available to Archimedes, BACON.4 can also generate this law, though we would hardly argue that it follows the same line of reasoning as did Archimedes (BACON seldom takes baths). Let us suppose that BACON.4 has experimental control over two nominal variables (the object being examined and the composition of that object) and one numerical variable (the volume v of liquid in an easily measured container). Like Archimedes, BACON.4 does not initially know the volumes of the objects, because of their irregular shapes. However, the only observable dependent variable—the combined volume, C, of the object and the liquid—will let the program devise a new measure.

The system begins by varying the volume of liquid in which a given object is immersed. The results of a number of such observations are presented in table 4.3. As before, each row in this table corresponds to an observation, while each column represents the observed values for a single variable. Two new terms, $S_{C,V}$ and $I_{C,V}$, are defined when the program notes a linear relation between the values of V and C. These correspond to the slope and the intercept of the line, respectively.

Table 4.4
Postulating the property of irregular volume.

Composition	Object	$S_{C,V}$	$I_{C,V}$	o	$I_{C,V}/o$
Silver	A	1.0	5.326	5.326	1.0
Silver	B	1.0	7.115	7.115	1.0
Silver	C	1.0	9.482	9.482	1.0
Gold	D	1.0	6.313	6.313	1.0
Gold	E	1.0	4.722	4.722	1.0
Gold	F	1.0	8.817	8.817	1.0
Lead	G	1.0	5.016	5.016	1.0
Lead	H	1.0	3.493	3.493	1.0
Lead	I	1.0	6.827	6.827	1.0

Table 4.4 summarizes the results of table 4.3 along with additional observations made when the composition is varied. The slope of the line $S_{C,V}$ is invariant, while different values of $I_{C,V}$ occur for each composition-object pair. At this point, BACON.4 has no numerical independent terms to relate to its dependent ones, so it defines an intrinsic property o (using the rule DEFINE-INTRINSIC) whose values are associated with each of these pairs. This term corresponds to the volume of the object that was placed in the water. On the basis of the initial values of the new term, the system notes a (tautological) linear relationship between $I_{C,V}$ and o. The slope of this line, $o/I_{C,V}$, has the constant value 1.0 for all objects. Moreover, since a complete factorial design is impossible (a given object can never be combined with more than one composition), the GENERALIZE-INTRINSIC rule can never apply, and BACON can only apply the production STORE-INTRINSIC to associate particular intrinsic values with particular combinations of the object and the composition. Despite this limitation, the program has succeeded in specifying a new technique for measuring the volumes of irregular objects, much as Archimedes did in the third century B.C.

Although BACON has failed to generalize the conditions for retrieving the values of its new intrinsic property, this term may still prove useful. Suppose that, at some later point, the program runs a different experiment involving the same independent variables—the object and the composition of the object—while the dependent term is the weight W of the object. Table 4.5 gives some data that might be recorded in such an experiment. If the same objects are used as before, the intrinsic value o associated with

Table 4.5
Relating weights to irregular volumes.

Composition	Object	W	o	W/o
Silver	A	55.923	5.326	10.5
Silver	B	74.708	7.115	10.5
Silver	C	99.561	9.482	10.5
Gold	D	121.841	6.313	19.3
Gold	E	91.135	4.722	19.3
Gold	F	170.168	8.817	19.3
Lead	G	57.182	5.016	11.4
Lead	H	39.820	3.493	11.4
Lead	I	77.828	6.827	11.4

Table 4.6
Postulating the property of density.

Composition	W/o	Density (d)	W/od
Silver	10.5	10.5	1.0
Gold	19.3	19.3	1.0
Lead	11.4	11.4	1.0

each object is retrieved in each case (by the rule RETRIEVE-INTRINSIC). Thus, when the composition is silver, BACON.4's trend detectors compare the values of W and o for the objects A, B, and C, noting a linear relation between these two terms. Since the intercept is zero, the slope of this line can be rewritten as W/o. The value of this term is stored at a higher level of description. Table 4.6 summarizes the slopes for each value of the composition. Since these are different for each composition, BACON postulates the higher-level intrinsic property d, basing its values on those of W/o and associating them with the nominal values of the composition. The values of the new term d correspond to the densities of silver, gold, and lead, respectively.

Snell's Law of Refraction

For our next example, let us turn to Snell's law of refraction, which involves the notion of symmetry. The invention of the telescope created the need for a sound theory of lens design, and this need attracted attention to the refraction of light. Kepler arrived at an approximate but not wholly correct

Table 4.7
Data obeying Snell's law.

Medium$_1$	Medium$_2$	$\sin A_1$	$\sin A_2$	$\sin A_1 / \sin A_2$
Vacuum	Vacuum	0.500	0.500	1.00
Vacuum	Vacuum	0.707	0.707	1.00
Vacuum	Vacuum	0.866	0.866	1.00
Vacuum	Water	0.500	0.665	0.75
Vacuum	Water	0.707	0.940	0.75
Vacuum	Water	0.866	1.152	0.75
Vacuum	Oil	0.500	0.735	0.68
Vacuum	Oil	0.707	1.039	0.68
Vacuum	Oil	0.866	1.273	0.68

law of refraction; in 1621 the Dutch astronomer Snell found the correct formula, which relates the angle of incidence, A_1, and the angle of refraction, A_2, of a ray of light as it meets a smooth, transparent interface between two media. The general form of Snell's law is

$$\sin A_1 / \sin A_2 = n_1 / n_2$$

where n_1 and n_2 are indices of refraction for two media relative to a common reference medium. Vacuum is the usual reference medium, with an index of refraction arbitrarily assigned as 1.0. With such a standàrd, water has an index of refraction of 1.33; oil, 1.47; quartz, 1.54; and ordinary glass, 1.66.

In rediscovering Snell's law, BACON.4 is given experimental control over the composition of the first medium, the composition of the second medium, and $\sin A_1$.[5] The first two of these take on nominal values; the third is numerical. The system is also told to use the numerical term $\sin A_2$ as the single dependent variable in this experiment. Table 4.7 shows some of the values BACON gathers when the first medium is set to vacuum. Since the system prefers complete factorial designs, it considers the situation in which both media are vacuum; this is equivalent to shining light through a single medium, so no refraction occurs in this case.

Upon considering the data in table 4.7, BACON.4 first notes a linear

---

5. BACON.4 does not have heuristics for considering trigonometric functions of variables directly. Thus, in the run described here we simply told the system to examine the sines. In the following chapter we will see how BACON can actually arrive at the sine term on its own in a rather subtle manner.

Table 4.8
Second-level data for Snell's law.

Medium$_1$	Medium$_2$	$\sin A_1/\sin A_2$	n_2	$\sin A_1/n_2 \sin A_2$
Vacuum	Vacuum	1.00	1.00	1.00
Vacuum	Water	0.75	0.75	1.00
Vacuum	Oil	0.68	0.68	1.00
Water	Vacuum	1.33	1.00	1.33
Water	Water	1.00	0.75	1.33
Water	Oil	0.90	0.68	1.33
Oil	Vacuum	1.47	1.00	1.47
Oil	Water	1.11	0.75	1.47
Oil	Oil	1.00	0.68	1.47

relation between the sines of the two angles. Since the intercept for this line is zero, the slope can be written as $\sin A_1/\sin A_2$. When the second medium is vacuum, this ratio has the value 1.0 (since no refraction occurs); when the second medium is water, the ratio is 0.75, and when oil is used it is 0.68. These regularities are summarized at the second level of description; the results are presented in table 4.8, along with the values of $\sin A_1/\sin A_2$ for other combinations of media.

At this point, since it is impossible to find a numerical law between the nominal values of medium$_2$ and $\sin A_1/\sin A_2$, BACON decides to postulate the intrinsic property n_2 and to base the values of this property on those of the sine ratio. Initially, the system finds a linear relation between the ratio of sines and n_2 when medium$_1$ is vacuum. However, when the first medium is water, the rule GENERALIZE-INTRINSIC tells BACON that it should generalize the retrieval conditions for n_2 to ignore the values of the first medium. As a result, the first set of intrinsic values is retrieved, and another (nontautological) linear relation is found, this time with a slope of 1.33. When medium$_1$ is set to oil, RETRIEVE-INTRINSIC recalls the same set of intrinsic values, and a third linear relation is noted, this one having the slope 1.47. Since each of these linear relations has a zero intercept, the slope term may be written as $\sin A_1/n_2 \sin A_2$. The values of this term are summarized in table 4.9.

Having arrived at the data summarized in table 4.9, BACON is again confronted with a nominal independent term and a numerical dependent term. However, the situation here differs somewhat from Ohm's law and Archimedes' law. BACON.4 has already defined the intrinsic property n_2,

Table 4.9
Third-level summary of Snell's data.

Medium$_1$	n_1	$\sin A_1 / n_2 \sin A_2$	$n_1 \sin A_1 / n_2 \sin A_2$
Vacuum	1.00	1.00	1.0
Water	0.75	1.33	1.0
Oil	0.68	1.47	1.0

and has generalized its retrieval conditions so that only medium$_2$ is considered. However, the first medium takes on nominal values from the same set as the second medium, and these two terms have the same type. BACON uses this knowledge (which is provided by the programmer) to infer intrinsic values for nominal values of the first medium as well.

Thus, since it knows n_2 to be 1.0 when medium$_2$ is vacuum, the system infers the analogous intrinsic property n_1 to have the same value when medium$_1$ is vacuum. Similary, the values 1.33 and 1.47 are retrieved when medium$_1$ is water and oil, respectively. As a result, BACON.4 is able to introduce the intrinsic term n_1 and determine its values without introducing a tautological law. Once it has values for this term, the system notes that the values of n_1 decrease as those of $\sin A_1 / n_2 \sin A_2$ increase. As a result, BACON defines the product $n_1 \sin A_1 / n_2 \sin A_2$ and finds it to have the constant value 1.0. Since this law completely summarizes the observed data, the system stops at this point.

It is instructive to relate BACON's formulation to the standard form of Snell's law: $\sin A_1 / \sin A_2 = n_1 / n_2$. Upon inspection, we find that the program's law transforms not into the standard form but into $\sin A_1 / \sin A_2 = n_2 / n_1$. However, nowhere has it been stated that BACON's n_1 and n_2 are identical to Snell's n_1 and n_2. Recalling the indices of refraction we used to generate the original data, we find that BACON has arrived at the reciprocal values. BACON's selection of a measurement scale extends beyond the introduction of simple coefficients. This explains the apparently upside-down relation, and with this insight the program's formulation is easily transformed into the standard version of Snell's law.

To summarize: The method of using intrinsic values from nominal terms having the same type allows BACON to sidestep the process of storing an initial set of values. As a result, the system is able to find an empirically valid law instead of the tautological law that is normally found when a new intrinsic term is introduced. The notion of variables with the same type is closely related to the concept of symmetry, and it could be argued that, in using the above strategy, BACON.4 is assuming that a symmetrical law will hold. For instance, one can imagine a universe in which the intrinsic value associated with water as the first medium differs from the intrinsic value for water as the second medium. Since BACON does not consider this possibility (we doubt that many scientists would either), it must be assuming implicitly that symmetry will in fact hold across different media.

Black's Law of Specific Heat

In addition to Snell's law of refraction, BACON.4 has used its intrinsic-property heuristic to arrive at a number of other laws from the history of physics that involve the notion of symmetry. One of these is the law of specific heat, which Joseph Black discovered in the 1760s (Magie 1935, pp. 134–145) when he systematically mixed liquids of different temperatures and observed the final temperatures of these mixtures. If T_1 and T_2 represent the initial temperatures of the two liquids, M_1 and M_2 stand for their masses, and T_f is the final temperature, Black's law can be stated as

$$T_f = \frac{c_1 M_1 T_1 + c_2 M_2 T_2}{c_1 M_1 + c_2 M_2},$$

where c_1 and c_2 represent the specific heats of the liquids being mixed. The specific heat is a numerical value associated with a particular liquid that summarizes the role the liquid plays in Black's equation. For example, if we let the specific heat of water be 1.0, then the value for mercury is 0.0332 and the value for ethyl alcohol is 0.456.

BACON.4's discovery of Black's law results from a lengthy but straightforward application of the techniques discussed above. The system is given experimental control of the two liquids, along with M_1, M_2, T_1, and T_2. The first two of these variables take nominal values; the last four take numerical values. The single dependent variable is T_f. Table 4.10 shows some noise-free data that are provided to BACON when it varies T_1 and T_2.

Upon examining the data contained in the first three rows of table 4.10, BACON notes a linear relation between T_2 and T_f. Accordingly, the system defines theoretical terms for the slope and the intercept of this line, which we will call simply a and b. For the first three rows ($T_1 = 50$), the slope term has the value 0.67 and the intercept is 16.67. These two values are stored at a second level of description, and additional (different) values

Table 4.10
First-level data for Black's specific-heat law.

Liquid$_1$	Liquid$_2$	M_1	M_2	T_1	T_2	T_f	a	b
A	B	1.0	1.0	50.0	50.0	50.00	0.67	16.67
A	B	1.0	1.0	50.0	60.0	56.67	0.67	16.67
A	B	1.0	1.0	50.0	70.0	63.33	0.67	16.67
A	B	1.0	1.0	60.0	50.0	53.33	0.67	20.00
A	B	1.0	1.0	60.0	60.0	60.00	0.67	20.00
A	B	1.0	1.0	60.0	70.0	66.67	0.67	20.00
A	B	1.0	1.0	70.0	50.0	56.67	0.67	23.33
A	B	1.0	1.0	70.0	60.0	63.33	0.67	23.33
A	B	1.0	1.0	70.0	70.0	70.00	0.67	23.33

Table 4.11
Second-level data for Black's specific-heat law.

Liquid$_1$	Liquid$_2$	M_1	M_2	T_1	a	b	d
A	B	1.0	1.0	50.0	0.67	16.67	0.33
A	B	1.0	1.0	60.0	0.67	20.00	0.33
A	B	1.0	1.0	70.0	0.67	23.33	0.33
A	B	1.0	2.0	50.0	0.80	10.00	0.20
A	B	1.0	2.0	60.0	0.80	12.00	0.20
A	B	1.0	2.0	70.0	0.80	14.00	0.20
A	B	1.0	3.0	50.0	0.86	7.14	0.14
A	B	1.0	3.0	60.0	0.86	8.57	0.14
A	B	1.0	3.0	70.0	0.86	10.00	0.14

for b are stored as new linear relations are found when the other rows
($T_1 = 60, 70$) in table 4.10 are examined. Thus far, BACON has postulated
that $T_f = aT_2 + b$, where a and b may be functions of any of the independent variables except T_2. (In fact, a cannot be related to T_1 either, since it
is constant across different values of this term; however, BACON does not
notice this regularity at the current level of description.)

Table 4.11 shows the (partial) second-level summary that BACON constructs from the original data. Using these higher-level data to explain the
new terms a and b, the system notes two regularities: The slope term a has
the constant value 0.67 when M_2 is 1.0 (though different constant values
are found as M_2 varies), and the intercept term b is related linearly to T_1,
with slope 0.33 and intercept 0 when M_2 is 1.0. Different slopes (let us call

Table 4.12
Third-level data for Black's specific-heat law.

Liquid$_1$	Liquid$_2$	M_1	M_2	a	M_2/a	j	k
A	B	1.0	1.0	0.67	1.5	1.0	-0.5
A	B	1.0	2.0	0.80	2.5	1.0	-0.5
A	B	1.0	3.0	0.86	3.5	1.0	-0.5

Table 4.13
Additional third-level data for Black's law.

Liquid$_1$	Liquid$_2$	M_1	M_2	d	dM_2	f	g
A	B	1.0	1.0	0.33	0.333	-0.5	0.5
A	B	1.0	2.0	0.20	0.400	-0.5	0.5
A	B	1.0	3.0	0.14	0.428	-0.5	0.5

this term d) occur for other values of M_2, but the intercept always remains zero, so we will ignore the latter term in our discussion. Tables 4.12 and 4.13 summarize these regularities at the third level of description. BACON has now found that $T_f = aT_2 + dT_1$. Its next task is to express a and d as functions of the remaining independent variables: M_2, M_1, Liquid$_2$, and Liquid$_1$.

Since the third-level regularities are somewhat more complex than the lower-level ones, we have summarized them in two tables (4.12 and 4.13). When BACON attempts to relate the slope a to M_2 (table 4.12), it notes that the terms increase together and considers the ratio M_2/a. Upon computing the values of this new term, the system finds a linear relation between M_2 and the ratio. The slope of this line (let us call it j) is 1.0; the intercept (let us call this k) is -0.5. Thus, we now have the law

$$M_2 = j(M_2/a) + k,$$

or

$$a = jM_2/(M_2 - k).$$

These results are summarized in table 4.14.

In a similar fashion, no simple relation emerges when BACON examines the values of the slope term d (table 4.13). Instead, the system notes that this term increases as M_2 decreases, and so defines the product dM_2.

Table 4.14
Fourth-level summary of data for Black's law.

Liquid$_1$	Liquid$_2$	M_1	j	k	f	g	p	q	r
A	B	1.0	1.0	-0.5	-0.5	0.5	-0.5	-0.5	0.5
A	B	2.0	1.0	-1.0	-1.0	1.0	-0.5	-0.5	0.5
A	B	3.0	1.0	-1.5	-1.5	1.5	-0.5	-0.5	0.5

Although this product does not have a constant value, it is related linearly to d itself:

$$dM_2 = fd + g.$$

This line has a slope f of -0.5 and an intercept g of 0.5. These relations, too, are summarized in table 4.14. BACON has now discovered that

$$d = \frac{g}{M_2 - f},$$

or

$$T_f = \frac{jM_2 T_2}{M_2 - k} + \frac{gT_1}{M_2 - f},$$

where the constants may depend on M_1, Liquid$_1$, and Liquid$_2$.

Upon reaching the fourth level of description, BACON must relate the four dependent terms ($j, k, f,$ and g) to the mass M_1. The first of these, j, has the constant value 1.0 (as it will have at even higher levels), but the remaining three terms vary. However, closer inspection reveals that each of $k, f,$ and g is linearly related to M_1, and that in each case the intercept is zero. Moreover, the resulting slope terms ($p, q,$ and r) differ only in their signs. Different values for these slopes occur as Liquid$_2$ is varied; the resulting values are summarized in table 4.15 (which, in contrast with the preceding tables, includes the results for all combinations of liquids used in the experiment). The law BACON has discovered can now be written as

$$T_f = \frac{jM_2 T_2}{M_2 - pM_1} + \frac{rM_1 T_1}{M_2 - qM_1}.$$

A glance at table 4.15 will show that, when the two liquids are the same (A, B, or C), we always have the values $p = -1$, $q = -1$, and $r = 1$. Moreover, we already know that $j = 1$. Hence, when two portions of the

Table 4.15
Fifth-level summary of data for Black's law.

Liquid$_1$	Liquid$_2$	p	q	r	$i_2{}^a$	$p/i_2 = u$	$q/i_2 = v$	$r/i_2 = w$
A	A	-1.00	-1.00	1.00	-1.00	1.00	1.00	-1.00
A	B	-0.50	-0.50	0.50	-0.50	1.00	1.00	-1.00
A	C	-0.25	-0.25	0.25	-0.25	1.00	1.00	-1.00
B	A	-2.00	-2.00	2.00	-1.00	2.00	2.00	-2.00
B	B	-1.00	-1.00	1.00	-0.50	2.00	2.00	-2.00
B	C	-0.50	-0.50	0.50	-0.25	2.00	2.00	-2.00
C	A	-4.00	-4.00	4.00	-1.00	4.00	4.00	-4.00
C	B	-2.00	-2.00	2.00	-0.50	4.00	4.00	-4.00
C	C	-1.00	-1.00	1.00	-0.25	4.00	4.00	-4.00

a. This intrinsic property is discussed in the text.

same liquid are mixed, Black's law takes the symmetric form

$$T_f = \frac{M_2 T_2 + M_1 T_1}{M_2 + M_1}.$$

In this form, the law was known to Black's predecessors Fahrenheit and Boerhaave. However, they failed to introduce the intrinsic term, specific heat, and thereby extend the law to the case where two substances are involved. Now let us see how BACON defines the new term and achieves this extension.

At this point, BACON finds itself with three numerical dependent terms (p, q, and r) and two nominal independent terms (the two liquids). In order to generate the independent numerical term it needs to formulate laws, the system postulates an intrinsic property (let us call this term i_2). BACON bases the values of i_2 on the values of p, though it could as easily have used the values of q or r. Examining the values of i_2 when Liquid$_1$ is A, the program finds a linear relation between p and the new intrinsic property. Of course, this tautological relation has a slope u of 1.0 and an intercept of 0. However, nearly identical (and empirically meaningful) relations are found between the new intrinsic variables i_2 and q, and between i_2 and r. The first relation has a slope v of 1.0 and an intercept of 0; the second has a slope w of -1.0 and an intercept of 0. Using the new intrinsic variable and slopes to replace p, q, and r, we have now arrived at

$$T_f = \frac{f M_2 T_2}{M_2 - u i_2 M_1} + \frac{w i_2 M_1 T_1}{M_2 - v i_2 M_1}.$$

Table 4.16
Sixth-level summary of data for Black's law.

Liquid$_1$	u	v	w	i_1	ui_1	vi_1	wi_1
A	1.0	1.0	-1.0	-1.00	-1.0	-1.0	1.0
B	2.0	2.0	-2.0	-0.50	-1.0	-1.0	1.0
C	4.0	4.0	-4.0	-0.25	-1.0	-1.0	1.0

Upon examining the values of p when Liquid$_1$ is B, BACON finds them linearly related to the intrinsic values associated with i_2. At a result, the retrieval conditions of i_2 are generalized, which makes them available for different values of Liquid$_1$. Thus, the system is able to note further linear relations between i_2 and the dependent terms p, q, and r. These are indentical to the relations found when Liquid$_1$ was A, except that the slopes (u, v, and w) are different. Table 4.16 summarizes the slope values found for different values of Liquid$_1$.

On reaching the sixth and final level of description, BACON finds one independent nominal term (Liquid$_1$) and three numerical dependent terms (u, v, and w). Normally the program would postulate some new intrinsic property at this point; however, since the two liquids are known to be of the same type, and since the intrinsic property i_2 has already been associated with Liquid$_2$, BACON uses the values of this term as its i_1. As a result, it is able to find nontautological relations between i_1 and each of the dependent terms. In each case, BACON notes that the dependent term decreases as i_1 increases, which leads to the definition of three product terms: ui_1, vi_1, and wi_1. Each of these terms has a constant value (-1.0, -1.0, and 1.0). After discovering these relations, the system stops, having summarized all the data it has gathered (table 4.16). Eliminating the values of u, v, and w by using the relations $u = -1/i_1$, $v = -1/i_1$, and $w = 1/i_1$, we get

$$T_f = \frac{jM_2T_2}{M_2 + (u_2/u_1)M_1} + \frac{(u_2/u_1)M_1T_1}{M_2 + (u_2/u_1)M_1}.$$

Now, if we interpret u as the reciprocal of the specific heat ($c_1 = 1/u_1$ and $c_2 = 1/u_2$), then the equation just written can be converted immediately into the familiar expression for Black's law with which we began our discussion of this example.

Table 4.17 brings together the steps that led BACON to the discovery of

Table 4.17
Relations discovered at successive levels for Black's law

Level 1	Vary T_2	$T_f = aT_2 + b$	$T_f = aT_2 + b$
Level 2	Vary T_1	$b = dT_1$ a is constant	$T_f = aT_2 + dT_1$
Level 3	Vary M_2	$M_2 = j(M_2/a) + k$ $dM_2 = fd + g$	$T_f = jM_2T_2/(M_2 - k)$ $+ gT_1/(M_2 - f)$
Level 4	Vary M_1	$k = pM_1$ $f = qM_1$ $g = rM_1$ j is constant	$T_f = jM_2T_2/(M_2 - pM_1)$ $+ rM_1T_1/(M_2 - qM_1)$
Level 5	Vary L_2	$p = ui_2$ $q = vi_2$ $r = wi_2$ j is constant	$T_f = jM_2T_2/(M_2 - ui_2M_1)$ $+ wi_2M_1T_1/(M_2 - vi_2M_1)$
Level 6	Vary L_1	$ui_1 = -1.0$ $vi_1 = -1.0$ $wi_1 = 1.0$ $wi_1 = 1.0$	$T_f = jM_2T_2/[M_2 + (i_2/i_1)M_1]$ $+ (i_2/i_1)M_1T_1/[M_2 + (i_2/i_1)M_1]$

the law and the invention of the concept of specific heat (or its reciprocal). At each level of the search, a new independent variable was considered, and the constants introduced previously were redefined in terms of this variable and new parameters (which were redefined, in turn, at the next level). The first column of the table shows the level, the second column the new independent variable that was considered, the third column the new relations that BACON discovered, and the fourth column the formula for T_f in terms of the highest-level constants thus far introduced.

BACON stopped one step short of converting the law into the familiar form. It did not wholly symmetrize the final expression by replacing i_1 and i_2 by their reciprocals and simplifying. A symmetrization heuristic to take such a step could be automated; however, this would require that the system be capable of noticing that the value of j is unity and not just an arbitrary constant. BACON already recognizes zeros and treats them in special ways. As we shall see, it also can distinguish integral from nonintegral values of variables. It would not appear unreasonable to incorporate a heuristic for replacing literal constants that are equal to unity with their values, but the version we have described does not include such a rule.

BACON.4 and Gravitational Mass

Late in the eighteenth century, Henry Cavendish (1766, 1784, 1785) designed an apparatus suitable for measuring the value of g, the universal constant of gravitation. (See Magie 1935, pp. 105–111.) This apparatus consisted of an object attached to an arm which was suspended from a quartz fiber, a second object which was attracted by the suspended object, and a mirror and a light source with which the torque produced by the attraction could be measured. Basically, this device was a more sensitive version of the torsion balance Coulomb had used in studying electrical attraction.

BACON.4 can use data collected in an experiment like Cavendish's to find the law of gravitational attraction. If m_1 is the mass of the suspended object, m_2 the mass of the movable object, D the distance between their centers of mass, and F the observed force between the two objects, the law of gravitational attraction can be stated as

$$F = gm_1m_2/D^2.$$

Since this law has exactly the same form as Coulomb's law, we know that BACON.3, given the force, the distance, and the two masses as numerical terms, would be able to discover the relation without difficulty. However, if the masses of the various objects used in the experiment were not known, BACON would have to treat the objects as nominal variables, in that it would be able to tell them apart but it would know nothing of their quantitative properties. As a result, it would bring its intrinsic-property heuristics to bear and infer the concept of mass from the values of the force and distance. Let us consider the details of this process in an experiment involving five objects, A, B, C, D, and E, whose unobservable masses are $M_A = 1.0$, $M_B = 2.0$, $M_C = 3.0$, $M_D = 4.0$, and $M_E = 5.0$.

BACON.4 begins by holding the two objects constant and varying the distance between them. Table 4.18 shows the data collected in such an experiment when the suspended object is A. In contrast with the situation in Snell's and Black's experiments, the two nominal terms cannot take on the same value, since a single object can never occupy two positions in space. This leads to some complications in determining the intrinsic values associated with the objects, which we will discuss shortly. However, BACON must first deal with the purely numerical task of relating the distance D to the force F.

In the first three rows of table 4.18 we see that the gravitational force

Table 4.18
Data obeying the law of gravitation.

Suspended object	Movable object	D (meters)	F (newtons)	FD (newton-meters)	FD^2
A	B	0.01	19.2	0.192	0.00192
A	B	0.02	4.8	0.096	0.00192
A	B	0.03	1.2	0.048	0.00192
A	C	0.01	28.8	0.288	0.00288
A	C	0.02	7.2	0.144	0.00288
A	C	0.03	1.8	0.027	0.00288
A	D	0.01	38.4	0.384	0.00384
A	D	0.02	9.6	0.192	0.00384
A	D	0.03	2.4	0.096	0.00384
A	E	0.01	48.0	0.480	0.00480
A	E	0.02	12.0	0.240	0.00480
A	E	0.03	3.0	0.120	0.00480

decreases as the distance increases, which leads the system to consider the product of F and D. Since this new term does not have a constant value, and because FD decreases when D increases, BACON calculates a second product, FD^2. This has a constant value of 0.00192 when the suspended object is A and the movable object is B. The program finds similar constants for the pairs of objects A and C, A and D, and A and E; table 4.19 summarizes these values at the second level of description.

Upon examination of the first five rows in table 4.19 (in which the suspended object is A), BACON notes that its independent term (the movable object) is nominal whereas its dependent term (FD^2) is numerical. Accordingly, the program postulates an intrinsic property (let us call it M_2) and bases the values of this new term on the numerical values of FD^2. Because BACON has no FD^2 value for the situation in which both objects are A (since this combination is impossible), at this point the system cannot assign any value for M_2 to A. However, BACON does find (tautologically) that the ratio FD^2/M_2 equals 1.0, and it infers that this relation holds in the hypothetical A-and-A case as well.[6]

The second five rows of table 4.19 show the values of FD^2 when the suspended object is B. In this case, BACON "observed" FD^2 for the com-

---

6. We have not discussed the rules that let BACON make this inference.

Table 4.19
Second-level summary of gravitation data.

Suspended object	Movable object	FD^2	Mass of object (M_2)	FD^2/M_2
A	A	—	—	(1.0)
A	B	0.00192	0.00192	1.0
A	C	0.00288	0.00288	1.0
A	D	0.00384	0.00384	1.0
A	E	0.00480	0.00480	1.0
B	A	0.00192	—	(2.0)
B	B	—	0.00192	(2.0)
B	C	0.00576	0.00288	2.0
B	D	0.00768	0.00384	2.0
B	E	0.00960	0.00480	2.0

bination B-A, but since it has no M_2 value for A it cannot compute the value of FD^2/M_2. For the hypothetical combination B-B, the system has an intrinsic property value for B; however, it cannot observe the value of FD^2 for this situation, so again FD^2/M_2 cannot be computed. The situation is better for the combinations B-C, B-D, and B-E, and BACON notes that the value of FD^2/M_2 is 2.0 in each of these cases. The program assumes that the same relation holds for the B-A and B-B combinations, and this assumption lets BACON determine the value of M_2 for A. Given $FD^2 = 0.00192$ for the B-A combination, and inferring that $FD^2/M_2 = 2.0$ for this case, we find

$$\frac{FD^2}{FD^2/M_2} = \frac{0.00192}{2.0} = 0.00096 = M_2.$$

This intrinsic value is stored with the nominal value A, and when later combinations involving this term are considered the numerical value is retrieved and used in computing FD^2/M_2.

The result of this reasoning process is the third-level summary shown in table 4.20. In this case, only one independent variable remains, the suspended object, and this must be related to the numerical term FD^2/M_2. BACON has already associated an intrinsic value for M_2 with each of the suspended objects in the table. Since it knows that the suspended object is in some sense analogous to the movable object, the program creates an analogous intrinsic term (let us call it M_1), which it attempts to relate to

Table 4.20
Third-level summary of gravitation data.

Suspended object	FD^2/M_2	M_1	$FD^2/M_1 M_2$
A	1.0	0.00096	1,041.67
B	2.0	0.00192	1,041.67
C	3.0	0.00288	1,041.67
D	4.0	0.00384	1,041.67
E	5.0	0.00480	1,041.67

FD^2. These terms are related linearly, with slope 1,041.67 and intercept 0, so BACON formulates the law

$$\frac{FD^2}{M_1 M_2} = 1,041.67.$$

Inverting this relation yields

$$\frac{M_1 M_2}{FD^2} = 9.6 \times 10^{-3},$$

a slight variation on the law of gravitational attraction presented above. The intrinsic properties M_1 and M_2 represent the *gravitational masses* of the various objects, measured in arbitrary units.

BACON.4 and Inertial Mass

BACON.4 can also discover mass in a second kind of experiment. Consider the case where two masses, m_1 and m_2, are connected by a perfectly elastic spring that has no inertia. If the objects are pulled apart and then released, the two masses will enter into harmonic oscillation. The velocities of the two objects can be measured at several points in their period. This situation is a special case of conservation of momentum, in which $m_1 V_1/m_2 V_2 = 1.0$. (For simplicity, we will define V as the absolute value of the velocity.) In order to arrive at this law, BACON.4 requires experimental control over nominal values for the first and second objects and over the times at which observations are made; it observes the two dependent values of V_1 and V_2 for various combinations of the independent values.

   In discovering this law, BACON.4 varies the times at which the velocities are measured and notes that the velocities V_1 and V_2 increase together.

Accordingly, it defines the term V_1/V_2, which does not vary with the time of the observation. Next the program postulates the intrinsic property m_2, which it associates with the nominal values of the second object. This term varies directly with V_1/V_2, leading BACON to consider the ratio $V_1/m_2 V_2$. This term has a value that is dependent only upon the first object. As in the gravitational-mass experiment, the system must determine the intrinsic value for one of the objects indirectly, since the same object cannot occupy both ends of the spring. Finally, BACON infers the intrinsic property m_1 by analogy with m_2, using the values of the latter. The values of m_1 vary directly with $V_1/m_2 V_2$, leading to the law $m_1 V_1/m_2 V_2 = 1.0$ (which was described above as a special case of conservation of momentum). The values of m_1 and m_2 correspond to the *inertial masses* of the objects used in the experiment.

Now that we have seen how BACON can discover the two notions of inertial and gravitational mass independently, let us consider the potential interaction between these two concepts. Suppose that we first presented BACON with the above experiment, leading it to the concept of inertial mass. Now suppose that we used the same objects in presenting the gravitation data. Rather than infer a new intrinsic property, BACON would first retrieve existing ones and look for relations. In this case, the inertial-mass values would lead directly to the gravitational law, without the need for introducing a separate notion of gravitational mass. Similarly, if the order of experiments were reversed, BACON.4 would incorporate gravitational-mass values into the spring experiment, without postulating inertial units. Since physicists do recognize two different aspects of mass, BACON's procedure may not be a plausible model of historical discovery. However, it does serve to illustrate the secondary role of the intrinsic-property heuristic in BACON, since the program introduces new terms only when its more conservative heuristics fail.

Summary of BACON.4's Discoveries

At this point, we summarize the main discoveries of BACON.4 and its intrinsic-property method. The following list gives the laws the system has found, along with the intrinsic properties postulated in each case.

• **Ohm's law of electrical circuits**   This law relates the current I in a circuit to characteristics of the wire and the battery from which it is constructed. The law can be stated as

$$I = v/r,$$

where the voltage v is an intrinsic property of the battery and the resistance r is an intrinsic property associated with the wire.

• **Archimedes' law of displacement**   This law relates an initial volume of liquid to the volume after an irregular object has been immersed. The law can be stated as

$$C = V + i,$$

where V is the intial volume, C is the volume after immersion, and i is an intrinsic property associated with the irregular object, representing its volume.

• **Snell's law of refraction**   This law relates the angle of incidence i and the angle of refraction r of a ray of light as it passes from one medium to another. The intrinsic properties are the indices of refraction of each medium, n_1 and n_2, and the law can be stated as

$$\sin i/\sin r = n_1/n_2.$$

• **Black's specific-heat law**   This law relates the temperatures T_1 and T_2 of two liquids, and their masses m_1 and m_2, to the final temperature T_f of the mixture. The intrinsic properties are the specific heats c_1 and c_2 of the two liquids, and the law can be stated as

$$c_1 m_1 T_1 + c_2 m_2 T_2 = (c_1 m_1 + c_2 m_2) T_f.$$

• **The law of conservation of momentum**   This law relates the velocities V_1 and V_2 of two objects o_1 and o_2 to each other, independent of the time they are observed. The intrinsic properties are the inertial masses of the objects, m_1 and m_2, and the law can be stated as

$$m_1 V_1 = m_2 V_2.$$

• **The law of gravitation**   BACON.4 discovered an experiment-based version of this law, which relates the attractive force F between two objects o_1 and o_2 to the distance d between them. The intrinsic properties are the gravitational masses of the objects, m_1 and m_2. The law can be stated as

$$F = Gm_1 m_2/d^2,$$

where G is a constant.

The diversity of these examples is encouraging, since it suggests that BACON's methods for handling intrinsic properties are reasonably general. In most cases, the retrieval conditions for intrinsic values were generalized before they led to nontautological laws. However, in the case of Archimedes' law we saw that intrinsic values may prove useful even when their conditions cannot be generalized. (We will see more examples of this in the following section.) Of course, there are limits to the current method's generality. For instance, it encounters difficulty when two intrinsic terms are associated with a single nominal variable. This is the reason we were forced to assume negligible internal resistance when dealing with the nominal version of Ohm's law. Extending the method to handle such cases is an important direction for future work.

In dealing with the last four of the above laws, we introduced another very general concept: the assumption of symmetry, which allowed BACON to generalize the retrieval conditions on its intrinsic properties without justification from the data. This enabled the system to employ existing intrinsic values rather than introduce new terms, and thus to discover empirically meaningful laws where it would otherwise have generated tautologies. However, the notion of symmetry in these cases was limited to the retrieval of intrinsic properties, and we know from the history of science that symmetry assumptions play a much broader role than they played in BACON.4. In the next chapter we shall further explore the uses of symmetry, and we shall find that it can greatly reduce BACON's search through the space of both data and laws. However, let us first consider the role of intrinsic properties in another domain.

Rediscovering Nineteenth-Century Chemistry

One is convinced of a theory's generality not only by the number of phenomena it explains but also by the diversity of those phenomena. As was shown in the preceding section, BACON.4 has enjoyed considerable success in rediscovering laws from physics. Since the program was designed with physical discovery in mind, it would be useful to have evidence of its capabilities in other domains. We felt that early chemistry would provide a challenging test for our theory of the discovery process. This section describes the results of that test. As it turned out, we were forced to include only one new heuristic in order for BACON.4 to obtain a number of important chemical laws.

Chemistry from Proust to Cannizzaro

Quantitative chemistry had its origins in the 1790s, when experimenters decided to focus their attention on the weight of objects instead of other attributes, such as color, texture, or hardness.[7] In 1797, Joseph Louis Proust proposed the *law of definite proportions*, which stated that a given element always contributed the same percentage to the weight of a given compound. Claude Louis Berthollet challenged this claim, pointing to counterexamples in which variable proportions occurred, such as mixtures of sugar and water. However, chemists soon came to distinguish between chemical and physical combinations (compounds and mixtures), and Proust's law was generally accepted for compounds by 1807.

In 1808, John Dalton set forth the *law of simple multiple proportions*. This claimed that, when element A combined with element B in different ways (i.e., forming different compounds), the various amounts of A combining with given amounts of B were always small integer multiples of the smallest amounts. For example, whereas 1.3 grams of oxygen combine with 1.0 gram of carbon to form carbon monoxide, 2.6 grams of oxygen combine with the same amount of carbon to form carbon dioxide.

In explaining the law of simple proportions, Dalton invoked the notion of *atoms* of elements combining to form particles of the resulting compound. Only certain combinations of atoms could occur, and this led to the integer relations that had been observed. To determine the formula of the compound, Dalton used his *rule of greatest simplicity*: If two elements combine in only a single way, assume a binary compound (such as NO); if two combinations are known, assume a binary and a ternary compound (e.g., NO_2 or N_2O). Using this assumption, Dalton calculated the relative atomic weights of the elements. Today we know that the rule of greatest simplicity was wrong in a number of instances. Dalton was aware of inconsistencies in his results, but no better approach presented itself at the time.

Meanwhile, Joseph Gay-Lussac was experimenting with chemical reactions among gases. In 1809 he announced that he had found a law of definite proportions for the *volumes* of gases. Moreover, he had found that the volumes of the materials contributing to and resulting from the reaction always occurred in small integer ratios with respect to each other. For example, 200 milliliters of hydrogen and 100 ml of oxygen combined to

7. An excellent account of this history can be found in chapters 28 and 29 of Arons 1965. For quotations from the sources mentioned in the text, see Leicester and Klickstein 1952.

form 200 ml of water vapor (under standard conditions of pressure and temperature). Gay-Lussac presented this as evidence for Dalton's atomic theory, as well as for the hypothesis that equal volumes of a gas contain equal numbers of particles regardless of composition. However, Dalton rejected this proposal—among other reasons, because he believed that all elementary gases were monatomic and that the particles of different substances were of different sizes.

Only two years later, in 1811, Amedeo Avogadro suggested that some elements might be *diatomic*—that in their isolated state they occurred as pairs of atoms. This required a distinction between *molecules*, which satisfied the "equal volumes, equal numbers" hypothesis, and *atoms*, which did not. Thus, hydrogen and oxygen were seen by Avogadro as diatomic elements, and water as the ternary compound H_2O. Unfortunately, Avogadro's contemporaries paid little attention to his suggestion, and nearly fifty years passed before its power was recognized.

In 1860 a paper by Stanislao Cannizzaro was distributed at the first International Chemical Congress at Karlsruhe. In this paper, Cannizzaro buttressed Avogadro's theory with a straightforward method for determining molecular formulas and relative atomic weights. He examined the percentage of the weight that an element (e.g., hydrogen) contributed to a number of compounds (e.g., water, hydrogen chloride). Upon multiplying these fractions by the density of the element at a standard temperature and pressure, he found all the resulting products to be small integer multiples of the smallest of the set. These divisors corresponded to the relative atomic weights of the elements, and Cannizzaro was able to derive the correct molecular formulas (e.g., H_2O for water) from his table.

Another possibly lawful regularity had been noted in 1815 by William Prout. Most of the computed atomic weights and combining ratios were very nearly multiples of those for hydrogen. Prout hypothesized that the higher elements might consist of clusters of hydrogen atoms. But the relations were not exact, and as better determinations of the atomic weights became available it was apparent that there were important exceptions (e.g., chlorine). Consequently, Prout's hypothesis was rejected by most chemists, and was not revived until, in the present century, the largest anomalies were explained by the discovery of isotopes.

Finding Common Divisors

Dalton's, Gay-Lussac's, and Cannizzaro's discoveries involved more than postulating intrinsic properties and noting recurring values. In addition, these men found in a number of cases that a set of values could be expressed as small integer multiples of one another. BACON.4, as described so far, has no heuristics for discovering such relations. Reluctantly, we added a new heuristic that searched for common divisors in proposed intrinsic values.[8]

A *common divisor* for a set of values is a number that, when divided into those values, generates a set of integers. The *greatest common divisor* of a set of values is simply the largest common divisor. The common divisor need not be an integer, and it will not be in the cases we examine. The greatest common divisor of a set may be found by using an extension of Euclid's algorithm. First, we select the smallest member in the set and divide this number into all numbers in the set, producing a revised set. For instance, suppose our original set of values is $\{1.11\ 1.85\ 2.96\}$. The smallest number in this set is 1.11, so we divide all members by this value, obtaining the new set $\{1.0\ 1.667\ 2.667\}$. If all members of the revised set were integers, we would stop and return 1.11 as the greatest common divisor. Since they are not, we find the smallest nonzero remainder in the revised set (0.667) and divide the current set by this remainder, producing still another set. In our example, dividing the set $\{1.0\ 1.667\ 2.667\}$ by 0.667 gives the new set $\{1.5\ 2.5\ 4.0\}$. If all members of this new set were integral, we would compute the product of the two divisors used so far ($1.11 \times 0.667 = 0.74$) and return this as our common divisor. Since not all the numbers are integers, we instead find the smallest remainder of the new set (0.5) and divide the members of the current set by this number, producing yet another set. Thus, the set $\{1.5\ 2.5\ 4.0\}$ divided by 0.5 gives the set $\{3.0\ 5.0\ 8.0\}$. In this case, all the members are integers, so we need perform no more divisions. To compute the common divisor of the original set, we multiply all the divisors used in reaching the integral set: $1.11 \times 0.667 \times 0.5 = 0.37$. Checking, we see that dividing the original set $\{1.11\ 1.85\ 2.96\}$ by 0.37 does indeed give us the integers 3, 5, and 8.

However, scientists do not always postulate integer proportions for intrinsic properties. For example, no one suggested that the specific heats of all liquids were evenly divisible by some common divisor. Clearly, there must be some criterion for determining when a "reasonable" common divisor has been found. For instance, one might insist that the divisor be

---

8. We added new mechanisms to BACON cautiously, with the goal of keeping our theory of discovery as simple as possible. Before adding a new heuristic, we attempted to ensure its generality by finding a number of cases in which it could be used. The generality of the new mechanism is discussed below.

a member of the original set. We rejected this heuristic, since one can imagine a chemist arriving at Prout's hypothesis without a familiarity with hydrogen.

A second approach would require that certain characteristics hold for the resulting integers. Thus, one might accept a common divisor only if it led to small integers, such as those less that 100. As soon as the method described above generated a nonintegral value greater than 100, the search would stop. A less restrictive criterion,[9] which includes smallness as a special case, requires that the interval between the smallest and the largest integers fall below a threshold. Thus, one would be as satisfied with integer values between 100 and 200 as with a set falling between 0 and 100. The search would then stop when the method generated a noninteger set with too large an interval. In addition, the system must have some means for distinguishing integers from nonintegers. This is required even in the absence of noise, since the calculations will introduce roundoff errors. To deal with such situations, BACON.4 includes a user-modifiable parameter that determines the degree of acceptable deviation from integer values. This parameter was set to 0.03 in the runs described below. Thus, if the remainder of a number is less than 0.03 or greater than 0.97, that number is considered to be an integer. If all the numbers are determined to be integers, the divisor has been found; if not, some remainder greater than 0.03 is selected as the new multiplier.

BACON.4 calls on this method for finding common divisors whenever a new set of dependent values is about to be assigned to an intrinsic property. Table 4.21 presents the two rules responsible for noting common divisors. If common divisors exist, one of these productions applies directly after the rule DEFINE-INTRINSIC has applied (when the property is initially defined) or directly after CONSIDER-INTRINSIC has applied (in cases where an intrinsic term already exists). In other words, the two common-divisor rules fire in place of STORE-INTRINSIC, which is responsible for storing intrinsic values when no common divisors exist. The conditions on the common-divisor rules are stated in such a manner that these rules will be preferred to STORE-INTRINSIC but will lose out to RETRIEVE-INTRINSIC. As a result, BACON considers common divisors only when it fails to retrieve existing intrinsic values because their conditions were not met.

9. This is the criterion currently implemented in BACON.4. We owe thanks to Marshall Atlas for suggesting this idea.

Table 4.21
BACON.4's rules for noting common divisors.

NOTE-COMMON-DIVISOR
If you want to consider intrinsic properties for X,
   and I is an intrinsic value associated with X based on Y,
   and the observed numerical values for Y were Y1, Y2, ..., Yn,
   and Y1, Y2, ..., Yn have the common divisor D,
   and the current set of independent values is C21, C22, ..., C2n,
   and the known irrelevant terms for I are T1, ..., Tn,
   and there exist no values of I under conditions C11, ..., C1n,
      for which C21, ..., C2n contain C11, ..., C1n,
then set the values of I to be V1/D, V2/D, ..., Vn/D
   and store them under the conditions C21, ..., C2n
      after removing the irrelevant terms T1, ..., Tn.

NOTE-INVERSE-DIVISOR
If you want to consider intrinsic properties for X,
   and I is an intrinsic value associated with X based on Y,
   and the observed numerical values for Y were Y1, Y2, ..., Yn,
   and the reciprocals of Y1, Y2, ..., Yn have the common divisor D,
   and the current set of independent values is C21, C22, ..., C2n,
   and the known irrelevant terms for I are T1, ..., Tn,
   and there exist no values of I under conditions C11, ..., C1n,
      for which C21, ..., C2n contain C11, ..., C1n,
then set the values of I to be 1/V1D, 1/V2D, ..., 1/VnD
   and store them under the conditions C21, ..., C2n
      after removing the irrelevant terms T1, ..., Tn.

The first of these rules, NOTE-COMMON-DIVISOR, applies when the observed values have a common divisor; the second rule, NOTE-INVERSE-DIVISOR, applies when a common divisor exists for the reciprocal of these values.[10] In the first case the new intrinsic values are computed to be the observed values divided by the common divisor; in the second case the reciprocals are divided in the same way. In both cases, the resulting integers are stored as the intrinsic values.

BACON encounters difficulty when it cannot generalize the retrieval conditions on its intrinsic values. In such cases, the system must propose new intrinsic values for each new situation; this leads to tautological linear relations with slopes of 1. Methods for generalizing retrieval conditions offered one path around these tautologies, and the common-divisor method offers another route: After BACON has computed a set of integer values, it looks for a linear relation between these values and the observed ones, just as it would in the non-divisor case. The resulting linear relation is still

---

10. Although it is possible for both situations to hold simultaneously, this seldom occurs. When it does, BACON gives priority to NOTE-COMMON-DIVISOR.

tautological, but the slope of this line equals the common divisor found in the current situation.

If different divisors occur in different situations, BACON will have differing values to consider when it moves to the next level of description. As a result, the system may be able to relate the values of the divisors to other terms even though the intrinsic values themselves may never be retrieved. Thus, the discovery of a common divisor may let the system break out of the tautological path that postulating intrinsic properties can produce. The following section shows the importance of this technique in a number of chemical discoveries.

BACON.4 on the Chemical Data

BACON.4 bases its understanding of chemistry on the results of various chemical reactions. In examining these reactions, the program treats three variables as independent: an element contributing to the reaction, the resulting compound, and the weight of the element used (W_e). For each combination of independent values, BACON.4 examines the associated values, of three dependent terms: the weight of the compound resulting from the reaction (W_c), the volume of the element (V_e), and the volume of the compound (V_c).[11] Thus, one can imagine an early chemist measuring out a quantity of an element by weight and combining it with others under conditions he knows will lead to a certain compound. Having done this, he measures the weight of the resulting compound, along with the volumes of both the compound and the element.

Table 4.22 shows some noise-free data supplied to the program when the element is hydrogen. If the weight of the element is varied first, BACON.4 notes linear relations between W_e and each of W_c, V_e, and V_c. Since the intercepts of these lines are zero, only the ratio terms W_e/W_c, W_e/V_e, and W_e/V_c are defined. Each of these ratios has a constant value for a given element-compound combination; this leads to the second-level summaries presented in tables 4.23 and 4.24.

Table 4.23 summarizes the values of W_e/W_c for hydrogen and the results from later experiments in which the elements are oxygen and nitrogen. Upon arriving at these second-level descriptions, BACON.4 notes that it has

---

11. All volumes are for the substances in gaseous form under standard conditions. Although it may seem odd to use the resulting compound as an independent term, this variable can take on different values for the same reacting substances. Thus, it seems reasonable to view the term as under observational control, just as we viewed the planets in our Keplerian example.

Table 4.22
First-level data for hydrogen.

Compound	W_e	W_c	V_e	V_c	W_e/W_c	W_e/V_e	W_e/V_c
Water	10.0	90.00	112.08	112.08	0.1111	0.0892	0.0892
Water	20.0	180.00	224.16	224.16	0.1111	0.0892	0.0892
Water	30.0	270.01	336.25	336.25	0.1111	0.0892	0.0892
Ammonia	10.0	56.79	112.08	74.72	0.1761	0.0892	0.1338
Ammonia	20.0	113.58	224.16	149.44	0.1761	0.0892	0.1338
Ammonia	30.0	170.37	336.25	224.16	0.1761	0.0892	0.1338
Ethylene	10.0	140.10	112.08	112.08	0.0714	0.0892	0.0892
Ethylene	20.0	280.21	224.16	224.16	0.0714	0.0892	0.0892
Ethylene	30.0	420.31	336.25	336.25	0.0714	0.0892	0.0892

Table 4.23
Second-level summary for weight proportions.

Element	Compound	W_e/W_c	i_1	$W_e/W_c i_1$
Hydrogen	Water	0.1111	0.1111	1.0
Hydrogen	Ammonia	0.1761	0.1761	1.0
Hydrogen	Ethylene	0.0714	0.0714	1.0
Oxygen	Nitrous oxide	0.3648	0.3648	1.0
Oxygen	Sulfur dioxide	0.5000	0.5000	1.0
Oxygen	Carbon dioxide	0.7396	0.7396	1.0
Nitrogen	Nitrous oxide	0.6378	0.6378	1.0
Nitrogen	Ammonia	0.8224	0.8224	1.0
Nitrogen	Nitric oxide	0.4664	0.4664	1.0

only nominal independent terms. This leads it to postulate the intrinsic property $i_1 = W_e/W_c$. These values have no reasonable common divisor.[12] Each intrinsic value is associated with a particular element-compound pair; these numbers correspond to the constant weight ratios first discovered by Joseph Proust. The program also defines the conjectured property $W_e/W_c i_1$. This is guaranteed to be 1.0 for the descriptions used in assigning values to i_1, but other values could occur in future experiments, thereby converting this ratio into a genuine intrinsic property.

The values of W_e/V_c for hydrogen, oxygen, and nitrogen are given in

12. In fact, the values for nitrogen in table 4.23 are evenly divisible by 0.032. However, this is not a general trend, and its occurrence does not significantly affect the program's behavior, so the values of W_e/W_c are used directly.

Table 4.24
Second-level summary for Cannizzaro numbers.

Element	Compound	W_e/V_c	i_2	$W_e/V_c i_1$
Hydrogen	Water	0.089	2.0	0.045
Hydrogen	Ammonia	1.338	3.0	0.045
Hydrogen	Ethylene	0.089	2.0	0.045
Oxygen	Nitrous oxide	0.715	1.0	0.715
Oxygen	Sulfur dioxide	1.430	2.0	0.715
Oxygen	Carbon dioxide	1.430	2.0	0.715
Nitrogen	Nitrous oxide	1.250	2.0	0.625
Nitrogen	Ammonia	0.625	1.0	0.625
Nitrogen	Nitric oxide	0.625	1.0	0.625

table 4.24. Here BACON.4 has defined the second intrinsic property, i_2, on the basis of the values of this ratio. However, this time useful common divisors are found: 0.0446 for hydrogen, 0.715 for oxygen, and 0.625 for nitrogen. The values of i_2 given in table 4.24 are simply the values of W_e/V_c divided by these numbers. Again, the values of the intrinsic property are associated with pairs of elements and compounds.

If one interprets these numbers as the coefficients of the element in the balanced equation for the chemical reaction determined by the pair, the value of i_2 for hydrogen and water will be 2 and that for oxygen and water will be 1. These are the numbers Cannizzaro found, by the same route, when he divided his products of densities and weight proportions by their common divisors. The program also defines the ratio $W_e/V_c i_2$, which has a constant value for each element; in fact, these values are precisely the greatest common divisors found for these elements.[13]

At this point, BACON.4 has discovered three invariants dependent only on the element. Table 4.25 summarizes these findings, and also gives the corresponding values for sodium. The first of these invariants states that the conjectured property, $W_e/W_c i_1$, is always 1.0; however, the rule, being tautological, introduces no new information. The second specifies the values of $W_e/V_c i_2$ associated with each element; since these are different, BACON.4 proposes the higher-level intrinsic term i_3. The fact that the values

13. In fact, BACON.4 examines the ratio V_c/W_e. In searching for common divisors, it considers both this term and its reciprocal. In this case, common divisors are found for the reciprocal, so the product $V_c i_2/W_e$ is defined instead of the ratio shown. We have presented the simpler picture in the interests of clarity.

Table 4.25
Relative atomic weights and densities of elements.

Element	$W_e/W_c i_1$	$W_e/V_c i_2$	i_3	$W_e/V_c i_2 i_3$	W_e/V_e	i_4	$W_e/V_e i_4$
Hydrogen	1.0	0.045	1.0	0.045	0.089	2.0	0.045
Oxygen	1.0	0.715	16.0	0.045	1.430	32.0	0.045
Nitrogen	1.0	0.625	14.0	0.045	1.250	28.0	0.045
Sodium[a]	1.0	1.027	23.0	0.045	1.027	23.0	0.045

a. BACON.4 was not actually run with the sodium data. We give them here because the inclusion of a monatomic gas makes clear the distinction that BACON.4 subsequently discovers between atomic and molecular weight. Compare the values of i_3 and i_4

of $W_e/V_c i_2$ are evenly divisible by 0.0446 leads the program to assign i_3 values of 1.0 for hydrogen, 16.0 for oxygen, 14.0 for nitrogen, and 23.0 for sodium—precisely the relative atomic weights that Cannizzaro derived from his table of densities and proportions. BACON.4 also defines the ratio $W_e/V_c i_2 i_3$ (a conjectured property with the value 0.0446), but this generates no new knowledge. The third regularity relates to the values of W_e/V_e. Earlier, BACON.4 found these values to be independent of the compound being considered but dependent on the element. Moreover, the recurring values are all divisible by 0.0446, so BACON.4 introduces yet another intrinsic property: i_4, the values of which are simply those of W_e/V_e divided by 0.0446. This gives values of 2.0 for hydrogen, 32.0 for oxygen, 28.0 for nitrogen, but 23.0 again for sodium (which, unlike the others, is a monatomic gas). These ratios may be interpreted as the *relative densities* of the elements in their gaseous form, which, according to Gay-Lussac's principle, are proportional to the corresponding molecular weights.

Finding Alternative Frameworks

In the preceding section we described BACON.4's chemical discoveries when it exerted experimental control over the weight of an element, W_e. However, one can imagine scenarios in which a scientist varies the values of W_c, V_e, or V_c instead. For example, whether one controls the weight or the volume of an element or compound is purely a matter of choice, and the characteristics of the compound are easily viewed as the independent variables if electrolysis is used to break that compound into its components

Replacing one independent term with another has an interesting effect on BACON.4. In all cases, the system still finds linear relations between the independent variable and the three dependent ones. However, recall that

Table 4.26
Alternative chemical frameworks generated by BACON.4 (the theoretical terms generated when different variables are taken as the independent term).

W_e	V_e	W_c	V_c
W_e/W_c	V_e/V_c	W_e/W_c	V_e/V_c
W_e/V_e	W_e/V_e	W_c/V_c	W_c/V_c
W_e/V_c	W_c/V_e	W_c/V_e	W_e/V_c

the program always relates dependent terms to independent or intrinsic ones rather than to one another. As a result, BACON.4 defines different theoretical terms and finds different associated constancies in each of the four situations. That is, the system arrives at different conceptual frameworks depending on the manner in which experiments are run.

Table 4.26 presents the first-level theoretical terms that result from the use of each term as an independent variable. In each case, BACON.4 defines three ratio terms and states the conditions under which these are constant. Each set of three laws is equivalent to the others in the sense that any triple can be derived from any other triple, though the program cannot actually carry out this derivation. Note that six ratios exist,[14] each occurring in two of the four possible combinations.

Three of these terms are especially interesting, since they did not occur in the run described above. One of these is W_c/V_c, the density of the compound. Another is V_e/V_c, the ratio of volumes for the element and the compound. Stating that this latter term is constant is equivalent to Gay-Lussac's law of definite proportions for volumes. Finally, the term W_c/V_e is simply the ratio of the two previously mentioned ratios.

Conclusions

In this chapter we have described the heuristics of BACON.4 and examined their application to a number of empirical laws from the history of physics and chemistry. The central notion was that of the intrinsic property, an inferred term whose numerical values are associated with the symbolic values of one or more nominal terms. We found that intrinsic values can be inferred from direct observations, can be stored in memory and retrieved

---

14. In fact, the reciprocals of these terms are sometimes defined. We have ignored this distinction for the sake of clarity in our comparison.

when appropriate, and must have their retrieval conditions generalized if BACON is to move beyond simple tautologies. Although these components were sufficient for rediscovering a number of laws, we found the notion of symmetry to be necessary for Snell's law, Black's law, and other relations. Finally, we found the idea of common divisors to be necessary when we attempted to apply the intrinsic-property methods to the discovery of chemical laws. However, the common-divisor method has also found application in physics. For instance, Robert A. Millikan determined the charge on the electron by calculating the common divisor of the electric charge required to levitate oil drops against gravity.

From the range and variety of the laws we have considered, we can conclude that the methods centering around intrinsic properties are indeed general and should prove useful in any branch of science concerned with quantitative empirical laws. However, the notions of intrinsic properties and common divisors are especially interesting, for they seem to move beyond simple summaries of the data into the beginnings of explanation. The current level of explanation is simple at best, but one can imagine them leading to deeper explanations as well. For instance, it was upon finding common divisors for the relative atomic weights that William Prout suggested that all atoms were composed of varying numbers of hydrogen atoms. Using similar forms of reasoning, future versions of the program might formulate structural models to explain the empirical laws it has found. We will have more to say on this topic in later chapters. For now, let us turn to the fifth and final version of BACON and the heuristics it employs to discover empirical laws.

5 Symmetry and Conservation

Each of the variants of BACON we have examined thus far, up through BACON.4, has been mainly driven by data, addressing itself to the part of the scientific process that starts with a set of data and then seeks to discover regularities in them. Moreover, the heuristics employed in these variants have been almost entirely free from theoretical presuppositions about the domains from which the data were drawn. A major goal of the research was to identify general discovery principles, and we felt that generality is more likely to reside in data-driven approaches than in theory-driven ones.

In this chapter we take steps toward incorporating into BACON search heuristics that amount to very general theoretical postulates applicable in several scientific domains. The new variant, BACON.5, still moves from data to laws, but it considers that the laws being sought may have certain convenient properties—specifically, symmetry and conservation. Symmetry and conservation lie at the very heart of physics, and the assumption of these properties has been a powerful aid in the discovery of many physical laws. BACON.5 discovers conservation laws through a simple form of analogical reasoning, postulating symmetries that speed its search for laws involving several variables.

As was true of the BACON variants examined above, BACON.5 is not intended as a detailed model of the history of particular discoveries. Rather, the system presents another one of many ways in which historical discoveries could have been made with the help of a few simple heuristics and with a moderate amount of computation. BACON.5's interest lies in its differences from the earlier variants and in the effect these differences have on its discovery process. We believe that performing experiments with different discovery methods will provide useful information about the intrinsic difficulty of discovery, as well as about the power of particular search heuristics.

Thus, we will begin by summarizing the new heuristics that distinguish BACON.5 from its predecessors, focusing on the system's data-collection strategies and its ability to take advantage of symmetry assumptions. After this, we will compare BACON.5's behavior in discovering three laws— Snell's law of refraction, Black's specific-heat law, and conservation of momentum—with that of BACON.4 in discovering the same laws, which was reported in chapter 4. Next we will examine BACON.5's rediscovery of Joule's law of energy conservation, using a simple method of reasoning by analogy. Finally, we will consider a somewhat different approach to discovering conservation laws that is even more strongly driven by theoretical assumptions. In these ways, we hope to provide some insight into the relation between data-driven and theory-driven discovery.

The Heuristics of BACON.5

The BACON.5 system includes all the heuristics used by its predecessor, BACON.4. Thus, it incorporates methods for discovering numerical relations between independent and dependent terms,[1] for recursing to higher levels of description, for postulating intrinsic properties and retrieving their values, and for noting common divisors. In the examples we will consider in this chapter, all these methods except the last will come into play.

In addition to the above discovery methods, BACON.5 incorporates a heuristic for reducing its search for laws in special cases. In many experimental situations, more objects than one are involved and each of these objects has a set of associated variables. In such cases, BACON.5 is given both the object associated with each term and the *type* of each variable. For instance, in Snell's law there are four terms: $medium_1$, $medium_2$, $sine_1$, and $sine_2$. The first two of these have type medium; the latter two have type sine. Similarly, the first and third terms are associated with object-1, while the second and fourth are attached to object-2. This information is necessary for BACON to reason about potential symmetries and analogies.[2] In order to simplify its reasoning along these lines, the program rearranges its experimental design so that all the independent terms associated with one of the objects are varied before the terms associated with other objects. This requirement puts some constraints on the experiments in which the symmetry heuristic can be used.

In cases where (as in the Snell example) two objects have the same types of associated terms, BACON.5 assumes that the final law will be symmetrical, though it cannot predict the actual form. As we noted, the system organizes its experiments so that all terms associated with one of the objects are varied first, and the symmetry heuristic can be used only in experiments where this is possible. In varying terms associated with the first object

---

1. An earlier version of BACON.5 (Langley, Bradshaw, and Simon 1981) employed a generalized variant of the differencing technique used in BACON.2. This let the system discover polynomial relations of the form $y^m = x^n + \cdots + c$ (where all exponents are integers). For the sake of continuity, the version of BACON.5 described in this chapter was rewritten to use the BACON.4 heuristics.

2. Gelernter (1959) was perhaps the first to exploit symmetry as a means for simplifying derivations, using it for this purpose in a program for proving theorems of geometry.

and in discovering laws relating them, BACON.5 follows exactly the same course as BACON.4. However, once it finds a constant theoretical term incorporating all variables associated with the first object (e.g., $sine_2/n_2$), BACON.5 assumes that an analogous term should be used for the other object (e.g., $sine_1/n_1$). All that remains is to find the relation between these two higher-level terms, and this can be done by varying systematically the value of the analogous term. When this is done, the higher-level terms take on different values, and BACON.5 can find a law relating them using its standard heuristics. The resulting law incorporates all the original terms in a symmetrical form.

Using this strategy, BACON can easily discover a number of symmetrical physical laws. Because it has strong expectations about the form of these laws, it can do so with a minimum of data. Thus, in the case of a symmetric law involving $2n$ independent variables, if the symmetry heuristic is not used BACON will normally have to make k^{2n} observations. Using the symmetry heuristic, only $k^n + a$ are required, where k is usually 3 and a is a small constant. In other cases, BACON.5 must use its standard techniques to relate two entirely different sets of variables, each associated with a different object. Later, a new task may be presented in which one set of terms is identical with a set from the previous problem. When this occurs, the system assumes that the theoretical term that proved useful before will be useful again. None of the analogous variables need be systematically varied, nor must the system search tediously for the appropriate combination of terms. As before, this heuristic reduces the volume of data that must be examined and directs search through the space of theoretical terms. We will discuss examples of each situation in the following section. However, let us first examine the rules implementing this method in more detail.

Table 5.1 presents English paraphrases of the five new rules required for BACON.5 to discover symmetric relations efficiently. The first of these rules is DEFINE-ANALOGOUS-TERM, which matches when the system is considering two objects each having the same associated variables and when some law (based on the theoretical term T_2) has been discovered relating all variables associated with one of the objects. In this case, BACON defines an analogous term (T_1) based on the variables associated with the other object and adds a goal to *check for symmetry* between the two terms T_1 and T_2.

The second production is REDESIGN-EXPERIMENT, which is responsible for reorganizing BACON.5's strategy for varying independent values after a potential symmetry has been noted. This rule's effect is subtle,

Table 5.1
BACON.5's rules for discovering symmetries.

DEFINE-ANALOGOUS-TERM
If you want to *find laws* at level L,
 and you expect term T_2 to have a constant value,
 and T_2 has the definition $A_2^b C_2^d \cdots N_2^m$,
 where $A_2, C_2, \ldots, N_2$ are terms associated with object O_2,
 and $A_1, C_1, \ldots, N_1$ are independent terms associated with object O_1,
then *define* T_1 as $A_1^b C_1^d \cdots N_1^m$,
 and *check for symmetry* between the terms T_1 and T_2.

REDESIGN-EXPERIMENT
If you want to *check for symmetry* between T_1 and T_2,
 and you want to incorporate terms $A_1, C_1, \ldots$ into laws,
 and the suggested values of A_1 are $V_1, V_2, \ldots, V_k$,
then *incorporate* the terms $C_1, \ldots$ into laws when $A = V_1$,
 and *iterate* through the values of $V_2, \ldots, V_k$ for A_1.

GATHER-ANALOGOUS-VALUES
If you want to *check for symmetry* between T_x and T_y,
 and T_x has the definition $Ax^b Cx^d \cdots Nx^m$,
 and you have values for $Ax, Cx, \ldots, Nx$,
then *gather values* for the term T_x.

CONFIRM-SYMMETRY
If you want to *check for symmetry* between T_1 and T_2,
 and you have recorded a set of values for the term T_1,
 and you have recorded a set of values for the term T_2,
 and the values of T_1 and T_2 are linearly related,
then *confirm* that a symmetry exists between T_1 and T_2.

REJECT-SYMMETRY
If you want to *check for symmetry* between T_1 and T_2,
 and you have recorded a set of values for the term T_1,
 and you have recorded a set of values for the term T_2,
then *reject* that any symmetry exists between T_1 and T_2,
 and *incorporate* all independent terms into laws.

---

since it applies in place of INITIALIZE-INDEPENDENT and UPDATE-INDEPENDENT and reorganizes the system's behavior simply by posting the *incorporate* and *interate* goals in a different order than normally occurs. The result is that BACON abandons its complete-factorial-design experiments, replacing them with a much sparser set of experimental combinations. For instance, given three independent variables X, Y, and Z, each having values 1, 2, and 3, the new goal structure would generate only three combinations of independent values: $[X = 1, Y = 1, Z = 1]$, $[X = 2, Y = 2, Z = 2]$, and $[X = 3, Y = 3, Z = 3]$. This restricted set of combinations is sufficient only because the symmetry assumption provides BACON with strong expectations about the form of the final law.

The production GATHER-ANALOGOUS-VALUES complements the second rule by telling the system when to replace a set of independent values with the higher-level term that it expects to be involved in the symmetry. Thus, if X and Y are both independent terms and T is defined as $X^2 Y^{-1}$, then this rule sets the goal to gather the values of T as soon as the values of both X and Y have been set. At this point the BACON.3 rules for computing the values of theoretical terms take control, ultimately adding the value of T to working memory.

The fourth rule, CONFIRM-SYMMETRY, notes when a linear relation exists between two analogous terms T_1 and T_2. This relation confirms the expected symmetry, and BACON.5 accepts its hypothesis. If none of the alternative symmetries are borne out, the final rule REJECT-SYMMETRY applies by default. This production rejects the symmetry hypothesis, adding this conclusion to memory to prevent it from being reconsidered later. In addition, it adds a goal to incorporate the various independent terms into laws, thus reinvoking BACON's normal strategy for gathering data and finding regularities.

The Discoveries of BACON.5

Having discussed BACON.5's strategies in the abstract, let us now trace some of the system's discoveries in detail, focusing on laws in which symmetry plays a role.

Snell's Law of Refraction

Our first example, Snell's law, is included to illustrate in the simplest way how the symmetry heuristic operates. To review the law: As a ray of light

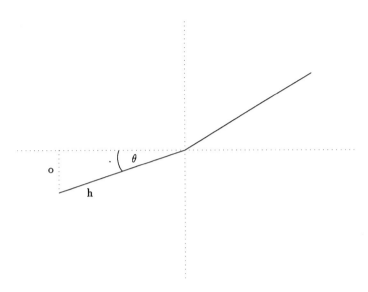

Figure 5.1

passes from one medium to another, the passage alters the direction in which the ray travels. Snell's law of refraction relates the initial and the final direction, as well as the media. If θ_1 is the incoming angle of incidence and θ_2 the outgoing angle of refraction, Snell's law can be stated as

$$\sin\theta_1/n_1 = \sin\theta_2/n_2.$$

In this equation, n_1 is the value of an intrinsic property of the first medium—the index of refraction—and n_2 is the analogous value for the second medium. The index of refraction for vacuum is normally assigned as the standard, 1.0; the values for water, oil, and glass are 1.33, 1.47, and 1.66, respectively.

In rediscovering Snell's law, BACON.5 is presented with two objects, each with three associated variables. The first of these variables is the medium, which takes nominal values such as vacuum, water, and oil. The second is the distance h from the boundary between the media to the point at which the light is measured. The final term is more complicated. Consider figure 5.1, in which the y axis corresponds to the boundary plane between the two media, and the origin corresponds to the point at which the ray of light crosses this boundary, so that the x axis intersects the ray at the origin point. Now find a point p on the ray that has distance h from the origin,

Table 5.2
First-level data obeying Snell's law.

medium$_1$	h_1	o_1	medium$_2$	h_2	o_2	o_2/h_2
Vacuum	40	10	Vacuum	40	10.00	0.25
Vacuum	40	10	Vacuum	50	12.50	0.25
Vacuum	40	10	Vacuum	60	15.00	0.25
Vacuum	40	10	Water	40	13.33	0.33
Vacuum	40	10	Water	50	16.67	0.33
Vacuum	40	10	Water	60	20.00	0.33
Vacuum	40	10	Oil	40	14.70	0.37
Vacuum	40	10	Oil	50	18.38	0.37
Vacuum	40	10	Oil	60	22.05	0.37

and define the variable o as the distance of this point p from the x axis. Thus, any combination of values for h and o determines a particular angle.

In this case, BACON is given experimental control of five variables: medium$_1$, h_1, o_1, medium$_2$, and h_2. Fixing h_1 and o_1 determines the angle of the incident ray. To find o_2 (the dependent variable) for a given experimental situation, one moves down the refracted ray of light for the distance h_2 from the boundary between the media; the value of o_2 is simply the distance of this point from the x axis.[3] This formulation of the task allows BACON.5 to discover Snell's law without knowledge of trigonometry. It can also discover the simpler four-term version of the law.

When presented with these terms, BACON.5 plans its experiment so that h_2 will be varied first, followed by medium$_2$, o_1, h_1, and medium$_1$, in that order. The program makes a special effort to group variables associated with the same object together, since this will simplify its reasoning about symmetry. Table 5.2 presents the first-level data collected during the resulting experiment. Comparing the values of o_2 and h_2 for each medium$_2$, the system finds a linear relation with a zero intercept. Accordingly, it defines the ratio o_2/h_2 which has the following constant values: 0.25 when medium$_2$ is vacuum, 0.33 when it is water, and 0.37 when it is oil. This term is equivalent to $\sin\theta_2/4.0$; the divisor appears because BACON was given $h_1 = 40.0$ and $o_1 = 10.0$ as its initial observations. The regularity discovered thus far has no relation to Snell's law; it simply expresses the fact that, if light moves in a straight line (o/h constant), then its path can

---

3. We owe thanks to Robert Akscyn for suggesting this approach.

Table 5.3
Second-level data obeying Snell's law

medium$_1$	h_1	o_1	medium$_2$	o_2/h_2	n_2	$o_2/h_2 n_2$
Vacuum	40	10	Glass	0.25	0.25	1.0
Vacuum	40	10	Water	0.33	0.33	1.0
Vacuum	40	10	Oil	0.37	0.37	1.0

Table 5.4
Highest-level data obeying Snell's law.

$o_1/h_1 n_1$	$o_2/h_2 n_2$	$o_2 h_1 n_1 / o_1 h_2 n_2$
1.00	1.00	1.0
1.20	1.20	1.0
1.35	1.35	1.0

be described by the sine (n) of the angle the path makes with the normal to the surface of the medium.

These regularities lead to the second-level symmary given in table 5.3. At this point, BACON.5 has a set of nominal independent values for medium$_2$ associated with a set of numerical dependent values for o_2/h_2. Since no more progress is possible until numbers are associated with the nominal symbols for the medium, the program postulates the intrinsic property n_2. The values of this term are taken to be those of o_2/h_2, and the ratio $o_2/h_2 n_2$ is defined. This new property has (by definition) the constant value 1.0. However, when the values of n_2 are retrieved later in the discovery process, it takes on different values, so BACON generalizes the conditions for retrieving this term.

Having related all the variables associated with the refracted ray, BACON.5 focuses on the set of terms for the incident ray. Assuming symmetry, the system does not bother to vary o_1 and h_1 systematically. Instead, the values of medium$_1$, h_1, and o_1 are varied in conjunction, and the corresponding values of $o_1/h_1 n_1$ are computed immediately. In addition, the values of $o_2/h_2 n_2$ are found for each situation, and the higher-level terms are compared, as shown in table 5.4. A linear relation with a zero intercept is noted, and the ratio $o_2 h_1 n_1 / o_1 h_2 n_2$ is found to have the constant value 1.0. Replacing o/h with $\sin\theta$, we see that this law becomes

$$n_1 \sin\theta_2 / n_2 \sin\theta_1 = 1.0,$$

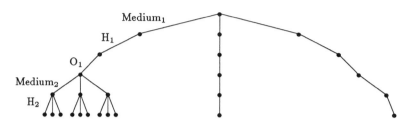

Figure 5.2

which is equivalent to Snell's law. The intrinsic properties n_1 and n_2 are proportional to the indices of refraction of the two media.

Figure 5.2 depicts BACON.5's search through the data space for this task. The subtree in the bottom left corner represents BACON's standard factorial design for experiments. The rest of the tree is much sparser, because the symmetry assumption enabled BACON to bypass the data-gathering process for two levels of description (those associated with o_1 and h_1) and to look immediately for some relation between the theoretical terms $o_1/h_1 n_1$ and $o_2/h_2 n_2$. The number of observations gathered was only 11 instead of the 243 that would have been required without the symmetry heuristic. The computer's net search and verification time for finding the law was reduced by a factor of 8.

In this case, only one symmetric relation was considered, since only one higher-level term (o/hn) was involved. However, some search through the space of hypotheses may remain even after the symmetry assumption has been made.

Conservation of Momentum

The momentum of an object is the product of its mass m and its velocity V; the total momentum of a group of objects is the sum of their individual momenta. In classical physics, when two or more objects collide the total momentum of the system is conserved. For two-object collisions this can be stated as

$$m_1 V_1 + m_2 V_2 = m_1 U_1 + m_2 U_2,$$

where m_1 and m_2 are the masses of the objects, V_1 and V_2 are their initial velocities, and U_1 and U_2 are their final velocities. This equation can be rewritten as

$$m_1(V_1 - U_1) = m_2(U_2 - V_2),$$

Table 5.5
First-level data obeying conservation of momentum.

object$_1$	V_1	U_1	object$_2$	V_2	U_2	$U_2 - V_2$
A	40	10	B	40	55.0	15.0
A	40	10	B	50	65.0	15.0
A	40	10	B	60	75.0	15.0
A	40	10	C	40	50.0	10.0
A	40	10	C	50	60.0	10.0
A	40	10	C	60	70.0	10.0
A	40	10	D	40	47.5	7.5
A	40	10	D	50	57.5	7.5
A	40	10	D	60	67.5	7.5

which says that the loss in momentum of one object is compensated by a gain in the momentum of the other object. In chapter 4 we considered a special case of this law in which the initial velocities were zero, so that we had

$$m_1 U_1 + m_2 U_2 = 0.$$

The collision experiment does not provide appropriate data for the use of BACON's symmetry heuristics. The method requires that the values of the velocities for the second object be constant while the law governing the velocities of the first object is being discovered. However, in the traditional version of the collision experiment the value of U_2 cannot be held constant when V_1 and V_2 are varied.

An alternative experimental design calls for two objects connected by a (massless) compressed spring. The objects, one behind the other, are propelled forward with nearly the same velocities. Because of the force of the spring, the object in front gradually increases its velocity, while the rear object decreases its velocity. Measurements of V_1 and V_2 are made at the initial moment; measurements of U_1 and U_2 are recorded when the velocity of the former reaches some predetermined value (10, in the present example). Under these conditions, all the variables except U_2 can be regarded as independent variables. The extra degree of freedom, as compared with the elastic collision experiment, derives from the fact that energy is not conserved but is provided by the spring. A set of possible observations from this arrangement is shown in table 5.5.

In discovering the general form of the relation, BACON.5 is informed of the values of three variables, each associated with two objects. The terms

Table 5.6
Second-level data obeying conservation of momentum.

object$_1$	V_1	U_1	object$_2$	a	$U_2 - aV_2$	k_2	$(U_2 - aV_2)/k_2$
A	40	10	B	1.0	15.0	15.0	1.0
A	40	10	C	1.0	10.0	10.0	1.0
A	40	10	D	1.0	7.5	7.5	1.0

object$_1$ (the rear object) and object$_2$ (the front object) take on the nominal values A, B, C, and D; these serve to distinguish specific objects from one another. The terms V_1, V_2, U_1, and U_2 are the initial and final velocities of the two objects. BACON.5 is not given information about the masses of the objects. The first five of the observables are under the system's experimental control; U_2 is viewed as dependent.

BACON.5 begins by arranging the variables so that V_2 is varied first, followed by object$_2$, U_1, V_1, and object$_1$. Some of the resulting values are presented in table 5.5, where BACON was provided with data based upon masses of 1.0 for object A, 2.0 for B, 3.0 for C, and 4.0 for D. Upon varying the values of V_2, the program notes a linear relation between U_2 and V_2 with a slope, a, of 1.0 and an intercept, b, of 15.0. (The intercept, b, is thus equivalent to $U_2 - aV_2$, a weighted difference of the final and initial velocities. However, the weight is always unity.) When a new value of object$_2$ (C) is examined, BACON.5 finds an analogous relation to hold between U_2 and V_2, with the same slope (1.0) and a new intercept (10.0). A linear relation also holds when object$_2$ is D, again with the same slope but with intercept 7.5. These second-level values are summarized in table 5.6.

At this level BACON is confronted with nominal independent values, which lead it to postulate the intrinsic property k_2, associated with object$_2$, and to assign it values based on those of the slope b (since these differ for different objects). The ratio $j = b/k_2$—equivalent to $(U_2 - aV_2)/k_2$—is also defined, and is found to be 1.0 (which follows from its definition). The values of k_2 are proportional to the reciprocals of m_2, the mass of the second object.

After relating k_2, V_2, and U_2, BACON.5 turns its attention to k_1, V_1, and U_1. Either or both of j and a—the two constant parameters in the third-level law $j = (U_2 - aV_2)/k_2$—may be functions of V_1 and U_1, and the symmetry heuristic conjectures that such a function should correspond to

Table 5.7
Highest-level data obeying conservation of momentum.

a_1	a_2	$j_1 j_2$	$\dfrac{(U_2 - a_2 V_2)}{k_2}$	$\dfrac{k_1(U_2 - a_2 V_2)}{k_2(U_1 - a_1 V_1)}$
1.0	1.0	-1.0	1.0	-1.0
1.0	1.0	-2.0	2.0	-1.0
1.0	1.0	-3.0	3.0	-1.0

the one just found, with the appropriate substitution of subscripts. Hence, there are two candidates:

$$j(V_1, U_1) = (U_1 - aV_1)/k_1$$

and

$$a(V_1, U_1) = (U_1 - jk_1)/V_1.$$

The first of these yields the equation

$$(U_1 - aV_1)/k_1 = (U_2 - aV_2)/k_2.$$

In contrast, the second yields

$$(U_1 - jk_1)/V_1 = (U_2 - jk_2)/V_2.$$

After generating these two hypotheses, the system gathers only the data it requires to distinguish between them.

The results are shown in table 5.7, where the a's are simply unity and the terms j_1 and j_2 are related linearly with slope -1 and intercept 0. Accordingly, BACON.5 settles on the symmetric relation

$$(U_1 - aV_1)/k_1 = -(U_2 - aV_2)/k_2,$$

which (after we replace k with its reciprocal and note that $a = 1$) is equivalent to the standard form of the law for conservation of momentum. Again BACON's symmetry assumption has greatly reduced the amount of data required to determine the final law; the system's search through the data space is identical in form to that for Snell's law, shown in figure 5.2.

Black's Specific-Heat Law

In chapter 4 we also traced BACON.4's discovery of Black's specific-heat law. If we wish to apply BACON.5's symmetry heuristic to the derivation of this law, we must (as in the previous example) modify the experiment that is to provide BACON with its data.

When two containers of liquid having different temperatures are brought into close contact, at any subsequent time, even before the final temperature equilibrium is established, the amount of heat lost by the hotter container must equal the amount gained by the cooler one. Hence, Black's law can be written in the form

$$c_1 M_1 T_1 + c_2 M_2 T_2 = c_1 M_1 F_1 + c_2 M_2 F_2,$$

where T_1 and T_2 are the initial temperatures, F_1 and F_2 are the temperatures at some later time, M_1 and M_2 are the masses of the two liquids, and c_1 and c_2 are intrinsic properties associated with various types of liquids (their specific heats). The equation can be recast as

$$c_1 M_1 (T_1 - F_1) = c_2 M_2 (F_2 - T_2),$$

which makes explicit that the heat lost from the one body is gained by the other (i.e., that the total quantity of heat in the system is conserved). In chapter 4 we dealt with the special case in which the two temperatures had achieved equilibrium and, since their values were then identical, could be represented as the single variable T_f.

In discovering the more general form of Black's law, BACON.5 is told about two objects, each with an associated liquid (taking nominal values such as water and oil), a mass M, an initial temperature T, and a final temperature F. All the variables are under experimental control except F_2, the single dependent term. The final temperature of the first liquid, F_1, can be manipulated observationally by observing it continuously and, when it reaches a specified value, measuring the temperature of the second liquid. Thus, one need not observe the liquids in equilibrium to discover Black's law.

The form of this law is quite similar to that of the law for conservation of momentum, and BACON.5's path of discovery is correspondingly similar. At the outset, the program groups together terms associated with each object, in order to simplify its reasoning about symmetry at a later stage. Upon varying T_2 and examining the resulting values of F_2, the system finds a linear relation with a slope of 1.0 (let us call this term a). This relation leads the system to consider the difference $F_2 - aT_2$, which has a constant value.

When BACON.5 varies M_2 at the next level, it finds that $F_2 - aT_2$ decreases as M_2 increases; their product, $M_2(F_2 - aT_2)$, is computed and is also found to be a constant. At the third level of description, the program finds itself attempting to relate nominal values to numerical ones. Its solution is to define an intrinsic property d_2 based on the values of $M_2(F_2 - aT_2)$. (This new property is proportional to the reciprocal of c_2, the specific heat of the second liquid.) The ratio $e = M_2(F_2 - aT_2)/d_2$ is immediately defined and is found to be the constant 1.0.

Since it has discovered the relations among the four terms associated with the first body, BACON.5 next considers the second body. As in the momentum example, there are two possible symmetries. One of these yields the symmetric equation

$$\frac{M_1(F_1 - aT_1)}{d_1} = \frac{M_2(F_2 - aT_2)}{d_2};$$

the other yields

$$\frac{F_1 - ed_1/M_1}{T_1} = \frac{F_2 - ed_2/M_2}{T_2}.$$

Upon gathering selected experimental combinations to test these two hypotheses, BACON finds that only the first symmetry is borne out by the data. Since the values of d are proportional to the reciprocals of the specific-heat values discovered by Black, we can replace $1/d$ in the first equation with the specific heat. This gives

$$c_1 M_1(F_1 - aT_1) = -c_2 M_2(F_2 - aT_2),$$

which can be expanded to give the standard form of Black's law when we remove the factor a, which is unity.

In rediscovering Black's law, the symmetry assumption produced even greater savings than for the previous two relations. In this case, BACON was attempting to relate eight separate variables, seven of which were under the system's experimental control. Since BACON requires at least three values for each independent term (to prevent the generation of tautological linear relations), this means the system would normally have had to examine $3^7 = 2,187$ experimental combinations.

In contrast, with the assumption of symmetry, BACON needed to carry out a complete factorial design for only three independent terms (liquid$_2$, M_2, and T_2), plus a few additional values to test the symmetry hypothesis. Thus, the system was required to examine only $3^3 + 2 = 29$ experimental combinations—a reduction by a factor of 75. Had none of the expected symmetries been supported by the data, BACON would have been forced to revert to the more exhaustive approach; however, testing for symmetry requires little effort, and the savings are well worth the additional work.

Joule's Law

In the 1840s James Prescott Joule set forth his law of energy conservation, which states that the total amount of energy present in any system remains constant over time—that is, energy can be transformed, but it cannot be lost or gained (Magie 1935, pp. 203–211). Joule tested his hypothesis in a variety of ways. In one experiment, heavy objects descended to turn a wheel whose motion heated a large container of water by friction. Comparing the potential energy lost by the lowered objects to the heat energy gained by the liquid, Joule found that the total energy remained the same. In a second experiment, Joule sent an electric current through water and measured the resulting change in temperature; the total energy was conserved in this case as well.

Using methods related to those for discovering symmetric relations, BACON.5 can generate both forms of Joule's law. In the first situation, the program is informed about two objects: a heavy ball and a container of liquid. Three independent terms are associated with the ball: its weight W_1, the height H_1 from which it is lowered, and N_1, the number of times it is lowered. The liquid is also associated with three controllable variables: the type of liquid L_2 occupying the container, its mass M_2, and its initial temperature T_2. In addition, a single dependent term, the final temperature F_2, is associated with the liquid.

As in its discovery of Black's law (itself a special case of Joule's law), BACON begins by varying T_2 and examining the resulting values of F_2. The difference $F_2 - T_2$ is found to be constant (the slope of the line relating the terms is 1), as is $M_2(F_2 - T_2)$ at the next level of description. Still later, the intrinsic property d_2 is defined, and then the ratio $M_2(F_2 - T_2)/d_2$.

At this point the program shifts to manipulating characteristics of the first object. Since different variables are involved, it must rely on its data-driven heuristics instead of jumping ahead through analogy. When the number N_1 is varied, a linear relation with intercept zero is noted; the ratio

$$M_2(F_2 - T_2)/d_2 N_1$$

is defined and found to be constant. This process repeats itself for the remaining terms, leading first to the ratio

$$M_2(F_2 - T_2)/d_2 N_1 W_1$$

and then to

$$M_2(F_2 - T_2)/d_2 N_1 W_1 H_1.$$

This last expression has a constant value, and the resulting hypothesis is equivalent to Joule's statement that the loss in potential energy, $N_1 W_1 H_1$, equals the gain in heat energy, $M_2(F_2 - T_2)/d_2$.

In discovering Joule's second relationship, BACON.5 is presented with the same container of liquid and a new object: an electric circuit. The liquid has the same associated terms as before; the circuit is associated with two independent variables: its resistance R and its current I. In generating its experimental design, the system recognizes the components of a familiar theoretical term. Thus, rather than varying the values of L_2, M_2, and T_2 systematically, it gathers data more selectively and computes the values of the term $M_2(F_2 - T_2)/d_2$ as soon as all its component terms have been set. This is done for a number of values of the current I_1, and the two sets of numbers are compared. Although $M_2(F_2 - T_2)/d_2$ and I_1 increase together, the ratio $M_2(F_2 - T_2)/d_2 I_1$ is not constant. However, the new term is related linearly to I_1, with an intercept of zero. The second ratio, $M_2(F_2 - T_2)/d_2 I_1^2$ is defined and found to be constant. Next, the resistance R_1 is varied; a linear relation with a zero intercept is discovered, and the ratio $M_2(F_2 - T_2)/d_2 I_1^2 R_1$ is defined. This complex term has a constant value, and thus BACON has arrived at Joule's second formulation of energy conservation. As in the symmetric cases, BACON has used its expectations to limit both the data it collected and its search for laws.

Theory-Driven Discovery of Conservation Laws

As we have seen, the assumption of symmetry can provide significant help in directing searches through the space of data and the space of laws. BACON.5's use of the symmetry assumption makes the system considerably more theory-driven than its predecessors, though it can still fall back on data-driven methods when necessary. However, BACON.5's symmetry heuristic still has a "syntactic" character. To see this, consider the four laws just discussed. Three of these involved some conserved quantity (the exception is Snell's law, which does not lend itself to such an interpretation), yet BACON has no real concept of conservation. In considering alternative symmetries, the system must solve for the conserved quantity (such as j) in the momentum example), but it does so without any understanding that conservation is involved. Something more than the symmetry heuristic appears to be required, though that assumption has served BACON very well.

To further our understanding of theory-driven discovery, we have constructed a simple system that is based on the notion of conservation. Like BACON, this program discovers quantitative empirical laws; however, it does so in a purely theory-driven manner, rather than using BACON.5's mixed approach.

Before examining the details of the system, we must define some terms.

Extensive and Intensive Properties

The theory of measurement distinguishes between two basically different types of variables. Suppose we have two objects A and B, and can measure the values of some variable X associated with these objects. Now suppose that A and B are combined to form a third object C, as in a chemical reaction.

We will call the variable *extensive* if the relationship $X_A + X_B = X_C$ holds; in other words, X is extensive if and only if it is conserved upon combination of the objects. Mass and volume (in many cases) are two well-known examples of extensive properties.

In general, a property is said to be *intensive* if it is not conserved. We will use the term in a somewhat more restricted way. For the present discussion, we will consider a variable X intensive if one of the relations $X_A < X_C < X_B$ and $X_B < X_C < X_A$ holds. In other words, a property is intensive if the value for the combined system falls between the initial values of the components, such that a weak form of averaging occurs. Density is a well-known example of such a property.

The relation between extensive properties and this restricted form of intensive property is straightforward. Consider the properties of mass (M), volume (V), and density (D). These terms are related by the equation $D = M/V$. From this it should be apparent that the ratio of two extensive properties is an intensive property. When the formula is rewritten as $M = VD$, the conservation law $M_A + M_B = M_C$ can be analyzed in terms of the weighted sum $V_A D_A + V_B D_B = V_C D_C$. This suggests a heuristic that might help in the discovery of conservation laws:

POSTULATE-EXTENSIVE
If you are trying to formulate a conservation law,
   and I is an intensive property,
   and E is an extensive property,
then postulate an extensive term C
   defined as the product of E and I,
   and see if C is conserved.

The reasoning here is that, since the ratio of two extensive terms is always an intensive one, there is a reasonable chance that a given intensive term can be expressed in this manner. If an intensive property and an extensive property can be observed directly, it is quite possible that their product will be an unobservable extensive term; this is equivalent to saying that it is conserved.

The BLACK System

In our previous derivations of Black's law, in this chapter and the preceding one, we did not say much about the history of the actual discovery, and we avoided claims that our derivations resembled the historical one. Indeed, the circumstances surrounding the discovery of Black's law in 1760 provide evidence that it was aided by a conceptual framework and was by no means completely data driven.

Using data reported in a standard chemistry textbook of his time (Hermann Boerhaave's) from an experiment performed at Boerhaave's request by Gabriel Fahrenheit, Black reinterpreted the data to formulate what we now know as Black's law for the temperature of mixtures. Since Fahrenheit reported his invention of the mercury thermometer in 1724 and died in 1736, Black's data were 25 to 35 years old.

It is an everyday experience that the temperature of hot water can be moderated by mixing it with cold. What Fahrenheit showed with his newly invented thermometer was that if equal volumes of water at different temperatures are mixed, the temperature of the mixture is the arithmetic average of the initial temperatures. Experiments had also shown that if the original amounts are unequal, the average has to be weighted by those amounts.

It was also reported by Boerhaave that if two objects of different substance are mixed, their final temperature will be some kind of average of their original temperatures. What Boerhaave failed to discover was the nature of this average. His data showed clearly that mercury, a heavy substance, influenced the final temperature less than an equal volume of a lighter substance, water. This fact appeared counterintuitive to Boerhaave, and the discrepancy in heat capacity per unit of volume was not large (although it was easily detected by the measuring instruments used). He opted for the simple average by volumes; the discrepancy in heat capacities by weight was so enormous that that possibility was ruled out.

Black, noting the discrepancy between the observations and the law based on them, attributed the error to confusion between heat and temperature. He remarked that the temperature equilibrium was sometimes supposed to imply an equal amount of heat per unit volume of each body. "But," he wrote, "this is taking a very hasty view of the subject. It is confounding the quantity of heat in different bodies with its general strength or intensity, although it is plain that these are two different things, and should always be distinguished when we are thinking of the distribution of heat." (Magie 1935, p. 135)

The idea of quantity of heat long predated Black. It had played a central role in the caloric theory. Although the very terms *hot* and *cold* as used in everyday language refer to heat intensity, this idea appears not to have been conceptualized clearly before the time of Black. It was his contribution, by introducing the concepts of specific heat and latent heat of melting and evaporation, to make clear the distinction between the extensive term *heat* and the intensive term *temperature.*

Black may well have approached the experimental data with the idea that quantity of heat is an extensive magnitude, and one that is conserved, already in his mind. He could also have had the idea that large quantities of substances would contain (other things being equal) greater quantities of heat than would small quantities of substances, and that hence one could define an intensive quantity by dividing the total heat by a substance's capacity for heat. Black identified this ratio with temperature.

The error of Black's predecessors lay in their identification of a large volume or weight with "heat capacity." Before the fact, both volume and mass were plausible candidates for the measure of heat capacity—volume because it defined the space within which the heat, or caloric, was held, and mass because it defined the "quantity of matter" of the heat-containing substance. Neither of these extensive quantities was consistent with the data from the experiments. By introducing a new property, with a different value for each substance, Black was able to express total heat as the product of an extensive variable (heat capacity) and an intensive variable (temperature). Heat capacity could, in turn, be expressed as a product of one of the traditionally accepted variables, mass and volume, and a new intensive quantity (specific heat). The key to Black's success was the introduction of this new intrinsic property.

We do not insist on the detailed accuracy of this account of how Black arrived at the concept of specific heat, for his textbook enjoys the clarity of hindsight and does not necessarily represent his state of mind at the time of the discovery. Nevertheless, this somewhat hypothetical sequence shows how the ideas of preceding theory could have guided Black's interpretation of new data.

We now outline a system that is capable of making use of conceptualizations of this kind in analyzing data and in discovering laws. We have named the system BLACK, since our main example of its operation involves the law of specific heat. The BLACK program knows about situations in which two objects combine to form a third, and its goal is to account for relations between the initial and the final configuration in terms of conservation laws.

For example, suppose BLACK were to be given information about its namesake's experiments. With information about the masses, volumes, temperatures, and compositions of these liquids, the system would try to explain the relative values in terms of one or more conservation laws. Upon examining the masses and volumes before and after the mixing, BLACK would discover their additivity and conclude that both mass and volume are extensive properties, and that the values of these terms could be explained by the simple conservation laws $M_A + M_B = M_C$ and $V_A + V_B = V_C$. However, upon examining the values of the temperature T, BLACK would be forced to infer that this property is intensive, since the final temperature always falls between the two initial values. The program would hypothesize (using the POSTULATE-EXTENSIVE rule from above) that some unobservable extensive term C is instead conserved, and that $C = MT$ or $C = VT$. (Either relation will work as well as the other.) In fact, as long as the two initial liquids have the same composition, both of these products are in fact conserved. However, when combinations of different substances are examined, this relation no longer holds. To deal with such situations, we must introduce a second heuristic:

POSTULATE-INTENSIVE
If C is a postulated extensive property
   defined as the product of E and I,
   and C is not conserved,
   and I is an intensive property,
   and E is an extensive property,
then postulate an intrinsic intensive term J,
   redefine C as the product of J, I, and E,
   and see if C is conserved.

In cases where the inferred extensive property is not actually conserved,
BLACK uses this rule to postulate a second property, J, and to redefine C
to be the product of T, M (or V), and J. This new property is both intrinsic
(i.e., it takes on numerical values that are associated with symbolic ones)
and intensive (i.e., it is not conserved). The values of this intrinsic property
can be found by solving simultaneous equations involving several substances; once found, the values can be used to check whether $C = JMT$ is
actually conserved. In this case, the quantity C (heat) is conserved, and
BLACK has arrived at one version of the specific-heat law, with J as the
specific heat.

However, in formulating this law, the system was forced to introduce the
intensive (and intrinsic) property J. Since BLACK's goal is to incorporate all
terms into some conservation law, it must deal with this term. BLACK
applies its various heuristics recursively to the new term, leading the system
to define a new, potentially extensive property, Q, as the product of J and
M. Upon checking the values of this term, the system finds that they are
conserved. Since no more unexplained intensive terms exist, the program
halts. The term Q corresponds to the *heat capacity* of a quantity of
liquid, and this property is indeed conserved. By focusing on conservation
laws, BLACK has rediscovered a law that BACON passed over in its more
syntactic analysis. Table 5.8 summarizes BLACK's steps in discovering these
conservation laws.

The BLACK system is equally successful in handling conservation of
momentum, which is not surprising in view of the similarity of the two
laws. Its application to Joule's relations is less clear, since different sets of
variables are involved, Still, the system provides some initial insights into
the theory-driven methods that we have been avoiding. Of course, there is
always a price to pay for additional power. Although BLACK's approach to
conservation laws is much more direct than BACON's method, it is also less

Table 5.8
BLACK's steps in arriving at the specific-heat law.

Relation discovered	Conclusions and actions
$V_1 + V_2 = V_f$	Volume (V) is extensive.
$M_1 + M_2 = M_f$	Mass (M) is extensive.
$T_1 < T_f < T_2$	Temperature (T) is intensive.
	Infer extensive $C = MT$.
$C_1 + C_2 \neq C_f$	$C = MT$ is not conserved.
	Infer intensive J; redefine $C = JMT$.
	Determine intrinsic values of J.
$C_1 + C_2 = C_f$	$C = JMT$ is conserved.
	Infer extensive $Q = MJ$.
$Q_1 + Q_2 = Q_f$	$Q = MJ$ is conserved.

general. Ideally, one would like to combine the approach to conservation taken by BLACK with the data-driven and syntactic schemes used in BACON, constructing a system that can use knowledge of conservation when appropriate but can employ weaker methods if necessary.

Conclusions

In this chapter we have described BACON.5 and BLACK, extensions to BACON.4 that incorporate heuristics for inferring symmetric relations and reasoning by analogy (in addition to those already present in BACON.4). These methods significantly reduced BACON's search for data, theoretical terms, and hypotheses. Moreover, they showed their generality by proving useful in discovering Snell's law and several conservation laws. It is possible that we could continue to extend BACON in this piecemeal way, adding a few heuristics at a time; no doubt we would learn much in the process. However, this approach would occasionally seem somewhat forced. (For instance, in this chapter we found that BACON's notion of conservation was largely syntactic, and in response we introduced BLACK, a theory-driven system designed specifically to discover conservation laws.) One could make a similar criticism of BACON.4's heuristic for noting common divisors. When John Dalton noted common divisors, he moved quickly to his atomic hypothesis; William Prout took a similar step on the basis of the relative atomic weights. In contrast, BACON constructs no such mental models; instead, it continues to play syntactic number games until it has completely summarized the data.

One of BACON's central deficiencies is that it has little notion of structure. The system represents both data and hypotheses as conjunctions of attribute-value pairs. This is why BACON.4 (which preceded BACON.5 historically and conceptually) did not take advantage of symmetry assumptions; the representation encouraged us to think of V_1 and V_2 as entirely different terms rather than as the same term associated with different objects. BACON.5 overcame this limitation by representing structure to a limited extent; this allowed the system to use the power of symmetry to reduce its search. Still, the structural framework used by BACON.5 cannot begin to support more sophisticated forms of reasoning, such as that required by Dalton's atomic hypothesis or Prout's proposal concerning the composition of the elements.

Another issue is BACON's focus on quantitative empirical laws. Certainly not all empirical laws are numerical in nature, and one can make a strong argument that qualitative laws will usually be discovered before the discovery of quantitative relations (Newell and Simon 1976). Similarly, not all discovery focuses on empirical laws. Once an empirical claim has been put forth, the scientist usually attempts to generate some theory or explanation of the law. Since many explanations are structural in character (the atomic theory of matter and the kinetic theory of gases are two well-known examples), we may, by addressing the issue of structural representations, simultaneously be dealing with one of the more important forms of explanation.

The data-driven, Baconian approach to discovery has served us well, and we do not intend to abandon the important methods that have been described thus far. However, it is time to move on to other aspects of the discovery process. Eventually we will return to BACON and its concern with quantitative, empirical laws; but we will do this with the insight gained from examining other facets of science to which we now turn.

III QUALITATIVE LAWS AND MODELS

In this part we introduce three new programs (GLAUBER, STAHL, and DALTON) that are capable of inducing qualitative laws from empirical data. These programs can also induce structural and explanatory models for certain phenomena.

6 Discovering Qualitative Laws

In the preceding three chapters, we examined the discovery of quantitative empirical laws. Although such discoveries play a significant role in the history of science, they are not the whole story. In this chapter and the two that follow, we shall focus on different forms of discovery that involve various kinds of qualitative reasoning. In each case, we shall summarize the class of discoveries with which we are concerned, provide examples of such discoveries from the history of science, and describe an artificial-intelligence system that is capable of making such discoveries. In the main, we will continue to focus on data-driven discovery.

In this chapter we shall take up the discovery of qualitative empirical laws and concepts. Our primary example will come from the history of chemistry, and our model of the qualitative discovery process is an AI system named GLAUBER. We will find that, along many dimensions, GLAUBER has much in common with BACON, despite its focus on qualitative rather than quantitative relations. After describing GLAUBER and providing some examples from the domain of chemistry, we will also consider the system's relation to some other AI discovery systems that operate in the domains of conceptual clustering and language acquisition. First, however, we shall review some events from the history of chemistry, since it was our interest in that area that led us to construct GLAUBER.

The discovery of quantitative laws has generally been preceded by the discovery of qualitative relations. Early physicists noted that colliding objects tended to change velocities before they determined the exact form of the relation, and plant and animal breeders knew that certain traits were passed on to offspring long before Gregor Mendel formulated the quantitative principles of inheritance. One of the best examples of this trend can be found in the history of chemistry, where qualitative laws of reaction were discovered decades before numerical relations were determined. The history of the theory of acids and bases provides particularly useful insights into the discovery of qualitative empirical laws and concepts.

During the seventeenth and eighteenth centuries, chemists made considerable progress in classifying substances on the basis of qualitative properties (Partington 1961–62). Researchers focused on such features as the tastes and textures of substances as well as on their interactions with other substances. They knew that the substance we now call hydrochloric acid had a sour taste, and that it combined with ammonia to form ammonium chloride, NH_4Cl (though the structure of this compound was of course not known). Moreover, they knew that sulfuric acid also tasted sour, and that it combined with ammonia to form ammonium sulfate, $(NH_4)_2SO_4$. From facts such as these, the early chemists defined classes such as acids, alkalis, and salts, and formulated laws involving these terms, such as "acids taste sour" and "acids react with alkalis to form salts." Eventually, they came to view both alkalis and metals as special cases of the more abstract concept of a *base*, and arrived at the more general law that "acids react with bases to form salts." Although some exceptions to these statements were known, chemists found the laws sufficiently general to use in making predictions and in classifying new substances. The definition of the classes *acid* and *alkali* and the formulation of laws involving these classes were at the center of the process of qualitative discovery.

The GLAUBER System

Our interest in the discovery of qualitative empirical laws led us to design and implement a second AI system concerned with this process. Since our main examples were derived from the early history of chemistry and from the theory of acids and bases, we named the system after Johann Rudolph Glauber, a seventeenth-century German chemist who played an important role in the development of acid-base theory. Let us begin by considering the form of the data input to the system and the types of laws that it generates. We will then turn to the mechanisms GLAUBER uses to transform data into laws. After we have described the system in the abstract, we will examine its operation on some of the data that were available to the early chemists.

The two versions of GLAUBER that have been implemented produce basically similar results when applied to the main example of this chapter. The account below is based on the second version; the first version is described in comparable detail in Langley et al. 1983. The two versions represent data and laws in identical ways, except that the first does not employ explicit quantifiers in its law statements. They differ with respect to the operators and search strategies they employ. After describing the second system and its applications, we will comment briefly on these differences.

GLAUBER's Representation of Data

In earlier chapters, BACON represented data as conjunctions of attribute-value pairs in which most attributes took on numeric values. In contrast,

GLAUBER operates on purely symbolic (qualitative) data. The system represents data using a predicate-argument notation similar to that used in semantic networks. Each fact or observation contains a predicate followed by one or more labeled arguments. An example will help clarify the representational scheme.

Suppose GLAUBER observes that the chemical hydrogen chloride (HCl) reacts with ammonia (NH_3) to form ammonium chloride (NH_4Cl).[1] This fact would be represented by the proposition

(reacts inputs $\{HCl\ NH_3\}$ outputs $\{NH_4Cl\}$).

Here the predicate is *reacts*, which takes two arguments: the *inputs* and the *outputs* of the reaction. GLAUBER represents the values of these attributes as sets (denoted by curly brackets), in which the order of elements is not significant. Thus, the proposition

(reacts inputs $\{NH_3\ HCl\}$ outputs $\{NH_4Cl\}$)

would be considered identical to the above fact. In our examples, we will use symbols such as HCl and NH_3 for the sake of clarity. GLAUBER does not know the meaning of these symbols or the internal structure of chemicals, such as ammonia. Its behavior would not change if we used symbols such as G00013 instead.

At first glance, GLAUBER's representation may seem identical to BACON's attribute-value scheme, save that sets can occur as values. However, the same symbols can occur in the arguments of several propositions, and this possibility makes for a significant difference. To see this, assume that GLAUBER inputs

(reacts inputs $\{HCl\ NH_3\}$ outputs $\{NH_4Cl\}$).

Now suppose that the system observes a second reaction, say

(reacts inputs $\{HCl\ KOH\}$ outputs $\{KCl\}$).

The occurrence of HCl in both propositions establishes a relation between the two facts of a sort that could not occur in BACON's simpler attribute-value representation. As will be shown later, GLAUBER takes advantage of such relations in its discovery process.

---

1. GLAUBER does not perform experiments. Rather, it takes a list of facts or observations provided by the programmer and searches for qualitative laws that summarize these data.

Relations (in terms of shared symbols) can also occur between facts involving predicates. For instance, the observation that hydrogen chloride tastes sour would be represented as

(has-quality object {HCl} tastes {sour}).

This fact provides another piece of information about the substance HCl that can be used in generating laws. An alternative representation of this information would use the predicate "sour" with the single argument "object." However, as we proceed through the example below, we will see why the first scheme is more suitable. It is clear that, to a certain extent, we have molded our representation to meet the specific needs of this application. We will have more to say on this matter in the final chapter.

GLAUBER's Representation of Laws

GLAUBER's goal is to find, given a set of facts, a set of laws that summarize the observed data. These laws should have the same form as the original facts, but specific substances should be replaced by common names that denote classes of substances, which provide generality. For instance, the qualitative law

(reacts inputs {acid alkali} outputs {salt})

has the same form as

(reacts inputs {HCl NaOH} outputs {NaCl}),

but HCl has been replaced by the common name *acid*, NaOH by *alkali*, and NaCl by *salt*. In order for such a law to have predictive power and make contact with the data, each class must have an associated list of members. Thus, the class of acids might contain the substances HCl and HNO_3, KOH and NaOH might be alkalis, and NaCl, KCl, $NaNO_3$, and KNO_3 might be classified as salts.

However, the proposition

(reacts inputs {acid alkali} outputs {salt})

contains some inherent ambiguity. Should this statement be interpreted to mean that "every acid combines with every alkali to form every salt"? It is to be hoped that it would not, since this assertion does not hold. In this case, we would like to say that "every acid combines with every alkali to form *some* salt." In order to distinguish these two quite different senses from one another (and from others as well), we must employ the universal quantifier ∀ ("for every") and the existential quantifier ∃ ("there exists"). Thus, we can represent the statement "every acid combines with every alkali to form some salt" as

∀ a ∈ acid ∀ k ∈ alkali ∃ s ∈ salt (reacts inputs $\{a\ k\}$ outputs $\{s\}$),

where ∈ means "is an element of." In the examples below, we will omit the set-membership notation and write simpler expressions such as

∀ acid ∀ alkali ∃ salt (reacts inputs {acid alkali} outputs {salt}).

Similarly, the statement "all acids taste sour" would be represented as

∀ acid (has-quality object {acid} taste {sour}).

The same class name may occur in different laws. Taken together, all laws that mention a given class provide an intensional definition of that class. This definition complements the extensional definition, the list of class members, since it can lead to predictions that go beyond the observed data. Also, the set of laws associated with a class is quite similar to the characterizations of concepts produced by many AI systems for learning from examples. Like BACON, GLAUBER has no explicit description of its goal state. Rather, GLAUBER knows it has achieved its goal state when it generates some description that adequately summarizes the data it has observed.

GLAUBER's Discovery Method

Like BACON, the GLAUBER system takes as its input a set of observations and attempts to formulate a set of general laws that summarize these data. Another similarity is that GLAUBER's discovery process can be usefully viewed in terms of search through a space of laws or hypotheses. Such a problem space is defined by the initial states from which search begins, by the operators used to generate new states, and by the test used to determine when the goal has been reached. We have already examined the first and last of these components, so let us now turn to GLAUBER's operators for proposing candidate laws.

In addition to the predicate and the attributes that GLAUBER's laws share with the facts on which they are based, these laws involve two additional structures: the classes referred to in each law and the quantifiers placed on each class in each law. Correspondingly, GLAUBER employs one operator for defining classes and a second operator for proposing quantifiers. We will call the first of these the FORM-CLASS operator and the second the DETERMINE-QUANTIFIER operator. Let us consider each in turn, and then consider how they are combined to produce an effective search process.

As its name implies, the operator FORM-CLASS proposes abstract classes for use in qualitative laws. Recall that at the outset GLAUBER has a set of propositions that vary in terms of their predicates, attributes, and values. Like most operators, FORM-CLASS can be instantiated in many different ways. In this case, each instantiation corresponds to a different combination of predicate, attribute, and value, and leads to different potential classes. For instance, on the basis of the fact

(reacts inputs {HCl NaOH} outputs {NaCl})

described above, it would propose three separate sets of classes. The first instantiation, based on the triple (reacts, inputs, HCl), would propose one class corresponding to the second input (NaOH) and another corresponding to the output (NaCl). Another instantiation of the FORM-CLASS operator is based on the triple (reacts, inputs, NaOH), and a third on the triple (reacts, outputs, NaCl).

Each such triple can be used to define one or more classes based on the facts in which that triple occurs. For example, suppose GLAUBER observes the following reactions:

(reacts inputs {HCl NaOH} outputs {NaCl}),

(reacts inputs {HCl KOH} outputs {KCl}),

(reacts inputs {HNO$_3$ NaOH} outputs {NaNO$_3$}),

(reacts inputs {HNO$_3$ KOH} outputs {KNO$_3$}).

Given these data, the triple (reacts, inputs, HCl) defines two classes, $A = \{NaOH, KOH\}$ and $B = \{NaCl, KCl\}$, while the triple (reacts, inputs, NaOH) defines two different classes, $C = \{HCl, HNO_3\}$ and $D = \{NaCl, NaNO_3\}$. Analogous classes (each with two elements) are defined by the triples (reacts, inputs, HNO$_3$) and (reacts, inputs, KOH). In contrast, the triple (reacts, outputs, NaCl) defines two single-element classes, $E = \{HCl\}$ and $F = \{NaOH\}$, since the substance NaCl occurs as the output of the reacts predicate in only one fact. The three other triples involving the output attribute also define classes containing one element.

When GLAUBER is presented with a set of observations, its first step is to form tentative classes based on all observed triples in the manner just described. Some of these classes are based on many observations, others on only one or a few. GLAUBER selects the instantiation (triple) of FORM-CLASS that covers the most data, and retains the classes associated with this choice for further processing. Now GLAUBER starts its substitution process, replacing all the occurrences of members of the classes retained with the corresponding class names. For instance, if the triple (reacts, inputs, HCl) were selected from the above data, two patterns would result:

(reacts inputs {HCl A} outputs {B})

and

(reacts inputs {HNO_3 A} outputs {B}).

Although the classes A and B were based on facts involving the substance HCl, the substitution process leads to their inclusion in facts involving the substance HNO_3. Thus, after the FORM-CLASS operator has been applied, GLAUBER not only has a set of initial abstract classes; it also has a set of patterns (hypotheses) that refer to those classes.

However, in their current form these hypotheses do not include quantifiers. Supplying these is the role of the operator DETERMINE-QUANTIFIER, which iterates through the newly generated hypotheses, determining whether each class mentioned in a hypothesis should be existentially or universally quantified. If a single class was introduced, then this class is universally quantified in the pattern on which the class was based. In this case the level of quantification is not an issue, since this is tautologically determined by the manner in which the class was defined. But if N classes are introduced, then N components of the law result, each containing one universally quantified class and with the quantifiers for the remaining classes undetermined. In the above example, two variations on the reaction law, (reacts inputs {A NaOH} outputs {B}), could be formulated:

$\forall$ A $\exists$ B (reacts inputs {A NaOH} outputs {B})

and

$\forall$ B $\exists$ A (reacts inputs {A NaOH} outputs {B}).

The first of these states that all members of class A react with at least one member of class B; the second states that all members of class B can be formed by at least one member of A in reaction with NaOH. The first quantifier in each law follows from the class definition, but the second quantifier must be determined empirically.

A similar issue arises when the FORM-CLASS operator generates additional hypotheses by replacing specific substances with classes in other facts. In these cases, all of the quantifiers must be tested against observations. For example, the law (has-quality object {A} taste {sour}) might hold for all members of A or for only a few members. The DETERMINE-QUANTIFIER operator examines the known facts and decides on the appropriate quantifier. If more than one class is involved, the possibility of multiple forms of the law must be considered. Thus, if a law were formed by substituting both A and B for members of these classes, GLAUBER might decide on a single law in which both were universally quantified, a single law in which both were existentially quantified, or two laws involving both existential and universal quantifiers.

Once GLAUBER has applied the FORM-CLASS and DETERMINE-QUANTIFIER operators, it has a revised set of facts and laws to which these operators can be applied recursively. The FORM-CLASS operator may apply to laws as well as to facts, provided the laws have identical quantifiers. For example, given the two laws

$\forall$ A $\exists$ B (reacts inputs {A NaOH} outputs {B})

and

$\forall$ A $\exists$ C (reacts inputs {A KOH} outputs {C}),

this operator would generate the more abstract law

$\forall$ A $\exists$ D (reacts inputs {A E} outputs {D}).

In addition, it would define the class E to have the members NaOH and KOH, and would define the class D with the classes B and C as subsets. DETERMINE-QUANTIFIER would then proceed to decide on the generality of this new abstract law, and the process would be repeated on the revised set of facts and laws. GLAUBER continues this alternation between finding laws and determining their generality until the goal state—a set of maximally general laws that account for as many of the original facts as possible—has been reached.

This process can be viewed as a form of hill-climbing through the space of possible laws and classes. At each point in the search, GLAUBER applies all instantiations of the appropriate operator and selects the best result. Thus, the system carries out a one-step look-ahead to determine the best course of action. GLAUBER's search control does not include backup capability, since its evaluation functions are sufficiently powerful to direct search along acceptable paths. Although hill-climbing methods can trap a system at local maxima, we have not encountered problems of this sort in our runs with chemical data.

To summarize: GLAUBER determines which classes to define by considering all known substances and classes and selecting the (predicate, attribute, value) triple that occurs in the largest number of facts or laws. Thus, if two facts have the predicate reacts and the symbol NaOH in the inputs slot, the triple (reacts, inputs, NaOH) will receive a score of 2. In the case of laws, GLAUBER uses as the score the total number of facts covered by those laws. GLAUBER indexes its facts and laws in terms of their arguments, so these scores are easily computed for each substance and class. Once this has been done, the system applies the FORM-CLASS operator to the facts with the highest score, with the constraint that existentially quantified classes are not considered.

In determining the placement of universal and existential quantifiers, GLAUBER examines the facts (or lower-level laws) on which the current law is based. The system generates all the laws or facts that would be produced by a universal quantifier for a given class. If enough of these have been observed (or inferred), then the universal quantifier is retained for that class; otherwise an existential quantifier is used. Thus, the system can be viewed as looking ahead one step in order to determine which move is most desirable. A certain externally specified percentage of the predicted facts must be observed for GLAUBER to generalize over a class. The program interprets missing facts as unobserved. The current system cannot handle disconfirming evidence, such as $\neg\exists$ salt (reacts inputs {HCl HNO$_3$} outputs {salt}), where $\neg\exists$ means "there does not exist."

Rediscovering the Concepts of Acids and Alkalis

Now that we have described GLAUBER in the abstract, let us examine its behavior when it is given a particular set of facts as input. These facts, presented in the top part of table 6.1 (Initial state, S1), are very similar to the facts that were known to seventeenth-century chemists before they

Table 6.1
States generated by GLAUBER in discovering acids and alkalis.

Initial state, S1
(reacts inp {HCl NaOH} outp {NaCl})
(reacts inp {HCl KOH} outp {KCl})
(reacts inp {HNO₃ NaOH} outp {NaNO₃})
(reacts inp {HNO₃ KOH} outp {KNO₃})
(has-qual object {HCl} taste {sour})
(has-qual object {HNO₃} taste {sour})
(has-qual object {NaCl} taste {salty})
(has-qual object {KCl} taste {salty})
(has-qual object {NaNO₃} taste {salty})
(has-qual object {KNO₃} taste {salty})
(has-qual object {NaOH} taste {bitter})
(has-qual object {KOH} taste {bitter})

FORM-CLASS and DETERMINE-QUANTIFIER lead to state S3
SALTS: {NaCl, KCl, NaNO₃, KNO₃}
∃ salt (reacts inp {HCl NaOH} outp {salt})
∃ salt (reacts inp {HCl KOH} outp {salt})
∃ salt (reacts inp {HNO₃ NaOH} outp {salt})
∃ salt (reacts inp {HNO₃ KOH} outp {salt})
∀ salt (has-qual object {salt} taste {salty})
(has-qual object {HCl} taste {sour})
(has-qual object {HNO₃} taste {sour})
(has-qual object {NaOH} taste {bitter})
(has-qual object {KOH} taste {bitter})

FORM-CLASS and DETERMINE-QUANTIFIER lead to state S5
SALTS: {NaCl, KCl, NaNO₃, KNO₃}
ACIDS: {HCL, HNO₃}
∀ acid (reacts inp {acid NaOH} outp {salt}) (has-qual object {NaOH} taste {bitter})
∀ acid ∃ salt (reacts inp {acid KOH} outp {salt}) (has-qual object {KOH} taste {bitter})
∀ salt (has-qual object {salt} taste {salty})
∀ acid (has-qual object {acid} taste {sour})

FORM-CLASS and DETERMINE-QUANTIFIER lead to final state S7
SALTS: {NaCL, KCl, NaNO₃, KNO₃}
ACIDS: {HCL, HNO₃}
ALKALIS: {NaOH, KOH}
∀ alkali ∀ acid ∃ salt (reacts inp {acid alkali} outp {salt})
∀ salt (has-qual object {salt} taste {salty})
∀ acid (has-qual object {acid} taste {sour})
∀ alkali (has-qual object {alkali} taste {bitter})

formulated the theory of acids and bases.[2] They consist of information about the tastes of substances and the reactions in which substances take part. As we shall see, GLAUBER arrives at a set of laws and classes very similar to those proposed by the early chemists. The data in the table are simplified for the sake of clarity in exposition; however, we have tested the system on larger sets of data and on sets with less regularity.

In this chapter we will not undertake to match in detail the sequence of steps taken by GLAUBER with the successive experiments and ruminations of early chemists that finally led to the emergence of a reasonably coherent classification of substances as acids, bases, and salts and to the understanding that acids and bases combine to form salts. The standard source for the known facts of the matter is Partington 1961–62. The existing historical evidence would hardly allow us to reconstruct the exact sequence of steps of conceptual clarification, but in order to be consistent with the history we have avoided relying, in our own treatment, on any facts about the properties of these substances or the reactions among them that were not well known by the middle of the seventeenth-century, when these ideas at last became clear. The chemists who were most important in enunciating them, in addition to Glauber, were Jan Baptista van Helmont and Otto Tachenius.

Given the twelve facts as inputs, GLAUBER begins by examining various (predicate, attribute, value) triples and determining which of these occurs in the greatest number of facts. It notes that the symbols HCl, HNO_3, NaOH, and KOH are each arguments of the *inputs* slot for two facts involving the *reacts* predicate. Similarly, the symbols sour and bitter each occur as argument of the *taste* slot in two *has-quality* facts. However, the highest-scoring symbol is salty, which occurs in four *has-quality* facts as the value for *taste*.[3] This triple is selected, and these four facts are replaced by the law (has-quality object {salt} taste {salty}), which has the same form as the original propositions but in which the differing values of the object

2. One might question whether these are facts or whether they are instead summaries of yet lower-level observations, such as the reactions and tastes of particular objects. Indeed, one could present GLAUBER with such lower-level data and hope it would form classes corresponding to substances like HCl and KOH. The presence of additional features, such as color and weight, would surely aid this process. Although we have not tested this prediction, we believe that, given such information, GLAUBER would be able to generate the "data" in table 6.1 from lower-level observations.

3. Had we represented taste information using predicates such as sour, bitter, and salty, GLAUBER would not have formulated this class. Since the system's heuristics look for shared values, substances' tastes must be stored as values instead of predicates.

slot have been replaced by the class name "salt." In addition, the four substances NaCl, KCl, NaNO$_3$, and KNO$_3$ are stored as members of the new class.

Besides proposing this law, the FORM-CLASS operator generates four additional hypotheses by substituting the symbol "salt" for members of this class into other facts. Thus, the facts (reacts inputs {HCl NaOH} outputs {NaCl}) and (reacts inputs {HCl KOH} outputs {KCl}) are replaced by (reacts inputs {HCl NaOH} outputs {salt}) and (reacts inputs {HCl KOH} outputs {salt}). Similarly, the facts (reacts inputs {HNO$_3$ NaOH} outputs {NaNO$_3$}) and (reacts inputs {HNO$_3$ KOH} outputs {KNO$_3$}) are replaced by (reacts inputs {HNO$_3$ NaOH} outputs {salt}) and (reacts inputs {HNO$_3$ KOH} outputs {salt}). Although the first of these laws is guaranteed to be universally quantified by the manner in which the salt class was defined, the generality of the other laws must be determined empirically. For example, if the law (reacts inputs {HCl NaOH} outputs {salt}) were universally quantified over the class of salts, then four facts would be predicted. Since only one of these predictions has been observed, GLAUBER employs an existential quantifier rather than a universal one. The same decision is made for the other laws formed by substitution; this leads to the laws and facts shown in the second section of table 6.1.

Given this new state of the world, state S3, GLAUBER again determines which triple occurs in the greatest number of propositions. In this case, the set of alternatives is slightly different from that on the earlier cycle, since the class name "salt" has replaced the individual members of that class. With the current set of facts and laws, six symbols tie for the honor: NaOH, KOH, HCl, HNO$_3$, sour, and bitter. NaOH occurs in the laws ∃salt (reacts inputs {HCl NaOH} outputs {salt}) and ∃salt (reacts inputs {HNO$_3$ NaOH} outputs {salt}); KOH occurs in the laws ∃salt (reacts inputs {HCl KOH} outputs {salt}) and ∃salt (reacts inputs {HNO$_3$ KOH} outputs {salt}). The salt symbol actually occurs in all four of these laws; however, since this class is existentially quantified in each of the laws, it is not considered. Since each of the viable options involves two laws (each based on one fact), GLAUBER selects one of them at random.

Let us follow the course that events take when the system chooses the pair of facts involving the symbol NaOH. The FORM-CLASS operator generates the law (reacts inputs {acid NaOH} outputs {salt}) and defines the new class "acid" as containing the elements HCl and HNO$_3$. Each of the two additional hypotheses that result from substitution—(reacts inputs

{acid KOH} outputs {salt}) and (has-quality object {acid} taste {sour})—
replaces two directly observed facts. After substitution, GLAUBER has four
laws and two facts in memory. However, the system must still determine
the generality of its new laws. The DETERMINE-QUANTIFIER operator
proceeds to consider the predictions made by each law when the law is
universally quantified over the new class of acids. Since all the predicted
facts have been observed, the universal quantifier is retained for each of
the new laws. This gives the set of facts and laws shown in the third section
of table 6.1 (state S5). At this point, only five symbols remain to be
considered: NaOH, KOH, bitter, and the classes salt and acid. The first
two occur only in single laws; the third occurs in two analogous facts. The
class name salt appears in two analogous laws, but it is ignored because of
its existential quantifier. However, the class name acid occurs in two
analogous laws, each of which is based on two facts; this gives acid a score
of 4. As a result, the two laws are passed to the FORM-CLASS operator,
and a higher-level law—(reacts inputs {acid alkali} outputs {salt})—is
formulated on this basis. In addition, the class alkali is defined as having
the members NaOH and KOH. A second law, (has-quality object {alkali}
taste {bitter}), is formed by substitution, and both laws are universally
quantified over the new class, the first by definition and the second empirically. At this point, GLAUBER has reached its goal of specifying a general
set of laws that summarize the original data. The final laws, shown in the
fourth section of table 6.1, are very similar to those proposed by the early
chemists.

When GLAUBER is given reactions involving metals as well as alkalis, it
defines the broader class of bases (containing both metals and alkalis as
members) and arrives at the central tenet that acids combine with bases to
form salts. As in the example above, the subclass of alkalis is identified by
taste; the subclass of metals is set apart by shiny appearance. Apart from
these differences, the overall discovery process is very similar to that
described above for the simpler task with alkalis alone.

The Two Versions of GLAUBER

The first version of GLAUBER we built differs from the one described here
with respect to its operators, the control of search, and the explicit use of
quantifiers. The operators of the first version are all components of what
has become the FORM-CLASS operator in the second. Their function is
to derive new classes, introduce new class names in patterns, and formulate

new hypotheses and laws in terms of the new classes. The heuristics they use are closely similar to those described for the **FORM-CLASS** operator in the version discussed above.

Whereas the search-control mechanisms of the first version define what is essentially a breadth-first search, the second version performs a best-first search, using a crude evaluation function to choose its next step. By "breadth-first" we mean that the first version generates all the hypotheses it can from the original data, generalizing each one as far as possible upon generation. It then combines into a single class pairs of classes having a sufficient number of common members. Having carried these procedures as far as possible, it then recurses, treating the patterns that have been generated as facts and applying its heuristics to them.

In the laws generated by the first version of GLAUBER, quantifiers are implicit. For example, in "acids react with alkalis to form salts," "acids" and "alkalis" are to be seen as universally quantified, and "salts" as existentially quantified. Quantification is made explicit in the second version in the particular way we have described, probably with some loss of generality. Further investigation will be needed to fix upon wholly appropriate rules for inferring quantifications from the data. In the next section, we will have a little more to say about quantification.

Limitations of the System

In its present form, GLAUBER has some important limitations which should be remedied in future versions. The first problem revolves around the program's treatment of quantifiers and their order. The expression $(\forall x \exists y \, P(x, y))$ is not equivalent to $(\exists y \, \text{A} \, x \, P(x, y))$; the second formula is more specific than the first, and thus makes stronger claims. Although GLAUBER can arrive at laws of the second form, this occurs only if it happens to define classes in a certain order; the system does not find maximally specific laws in all cases that it should. For instance, consider the third stage in table 6.1, in which GLAUBER defined the class "acid" and formulated the tautological law $\forall$ acid $\exists$ salt (reacts inputs {acid NaOH} outputs {salt}). Although this "law" was guaranteed to hold by the manner in which acids were defined, an even stronger law might hold. This would be the case if the same salt were the output for every acid-NaOH reaction that had been observed. The stronger law could then be stated as $\exists$ salt $\forall$ acid (reacts inputs {acid NaOH} outputs {salt}). In fact, this more specific law does not describe the data, but one can imagine cases where it would, and future versions of GLAUBER should be able to handle them.

A second problem involving the order of quantifiers concerns complementary laws, such as $\forall x \exists y \; P(x, y)$ and $\forall y \exists x \; P(x, y)$. We have seen that such laws are considered when two classes are defined in the same step; however, there are other cases in which one would like this to occur. For example, table 6.1 summarizes GLAUBER's discovery of the law $\forall$ alkali $\forall$ acid $\exists$ salt (reacts inputs {acid alkali} outputs {salt}). This states that all acids and alkalis react to form some salt. However, the original data also support the complementary law, $\forall$ salt $\exists$ alkali $\exists$ acid (reacts inputs {acid alkali} outputs {salt}), which states that all salts are the product of a reaction between some acid and some alkali. GLAUBER could have generated this law had its heuristics taken it down an alternative path (first defining acids, then alkalis, and finally salts), but the existing version could never generate both laws in the same run.

Other limitations relate to the system's evaluation function for directing search through the space of classes and laws. The current version iterates through the set of (predicate, attribute, value) triples and selects the triple that occurs in the greatest number of facts. This leads GLAUBER to prefer large classes to small ones, which in turn leads to laws with greater generality (in the sense that they cover more of the observed facts). However, recall that once GLAUBER defines a new class on the basis of some law it then creates additional laws by substituting the class for its members in other facts. This suggests a broader definition of generality, including all facts predicted by any law involving the new class. This analysis leads to two methods for preferring one class over another. The most obvious approach involves computing the percentage of predictions that are actually borne out by observations; we shall call this the *predictive power* of a class and its associated laws. The second method involves computing the total number of facts predicted by a class and its related laws; we shall call this the *predictive potential* of the class.

Obviously, a law that predicts a few observed reactions but predicts many unobserved ones is undesirable; this suggests that predictive power should be used to weed out grossly unacceptable classes. However, when the scores on this dimension are roughly equal, sets of laws with greater predictive potential should be preferred, since these lead to many predictions that, if satisfied, will lead to an increase in predictive power. One way to implement this scheme would have GLAUBER generate the potential classes and their associated laws, in order to determine their predictive power and potential. The system would then have to consider whether these laws should be quantified existentially or universally in order to maximize their scores. In other words, the system would have to apply the FORM-CLASS operator in all possible ways, and then apply the DETERMINE-QUANTIFIER operator in all possible ways, in order to determine the best path to follow. This is equivalent to a two-step look-ahead in the search tree, and it would involve considerably more computation time than the current simple strategy. Although the details of this scheme remain to be elaborated, the basic idea of defining classes that account for the most data seems a plausible approach.

However, in order to implement this strategy, we would first have to deal with two other limitations of the current system. The distinction between predictive power and predictive potential makes sense only if one can test predictions, and the testing of predictions makes sense only if such predictions can fail. This means that GLAUBER must be able to represent negated facts or "failed" observations. For instance, if the substance KOH were added to the alkali class solely on the basis of its taste, we might predict that KOH would react with every acid to produce some salt. This abstract prediction can be stated as ∀ acid ∃ salt (reacts inputs {acid KOH} outputs {salt}).

If we also know that the substances HCl and HNO_3 are acids, then two more specific predictions can be made: ∃ salt (reacts inputs {HCl KOH} outputs {salt}) and ∃ salt (reacts inputs {HNO_3 KOH} outputs {salt}). These predictions can be tested by combining the pairs of chemicals, seeing if they react, and seeing whether the output satisfies the definition of a salt. If the substances fail to react, we must represent this information in some format that GLAUBER can use, such as ∀ substance ¬ (reacts inputs {HCl KOH} outputs {substance}) or (reacts inputs {HCl KOH} outputs { }). The exact representation matters little, as long as GLAUBER knows how to interpret it. Nearly any representation is preferable to the current scheme, in which the system cannot distinguish between failed reactions and those that have simply not been observed.

In addition, an improved GLAUBER must be able to design and run simple experiments, and this requires the system to distinguish between independent and dependent terms. For each predicate, GLAUBER must know the attributes (and values) over which it has experimental control, and which attributes it can only observe. In the case of the reacts predicate, one has control over all values of the inputs attribute, whereas the values of the ouptuts attribute can only be observed. For the has-quality predicate, one has control over the object being tasted, but the resulting taste can only be noted. Assuming such knowledge, one can easily enable GLAUBER to generate a simple factorial design (similar to that used by BACON), and use it to request an initial set of observations. However, after some tentative classes and laws have been formulated, these can be used to generate predictions, which can lead directly to new experiments. Depending on the results of these forays, some laws may be rejected in favor of others, which would lead to yet other predictions and experiments.

This proposal suggests still other modifications to GLAUBER. The current implementation assumes that all data are present at the outset, and the system puts these data to good use in directing search through the space of laws. However, the existing version of GLAUBER is unable to respond to new data, even if these disconfirm the hypotheses it has formed. Given a data-gathering scheme like that just described, a revised version of the system might employ more incremental discovery methods. These might operate in the following fashion.

The revised GLAUBER would begin by selecting some predicate that involves only one independent term, such as the has-quality predicate, and applying this to various substances. On the basis of the resulting observations, the system would define initial classes and form some tentative laws, such as ∀ acid (has-quality object {acid} taste {sour}). Since only one predicate would have been observed, each of the initial classes would have only one law associated with it. After this trial period, GLAUBER would be able to run experiments using different predicates, such as reacts, in the hope that its initial classes would lead it to further regularities.

On the basis of its initial classes, the system could form a number of experimental *templates*, such as (reacts inputs {acid acid} outputs {?}, (reacts inputs {acid alkali} outputs {?}), and (reacts inputs {acid salt} outputs {?}). Each of these could be instantiated to produce specific experimental combinations, and the results could be examined. In many cases, no reaction would occur, and the template responsible would be abandoned after a few instances. In the present case, only one template leads to interesting results: Not only do acids combine with alkalis, but the substance generated usually seems to be a salt. This law would thus be added to the intensional definition for each of the classes involved. As more data were gathered, GLAUBER might find substances that combine with alkalis to form salts but that have no sour taste. If this were to occur often enough, the reacts law might become more central to the definition of acids than the law involving taste. This would seem to be a more plausible account of the actual historical development of the concept of acid than that provided by the current version of GLAUBER.

The incremental acquisition of data would require yet another revision: It would force us to replace GLAUBER's simple hill-climbing strategy with a more robust search method. At any given point, one set of classes and laws might best summarize the data that had been observed. However, as predictions were tested and sometimes disconfirmed and as new (possibly unexpected) observations were made, the current hypotheses might become untenable and alternative accounts might become preferable. Future in-carnations of GLAUBER should employ a version of the best-first search, in which old options are retained for expansion as new evidence becomes available.

GLAUBER's Relation to Other Discovery Systems

Before leaving GLAUBER, we should spend some time examining its relation to other machine learning and discovery systems. Such an analysis will serve two related functions. First, it will locate GLAUBER's discovery task within the space of learning tasks that have been studied; second, it will locate GLAUBER's methods within the space of learning and discovery techniques.

The Task of Conceptual Clustering

In the literature on machine learning, a variety of distinct learning tasks have been identified. These include learning from examples, language acquisition, learning search heuristics, and conceptual clustering. Langley and Carbonell (1984) provide an overview of these learning tasks and the relations among them. In the following pages we will focus on the task of conceptual clustering, since this comes closest to the discovery task con-fronting the GLAUBER system.

Michalski and Stepp (1983) are responsible for the term "conceptual clustering" and were the first to formulate clearly the class of discovery tasks denoted by this term. They proposed the notion of conceptual clustering as an alternative to traditional statistical methods for numerical taxonomy and cluster analysis (Everitt 1984). In both cases, a set of objects and their associated descriptions are presented, and the goal is to generate some taxonomic scheme that groups similar objects together. For instance, one might be given a variety of animal species, along with their measurements on various dimensions. In this case, the goal would be a hierarchical classification scheme in which species were grouped into genera, families, and the like.

In traditional approaches, the analysis would stop at this point, with the observed objects grouped at varying levels of aggregation. However, Michalski and Stepp proposed that it would also be very useful to characterize each group in terms of some general description. Moreover, traditional methods usually employed a simple distance measure (between the positions of objects in an N-dimensional space) to direct the search for groupings. Michalski and Stepp suggested that if concept descriptions were constructed as well, the quality of these descriptions could be used to direct the search for a useful taxonomy.

This formulation of the task of conceptual clustering suggests two distinct but related subtasks: *aggregation*, which involves grouping a set of objects into (usually disjoint) subclasses, and *characterization*, which involves finding some general description for each aggregate that covers members of that group but does not cover members of any other group. The characterization task has been widely studied under the label of "learning from examples," and various methods for solving this problem have been explored (Winston 1975; Hayes-Roth and McDermott 1978; Mitchell 1977; Anzai and Simon 1979; Anderson et al. 1979; Langley 1982). In learning from examples, the aggregation problem is made trivial, since instances or objects are classified by a tutor. Thus, the problem of conceptual clustering can be viewed as a more difficult version of learning from examples, in which one must solve the aggregation problem in addition to finding an adequate characterization.

The task of conceptual clustering differs from that of learning from examples along another dimension as well: In the latter only one level of concepts or descriptions must be discovered, but in conceptual clustering a hierarchy of such descriptions must be generated. This introduces a whole new dimension along which methods for conceptual clustering may vary, as we will see when we compare some existing systems. Issues also arise about the interaction among submethods for aggregation, characterization, and hierarchy construction. Now that we have considered conceptual clustering and its position in the space of learning tasks, let us examine some specific AI systems that address this problem.

Methods for Conceptual Clustering

Mitchell (1979, 1982) has argued that learning methods can be analyzed usefully in terms of the search methods they employ, and we will follow his advice in our discussion of conceptual-clustering systems. In each case, we describe the system in the abstract and then restate its approach as search. Since we have identified three major subtasks, we consider each system's response to the search inherent in aggregation, characterization, and hierarchy construction.

Michalski and Stepp's (1983) CLUSTER/2 is by far the best-known conceptual clustering program. This system constructs its taxonomic hierarchy from the top down, finding aggregations and characterizations at each level. Given a set of objects, CLUSTER/2 first selects N objects randomly as *seeds* around which to "grow" clusters of objects. To this end, it employs a general-to-specific characterization technique that finds some description that covers each seed but no other. Other objects covered by the description that are not seeds are placed in the same class as the seed. However, the process does not stop here. CLUSTER next selects a new seed from each of the groups[4] and repeats the process, finding a new description for each seed and possibly reassigning some of the objects to new groups. This continues until the seeds stabilize, giving an optimal set of disjoint classes. At this point, CLUSTER/2 uses a specific-to-general characterization technique that produces a more conservative description of the clusters than the method used on seeds. The system repeats this process for different values of N, giving alternative partitions of the object set, each with associated descriptions. These descriptions are used in deciding among the competitors, and the best partition is used to create the first branches in the taxonomic hierarchy. CLUSTER/2 then applies the above process recursively to each of the resulting classes, finding partitions of each set, and providing the partitions with descriptions. Each such partition leads to additional branches at lower levels of the tree, and this process of subdivision continues until further partitions cease to provide useful summaries of the data.

Now let us redescribe CLUSTER/2 in terms of our three levels of search, and examine the relations among these levels. The system selects an initial

---

4. If the quality of the clusters (in terms of their descriptions) has improved over the previous round, this object is picked from the "center" of the group; otherwise, it is picked from the "edge."

set of seed objects at random, but these seeds do not constitute complete aggregations. Rather, CLUSTER/2 employs a characterization method (which involves searching through a space of concept descriptions) to find some description for each seed. Each such description determines an aggregate for the seed on which it is based. However, these are not the final groupings. From each aggregate, CLUSTER/2 selects a new seed and the process is repeated, generating a new set of descriptions and a new set of aggregates. Thus, the system uses a hill-climbing strategy in which each step involves finding an improved set of characterizations and their associated aggregates. There is a "search" for aggregations, but this is subsumed within the search for descriptions.

CLUSTER/2's higher-level search through the space of taxonomies is easier to follow. The system begins with a single, all-encompassing class and successively divides it into lower-level classes. However; these classes are entirely determined by the process of aggregation and characterization just described, so no additional search control is required at this level.

Langley and Sage (1984) have described DISCON, a conceptual-clustering system that takes a quite different approach. DISCON also constructs taxonomies from the top downward, but it uses knowledge of attributes and their values rather than employ the more data-driven approach of Michalski and Stepp's system. DISCON carries out an exhaustive search through the space of taxonomic hierarchies, evaluating completed trees in terms of their complexity. This search process constructs an AND/OR graph, in which OR branches correspond to alternative attributes and AND branches correspond to the values of an attribute. DISCON prefers simpler taxonomies to more complex ones that cover the same observations, and so selects the tree with the fewest nodes. Since the system carries out an exhaustive look-ahead, it is guaranteed to find the simplest summary of the data, though this method is expensive when many attributes are involved.

DISCON differs from Michalski and Stepp's CLUSTER/2 system along a number of dimensions. In CLUSTER/2, the main search passes through the space of aggregations, and the results of a secondary search through the space of concept descriptions are used to direct the first search. In DISCON, the main search takes place in the space of taxonomic hierarchies. At each level of the hierarchy, the systems tries to select the best description, but the quality of each description depends on the quality of the entire hierarchy. As a result, the evaluation must wait until complete trees have been constructed. Moreover, each "description" is limited to a single attribute-value pair, rather than the arbitrary conjuncts and disjuncts of Michalski and Stepp's program. In CLUSTER/2, the search through the space of hierarchies is degenerate, with all search occurring in the aggregation and characterization spaces. In DISCON, the search through these latter spaces is degenerate, with all true search occurring in the space of hierarchies. This distinction between the spaces they search accounts for the vastly different flavor of the descriptions produced by these systems.

In many ways, RUMMAGE (1984) is a compromise between CLUSTER/2 and DISCON. Like DISCON, RUMMAGE considers only descriptions that consist of single attribute-value pairs. However, rather than carry out an exhaustive look-ahead through the space of hierarchies, RUMMAGE employs an evaluation function that requires only one-step look-aheads. Thus, at each stage in constructing its taxonomic hierarchy, it considers all unused attributes in terms of their ability to summarize the current set of objects. For each value of an attribute, RUMMAGE constructs a description of the objects having that value. The program then computes a complexity score for all values of the attribute, and it selects the attribute with the lowest score.

GLAUBER as a Conceptual Clustering System

Now that we have examined some other approaches to the task of conceptual clustering, we can describe GLAUBER in the same terms. Upon reflection, we see that the system has clear responses to the problems of aggregation and characterization. The FORM-CLASS operator and the heuristics for selecting a particular class deal with the aggregation issue. Similarly, the DETERMINE-QUANTIFIER operator deals with characterization, with some help from the substitution process within the FORM-CLASS mechanism. Unlike other conceptual-clustering systems, GLAUBER does not attempt to partition objects into disjoint classes all at once. In the acid-alkali example, GLAUBER first formed the class of salts and its associated laws, and then found the class of acids; only at the end did it formulate the class of alkalis. Since the system substitutes the class name for all instances of the class, it is guaranteed to find disjoint classes—but not in the traditional manner.

A second difference is that GLAUBER does not classify the structures it is given. (In the chemical example, these structures were reaction and taste events.) Rather, it forms classes from the objects occurring in these structures. Thus, GLAUBER deals with inherently relational descriptions, whereas CLUSTER/2, DISCON, and RUMMAGE all assume attribute-value representations. But the difference is more subtle than it may appear at first. One can imagine relational descriptions of objects, such as chairs or tables, that would still lead one to classify the objects themselves rather than their components. The important point is that GLAUBER uses relations among the objects being classified in determining its taxonomic hierarchy, and this leads it to use quite different methods than other conceptual-clustering systems.

Another issue relates to the direction of GLAUBER's search through the space of hierarchies. Although one cannot tell from the acid-alkali example (which involves only one level of classes), the system constructs its taxonomies from the bottom up, rather than in the top-down fashion of RUMMAGE, DISCON, and CLUSTER/2. This difference comes into play when reactions involving metals as well as alkalis are included.

Two final differences arise from the nature of GLAUBER's concept descriptions. First, the intensional definitions of classes may include existential quantifiers as well as universal ones. This is possible because GLAUBER's laws can relate different classes to one another, and these relations may hold only among subsets of class members. Since other conceptual-clustering systems generate descriptions of isolated objects, existential quantifiers have no role to play. Second, GLAUBER's descriptions need not be perfect. If a law holds for most members in a class, it may still be universally quantified. This allows the system's concept definitions to have a "fuzzy" quality, as do many real-world concepts.

In summary: GLAUBER has many similarities to AI systems for conceptual clustering, but there are also some significant differences. In many ways, GLAUBER seems to have a somewhat different discovery task than CLUSTER/2, DISCON, and RUMMAGE. All four systems are concerned with forming classes and descriptions for those classes, but GLAUBER involves searching for relations between objects whereas the other three systems focus on isolated objects. Almost certainly, this difference arises from the sample problems from which the systems were developed. The "mainstream" conceptual-clustering systems emerged in response to work in numerical taxonomy, which was created to deal with biological data. In contrast, we developed GLAUBER in order to understand the mechanisms of discovery in early chemistry, where the "properties" of substances included their reactivity with other substances. Whether the two approaches can be combined to produce a more robust discovery method is an interesting question for future research.

Some Other Discovery Systems

GLAUBER can be viewed as a conceptual-clustering system whose discovery task differs somewhat from the standard definition of the problem of conceptual clustering. Before closing our survey, we should briefly consider some other AI systems that are not usually viewed as conceptual-clustering programs yet which have much in common with GLAUBER. A number of these systems operate in the domain of language acquisition.

One of the most interesting (though perhaps the least known) of these systems is SNPR (Wolff 1978). In implementing this system, Wolff explored an approach to the learning of grammar that incorporates methods very similar to those used in GLAUBER. SNPR begins with a sequence of letters and, on the basis of common sequences of symbols, defines *chunks* in terms of these sequences. For example, given the sequence "thedogchasedthe-catthecatchasedthedog . . . ," the program defines as chunks "the," "dog," "cat," and "chased." Whenever a chunk is created, the component symbols are replaced by the symbol for that chunk. In this case, the sequence "the-dog-chased-the-cat-the-cat-chased-the-dog" would result. In addition, when a number of different symbols (letters or chunks) are found to precede or follow a common symbol, a disjunctive class is defined in terms of the first set. For instance, in the above sequence we find the subsequences "the-dog-chased" and "the-cat-chased." On the basis of this regularity, Wolff's program would define the disjunctive class

noun = {dog, cat}.

The symbol for this new class would then be substituted into the letter sequence for the member symbols. In this case, the sequence "the-noun-chased-the-noun-the-noun-chased-the-noun" would be generated. These two basic methods are applied recursively, so that chunks can be defined in terms of disjunctive classes and vice versa. Thus, given the last sequence, the chunk

sentence = the-noun-chased-the-noun

would be defined, giving the final sequence

sentence-sentence.

From the above it can be seen that Wolff's learning system employs two operators: one for forming disjunctive classes, such as "noun," and another for defining chunks or *conjunctive* classes, such as "dog." The first of these is identical to GLAUBER's operator for forming disjunctive classes such as "acid" and "alkali." [5] The main difference between the two systems' use of this operator lies in the heuristics used to form such disjuncts. Whereas Wolff employed adjacency criteria, which are well suited to the language-acquisition domain, GLAUBER uses the notion of shared arguments, which is more appropriate for relational domains. In contrast, the second operator in Wolff's method has no analog in GLAUBER's repertoire. This suggests a gap in our discovery system's capabilities.

In our review of conceptual clustering, we divided the concept-learning task into two components: a process of aggregation and a process of characterization. However, we failed to distinguish between two quite different notions of aggregation. In the first form of aggregation, one must determine which objects or events should be grouped together as *instances* of a single concept or class. This is the aggregation problem addressed by conceptual-clustering systems such as CLUSTER/2, DISCON, and RUMMAGE, as well as GLAUBER. In the second form of aggregation, one must determine which objects or events should be grouped together as *parts* of a higher-level object or event. Both problems are trivialized in the task of learning from examples, since the tutor groups objects into classes and specifies the parts of each object. Traditional approaches to conceptual clustering deal with instance aggregation but ignore part aggregation.

An obvious way to extend GLAUBER would be to let it form conjunctive classes or chunks, in addition to the disjunctive classes it already forms. Let us consider an example from the domain of genetics that requires this form of reasoning. Suppose the system observes, as did Mendel (1865), that when certain green garden peas were self-fertilized they produced only green offspring, but when other green peas were self-fertilized they produced both green and yellow offspring. These operations can be represented with propositions such as (parent of {pea-2} is {pea-1}), (has-quality object {pea-1} color {green}), and (has-quality object {pea-2} color {yellow}). In this case, we would like GLAUBER to divide the green peas into two classes

5. Rather, we should say that GLAUBER's operator is identical to Wolff's operator, since Wolff's work preceded ours by many years. Although the original version of GLAUBER was developed independent of Wolff's approach, the current system borrows considerably from his results in the domain of grammar learning. Also note that, like GLAUBER, the SNPR system operates in a bottom-up fashion rather than the top-down manner used in most conceptual-clustering systems.

based not on their own directly observable features (since these are identical) but on the features of their offspring. We can accomplish this by first defining the higher-level predicate child-has-quality, and defining this chunk by the rule

(child-has-quality parent {X} child {Y} color {Z})
→ (parent of {Y} is {X}) & (has-quality object {Y} color {Z}).

Given such a predicate, GLAUBER could rewrite its direct observations at a higher level of aggregation and form disjunctive classes based on the resulting propositions. As a result, the system would be able to formulate laws such as

∀ pure-green (child-has-quality parent {pure-green} child {pure-green} color {green}).

This states that all members of the "pure-green" class have offspring that are also members of that class, and that these offspring are green in color. This is equivalent to stating that pure-strain green peas always breed true with respect to color. (We have not suggested heuristics for directing GLAUBER's search through the space of conjunctive classes. Wolff's system employed a data-intensive method similar to our technique for selecting disjunctive classes. Such a method might work for an extended nonincremental version of GLAUBER, but it would not be useful for the incremental version outlined in the preceding section.)

Three other AI language-learning systems formed both disjunctive and conjunctive classes like those generated by SNPR: ZBIE (Siklossy 1968), LAS (Anderson 1977), and ACT* (Anderson 1983). However, these systems assumed that word chunks were already known and that the learner could tell where sentences began and ended, whereas Wolff's system induced both of these things. In addition, ZBIE and LAS assumed that each sample sentence was accompanied by its meaning, and that the goal of the learning system was to acquire some mapping between sentences and their meanings. Siklossy represented meaning using a propositional notation whereas Anderson used semantic networks, but both used this information to constrain the learning process severely.

ZBIE and LAS employed a method for forming disjunctive classes that is a mixture of the methods used by SNPR and GLAUBER. Suppose the word X precedes the word Z in one sentence, and that Y precedes Z in another sentence. ZBIE and LAS would consider creating a disjunctive class at this point, but would not follow through before examining the meaning of each sentence. Assume that X, Y, and Z stand for the concepts associated with the words X, Y, and Z. The systems would create the class (or add a word to it, if it already existed) only if X and Y occurred in the same relation to Z in the meanings of the two sentences. Thus, ZBIE and LAS required converging evidence from two sources—sequential linguistic information and relational semantic information—before forming a disjunctive class such as "subject" or "verb." In contrast, SNPR relied on only the first form of information, and GLAUBER only the second. (From our description, ZBIE and LAS sound very similar. They actually differ in many ways, including their representations of grammar and their solutions to the part-aggregation problem. However, we have focused here on their handling of instance aggregation, since this holds the most relevance to GLAUBER.)

GLAUBER also bears some resemblance to Brown's (1973) discovery system, which operated in the domain of kinship relations. This system noted relations that held empirically among predicates in its data base. For instance, it might discover that whenever the relation brother(X, Y) holds, the relations parent(Z, X) and parent(Z, Y) also hold. Such relations are actually more like relational versions of Wolff's sequential chunks than like GLAUBER's disjunctive classes, which Brown's program did not define. Also, Brown's system focused on finding redundancies among facts in a data base rather than on creating higher-level terms to summarize a set of observations.

Emde, Habel, and Rollinger (1983) addressed a problem very similar to Brown's task. Their method examines whether predicates obey certain higher-level relations, such as transitivity or invertability. Although this approach leads to laws very similar to those found by Brown, their model-driven discovery method contrasts with the data-driven technique used in the earlier system.

Conclusions

Our interest in the discovery of qualitative empirical laws led us to design and implement GLAUBER, an AI system that operates in that domain. Given a set of observations, GLAUBER defines abstract classes and formulates laws stated in terms of those classes. Our approach was driven by examples from the history of early chemistry, especially the development of the theory of acids and bases. Although the existing version of GLAUBER covers many of these discoveries, it has numerous limitations that should be remedied in future versions of the system. These include the need for improved evaluation methods, the need for the ability to distinguish between unobserved and unsuccessful reactions, and the need to be able to run simple experiments in order to test predictions. These needs suggest two others: the need for methods for the incremental discovery of classes and laws, and the need for a search organization more robust than the current hill-climbing scheme.

GLAUBER's relations to other AI discovery systems are of considerable interest. We found that GLAUBER has much in common with conceptual-clustering systems such as Michalski and Stepp's CLUSTER/2, but we found significant differences as well. These included differences in the representation of data and laws and in the details of search through the space of laws and classes. GLAUBER is also closely related to AI language-acquisition systems, particularly Wolff's SNPR. In this case, the differences between the systems suggested another extension of GLAUBER: the inclusion of an operator that forms conjunctive classes or chunks that will let the system restate observations at higher levels of aggregation.

As usual, more work remains to be done. We intend to implement a revised version of GLAUBER that incorporates many of the extensions we have outlined. However, the current instantiation of the system has already provided us with an interesting account of the qualitative discovery process, and it has led to a variety of questions that we plan to pursue in our research.

7 Constructing Componential Models

In addition to the qualitative and quantitative description of chemical reactions, another goal of the early chemists was to determine the components of various substances. Information about chemical reactions also proved quite useful in this regard.

Finding components was, from the outset, an important facet of the atomic theory, in that it postulated primitive building blocks for the observed substances (although it took no stance on whether these building blocks were particulate or continuous in nature). Componential models provide simple explanations of the hidden structures of individual substances, which are clearly distinct from the descriptive summaries generated by BACON and GLAUBER.

A typical example of the eighteenth-century componential model is "marine acid consists of inflammable air and chlorine." [1] No matter how simple such componential models were, it was very difficult to construct a coherent set of them for all the substances known by the end of the eighteenth century. A great variety of alternative componential models were devised during this period, and there were lengthy disputes among their proponents. For example, eighteenth-century chemistry produced two quite different sets of models for basic combustion processes. The first set was collectively called the phlogiston theory, while the second set (which was developed several decades later and replaced the first after more than ten years of competition) was known as the oxygen theory. Each of these theories encountered several major obstacles, but for a long time their adherents found ways around them.

Testing Models of Historical Discovery

The frequent occurrence of alternative accounts of the same data suggests an important requirement on computational models of the discovery process: Such models should be able to arrive at plausible laws or explanations even if these were ultimately rejected in favor of others. The ability to reconstruct different and even competing frameworks, especially ones that

---

1. In today's terminology, marine acid is hydrochloric acid (HCl), and inflammable air is hydrogen (H). In this chapter we have retained the original terminology in order to avoid the use of cues that the eighteenth-century chemists did not posses, and hence to provide additional insight into their ways of thinking. It may be difficult to think in the language of eighteenth-century chemistry; however, the computer system we shall describe is equally adept with modern and traditional terminology.

persisted over long periods, is an important test of the historical and psychological adequacy of a theory of discovery.

Much of the earlier work on computational models of discovery (including our own) explains only how discoveries *might have* been made, and claims no detailed historical accuracy. Although the successful rediscovery of a concept by AM (Lenat 1977) or a law by BACON certainly demonstrates one path to that discovery, it does not demonstrate that this path was taken historically. One way to ensure greater historical validity is to build a model that accounts for a historical *sequence* of discoveries rather than for isolated and selected events. This provides a much stronger test for the theory of discovery, especially when the historical data lend themselves to more than one interpretation.

In our experiments with BACON we encountered at least three instances where, in the actual history of the matter, the data—essentially the same data that were available to BACON—were interpreted erroneously before the "correct" law was discovered: Kepler at first concluded that the periods of the planets varied with the squares of their distances from the Sun, and arrived at the $\frac{3}{2}$-power law only when he reexamined the data ten years later. Kepler also proposed a law of refraction that was only an approximation to Snell's sine law, which is accepted today. And, as we have seen, Boerhaave thought that heat capacity depended only on the volume of a body, and not on a special property (its specific heat). In all of these cases, the error arose from accepting "loose" fits of a law to data, and the later, correct formulation provided a law that fit the data much more closely. If we wished to simulate this phenomenon with BACON, we would only have to set the error allowance generously at the outset, then set stricter limits after an initial law had been found. However, the differences between competing interpretations of data to be considered in this chapter are more subtle and do not depend simply on how strict a fit of law to data is demanded.

What historical evidence should be used to test whether a theory of discovery models the scientific thinking in a particular epoch successfully? Is every instance of scientific reasoning relevant? Perhaps not. A scientist may make a mistake in a particular application of his method, and we cannot expect to simulate all such errors. However, conclusions—even mistaken ones—that were accepted over a long period of time and by several leading scientists are likely candidates for confirmatory tests. If one's model of discovery aims at grasping the main currents of reasoning in a given epoch, then reproducing the errors that were typical of that epoch is diagnostic. Here "errors" means conclusions that were later rejected but that temporarily enjoyed widespread acceptance. Our model should account for the systematically collected evidence of scientific practice during the period. In this way we ensure that the evidence was not chosen arbitrarily, and that the system's reconstruction is not ad hoc, fitting only the examples that we selected.

An *incremental* discovery system is particularly well suited for this type of evaluation. We can provide the system with data piecemeal, in the order in which experiments were actually made in history. Then we can see how the inferences the system derives from earlier evidence interact with the later evidence. This technique provides a strong test of the reconstruction, for the inferences used in later discoveries are created by the system itself, not by the programmer. In this way we protect ourselves against the unconscious (and conscious) introduction of ad hoc assumptions.

A system that models historical developments can serve several purposes. First, it can answer many specific questions about a particular epoch. In the case of eighteenth-century chemistry, these include notorious questions about the conflict between the phlogiston and oxygen theories. For example, was the phlogiston theory a mistake resulting from inadequate thinking and maintained by blindness or conservatism, or was it a plausible set of inferences from the available data? What (if anything) was superior in Lavoisier's method, and what accounted for the final success of his oxygen theory? Second, a detailed model of discovery can be a source of analogies for the construction of similar systems. For example, its specific procedural criteria for choosing among multiple interpretations of data can be applied to other domains. Analogous extrapolation may be attempted with criteria for recognizing inconsistencies, for recovering from errors, and so forth. Third, simulations of historic episodes provide concrete evidence about the evolution of the scientific method. If methods can be specified at the precise level of procedures that enter into operative simulation programs, it becomes clear what methods are being used at any given time, and how these methods change over time.

Beginnings of the Phlogiston Theory

The phlogiston theory originated near the end of the seventeenth century. It was developed by the German chemist Georg Ernst Stahl from the ancient view that fire, heat, and light are different manifestations of a common principle that leaves a body during combustion. He called this principle *phlogiston* and initiated an extensive use of the concept in reasoning about chemical reactions. After undergoing several transformations, the phlogiston theory was widely accepted until the 1780s, when it was rapidly supplanted by the oxygen theory.[2]

In the phlogiston theory, any reaction involving combustion was viewed as a decomposition of the burned body. For instance, Stahl interpreted the burning of charcoal as involving its decomposition into the matter of fire (another term for phlogiston) and ash.[3] Early phlogistians were not able to isolate phlogiston, but the generation of fire during combustion seemed to be a good observational reason for admitting the production of a substance from the burning body. Later, the existence of phlogiston was supported by a considerable body of evidence, as this substance proved useful in explaining many additional reactions.

One of the early successes of the phlogiston theory was its explanation of the smelting of iron from iron ore (calx of iron) and charcoal when the latter substances were heated together. According to the phlogistians, this well-known process involved the decomposition of charcoal into phlogiston and ash, followed by the combination of phlogiston with calx of iron to form iron. Similar explanations were proposed for the other metals that could be reduced from their calxes when heated in the presence of charcoal.

The STAHL Program

Having reviewed briefly one episode from the initial development of the phlogiston theory, let us now consider a computational model of this development. Our model is implemented as a running computer program named STAHL, after the originator of the phlogiston theory. We will describe the system at a number of levels: in terms of its inputs and outputs, in terms of its intermediate data representation and the rules it employs, and in terms of the control structure for applying those rules.

2. On the history of the phlogiston theory see Koertge 1969; Musgrave 1976; Partington 1961–62; Zytkow and Lewenstam 1982. Throughout this chapter we will recount only as much of chemical history as is essential for purposes of comparison with the behavior of the simulation program STAHL. The references in this footnote will provide the reader with a more complete account. On topics other than phlogiston, Partington is a reliable source of facts, although some of his interpretations are now being challenged.
3. Several decades later, in the second half of the eighteenth century, fixed air (carbon dioxide) was discovered and recognized as a product of burning charcoal.

STAHL's Inputs and Outputs

The STAHL system accepts an ordered list of chemical reactions as input, and generates as output a list of chemical elements and the compounds in which they are components. For STAHL, as for human chemists, "being an element" is a property relative to the chemical reactions available. Thus, from descriptions it is given of chemical reactions, STAHL derives componential models of the substances involved in those reactions.[4] The program may be viewed as representing a chemist-theoretician who considers empirical data and postulates components for the chemicals involved in the data. In doing this, the program addresses the same task addressed by G. E. Stahl, who wrote: "Universal chemistry is the Art of resolving mixt, compound, or aggregate Bodies into their Principles; and of composing such Bodies from those Principles." (Stahl 1730)   Stahl's concern was shared by his colleagues and followers. The constitution of substances was a vital problem to every chemist of the eighteenth century, and most of the disputes and theoretical developments in that century focused on componential models.

Like GLAUBER, STAHL accepts qualitative facts as input and generates qualitative statements as output. However, STAHL's conclusions are explanations of the structures of individual substances, and are quite different from the descriptive summaries (generalizations) produced by GLAUBER. The system's initial state consists of a set of reactions, represented in the same schema-like format used by GLAUBER. For instance, the reaction of burning charcoal in the presence of air would be represented as

(reacts inputs {charcoal air} outputs {phlogiston ash air}),

with the braces indicating that the order of elements is irrelevant. The inputs and outputs of the reactions given to STAHL are to be regarded as observable substances. STAHL does not explain how the observers chose the substances in terms of which they described the reactions; these choices are already assumed in the descriptions of inputs and outputs. What STAHL explains is how, with the same set of heuristics for reasoning but with different descriptions of the observations, different theories could account for the same set of experiments.

STAHL represents its inferences—the components of nonelemental substances involved in the given reactions—in the same form as the initial reactions. Thus, the conclusion that charcoal is composed of phlogiston

4. The current version of STAHL does not design its own experiments, though extending the model to include this ability is an obvious direction for future research.

and ash would be stated as the following componential model:

(components-of {charcoal} are {phlogiston ash}).

The intermediate states of STAHL's computation consist of transformed versions of the initial reactions, and inferences about the components of some substances.

The Heuristics of STAHL

STAHL incorporates several inference rules for analyzing chemical reactions and building componential models. The most basic of these rules deals with simple synthesis and decomposition reactions and allows the system to infer unambiguously the components of a compound. It can be stated as follows:

INFER-COMPONENTS
If A and B react to form C,
** or if C decomposes into A and B,**
then infer that C is composed of A and B.

This rule can be used to determine the components of charcoal. Given the information that charcoal decomposes to form phlogiston and ash, STAHL would infer that the first substance is composed of the latter two. STAHL does not draw any conclusions about the *amount* of phlogiston and ash contributing to charcoal; it concludes only that they contribute something. Of course, the INFER-COMPONENTS rule is not limited to reactions involving pairs of elements; it can also deal with cases in which three or more substances unite to form a single compound. In the special case where a single substance occurs on both sides of a reaction, STAHL infers that they are identical.

If all chemical reactions were as simple as those shown above, STAHL's task would be easy indeed. However, more complex reactions were common even in the early days of chemistry, and STAHL includes additional rules for dealing with them. The purpose of these rules is to transform complex reactions so they can eventually be matched by the INFER-COMPONENTS rule given above. One such operator is responsible for "canceling out" substances that occur on both sides of a reaction. The reduction heuristic that proposes this inference can be paraphrased as

REDUCE
If A occurs on both sides of a reaction,
then remove A from the reaction.

This heuristic produces a simplified version of a reaction. For instance, if STAHL were given a more complete description of the charcoal burning reaction

(reacts inputs {charcoal air} outputs {phlogiston ash air}),

the REDUCE rule would apply, giving the simplified reaction

(reacts inputs {charcoal} outputs {phlogiston ash}).

This revised description would then be used by the INFER-COMPONENTS rule to infer that charcoal is composed of phlogiston and ash.

A third rule that STAHL incorporates leads at first to more complex statements of reactions, but may make it possible to apply the REDUCE rule. It can be stated as

SUBSTITUTE
If A occurs in a reaction,
  and A is composed of B and C,
then replace A with B and C.

The SUBSTITUTE rule draws on information about the components of a substance that was inferred earlier. For instance, STAHL may know that charcoal is composed of phlogiston and ash, and that (reacts inputs {calx-of-iron charcoal} outputs {iron ash}). In this case, the SUBSTITUTE rule would let STAHL rewrite the reaction as (reacts inputs {calx-of-iron phlogiston ash} outputs {iron ash}). Given this formulation, the REDUCE rule would lead to (reacts inputs {calx-of-iron phlogiston} outputs {iron}), and the INFER-COMPONENTS rule would conclude that iron is composed of calx-of-iron and phlogiston. As before, the SUBSTITUTE rule is not restricted to substances composed of two elements, but works equally well for more complex structures.

Example: The Early Phlogiston Theory

Let us summarize the above inferences by examining the whole path taken by STAHL in arriving at the componential models of charcoal and iron of the early phlogiston theory. We present the system with two facts:

(reacts inputs {charcoal air} outputs {phlogiston ash air})

and

(reacts inputs {calx-of-iron charcoal air} outputs {iron ash air}).

One may question the exact representation of these facts, but clearly something very much like this was believed during the period in which the phlogiston theory was developed. We will address the inputs presented to the system in more detail below.

Given the above information, STAHL immediately applies its REDUCE operator to the first fact, giving the revised reaction (reacts inputs {charcoal} outputs {phlogiston ash}). This revision, combined with the INFER-COMPONENTS rule, leads to the inference that charcoal is composed of phlogiston and ash, which was one tenet of the early phlogiston theory. The system then applies its REDUCE operator to the second fact, giving the reduced reaction (reacts inputs {calx-of-iron charcoal} outputs {iron ash}). Having arrived at this conclusion, STAHL applies the SUBSTITUTE rule, generating the expanded description (reacts inputs {calx-of-iron ash phlogiston} outputs {iron ash}). At this point, the REDUCE rule is used to remove ash from both sides of the equation, giving (reacts inputs {calx-of-iron phlogiston} outputs {iron}). Finally, the INFER-COMPONENTS operator leads STAHL to infer that iron is a compound composed of calx-of-iron and phlogiston. Table 7.1 summarizes the states visited by the system in arriving at these conclusions, and the operators used to generate them.

Comments on STAHL's Inputs

Before we discuss additional models formulated by STAHL, we should comment on the way reactions are described in our examples.

We have been careful to use representations for reactions that have some justification in the literature of the period. For instance, by explicitly listing phlogiston as one of the products of combustion we follow the early chemists' understanding of combustion. The disengagement of fire was such a clear phenomenon that there was little doubt at the time that some form of matter left the combustible and escaped in the form of fire. Lavoisier agreed, too, that a substance disengages during combustion. He called this substance *caloric*, but he believed that it came from oxygen rather than from the combustible substance.

After chemists began to study combustion within closed vessels, they realized that air was necessary for combustion to occur. However, they did not at first believe that air changed its chemical identity during combustion. Rather, they decided that it played an auxiliary role, similar to that played

Table 7.1
STAHL's steps in formulating the phlogiston model.

Initial state S1:
(reacts inputs {charcoal air} outputs {phlogiston ash air})
(reacts inputs {calx-of-iron charcoal air} outputs {iron ash air})

REDUCE leads to state S2:
(reacts inputs {charcoal} outputs {phlogiston ash})
(reacts inputs {calx-of-iron charcoal air} outputs {iron ash air})

INFER-COMPONENTS leads to state S3:
(components of {charcoal} are {phlogiston ash})
(reacts inputs {calx-of-iron charcoal air} outputs {iron ash air})

REDUCE leads to state S4:
(components of {charcoal} are {phlogiston ash})
(reacts inputs {calx-of-iron charcoal} outputs {iron ash})

SUBSTITUTE leads to state S5:
(components of {charcoal} are {phlogiston ash})
(reacts inputs {calx-of-iron phlogiston ash} outputs {iron ash})

REDUCE leads to state S6:
(components of {charcoal} are {phlogiston ash})
(reacts inputs {calx-of-iron phlogiston} outputs {iron})

INFER-COMPONENTS leads to final state S7:
(components of {charcoal} are {phlogiston ash})
(components of {iron} are {calx-of-iron phlogiston})

by water in reactions involving acids, alkalis, and salts. Thus, even when they started with empirically more complete descriptions of combustion, such as "In the presence of air, charcoal burns to release phlogiston and to form ash," they disregarded air in the analysis of the reaction. The inference can be explained by STAHL's reduction heuristic, which removes the occurrence of air from both sides of the reaction. As a result, STAHL makes similar "errors" in reasoning, thus providing a simple account of the process by which chemists developed phlogiston-based models of combustion. (Such confusions are common in the history of chemistry; around 1810 a similar error, related to the presence of water, led the followers of Lavoisier to believe that sodium was a compound of soda and hydrogen.)

The phlogistians noted that some residual ash was left after the combustion of charcoal. Since a similar residuum was the product of any combustion, they inferred that phlogiston could never be found in pure form. (For Stahl, the purest donor of phlogiston was the soot from burning turpentine.) Thus, we will include a residual ash in all our descriptions of early-eighteenth-century reactions. Later in the century, as the samples of chemicals became purer, the "observed" reactions took on a different form, in which most of the residual substances were disregarded.

Incremental Processing of Data

One of STAHL's characteristic features is the manner in which its heuristics interact. The SUBSTITUTE rule requires knowledge of a substance's composition, so some inferences about composition must be made before it can be used. However, as we have also seen, complex reactions must be rewritten by the REDUCE and SUBSTITUTE rules before composition inferences can be made. This interdependence leads to a "bootstrapping" effect, in which inferences made by one of the rules make possible further inferences; these allow additional inferences, and so forth, until as many conclusions as possible have been reached. This process generally begins with one or more simple reactions to which INFER-COMPONENTS is applied, but after this the particular path taken depends on the data available to the system.

There is no limit to the length of the list of reactions that STAHL can work on, and after the list has been processed STAHL can take additional data and draw further conclusions from them, repeating this process at will. The more conclusions STAHL has collected, the more powerful its reasoning becomes, as it applies the componential models it has inferred to the analysis of other reactions. This incremental processing makes it possible to model long episodes in the history of chemistry. In our examples, the packages of data input to STAHL are ordered historically to reflect the growing experimental capabilties of chemistry throughout the eighteenth century. Let us consider some of the other phlogiston-related inferences replicated by STAHL.

Phlogiston in Lead and Sulfur

The early chemists believed that all combustible bodies contained phlogiston, since they emitted fire and heat upon burning. In addition, they believed that any metal produced in a reaction similar to that of charcoal and calx-of-iron also contained phlogiston. STAHL makes analogous inferences for these reactions.

For example, suppose we give the system the situation[5]

---

5. Litharge: an oxide of lead with the chemical formula PbO.

(reacts inputs {charcoal litharge} outputs {lead ash})

and the results from table 7.1. Given this reaction, together with the previous results, STAHL would apply the SUBSTITUTE rule to replace charcoal with its components, followed by REDUCE to cancel out both occurrences of ash. Finally, it would use INFER-COMPONENTS to conclude that lead is composed of litharge and phlogiston.

STAHL models the phlogistians' belief (Partington 1961–62, p. 671) that sulfur consisted of phlogiston and vitriolic acid by referring to the following reactions:[6]

(reacts inputs {vitriolic-acid potash} outputs {vitriolated-tartar}),

(reacts inputs {sulfur potash} outputs {liver-of-sulfur}),

(reacts inputs {vitriolated-tartar charcoal} outputs {liver-of-sulfur}).

Knowing already that charcoal contains phlogiston, STAHL reaches the same conclusion about the composition of sulfur as did G. E. Stahl: that sulfur consists of vitriolic acid and phlogiston (and ash, unless we see it as one of the products of the last of the above reactions, or disregard it, or use soot as an almost pure source of phlogiston). In this example, STAHL applies the INFER-COMPONENTS rule three times and, after reaching the second decomposition of liver-of-sulfur, applies SUBSTITUTE to the final reaction, giving

(reacts inputs {sulfur potash} outputs {vitriolated-tartar charcoal}).

At this point STAHL applies SUBSTITUTE, replacing first vitriolated tartar and then charcoal with their components. Finally, it employs REDUCE to eliminate potash from both sides of the reaction, obtaining the conclusion that sulfur is composed of phlogiston, vitriolic acid, and ash.

Identification Heuristics

Although STAHL's three basic rules—INFER-COMPONENTS, SUB-STITUTE, and REDUCE—account for many of the inferences that led to the phlogiston theory, they do not cover all such conclusions. The history of chemistry abounds with cases in which a substance was discovered in two different contexts, was originally thought to be two distinct

---

6. Vitriolic acid: sulfuric acid. Vitriolated tartar: potassium sulfate. Liver of sulfur: a carbonate of sulfur.

substances, and was eventually identified as a single substance. STAHL employs two heuristics to model this form of reasoning.[7] The first can be stated as

IDENTIFY-COMPONENTS
If A is composed of B and C,
  and A is composed of B and D,
  and neither C contains D nor D contains C,
then identify C with D.

This heuristic matches when STAHL concludes that a compound can be decomposed in two different ways, but with the decompositions differing by a only single substance. For instance, the identification of phlogiston with inflammable air played an important role in the development of the phlogiston theory. We will see shortly how this identification can be achieved with the rule IDENTIFY-COMPONENTS. The second heuristic is very similar, except that it applies when two apparently different compounds are found to have the same components. It can be paraphrased as

IDENTIFY-COMPOUNDS
If A is composed of C and D,
  and B is composed of C and D,
  and neither A contains B nor B contains A,
then identify A with B.

By the application of this rule, lime can be identified chemically with chalk and with calcite.

The early chemists acknowledged that changes similar to burning could be produced by the action of acids. Detailed studies of reactions involving solution in acids led to evidence confirming the phlogiston theory, and eventually, after the discovery of "inflammable air" (hydrogen) in 1766, to the identification of inflammable air with phlogiston. Before we can demonstrate the application of STAHL's identification heuristics in this context, we must consider STAHL's response to the chemical reactions involved in the discovery of inflammable air. Consider the reactions[8]

---

7. The philosophical criterion of Leibniz says that two things are identical if all their properties are the same. For chemical identity it would be enough if two substances had all chemical properties the same. STAHL operates on even weaker criteria of identity, as it does not make use of such properties as color or shape. Does this handicap the system in identifying substances? Not necessarily. Color or shape are not as essential chemical properties as participation in reactions.
8. Vitriol of iron: iron sulfate.

(reacts inputs {iron sulfuric-acid water} outputs {vitriol-of-iron inflammable-air water})

and

(reacts inputs {calx-of-iron sulfuric-acid water} outputs {vitriol-of-iron water}).

Given these facts in addition to some earlier inferences, STAHL removes the water from both reactions using the REDUCE rule. This simplifies the second reaction enough that the system can apply the INFER-COMPONENTS rule and can conclude that vitriol of iron is composed of calx of iron and sulfuric acid. This lets STAHL substitute the components of vitriol of iron into the first reaction to obtain the following: (reacts inputs {iron sulfuric-acid} outputs {calx-of-iron sulfuric-acid inflammable-air}). After using the REDUCE rule to eliminate sulfuric acid from both sides of this expression, STAHL infers that iron consists of calx of iron and in-flammable air. However, STAHL knows from the reactions described above that iron can also be decomposed into calx of iron and phlogi-ston. Thus, using the first of its identification heuristics (IDENTIFY-COMPONENTS), the system infers that inflammable air and phlogiston are identical. Both the reasoning and the conclusions of STAHL in this example are very similar to those of Cavendish and other phlogiston theorists during the 1760s.

In addition to individual reactions, the eighteenth-century chemists formulated schemes of reactions,[9] such as

metal + acid → inflammable air + salt   (7.1)

and

metallic-calx + acid → salt.   (7.2)

Metals were considered to be combinations of metallic calxes with phlogis-ton, and salts were believed to consist of bases and acids. Metallic calxes were classified as bases. From these assumptions, the identification of inflammable air with phlogiston gives the following underlying structure to reaction 7.1:

9. GLAUBER generates just such relational laws from specific reactions, and it might be used in conjunction with STAHL to model the generation of these higher-level chemical inferences. The ways in which GLAUBER and STAHL might interact are discussed further in chapter 9.

(phlogiston * metallic calx) + acid → phlogiston + (metallic calx * acid),

where the asterisk denotes chemical union and the "plus" sign denotes concatenation of two substances. This schema explained to the phlogistians why the changes produced by acids were similar to calcination and combustion. It also makes clear that no "inflammable air" effervesces in reaction 7.2 because, instead of a metal, its calx (metal deprived of phlogiston) is used in that reaction. Although STAHL is unable to generate laws from individual descriptions, it can construct componential models based on general schemes of reactions. Thus, on the basis of reactions 7.1 and 7.2, STAHL infers that salt consists of metallic calx and acid, and that metal consists of metallic calx and inflammable air. If STAHL also knows that metal consists of metallic calx and phlogiston, if concludes that phlogiston is identical with inflammable air.

Evidence for STAHL's Heuristics

As we have seen, STAHL's heuristics lead to conclusions very similar to those reached by the chemists of the eighteenth century. But are these the heuristics that were actually used by those chemists? Let us consider the evidence that they are.

Our motivation for using the INFER-COMPONENTS rule as the sole basis for structural conclusions relies on the nonambiguity of simple reactions and on empirical access to all the substances involved. Everywhere in the history of chemistry where a synthesis or decomposition reaction was interpreted, its conclusions were generally accepted unless somebody could show that some "hidden" reactant had been disregarded. For example, the discovery that calx of mercury decomposed into mercury and oxygen forced the phlogistians to alter their theory and to reject the notion that metallic calxes were elements.

However, the conclusions of INFER-COMPONENTS are not as certain when this rule is applied to the description of a reaction to which REDUCE was earlier applied. The REDUCE rule simplifies descriptions of reactions, thus making it possible to draw useful structural conclusions. However, there are situations in which REDUCE produces erroneous conclusions. For example, given the reactions

(reacts inputs {copper vitriolic-acid}
    outputs {sulfurous-acid vitriol-of-copper})   (7.3)

and

(reacts inputs {sulfurous-acid} outputs {vitriolic-acid phlogiston}), (7.4)

the program infers that

copper consists of vitriol-of-copper and phlogiston. (7.5)

Only if provided with knowledge about the composition of vitriol of copper (which consists of vitriolic acid and calx of copper) could the system make the correct reduction and infer that

copper consists of calx-of-copper and phlogiston. (7.6)

In other words, the REDUCE rule leads to errors in cases where different amounts of a substance are observed before and after a reaction. From our point of view, such mistaken behavior on STAHL's part is desirable, since similar errors were common in the eighteenth century and the REDUCE heuristic provides a simple account of their origin.[10] However, these errors were eventually noted and corrected, and STAHL must have a similar resilience if it is to retain historical accuracy. We will consider the system's error-recovery methods in a later section.

Using the REDUCE rule, we can model several important cases of reasoning in which similar errors were actually made. Water or air that was present on both sides of a reaction was routinely canceled until it became clear that these substances not only were necessary environments of reactions but also had their chemical structures changed during reaction. Even long after the oxygen-phlogiston dispute had been resolved, at the beginning of the nineteenth century, we can see examples of this error. After Humphry Davy decomposed potash into potassium and oxygen in 1807, Joseph Gay-Lussac and Louis Thenard (1808, 1810) argued that potassium was a compound of potash with hydrogen. Their goal was to defend Lavoisier's view of oxygen as the principle of acidity. Given the appropriate data, STAHL repeats their reasoning. From the premises

(reacts inputs {potassium water} outputs {caustic-potash hydrogen
    water}),

(reacts inputs {caustic-potash water} outputs {potassium oxygen}),

10. One can imagine more conservative versions of the heuristic that would require equal amounts of the canceled substance to occur on each side of the reaction. However, since this form of the rule would require quantitative data, it would fail to explain most of the eighteenth-century qualitative inferences.

(reacts inputs {potassium ammonia} outputs {hydrogen green-solid}),

and

(reacts inputs {green-solid water} outputs {caustic-potash ammonia
    water}),

STAHL reaches the same conclusion as Gay-Lussac and Thenard: that potassium consists of caustic potash and hydrogen. The second reaction here is a modification of Davy's description (justified by disbelief in the success of Davy's attempts at making caustic potash absolutely dry before applying his source of electricity). In fact, the conclusion of Gay-Lussac and Thenard can be derived from the first premise, from the second premise (using the assumption that water consists of hydrogen and oxygen), or from the final two reactions.

We could postulate rules that would make conjectures about the components of chemicals by hypothesizing the exchange of hidden substances during reactions. Such rules could be useful for modeling chemical research in the seventeenth century or earlier, but there seems to be neither a historical justification nor an inferential need for such rules in dealing with eighteenth-century chemistry.

The Control Structure of STAHL

Applying the heuristics of STAHL to a set of reactions may lead to different conclusions along alternate inference paths, to inconsistencies, or to infinite recursion. STAHL avoids many of these difficulties by employing a particular control structure, which we consider in detail below. However, this strategy is not sufficient to avoid all difficulties, so the system also contains an error-recovery mechanism.

The emergence of such difficulties should not be regarded as a deficiency of STAHL. Similar difficulties have been common in the history of chemistry. Whereas many of these difficulties were resolved only with the help of new methods of inquiry and new experimental evidence, STAHL is limited to working with the data it is given.

Testing Models for Consistency

STAHL processes one reaction at a time, generating as many inferences as possible from this new information. After the system has applied all its rules to the reaction, it checks the resulting componential models for internal consistency and for consistency with the componential models that have been accumulated from previous analyses. For instance, STAHL might infer that A consists of B and C *and* that A consists of B, C, and D. Obviously, both componential models cannot be correct. In still other cases, the system may generate an individual conclusion that is internally inconsistent. Two examples of such inferences are (reacts inputs { } outputs {A}) and (reacts inputs {A} outputs { }). In each of these cases, the principle of conservation of types of substances is violated. The source of these "inconsistencies" is either an error in the input to STAHL or an inappropriate application of REDUCE. STAHL's methods for avoiding such difficulties, and for recovering from them when they occur, will be discussed below.

If STAHL fails to construct a componential model based on a given reaction, it drops any intermediate conclusions and remembers the reaction in its original form until new information becomes available. This conservative procedure provides some protection against errors introduced by REDUCE, since the availability of more componential models at the later time will lower the chance of error in both intermediate and final conclusions. Such a practice seems to be historically justified, since the chemical reactions were considered over and over again and were recorded in their original perceived form rather than in a form partially transformed by analysis.

If the application of REDUCE brings the description of a reaction into the form (reacts inputs { } outputs { }), this means that the input and the output of the reaction have canceled each other by reduction. This welcome outcome confirms the structural knowledge collected by STAHL in the earlier phases of computation. (More precise, the part of the knowledge that was used in applying the SUBSTITUTE rule to the initial form of the reaction has been confirmed.)

Difficulties Arising from Multiple Inference Paths

When several heuristics can be applied to the same reaction, they sometimes produce different results. For example, suppose STAHL knows that (components-of {sulfurous-acid} are {vitriolic-acid phlogiston}) and then is given the reaction (reacts inputs {sulfur air} outputs {sulfurous-acid phlogiston air}). Applying the REDUCE rule and then INFER-COMPONENTS, the system would conclude that (components-of {sulfur} are {sulfurous-acid phlogiston}). In contrast, applying SUB-STITUTE, REDUCE, and INFER-COMPONENTS, it would conclude that (components-of {sulfur} are {vitriolic-acid phlogiston}). Both conclusions are correct within the framework of the phlogiston theory. In fact, using the first conclusion together with the premise that sulfurous acid consists of vitriolic acid and phlogiston, one can infer (and thus explain) the second conclusion. However, the reverse is not true; from the second conclusion, one cannot infer, and hence cannot explain, the first.

STAHL employs a well-defined control structure to deal with inconsistency in conclusions and with the choice among multiple conclusions reached through alternative inference paths. For every new reaction it encounters, STAHL tries to apply several methods (inference paths) and then to test and compare the results. The first method STAHL tries to apply is INFER-COMPONENTS. Its result is not a matter of dispute, as the conclusion is based on direct empirical data. If INFER-COMPONENTS cannot be applied, STAHL tries other methods—basically (a) apply REDUCE first, then INFER-COMPONENTS, and (b) apply SUB-STITUTE first, then REDUCE, and finally INFER-COMPONENTS. In fact, the number of alternative conclusions obtained from a reaction may be even greater, since SUBSTITUTE can be applied to different chemicals involved in a given reaction, or can be applied several times in succession. Neither method a nor method b is *a priori* superior to the other. That is, there are cases in which method a brings the correct result and the result of application of b is incorrect and cases in which method b produces the correct conclusion. For this reason, both methods have to be considered whenever possible.

After STAHL has applied all these methods to the current reaction, it checks the results for consistency with the componential models accumulated from previous analyses. The system then divides these into acceptable and unacceptable results, depending on whether they pass the test of consistency. There may also be no result (that is, no conclusion in the form of a componential model) when a method is applied to a reaction. If there is exactly one acceptable result, it is accepted by the system. If there are no acceptable results but some that are unacceptable, STAHL enters its automated self-correction procedure, which will be described in the next subsection.

If STAHL obtains multiple acceptable results, it tries to choose the best of them. The best result is one that is acceptable and that explains away all the other acceptable results on the basis of the following mechanism: Suppose that R1 and R2 are two different componential models obtained from a reaction by the use of inference paths P1 and P2, respectively, and D is the set of componential models inferred by the system in the past. In order to choose between R1 and R2, STAHL substitutes R2 into the current reaction and then tries to apply P1 once again, using D as before. If the reaction is now reduced to empty input and empty output, it can be argued that R2 has received an additional confirmation. If the reaction is now transformed into an inconsistent conclusion, it can be argued that R2 is to blame. Of course, by symmetry, the second inference path, P2, is examined next, together with R1. If either R1 or R2 is found to be better, it is accepted and added to the set D of the confirmed componential models. If neither R1 nor R2 is found to be better by this procedure, then both inferences are rejected and the reaction that led to them is reconsidered after new data become available.

In the light of this procedure, let us reconsider the example of burning sulfur. Reconsidering the second result, (components-of {sulfur} are {vitriolic-acid phlogiston}), STAHL substitutes it into the sulfur burning reaction. The application of the first inference path (REDUCE followed by INFER-COMPONENTS) ends with a dubious claim that vitriolic acid is identical with sulphurous acid. Reconsidering the first result, (components-of {sulfur} are {sulfurous-acid phlogiston}), the system substitutes it into the sulfur-burning reaction and repeats the second inference path. The initial reaction is reduced to empty input and empty output, thereby confirming the premises. Thus, the first result is accepted and the second rejected. In this case, STAHL will later rederive the rejected conclusion by substituting the previously known components of sulfurous acid (vitriolic-acid and phlogiston) into the componential model for sulfur. Usually, however, the rejected conclusion is not later reinstated.

Using a reaction involving potassium—considered by Gay-Lussac and Thenard—in which (reacts inputs {potassium water} outputs {caustic-potash hydrogen water}), let us consider briefly another case of competing inferences. By applying the first inference path, STAHL infers that potassium consists of caustic potash and hydrogen. Knowing that water consists of hydrogen and oxygen and applying the second inference path, STAHL concludes that potassium is identical with caustic potash. Now STAHL reconsiders both inferences. Using the second result and the first inference path, it obtains the inconsistent result (reacts inputs { } outputs {hydrogen}). However, when the first result and the second inference path are used, the initial reaction reduces to empty input and empty output. Thus, the system rejects the second result and chooses the first one, obtaining Gay-Lussac's model of potassium as a compound of caustic potash and hydrogen.

STAHL adds consistent results to its data base for use in future reasoning; it rejects problematic inferences, and it passes inconsistent results on to its error-recovery mechanisms. Although a given reaction may not lead to inferences when first introduced, it is retained in memory and may cause STAHL to draw new conclusions when additional data are added. At each point in its processing, the system's memory contains a list of beliefs about which substances are primitive elements and about the components of nonelemental substances.

When all the reactions have been considered, some of them may remain unanalyzed. In this case, STAHL applies the same cycle to the remaining data recursively. When no more componential models can be found, the system prints out the structural knowledge it has inferred and halts.

Recovering from Inconsistencies

As mentioned, STAHL recognizes two types of inconsistency: models for the same substances but with different components, and reduced reactions with inputs but no output or with outputs but no input. Upon realizing that it has generated such an error, the system collects all the original reactions that contain the substances involved in the inconsistency. It then reconsiders the reactions—this time using all the structural knowledge it had already collected, omitting only the inconsistent componential models. Since the knowledge of the system is now larger than at the time when these reactions were first considered, most of these reactions will quickly reduce to the form of empty input and output. However, this will not occur for all of the data, and usually the resultant componential models will be consistent and the problem resolved.

Let us reconsider the example of vitriol of copper (reactions 7.3 and 7.4). The system inferred that copper consists of vitriol of copper and phlogiston (7.5) and then inferred, on the basis of other evidence, that copper consists of calx of copper and phlogiston (7.6). Suppose that, still later, STAHL concluded that vitriol of copper consists of calx of copper and vitriolic acid. This model, combined by inheritance (substitution) with inference 7.5, generates a result inconsistent with inference 7.6, and this triggers the recovery mechanism. As a result, STAHL reconsiders its knowledge that copper and vitriolic acid react to form sulfurous acid and vitriol of copper (7.3) and that sulfurous acid decomposes into vitriolic acid and phlogiston (7.4). On the basis of its knowledge of the components of vitriol of copper, the system concludes that copper consists of calx of copper and phlogiston. Therefore, inference 7.5 is rejected and inference 7.6 is retained, because STAHL is able to apply the componential model of vitriol of copper—an additional piece of knowledge that was inferred in the meantime.

This process is different from the method of dependency-directed backtracking used in some nonmonotonic reasoning systems (Stallman and Sussman 1977; Doyle 1979). STAHL does not keep track of its inferences, because it models a collective subject over spans of decades rather than a single chemist in time limited to days or weeks. Even a single chemist would have a hard time remembering which inference path he used fifteen years before, and it would be often impossible for him to know another chemist's exact way of reasoning. Dependency-directed backtracking is much more efficient then the scheme used by STAHL; however, science is not organized as neatly as computer data bases, and such strong methods are more difficult to employ.

Dealing with Circular Definitions

It has already been mentioned as a possibility that STAHL may enter an infinite loop or recursion. For instance, given certain reactions involving mercury, calx of mercury, and oxygen,[11] STAHL eventually makes two inferences:

(components of {mercury} are {calx-of-mercury phlogiston})

and

(components of {calx-of-mercury} are {mercury oxygen}).

Taken together, these two inferences imply that mercury is composed of oxygen, phlogiston, and itself. It seems undesirable that an explanatory model should reach such a conclusion.

Infinite recursion does not indicate logical inconsistency. The program applies SUBSTITUTE indefinitely, but at no point does this produce

11. Later versions of the phlogiston theory included oxygen as an element but retained phlogiston as their central feature.

logically contradictory results. Why then do we regard this situation as unsatisfactory? First, an infinite substitution violates our intuitions about the nature of elements (that is, of the existence of primitive substances from which all others are composed). Second, infinite recursion is technically bothersome. It forces the programmer to interrupt processing in an ad hoc manner if he wants the program to continue down more useful paths. Any intervention by the programmer violates the goal of an independently acting computational model.

The recovery method used by STAHL involves four basic components: recognizing the trouble, localizing its source, choosing the recovery procedure, and finally applying the procedure and checking whether the problem has been corrected. As before, we have attempted to implement this process so that it simulates the historical developments in chemistry as closely as possible.

STAHL recognizes cases of infinite recursion by keeping track of the number of levels it has recursed and exiting after reaching a threshold. Upon exiting, the system collects structural facts that may be responsible for the difficulty. In the case of the decomposition of red precipitate of mercury, these facts are (a) that mercury consists of calx of mercury and phlogiston and (b) that calx of mercury consists of mercury and oxygen. Now the system identifies the reactions from which these componential models were drawn, and it divides the componential models into those obtained by direct inference from simple reactions and those supported by the use of the SUBSTITUTE-REDUCE technique. The latter models are more dubious, as they are "less observational" than the inferences in the first group. In our example, fact b is recognized as observational and fact a as derived. The derived fact is reinterpreted under a general strategy: "In case of inconsistency, make a conceptual distinction." In our case, the derived component of fact a is the underlying structure of mercury. Then, calx of mercury is the only substance recurring in facts a and b that is a candidate for reinterpretation. STAHL replaces it in fact a with the new substance "calx-of mercury-proper" (of course, this name is specified by the programmer).[12] As a result, fact a is replaced by "mercury consists of

12. In some sense, this process of discrimination is similar to BACON's introduction of new intrinsic properties when it encounters a situation in which its numerical methods fail to apply. As with BACON, such concepts introduced by STAHL may appear tautological when first introduced, but become respectable to the extent that they prove useful in dealing with other situations besides the one that led to their introduction.

calx-of-mercury-proper and phlogiston," while fact b remains unchanged.

After introducing a conceptual distinction such as this, STAHL replays the inference process that led to the infinite recursion in order to ensure that the alteration has had the desired effect. If it has, the system then resumes its main mode and continues processing new reactions.

STAHL's strategy for dealing with infinite recursions reproduces historic lines of reasoning for the case of metallic calxes. Still, it might be an ad hoc solution, created to deal with this particular problem. We can claim that our solution represents a method characteristic of eighteenth-century chemistry only if the same mechanism deals adequately with other historical cases. Let us consider an episode that occurred three decades later and involved the followers of Lavoisier.

As was mentioned above, Gay-Lussac and Thenard claimed that potassium consisted of potash and hydrogen, and Davy demonstrated that by the use of electricity potash could be decomposed into potassium and oxygen. These componential models formed a troublesome pair, analogous to the one involving mercury and its calx that had given the phlogistians a hard time 35 years earlier. The solution of Gay-Lussac and Thenard was also analogous to that developed by the phlogistians. They claimed that in Davy's experiment the potash had not been pure but had been saturated with water. Here STAHL applies the same reasoning as in the case of calx of mercury and infers that Davy's potash consisted of potash proper and water.

Beyond the Phlogiston Theory

Now that we have examined STAHL's behavior in the context of the phlogiston theory, let us see whether the same reasoning can be used to model different episodes in the history of chemistry, such as the development of Lavoisier's oxygen theory of combustion and its implications for the phlogiston theory. But before we investigate the oxygen theory, let us consider some work by Joseph Black and Claude Berthollet.

Black on Magnesia Alba

In his important work on alkaline substances and fixed air (carbon dioxide), Black (1756) drew several important conclusions about the underlying structures of alkaline substances, and made an analogy between fixed air and acids based on the similar patterns of their reactions with alkalies.

We have chosen the following eight reactions to model Black's reasoning:

(reacts inputs {lime} outputs {quicklime fixed-air}),

(reacts inputs {quicklime magnesia-alba} outputs {lime calcined-magnesia}),[13]

(reacts inputs {quicklime salt-of-tartar} outputs {lime caustic-potash}),

(reacts inputs {lime vitriolic-acid} outputs {gypsum fixed-air}),

(reacts inputs {magnesia-alba vitriolic-acid} outputs {epsom-salt fixed-air}),

(reacts inputs {quicklime vitriolic-acid} outputs {gypsum}),

(reacts inputs {calcined-magnesia vitriolic-acid} outputs {epsom-salt}),

(reacts inputs {caustic-potash epsom-salt} outputs {calcined-magnesia vitriolated-tartar}).

Let us consider in detail the operation of STAHL's heuristics on the first two of these reactions. The INFER-COMPONENTS rule applies first, leading to the inference that lime ($CaCO_3$) is composed of quicklime (CaO) and fixed air (CO_2). This result enables the SUBSTITUTE heuristic to match, producing a temporarily more complex version of the second reaction:

(reacts inputs {quicklime magnesia-alba} outputs {quicklime fixed-air calcined-magnesia}).

However, since the substance quicklime occurs in both sides of the modified reaction, the REDUCE rule applies, transforming it into the simpler form

(reacts inputs {magnesia-alba} outputs {fixed-air calcined-magnesia}).

Finally, this reduced form allows the INFER-COMPONENTS rule to infer that magnesia alba is composed of fixed air (CO_2) and calcined magnesia (MgO). At this point, since no more of its heuristics apply, STAHL concludes that it has formulated as many componential models as the data allow, and halts its operation. The system's behavior on this example is summarized in table 7.2.

Considering the remaining six reactions and following similar lines of

13. Magnesia alba is magnesium carbonate, $MgCO_3$.

Table 7.2
Inferring the composition of lime and magnesia alba.

Initial State S1:
(reacts inputs {lime} outputs {quicklime fixed-air})
(reacts inputs {quicklime magnesia-alba} outputs {lime calcined-magnesia})

INFER-COMPONENTS leads to state S2:
Components-of {lime} are {quicklime fixed-air})
(reacts inputs {quicklime magnesia-alba} outputs {lime calcined-magnesia})

SUBSTITUTE leads to state S3:
(components-of {lime} are {quicklime fixed-air})
(reacts inputs {quicklime magnesia-alba} outputs {quicklime fixed-air calcined-magnesia})

REDUCE leads to state S4:
(components-of {lime} are {quicklime fixed-air})
(reacts inputs {magnesia-alba} outputs {fixed-air calcined-magnesia})

INFER-COMPONENTS leads to final state S5:
(components-of {lime} are {quicklime fixed-air})
(components-of {magnesia-alba} are {fixed-air calcined-magnesia})

reasoning, STAHL arrives at the following conclusions:

lime consists of quick-lime and fixed-air,

magnesia-alba consists of calcined-magnesia and fixed-air,

salt-of-tartar consists of caustic-potash and fixed-air,

gypsum consists of quick-lime and vitriolic-acid,

epsom-salt consists of calcined-magnesia and vitriolic-acid,

vitriolated-tartar consists of caustic-potash and vitriolic-acid.

Providing STAHL with the additional reactions (reacts inputs {calcite vitriolic-acid} outputs {gypsum fixed-air}) and (reacts inputs {chalk vitriolic-acid} outputs {gypsum fixed-air}) enables it to draw the conclusions that chalk consist of quicklime and fixed air and that calcite consists of quicklime and fixed air, and then to identify lime with chalk and with calcite by applying its IDENTIFY-COMPOUNDS rule.

In addition to all these componential models, Black formulated general laws such as "a caustic alkali becomes mild after being saturated with fixed air." In order to generate such laws, STAHL would have to define general classes and qualitative laws that summarized conclusions about individual substances. This form of reasoning is similar to that employed by GLAUBER, so one can imagine a version of STAHL combined with GLAUBER to replicate this aspect of Black's reasoning. (See chapter 9.)

Berthollet on Chlorine

In 1774, Karl Wilhelm Scheele added marine acid (hydrochloric acid) to manganese (actually manganese dioxide), obtaining a brownish liquid (Scheele 1786). On heating, the liquid became colorless and a gas was expelled, signaling a chemical change that Scheele interpreted as a transfer of phlogiston from the acid to the oxide. We can write this as

(reacts inputs {manganese marine-acid} outputs {phlogisticated-
   manganese dephlogisticated-marine-acid}).

Scheele interpreted the expelled gas (which we call chlorine) as "dephlo-
gisticated" marine acid (i.e., marine acid with all phlogiston removed), but Lavoisier and his followers viewed the substance as a compound of marine acid and oxygen. Berthollet (1788) conducted several experiments, which convinced him that Lavoisier's view was correct. His results can be stated as

(reacts inputs {chlorine water} outputs {oxymuriatic-acid water}),

(reacts inputs {oxymuriatic-acid water} outputs {muriatic-acid oxygen
   water}),

(reacts inputs {black-manganese) outputs {calcined-manganese
   oxygen}),

(reacts inputs {black-manganese muriatic-acid water} outputs {salt-of-
   manganese chlorine water}),

(reacts inputs {calcined-manganese muriatic-acid water} outputs {salt-
   of-manganese water}).

When presented with these reactions, STAHL reaches a conclusion similar to that of Berthollet: that chlorine consists of muriatic-acid and oxygen. This inference can be drawn from the first two reactions. It is also confirmed by the last three reactions, since the fourth reaction will finally reduce to (reacts inputs { } outputs { }) when STAHL applies to it Berthollet's model of chlorine.

Lavoisier's Caloric Theory and the Discovery of Oxygen

In 1773 Joseph Priestley (1774) experimented with the red calx of mercury (called red precipitate) and obtained the element oxygen, which

phlogistians later termed dephlogisticated air. This important reaction can be stated as

(reacts inputs {red-calx-of-mercury} outputs {mercury oxygen}).

The conclusions of this experiment challenged the claim that metallic calxes were elements. Priestley's result also challenged the phlogistians to identify the source of the phlogiston that produced mercury, one of the products of the reaction. In response to these difficulties, and in response to Cavendish's (1784, 1785) findings on the composition of water, the theory of phlogiston was modified and improved over the years from 1775 to 1785.

The impact of Priestley's experiment was discussed in the section on circular definitions. Interestingly, the very experiment that caused the phlogistians to change their theory leads STAHL into a troublesome infinite loop. We made STAHL recover from this crisis in essentially the same way that the phlogistians did. Then STAHL was able to follow the further development of the phlogiston theory, including the final version proposed by Cavendish (1784, 1785).

Now that we have STAHL's response to these new findings within the framework of the phlogiston theory, let us outline the development of Lavoisier's (1789) oxygen theory. STAHL can easily reconstruct what is usually accepted as Lavoisier's reasoning on oxides and oxidation. Given the reactions

(reacts inputs {calx-of-lead} outputs {lead oxygen})

and

(reacts inputs {calx-of-lead charcoal} outputs {lead fixed-air}),

STAHL reaches the conclusions that calx of lead consists of lead and oxygen and that fixed air consists of charcoal and oxygen. STAHL's ability to reconstruct these conclusions about combustion calls into question Lavoisier's claim that exact, quantitative measurements are both necessary and sufficient to prove the correctness of his theory of combustion and to reject the views of the phlogistians. In fact, weighing was not performed as carefully as was claimed by proponents of the quantitative method, either during the culmination of the phlogiston-oxygen dispute in 1780s or 20 years later.

The conclusions just cited are not quite those reached by Lavoisier. But we cannot blame STAHL, since the patterns of the reactions that we gave to the system are also not Lavoisier's. For Lavoisier, combustion was a decomposition of oxygen-gas, and the pattern of combustion and reduction was

combustible + oxygen-gas → oxide + caloric,

where oxygen-gas consists of oxygen-principle and caloric.[14] Calcination of metals was conceived in the same way:

metal + oxygen-gas → metallic-oxide + caloric,

where metallic-oxide is a compound of oxygen-principle and metal. Lavoisier viewed the creation of acids in a similar way. For him, caloric was an important chemical agent, and his descriptions of combustion and calcination reactions all involved it. Such reactions can be written as

(reacts inputs {calx-of-lead caloric} outputs {lead oxygen-gas}),

(reacts inputs {calx-of-lead charcoal caloric} outputs {lead fixed-air}),

(reacts inputs {charcoal oxygen-gas} outputs {fixed-air caloric}),

(reacts inputs {water charcoal caloric} outputs {hydrogen-gas fixed-air}),

and

(reacts inputs {water iron caloric} outputs {hydrogen-gas oxide-of-iron}).
$$(7.7)$$

These data are not sufficient for STAHL to draw any conclusions, and they were indeed not sufficient for Lavoisier to argue that the caloric in the third reaction came from oxygen gas rather than from charcoal. Lavoisier's belief that oxygen gas contained caloric was based on his earlier idea of caloric as the principle of the gaseous form of matter. He noticed that in many reactions in which the input is heated, some kind of air is disengaged, and that in reactions in which an air is absorbed, fire or heat is disengaged. In short: Fire in, gas out; fire out, gas in. In conclusion: Any gas contains caloric.

14. From a phenomenological standpoint (as Lavoisier himself noted), caloric—like phlogiston—evidenced itself as "matter of fire." But whereas the phlogistians found the source of the "matter of fire" in the combustible or the metal, Lavoisier found it in the oxygen gas. This change of interpretation could not have taken place before oxygen was determined to be an actual participant in (and not a mere condition for) the combustion or calcination process. Nor did the introduction of oxygen into the descriptions of the reactions immediately require a reinterpretation of the source of the "matter of fire."

STAHL has no capability for considering properties like "gaseous-form," and is not able to generalize about classes of substances. However, if we supply STAHL with statements like "Oxygen-gas consists of oxygen-principle and caloric," then many of STAHL's findings on the composition of substances are the same as Lavoisier's. For example, STAHL concludes from this statement and from the first of reactions 7.7 that calx of lead is composed of lead and oxygen-principle. Lavoisier's reasoning is difficult to model with STAHL, because the French chemist made extensive use of generalizations (all acids contain oxygen, all gases contain caloric) and on several occasions accepted the conclusions of a generalization rather than facts that contradicted it.

The Final Years of Phlogiston

Between 1785 and 1795, most of the supporters of the phlogiston theory abandoned it and accepted the theory of oxygen instead, although they did so to varying extents. Historians and philosophers of science have proposed many explanations of this development (see, e.g., Musgrave 1976; Krajewski 1977; Zytkow and Lewenstam 1982), but their accounts are beyond the scope of the current version of STAHL. STAHL can, however, provide justification for a theory proposed during this transitional period that was meant to satisfy both sides in the conflict by suggesting that each of the two theories embodied some truth.

Suppose we provide STAHL with the following information: (a) Lavoisier's general pattern for calcination of metals (see the preceding section), (b) his belief that metallic-oxide consisted of metal and oxygen-principle, (c) his belief that oxygen-gas consisted of oxygen-principle and caloric, and (d) the componential model of metals of the phlogiston theory in its 1780s version (that is, the claim that a metal consisted of its proper calx and phlogiston). Upon substituting b, c, and d into a, STAHL would produce the general structure

(metallic-calx-proper * phlogiston) + (oxygen-principle * caloric)
→ (metallic-calx-proper * phlogiston * oxygen-principle) + caloric,

which can be reduced to empty input and output, confirming the admissibility of its premises. This schema, proposed by John Gadolin in the 1790s, fits the empirical data as well as either the oxygen or the phlogiston theory. Although this theory never gained wide acceptance, it shows that there was no inherent reason why the notions of phlogiston and oxygen could not be combined in a single framework.

Limitations of Stahl

Although STAHL incorporates an important part of the eighteenth-century methods for theorizing about the composition of substances, there are several aspects of eighteenth-century reasoning that the system cannot handle. A number of these limitations were mentioned above. Some of them are easy to remedy; overcoming others would require substantial additions to the model.

As we have seen, the early chemists formulated general laws, such as Lavoisier's statement that combustion involved the combination of combustible substances with oxygen to generate an oxide and caloric. STAHL cannot make generalizations, but general qualitative laws are the main concern of GLAUBER, which uses exactly the same format for its data as STAHL. Thus, one can imagine a combined system in which the STAHL component passes its results to the GLAUBER component, which would then formulate general laws like Lavoisier's. In turn, laws produced by GLAUBER could be passed back to STAHL, which treats general terms such as metal, acid, and alkali in exactly the same way it treats specific substances such as iron, chlorine, and potash. (See chapter 9.) For example, given the schema

(reacts inputs {caustic-alkali fixed-air} outputs {mild-alkali}),

which might be generated by the GLAUBER system, STAHL would conclude that mild alkali consists of caustic alkali and fixed air.

The current version of STAHL does not deal with *affinities* (measures of the relative attractions of different substances of one class for the substances of another). Affinities were the subject of a very lively (and inconclusive) controversy during the eighteenth century. We believe that the ability to make inferences about affinity could be added to STAHL with very little effort. After collecting facts on the internal structures of chemicals, STAHL is in an ideal position to reconsider the reactions already processed and to look for exchange reactions of the form[15]

$(A * B) + C \rightarrow A + (B * C),$

which are the major source of inferences about affinity. The program need only be supplemented by a few additional heuristics and perhaps some adjustments to its control mechanism.

---

15. The example cited shows B having a great affinity for C than for A, and C having a greater affinity for B than for A.

At similarly low cost, STAHL could be supplemented with two other facilities. First, it could be extended to explain reactions themselves by applying the SUBSTITUTE rule to the description of the reaction, giving forms like that for the exchange relation above. Second, it could be modified to predict the outputs of a reaction from its inputs, using componential models and its knowledge of affinities.

In its current form, STAHL cannot consider properties of substances such ⸰ as shape, taste, and color. There are several episodes from the history of chemistry in which such properties were used in arguing about components of chemicals. For Lavoisier, acid taste was a very strong argument for the presence of oxygen in a substance and aeriform state indicated the presence of caloric. STAHL is not able to reach these conclusions, but it can accept them in the form of explicitly added componential models:

(components-of {acid} are {acid-radical oxygen-principle})

and

(components-of {gas} are {gas-radical caloric}).

It can use these models as premises for further inferences. The example of caloric as the principle of elastic fluids was considered above.

Another limitation is that the present incarnation of STAHL must rely entirely on data provided by an experimenter. In the course of using its error-recovery mechanisms it may question some of these data, but the task of verifying and improving them is then passed back to the experimenter. An experimenter must be able to recognize (identify) substances and able to produce a given reaction. He is also responsible for selecting the right amounts of substances so that neither input substance remains in the output. This is essential; STAHL would fail miserably in dealing with reactions that contained redundant amounts of a substance. This again raises the issue of quantitative measurement, which was applied by both sides in the phlogiston conflict. However indirectly, the early chemists (and STAHL) used the results of precise weight measurements in order to make their reactions as simple as possible. For example, (reacts inputs {sulfur iron} outputs {sulfur sulfuretted-iron}) can be simplified to the form (reacts inputs {sulfur iron} outputs {sulfuretted-iron}) if proper quantities of sulfur and iron enter the reaction. This process of refining chemical reactions was an important part of the experimental art during the 1770s and the 1780s; the phlogistians used balances no less accurate than Lavoisier's, and they estimated empirical error realistically (Cavendish 1784, 1785; see also Nicholson's preface to Kirwan 1789).

Finally, STAHL is limited to considering one line of theoretical development at a time; it is not able to compare two different views. The current version routinely considers different inference paths for each reaction, and chooses the best componential model, but it does not keep different solutions for further consideration. Therefore it cannot choose between theories, and in particular it cannot model the resolution of the oxygen-phlogiston conflict in favor of either side. Future versions of the system should be able to retain at least a few competing sets of models and test them on their ability to explain new reactions.

Conclusion

In discussing BACON we claimed only that the system embodies mechanisms that are sufficient for making certain kinds of discoveries. Although we used historical examples to test the capabilities of these mechanisms, we did not claim that they follow closely the original path of historical discovery. In the case of STAHL, we believe the claims can go a little farther. The program traces in detail several historical paths of discovery. It provides an explication of alternative conceptualizations of a research domain, and hence of alternative assumptions that characterized competing schools of thought.

STAHL incorporates specific knowledge about the constitution of objects and the conservation of basic substances. It constructs explanations in the form of descriptions of underlying structures of substances and reactions. At the beginning it is driven by data, but after it has made conjectures about the hidden structures it is also driven by these conjectures—that is, by theory. It employs general-purpose heuristics, and it can use them to choose among multiple conclusions and to deal with some of the inconsistencies in its results.

Applying STAHL to the study of eighteenth-century chemical theorizing, we find considerable consistency in the modes of reasoning used by different chemists, even when they reached different conclusions. In the case of the conflict between the phlogiston and the oxygen theory of combustion, it appears that the proponents of the two theories reasoned in essentially similar ways and differed mainly in their assumptions. The phlogistians believed "matter of fire" to be an essential constituent of metals that was driven off during calcination. The oxygen theorists assumed "matter of fire" (which they renamed "caloric") to be an essential constituent of "pure air" that was driven off when the air combined with combustible material. Because of the difference in assumptions, the same rules of reasoning applied to the same reaction could bring different conclusions.

The reasoning embodied in STAHL's heuristics is not peculiar to the theory of combustion. By examining other events of eighteenth-century chemistry, such as Black's analysis of magnesia alba, we have shown that the same principles of inference were used by chemists quite widely in their search for consistent accounts of the chemical substances and their reactions.

8 Formulating Structural Models

As an area of science matures, researchers progress from descriptions to explanations (Hempel 1965). Although the dividing line between these forms of understanding is fuzzy, some examples clearly lie at the explanatory end of the spectrum. For instance, the kinetic theory of heat provides an explanation of both Black's law and the ideal-gas law. A simpler example (though it was no less impressive at the time it was proposed) is Dalton's atomic theory, which provides explanations for the law of simple multiple proportions and Gay-Lussac's law of combining volumes. Each of these examples involves a structural model in which macroscopic phenomena are described in terms of their inferred components. Although this is not the only form of scientific explanation, the notion of structural models seems significant enough to merit detailed exploration. We will take the atomic theory as our main example.

In chapter 4, BACON.4 rediscovered, in a wholly data-driven manner, the concepts of molecular and atomic weight, and assigned correct weights to many substances. The analysis was purely phenomenological and descriptive, involving no appeal to a particulate model of chemical elements and compounds. What took the place of the atomic model was a heuristic that searched for small integer ratios among corresponding properties (e.g., combining weights and volumes) of substances. The method of BACON.4 was not unlike the method used by Cannizzaro in 1860 to calculate atomic weights, also without explicit appeal to an atomic hypothesis (although there is no question but that Cannizzaro actually arrived at his idea by way of Avogadro's atomic theory).

Now we will return to history and examine the role that theory actually played in determining (and impeding the determination of) atomic weights. The main events were reviewed in chapter 4 from the phenomenological standpoint of that chapter. We reconsider them briefly here in terms of the underlying explanatory models that were proposed and debated.

The Atomic Theory Revisited

As we have seen, a portion of the atomic hypothesis was implicit in componential models such as the phlogiston theory; however, the full version of the atomic model was first published by John Dalton in 1808. In order to explain the law of multiple proportions, Dalton assumed that substances were composed of particles called atoms, and focused on the numbers of particles making up a molecule of each substance and on their weights.

The key point in Dalton's atomic theory was that chemical compounds were of particulate nature, being combinations of small numbers of particles of their constituent elements. All elementary particles of a given chemical substance, it was further assumed, were identical in weight, size, and other properties. Thus, Dalton took a particle of water to consist of one particle of oxgen and one of hydrogen.

In those cases where a pair of elements formed more than one compound, Dalton found that one gram of one of the elements was always combined with such weights of the other that these weights could be expressed as small integral multiples of some number. For example, the weights of lead combined with one gram of oxygen in various oxides of lead were 2×3.234 (minium), 3×3.234 (litharge), and 4×3.234 (lead dioxide). According to Dalton's principles, these ratios are compatible with the formulas PbO_2, Pb_3O_4, and PbO. (They are also compatible with Pb_2O, Pb_3O, and Pb_4O, for Dalton's hypothesis does not provide a unique criterion of "simplicity.") Similarly, the weights of oxygen per gram of nitrogen in some common oxides of nitrogen are 0.71, 1.42, and 2.84, which are consistent with the formulas N_2O, NO, and NO_2, the simplest molecules (binary and ternary) that can be formed from these elements.

Dalton had a number of theoretical reasons for preferring binary to ternary formulas, and ternary formulas to those still more complex. These reasons were largely derived from a theory of gaseous mixtures he had developed earlier to account for atmospheric phenomena and for the solution of gases in liquids. The theory required that the particles of the different elementary components of a gaseous mixture be of different weights, and that particles of like nature repel one another. Because of this repulsion, it would be difficult for several particles of a single substance to coexist in the particle of a compound (a molecule).

Dalton employed his *rule of greatest simplicity* to apply the atomic theory to specific cases. This heuristic worked in many cases but led to incorrect conclusions in others. For instance, it led Dalton to conclude that water was composed of a single hydrogen atom and a single oxygen atom.

In contrast, Avogadro (1811) employed Gay-Lussac's (1809) law of combining volumes, along with the assumption that equal volumes of gases contained equal numbers of particles. Gay-Lussac had found that the volumes of reacting gases, under the same conditions of temperature and pressure, were always in ratios of small integers, as they were also in relation to the gaseous products of such reactions; thus, two volumes of hydrogen and one of oxygen produced two volumes of water vapor. If it is further assumed (as it was by Avogadro) that equal volumes of gases contain equal numbers of particles, then two particles of hydrogen join one of oxygen to form two of water. But Dalton called this impossible, since in this interpretation there was only one particle of oxygen to divide between every two particles of water. Avogadro cut the Gordian knot by postulating two levels of particles: molecules (the particles referred to in Gay-Lussac's law of combining volumes) and atoms (the "ultimate" constituents). If the oxygen molecule were diatomic, then it could be divided, and one of the constituent atoms could be contributed to each of the water molecules, giving the formula HO for water. (The hydrogen molecule was assumed to be monatomic.)

Using these assumptions, Avogadro inferred a diatomic model for oxygen and a different structure for water. Although Avogadro's hypothesis is accepted today, it was rejected or ignored by his contemporaries. Among the reasons for rejection was Dalton's belief, mentioned above, that different atoms of the same element would repel one another, and that hence they could not form a multi-atom molecule. This is another case, similar to the case of combustion, in which two hypotheses provided plausible accounts of phenomena, making the area an ideal one in which to test a discovery system concerned with the formulation of structural models.

It is of some interest that, whereas data-driven search with the integer-ratio heuristic led BACON.4 rapidly to atomic weights and the molecule-atom distinction, Dalton's theory—which was correct in its basic atomic premise but wrong in its detailed structural hypothesis—both led to the search for atomic weights (or combining weights) and seriously impeded their disambiguation. A new advance in theory—Avogadro's reformulation of the atomic hypothesis postulating two layers of particles, molecules, and atoms—was needed to put matters back on the track. For Avogadro to accomplish this, he had to have an unshakeable faith in both the atomic hypothesis and Gay-Lussac's findings, and a consequent need to reconcile them. His solution was the postulate that equal volumes of gas contain equal numbers of molecules, which he justified by the argument (Leicester and Klickstein 1952, p. 232) that "it would scarcely be possible to conceive that the law regulating the distances of particles could give us in all cases relations so simple as those which the facts [due to Gay-Lussac] compel us to acknowledge between the volume and the number of particles."

The DALTON System

Our interest in structural models has led us to construct a discovery system concerned with this issue. Since John Dalton was one of the earliest proponents of atomic models, we have named the system DALTON. In accordance with our discussion of the other discovery systems, we will describe DALTON in terms of heuristic search—in this case, search through a space of possible structural models. As before, we begin by considering the system's inputs and outputs and the manner in which it represents this information. After this, we turn to the operators DALTON employs to generate new states and to the search scheme and heuristics it uses to direct the search process.

The DALTON system we will describe does not invent the atomic hypothesis. (Neither did John Dalton.) Rather, it employs a representation of chemical reactions and substances that embodies the hypothesis. This representation also incorporates the distinction, invented by Avogadro, between molecules and atoms.[1] Thus, DALTON can be regarded as a theory-driven system for reaching the conclusions about atomic weights that BACON.4 derived in a data-driven way.

Representing Structural Models

DALTON begins with information similar to that available to chemists in the year 1800: a set of chemical reactions and knowledge (or inferences) about the components of the substances involved in each reaction. For instance, DALTON is told that hydrogen reacts with oxygen to form water, and that hydrogen reacts with nitrogen to form ammonia. It is also told that water has hydrogen and oxygen as its components, whereas ammonia has hydrogen and nitrogen. Thus, DALTON accepts as input the type of information that STAHL generates as output. (This suggests that these systems could easily be linked. We will discuss this possibility in the next chapter.) Finally, DALTON is informed that hydrogen, oxygen, and nitrogen are elements, which implies that they have no components other than themselves.

DALTON represents this information in a manner identical to that used by GLAUBER and STAHL. Thus, the water reaction is stored as (reacts inputs

---

1. To remove this distinction and provide a pure "Daltonian" version of DALTON, we can add a constraint to the system that admits only monatomic molecules of the elements. However, this trick does not account for Avogadro's insight in introducing the distinction.

{hydrogen oxygen} outputs {water}), and the knowledge that ammonia is composed of hydrogen and nitrogen as (components of {ammonia} are {hydrogen nitrogen}). As before, the set notation indicates that the order of elements in a list is not significant.

DALTON's goal is to develop a structural model for each reaction and the substances involved in it. Moreover, the system knows that two quantities are important in a reaction: the number of molecules of each substance that take part in the simplest form of the reaction and the number of particles (or atoms) of each element in a given molecule. Thus, the DALTON program begins with a better notion of the true situation than did its namesake, who did not make the distinction between atoms and molecules. Finally, DALTON assumes that different molecules of a given element always have the same internal structure, whether they occur in the same reaction or in different ones. For instance, the system might hypothesize that hydrogen molecules consist of two hydrogen atoms whether they are reacting with nitrogen or with oxygen.

The program represents its structural models at several different levels of abstraction. At the highest level are the reactions themselves, specifying neither the number of molecules nor their internal structure. Thus, the expression

(reacts inputs {hydrogen oxygen} outputs {water})

can be viewed as a structural model that remains to be instantiated. In order to save space, we will use the shorthand notation

(hydrogen oxygen → water),

with inputs to the left of the arrow and outputs to the right.

DALTON assumes that the number of molecules is to be specified first. Thus, a more detailed model of the water reaction might state that it involves two molecules of hydrogen. This hypothesis would be represented as (reacts inputs {{H H} oxygen} outputs {water}), where H stands for one molecule of hydrogen. In our shorter notation, this would be written ({H H} oxygen → water). The number of molecules can be specified independently for each substance. A more detailed model of the water reaction would instantiate the number of molecules for all three substances, ({H H} {O} → {W W}). This structure asserts that the water reaction involves two molecules of hydrogen, and two of water.

Once decisions have been reached about the numbers of molecules,

DALTON can proceed to specify the internal structure of each molecule. This specification is represented with another level of brackets and with lower-case letters designating atoms, e.g.

$(\{\{h\ h\}\{h\ h\}\}\{O\} \rightarrow \{W\ W\})$.

Here the molecule of hydrogen has been hypothesized to consist of two hydrogen atoms. Again, the decisions about the atomic structure of the molecules are made for each substance individually, but eventually the system arrives at a completely instantiated model of the water reaction. For example, the currently accepted model, in which two diatomic molecules of hydrogen combine with one diatomic molecule of oxygen to form water, would be stated as $(\{\{h\ h\}\{h\ h\}\}\{\{o\ o\}\} \rightarrow \{\{h\ h\ o\}\{h\ h\ o\}\})$. Of course, other models of this reaction can be constructed, as we will see shortly.

Operators for Constructing Models

The representational scheme we have described suggests two natural operators for formulating structural models: one for specifying the number of molecules of each substance participating in a reaction and another for specifying the atomic structure of each molecule. The rule for implementing the first of these is straightforward: If the number of molecules of a substance is unspecified, then hypothesize that the number equals some small integer (from 1 to 4, say). Each such integer (and each substance-reaction pair) provides a different instantiation produced by this SPECIFY-MOLECULES operator. For instance, one instantiation would propose a single molecule of oxygen in the water reaction, another would propose two molecules, and so forth. How these instantiations are ordered will be discussed shortly.

DALTON implements the second operator, the one specifying the atomic structure of a molecule, by means of two more specialized rules. The rule SPECIFY-ELEMENT applies only to substances known to be elements, such as hydrogen and oxygen. If the number of atoms for some element is unspecified, the rule hypothesizes that this number is some small integer (from 1 to 4, say).[2] Each element-integer pair produces a different instantiation of this rule and hence a different structural hypothesis about the element. For example, one instantiation would propose a monatomic

---

2. As indicated earlier, this rule could be replaced by the "Daltonian" rule that all molecules of elements are monatomic.

oxygen molecule, another would propose a diatomic molecule, and so forth.

A third rule, SPECIFY-COMPOUND, applies only to compounds, (such as water and ammonia) and operates more efficiently than the first two rules. This rule assumes that all but one of the molecular structures in a reaction have been specified, together with the number of molecules for each substance in the reaction. Thus, only the atomic structure of one molecule remains to be determined. The SPECIFY-COMPOUND rule also assumes that the total number of particles of each kind in a reaction is conserved: For each type of atom, the number of atoms present in the input to the reaction must equal the number in the output. Given these data and assumptions, the rule determines whether the conservation assumption can be satisfied; if so, it specifies a molecular structure that will balance the equation.[3] For example, given the structure $(\{\{h\ h\}\{h\ h\}\}\{\{o\ o\}\} \rightarrow \{W\ W\})$, SPECIFY-COMPOUND would generate the model $(\{\{h\ h\}\{h\ h\}\}\{\{o\ o\}\} \rightarrow \{\{h\ h\ o\}\{h\ h\ o\}\})$, in which there are four hydrogen atoms and two oxygen atoms on each side of the equation.

The importance of the conservation assumption in SPECIFY-COMPOUND can be seen clearly from the mythical example $(\{\{h\ h\}\{h\ h\}\}\{\{o\}\} \rightarrow \{W\ W\})$. Since there are two identical water molecules in the output of the reaction, their oxygen content must be identical. But there is only a single oxygen atom in the input, and this cannot be divided between the two water molecules. Hence, the conservation assumption calls for a revision of the input side of the model (such as the addition of another oxygen atom to the oxygen molecule, or the addition of another oxygen molecule). These three operators, in combination with the information about reactions and the components of substances that is provided to the system, define a *space* of structural models. DALTON organizes its search through this space in a depth-first manner, focusing on one reaction at a time. For each reaction, the system first specifies the number of molecules, instantiating these one at a time. Only after all substances in a reaction have been dealt with does DALTON turn to the atomic structure of each molecule, first specifying the molecular composition of elements and then focusing on the compound.

---

3. In its present form, the rule can be used to generate a final model only for reactions producing a single compound as output, and DALTON runs only on this class of problems. For reactions with multiple outputs, the system would have to rely on a less powerful generate-and-test strategy, with a consequent increase in the amount of search it would require.

We noted earlier that at each point in the search the SPECIFY-MOLECULE and SPECIFY-ELEMENT rules can provide multiple instantiations. DALTON must search among these alternatives in some principled manner. Its response is to instantiate by always selecting the smallest integer that has not previously been tried. Thus, the system considers simpler models before resorting to more complex ones. For instance, models of the water reaction specifying one oxygen molecule will be considered before those specifying two or three molecules, and monatomic models of the molecules of an element will be considered before diatomic models or models with larger numbers of atoms. DALTON applies the SPECIFY-COMPOUND rule (and thus the conservation assumption) as soon as the model for a reaction is sufficiently constrained for it to be used. As we have already seen, some partial models cannot be instantiated in any way that will satisfy the conservation constraint; thus, DALTON must be able to backtrack and consider other paths to a complete model.

One additional constraint makes the process of constructing models challenging. Consistency requires that the model of the molecule of a substance be the same for all reactions in which it is present. For example, if hydrogen is assumed to be monatomic in the water reaction, it must also be monatomic in the ammonia reaction. In general, this requirement simplifies the search process, since models that have already been constructed will constrain the construction of later ones. However, a conservative model constructed for one reaction may not be extendable to a later reaction. In such cases, DALTON must revise its earlier model if it is to construct a consistent explanation for both reactions. This involves a form of backtracking, though not the simple form discussed above; some existing models may be retained during the backtracking process. An example of this backup method will be given shortly.)

DALTON has been described here in terms of the heuristics of search. Its task, formulating structural models of chemical reactions, can also be viewed as a constraint satisfaction problem. In this respect, it is very similar to other AI tasks that involve finding some structure that satisfies a set of assumptions. These include the line-labeling task of Waltz (1975), the cryptarithmetic problems of Newell and Simon (1972), MOLGEN's task of planning experiments in molecular genetics (Stefik 1979), and the task of configuring computers discussed in McDermott 1982. As we have seen, DALTON's constraints are of two forms: the conservation assumption and the assumption of consistency across reactions. As we will see in the examples that are examined below, each of these constraints can produce a need for backtracking.

Modeling the Water Reaction

Now that we have examined DALTON's problem space and search control in the abstract, let us consider their use in some examples. Suppose the system is asked to construct a model of the water reaction, and that it is given only the information that water is composed of hydrogen and oxygen and that hydrogen and oxygen are primitive elements (and thus composed of themselves). The program must determine the number of hydrogen, oxygen, and water molecules in the reaction, and the numbers and kinds of particles in each type of molecule. We first consider how the version of DALTON described above generates a monatomic model of the water reaction. After this, we examine the effect of adding a constraint based on Gay-Lussac's law of combining volumes, and the quite different diatomic model that then results.

Constructing a Monatomic Model

As we have seen, DALTON begins with a very abstract model in which no commitments are made, and successively refines this model as it proceeds. In this case the initial model has the form (hydrogen oxygen → water), which leads the system to apply its SPECIFY-MOLECULE rule to hypothesize the number of hydrogen molecules involved. Lacking any criterion other than complexity, the system chooses the simplest hypothesis and assumes that a single hydrogen molecule is required. If this choice later causes difficulty, the model builder can back up and try another path. Similar initial choices are made for oxygen and water, so that the partially specified model includes one molecule each. This is represented by the proposition ({H} {O} → {W}), in which brackets indicate molecules.

Now, as it must determine the internal structure of the hydrogen and oxygen molecules, DALTON applies the SPECIFY-ELEMENT rule. As before, its preference for simplicity leads it to assume initially that both hydrogen and oxygen consist of a single elementary particle (say h and o), giving the model ({{h}} {{o}} → {W}). At this point, since only the molecular structure of water remains to be determined, the program invokes its conservation-based rule, SPECIFY-COMPOUND, to this end. This routine checks to see if the model can be finalized in such a way that

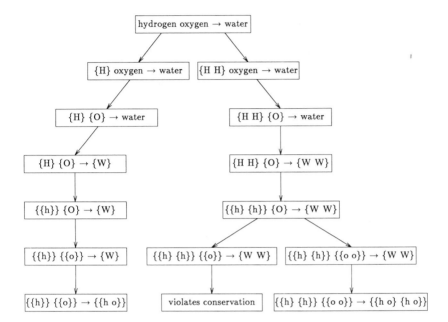

Figure 8.1

conservation is obeyed. If this is possible, DALTON outputs the completed model and halts; if the conservation principle cannot be satisfied, the system backs up and considers other possibilities.

In this case, the conservation operator tells DALTON that the water molecule must be composed of one hydrogen atom and one oxygen atom, and that the final model must have the form ($\{\{h\}\}\{\{o\}\} \to \{\{h\ o\}\}$). This model is equivalent to the one originally formulated by John Dalton. Figure 8.1 presents some of the paths available in the space of molecular models. In arriving at the monatomic model just described, DALTON takes the left path; since this leads to an acceptable solution, no backtracking is required.[4]

4. Our program, DALTON, arrives in this case at precisely the same model (now regarded as erroneous) that John Dalton arrived at, because it employs the heuristic, proposed by Dalton, of greatest simplicity—that is, of adopting the simplest model that satisfies the constraints. The result depends strongly on the particular reactions that are considered. For example, if Dalton had analyzed hydrogen peroxide (H_2O_2) before water, he would have assigned the formula HO to peroxide, and then would have been led to the formula H_2O for water. DALTON would do the same.

A Diatomic Model of the Water Reaction

As we have seen, DALTON's basic strategy is to carry out a depth-first search through the space of models, ordering the search so that simple models are considered first. However, when enough of the model has been specified, a theory-driven heuristic (implementing the conservation assumption) takes over and finalizes the model. DALTON can also employ theory-driven methods at other stages in its search process, and these methods can alter the system's behavior in significant ways. In the above run, DALTON had no theoretical biases other than a belief in conservation of particles and a desire to construct as simple a model as possible. However, if we give the system some additional information about the water reaction, its behavior changes significantly.

Avogadro, who was aware of Gay-Lussac's results, believed firmly that the combining volumes he observed were related to the number of molecules involved in the reaction. To model this knowledge, we can add the following heuristic:

INFER-MULTIPLES
If you want to know the number of molecules of X involved in a reaction,
**   and the combining volume of X was V,**
then consider only multiples of V as possibilities.

In the water reaction, two volumes of hydrogen combine with one volume of oxygen to form two volumes of water vapor. Given the above rule, and knowledge of these combining volumes, the revised system (let us call it DALTON*) instead postulates two molecules of both hydrogen and water (and if this were later found to be unsatisfactory, would propose four and then six), while retaining the assumption of one oxygen molecule. Thus, at the third level in the search tree, DALTON* has the partially specified model ({H H} {O} → {W W}).

At this point the revised system moves to consider the internal structure of the hydrogen molecule, assuming that it is composed of a single particle. It then proceeds to make a similar assumption for the structure of oxygen. However, for the resulting model, ({{h} {h}} {{o}} → {W W}), there exists no decomposition of water in terms of hydrogen and oxygen that satisfies the conservation assumption. In response to this situation, DALTON* backs up and considers another alternative. The system next hypothesizes that the oxygen molecule is composed of two particles. Since this allows conservation to be satisfied, a final model is constructed in which oxygen is diatomic and hydrogen is monatomic: ({{h}{h}}{{o o}} → {{h o}{h o}}). (These two search paths are shown on the right side of figure 8.1.) Although this model differs from the modern-day one, it is consistent with Gay-Lussac's data, and it encounters difficulty only when other reactions are considered; for example, the monatomic assuption for hydrogen does not work for the ammonia reaction.

Modeling Multiple Reactions

Now that we have seen how DALTON behaves in the case of an isolated reaction, let us consider its response to the constraints introduced by multiple reactions. As was mentioned above, multiple constraints appear because one must assume the same structure for a substance across different reactions. For instance, the structure DALTON hypothesizes for hydrogen when it combines with oxygen to form water may simply not work in the model for the ammonia reaction. In order to understand the process by which DALTON recovers from such situations, we must examine the system's operation in greater detail.

Like most of the programs we have described, DALTON is stated as a production system. In default mode, the system uses the rules SPECIFY-MOLECULE, SPECIFY-ELEMENT, and SPECIFY-COMPOUND to formulate simpler models first and then to formulate more complicated ones as they become necessary. However, if new condition-action rules are added to the system, they take precedence over the default rules and can direct search down paths that might otherwise not be considered, as when the rule INFER-MULTIPLES led to a different model of the water reaction than would otherwise have been constructed. In that case we inserted the rule manually; DALTON, however, has the capacity to add rules on its own initiative, in the following manner: Once DALTON has generated a successful model for a reaction, it converts this knowledge into productions. For instance, having arrived at the diatomic explanation of water given above, the program would store one rule for the molecules of hydrogen, another for the oxygen molecules, and a third for the water molecules. (See the first three productions in table 8.1) If the system is asked to explain the water reaction at a later date, it will be able to recall the number of molecules without search.

DALTON also constructs productions describing the internal structure of

Table 8.1
Rules summarizing DALTON's diatomic model of the water reaction.

HYDROGEN-WATER-2
If you want to know the number of molecules of hydrogen
   in the water reaction,
then hypothesize 2 molecules of hydrogen.

OXYGEN-WATER-1
If you want to know the number of molecules of oxygen
   in the water reaction,
then hypothesize 1 molecules of oxygen.

WATER-WATER-2
If you want to know the number of molecules of water
   in the water reaction,
then hypothesize 2 molecules of water.

HYDROGEN-1
If you want to know the molecular structure of hydrogen
then hypothesize the structure $\{h\}$.

OXYGEN-2
If you want to know the molecular structure of oxygen
then hypothesize the structure $\{o\ o\}$.

---

each molecule in the reaction. Table 8.1 presents the five rules created during generation of the diatomic model of the water reaction described above. Basically, these rules constitute a procedural representation of the model ($\{\{h\}\{h\}\}\{\{o\ o\}\} \to \{\{h\ o\}\{h\ o\}\}$), since they will regenerate this model when given the reaction (hydrogen oxygen $\to$ water).

The rules for specifying the structure of hydrogen and oxygen molecules are more general than the others, for they make no mention of the reaction itself. As a consequence, they will affect the search process in other reactions that involve these substances. For instance, the HYDROGEN-1 rule comes into play in modeling the ammonia reaction. When DALTON attempts to model this reaction (after successfully modeling the production of water), it begins by applying INFER-MULTIPLES to determine the number of molecules involved. After three applications of this production, the system has the model ($\{H\ H\ H\}\{N\} \to \{A\ A\}$).

At this point the learned rule HYDROGEN-1 applies, suggesting a monatomic structure for hydrogen molecules. Since no analogous rule exists for nitrogen, the rule SPECIFY-ELEMENT applies, suggesting a monatomic structure for this substance as well. This leads to the model ($\{\{h\}\{h\}\{h\}\}\{\{n\}\} \to \{A\ A\}$), but this also cannot satisfy the conservation principle, since the right side requires an even number each of hydrogen and nitrogen atoms but there is an odd number of each on the left side.

DALTON's only choice is to reject the monatomic assumption for hydrogen that served it in explaining the water reaction, and to replace it with a diatomic assumption. To do so, it deletes the rule HYDROGEN-1 and replaces it with an analogous rule, HYDROGEN-2, that proposes the new structure. The system must now reconsider the possibilities for nitrogen. Again it tries a monatomic hypothesis, producing the model ({{h h}{h h}{h h}}{{n}} → {A A}). However, the SPECIFY-COMPOUND rule now fails to fit this scheme into the conservation requirement, forcing DALTON to backtrack once more and consider a diatomic structure for nitrogen. This combination finally leads to a complete model obeying the conservation law:

({{h h}{h h}{h h}}{{ n n}} → {{h h h n}{h h h n}}).

Thus, DALTON has now modeled the ammonia reaction successfully.

However, since DALTON has replaced one of the rules generated during its experience with the water reaction, it must now update that model, making sure that the new rule works there as well. Since the other rules remain, DALTON assigns the same number of molecules as before, giving the model ({H H}{O} → {W W}). At this point, the rule HYDROGEN-2 applies, giving the more detailed model ({{h h}{h h}}{O} → {W W}). However, since the rule OXYGEN-2 remains as before, DALTON is led to a diatomic structure for oxygen. Note that DALTON did not backtrack blindly in the ammonia case but changed only the rules relevant to that reaction, leaving other rules (e.g., OXYGEN-2) as they were. Finally, the SPECIFY-COMPOUND rule employs its knowledge of conservation to generate the complete model,

({{h h}{h h}}{{o o}} → {{h h o}{h h o}}),

which is the modern account of the water reaction.

In this example, the rule generated during the ammonia episode also worked when DALTON returned to the water reaction. However, this is not guaranteed to happen. Had DALTON run into further difficulty during its second attempt with water, the process would have been repeated, with DALTON considering ever more complicated molecular structures (up to a limit) until a single model of hydrogen was found that successfully explained both reactions.

John Dalton's Rule of Greatest Simplicity

John Dalton reduced the ambiguity in the assignment of atomic weights by assigning the simplest formulas first. As we have seen, the DALTON program also applies this principle to single reactions. But John Dalton, taking into account data on combining weights, used it in a stronger form to impose additional constraints on acceptable formulas. Earlier, we mentioned the three oxides of nitrogen in which 0.71, 1.42, and 2.82 grams of oxygen unite with one gram of nitrogen. The ratios are $1:2:4$. Accordingly, John Dalton assigned the formulas N_2O, NO, and NO_2. The data are also consistent with N_4O, N_2O, and NO, respectively, or NO, NO_2, and NO_4, but the latter assignments call for quinquenary molecules, which by Dalton's criteria were far less probable than ternary ones.

A constraint of this kind could readily be incorporated in DALTON, which would then have to be provided with data on combining weights. This constraint would also operate over different sets of substances. Consider the relations among water, ammonia, and nitric oxide (NO). Without a constraint on combining volumes, DALTON would assign the formulas {h o}, {h n}, and {n o}, respectively. The combining weights (1 : 8 for hydrogen and oxygen in water, 1 : 4.67 for hydrogen and nitrogen in ammonia, and 7 : 8 for nitrogen and oxygen in nitric oxide) suggest contradictory atomic weights: Taking the atomic weight of hydrogen as 1, we find from the formula {h o} and the associated combining weight 1 : 8 an atomic weight of 8 for oxygen. Similarly, from the formula {h n} and the combining weight 1 : 4.67, we obtain an atomic weight of 4.67 for nitrogen. However, in the case of the formula {n o}, the atomic weight of 4.67 for nitrogen and the combining weight 7 : 8 imply that the atomic weight of oxygen must be $8/7 \times 4.67 = 5.33$, which contradicts the value of 8 obtained from the first reaction.

Under the consistency constraint, DALTON would be forced to search for formulas that would resolve this contradiction. The search might be guided by looking for least common denominators, as BACON.4 does (e.g., nitrogen has a combining weight of 7 in {n o} and of 4.67 in {h n}, but $7 = 2.33 \times 3$; $4.67 = 2.33 \times 2$). Depending on the order of search, the formulas might be revised (correctly) to H_2O, H_3N, and NO, with atomic weights of $H = 1$, $O = 16$, and $N = 14$, which are consistent with the combining weights of 1 : 8 for H_2O, 1 : 4.67 for H_3N, and 7 : 8 for NO; or revised (incorrectly) to HO, H_3N, and NO_2, with atomic weights of $H = 1$, $O = 8$, and $N = 14$, which are consistent with the same combining weights. Ambiguity would be reduced, but not eliminated, for the alternatives given above cannot be distinguished by the simplicity criterion.

Applications to Other Domains

A theory of discovery, like any other theory, should be formulated in as general a manner as possible. Thus, it is natural to ask whether DALTON's representation and heuristics can be employed for other discovery tasks that call for structural inference. Two other domains present themselves as obvious candidates, since the data in both can be described in the language of reactions and since both require the creation of structural models to explain these reactions in terms of underlying substances and components. Moreover, the "substances" in both cases are particulate in nature. The first of these domains is elementary-particle physics; the second is classical genetics.

We must not expect the version of DALTON that has been described in this chapter to be adequate for these tasks, but we will propose some extensions to the representation and the heuristics of DALTON that might enable the system to deal with phenomena in these domains. Since our ideas have not been implemented in a running program, they will necessarily be somewhat sketchy. We do not wish to imply that DALTON is ready to tackle the puzzles of elementary-particle theory. Our aim, instead, is to try to throw light on the inference processes that have been employed in twentieth-century particle physics and in early genetic research, and to show the close relation of these inference processes to those we have described for early-nineteenth-century chemistry.

Particle Physics

Much of the basic data in particle physics comes from the collisions and disintegrations of particles as recorded in a cloud chamber, a bubble chamber, or some similar detection device. The events themselves are either "spontaneous" (e.g., caused by natural radioactivity) or induced by bombarding target substances with high-energy particles. The latter may either be obtained from natural sources (e.g., cosmic rays) or produced by some kind of particle accelerator. From the tracks of particles that are recorded in experiments, the masses, electrical charges, and velocities of the particles are inferred. We will regard these properties of the particles as obervable, ignoring the inference processes required to estimate them, and we will represent the changes in particles and the interactions among them as reactions.

A first task of experimental particle physic is to record the kinds of reactions that actually occur, and to catalog and classify them. Early examples are the reactions produced by the bombardment of atoms with helium particles. In DALTON's language, such a reaction could be represented by

$$^{A}R + \alpha \rightarrow {}^{A+3}R + p,$$

where ^{A}R is an atom of atomic weight A, α is an alpha particle (a helium nucleus of atomic weight 4), ^{A+3}R is an atom of atomic weight $A + 3$, and p is a proton (a hydrogen nucleus of atomic weight 1). Thus, the bombarded atom combines with the helium nucleus to produce a heavier atom, and a proton is ejected.

The radioactive reactions—the first transmutations of elements that were discovered—were even simpler, involving the disintegration of an atom into one of lower atomic weight, for example with the emission of a proton, a helium nucleus, and a photon. The same kind of representation suffices for these, e.g.

$$^{A}R \rightarrow p + \alpha + {}^{A-5}R + \beta.$$

One important task of data-driven inference here is to find rules that specify which reactions, of all the conceivable ones, actually take place. These restriction rules may be based, for example, on the idea of conserving the total values of properties that are attributed to the component particles (mass, charge, proton number, and so on). Although some of these conservation laws predate particle physics, others have been derived through the introduction of new properties inferred from the data themselves and from the laws of quantum mechanics. Among these new properties are spin, isotopic spin, strangeness, and charm.

A discovery that certain properties may be conserved only under particular conditions can lead to a classification of reactions and to restriction rules requiring conservation of particular properties under transformation by particular classes of reactions. The current classification of reactions—strong, electromagnetic, weak, and gravitational—can be derived from energy considerations, independent of the conservation laws, thus giving converging evidence for the conditional restrictions.

A different theoretical enterprise, and one that has burgeoned as the number of different kinds of observed particles has continued to grow, has been the postulating of a still more elementary class of particles out of which the previously observed "elementary" particles could be composed. The step here is not wholly unlike the one that took chemistry from compounds to elements, and physics from atoms to the first level of elementary particles (photons, electrons, neutrons, and protons). For example, the proton is now viewed as composed of smaller particles called quarks—initially, two u quarks and one d quark. Currently accepted theory postulates as many as twelve kinds of quarks, combinations of pairs and triplets of which can account for a substantial variety of observable particles.

Along one dimension, inferring the quark theory is simpler than the task that confronted the early chemists. Since most of the reacting substances can be "directly" observed in photographs from a cloud chamber or some other recording system, physicists know exactly how many particles of each kind take part in a reaction; they do not have to infer how many molecules or atoms are participating. However, two other aspects of the task of inferring elementary particles make it more difficult than its chemical analog.

First, the current version of DALTON requires knowledge of the components of a substance, or knowledge that the substance is elementary. However, the "elements" of quark theory are not necessarily directly observable themselves; hence, in order to explain particle interactions, physicists have had to postulate entirely new substances that have never been seen. In order to regenerate the quark theory, DALTON must be modified to search the larger space of models in which such decompositions can occur. In contemporary physics, that search is driven partly by the supposition that the fundamental sets of particles form finite groups, so that the search takes place in the space of such groups. Alternatively, one can imagine a modified version of STAHL capable of determining the unseen elementary components of observed particles, with DALTON retaining its focus on the number of particles involved. The task remains a constraint-satisfaction problem, with particular reactions obeying the same constraints as in the chemical domain: that the total number of elementary particles of each type must be conserved, and that the structure for each observed particle must be consistent across reactions. However, since the substances observed are usually compounds, one must employ a generate-and-test method to find models satisfying the constraints.

The second complication concerns attributes of the elementary particles themselves. The process of moving downward to the quark level endows the quarks with the same kinds of properties as the particles composed of them, so that new constraints arise from the requirement that these properties (e.g., mass, charge, spin, strangeness, charm) be conserved in the composition. For instance, the mass of a proton is equal to the summed mass of two *u* quarks and one *d* quark, and similar relations hold for charge and spin.[5] In most ways, these additional restrictions reduce the amount of search that DALTON would require, since many possibilities are ruled out by the conservation laws early in the search process.

If DALTON were to be extended to handle such quantitative attributes as mass and charge, it might be able to account for another historical discovery: the caloric theory of heat. As we saw in our earlier discussions of Black's law, the conserved numerical quantities of mass, heat capacity, and heat are used to explain changes in the nonconserved quantity of temperature. However, if the conserved quantity, heat, is regarded as a substance, we have the caloric theory.

Classical Mendelian Genetics

A less obvious application of DALTON involves the field of classical genetics. For example, the hereditary rules for garden peas, first set forth by Gregor Mendel (1865), can be viewed as reactions in which characteristics of the parents are transformed into characteristics of the offspring. Given the first extension described above (the ability to find elements by decomposition), along with a suitable replacement for the conservation assumption (since this does not apply in reproductive systems), DALTON should be able to arrive at the two-trait model originally formulated by Mendel. For example, let us suppose that the system is provided with genotypic statements of the results of inbreeding and crossbreeding, which might be induced by another discovery system (e.g. GLAUBER) from phenotypic descriptions of these reactions.

If we let G stand for green peas that produce only green offspring, Y

---

5. What is presented here is a simplified view of the quark theory, since the version of DALTON we are sketching could generate only such a simplified version. In the full physical theory, the predicted mass of a proton is not exactly equal to the sum of its component masses, but takes into account the binding energy. Similarly, the predicted spin number for particles is not precisely the summed spins of the component quarks, but is derived from quantum-mechanical considerations about the nature of spin numbers.

stand for yellow peas that produce only yellow offspring, and G' stand for green peas that produce mixed offspring, then four basic reactions suffice to describe Mendel's observations. In our shorthand notation for chemical reactions, these are the following:

$$(G\ G \to G), \qquad\qquad\qquad\qquad\qquad\qquad\qquad (8.1)$$

$$(Y\ Y \to Y), \qquad\qquad\qquad\qquad\qquad\qquad\qquad (8.2)$$

$$(G\ Y \to G'), \qquad\qquad\qquad\qquad\qquad\qquad\qquad (8.3)$$

$$(G'\ G' \to G\ G'\ Y). \qquad\qquad\qquad\qquad\qquad\qquad (8.4)$$

Reactions 8.1 and 8.2 state that pure-strain green peas produce only green offspring and that pure yellow peas always generate yellow offspring. Reaction 8.3 states that crossing pure green and pure yellow peas produces only mixed green offspring. Reaction 8.4 states that breeding hybrid green peas generates offspring in all three classes. Given these reactions, an extended version of DALTON should be able to infer that two primitive traits (say g and y) are required, and to decide that the genotype G can be modeled by the "molecular" pair (g g), that Y can be modeled by the pair (y y), and that G' can be modeled by the pair (g y). Thus, the above reactions would be rewritten as

$$(\{g\ g\}\{g\ g\} \to \{g\ g\}), \qquad\qquad\qquad\qquad\qquad (8.5)$$

$$(\{y\ y\}\{y\ y\} \to \{y\ y\}), \qquad\qquad\qquad\qquad\qquad (8.6)$$

$$(\{g\ g\}\{y\ y\} \to \{g\ y\}), \qquad\qquad\qquad\qquad\qquad (8.7)$$

$$(\{g\ y\}\{g\ y\} \to \{g\ g\}\{g\ y\}\{y\ y\}). \qquad\qquad\qquad (8.8)$$

As we envision it, the system's explanation of these reactions would not involve the notion of dominance, nor would it predict the proportions in which the various genotypes are observed, but it would account for the basic qualitative relations between parents and offspring.

   The above models also suggest a natural replacement for the conservation assumption. In the domain of genetics, all possible combinations that can be formed from the components on the left of a reaction must occur on the right of the reaction. Thus, in each of reactions 8.5, 8.6, and 8.7 only one combination is possible—a different one in each case. However, in reaction 8.8 there are three ways to combine the elements on the left side, so all of these combinations must occur on the right side of the equation. This constraint is quite different in form from a conservation principle, but it is still a constraint and so it can be used in limiting the search for models.

DALTON's Relation to DENDRAL

DENDRAL (Feigenbaum et al. 1971), one of the first AI systems to incorporate extensive amounts of domain-specific knowledge, operated in the domain of organic chemistry and was also concerned with formulating structural models of substances. DENDRAL accepted two pieces of information: the chemical formula for a molecule (such as $C_6H_{16}O$) and its mass spectrogram (a graph mapping the masses of submolecules, obtained by decomposing the substance, against their frequencies of occurrence). DENDRAL's goal was to infer the structure of a compound in terms of the connections of its elementary components. Since there are many different ways to connect a set of atoms (millions for reasonably complex compounds), this task has the potential to generate considerable search.

DENDRAL's response to this search problem was to use knowledge of organic chemistry to constrain the possibilities. The system operated in three major stages. First, it examined the mass spectrogram to determine what substructures had to be in the molecule and what substructures could not be in it. It obtained this information by noting all major peaks in the mass spectrogram and retrieving the chemical structures it knew would produce subsets of these peaks. In the second stage, DENDRAL proceeded to consider different combinations of these substructures, adding to them until the original formula was achieved. During this process, it used knowledge of stable and unstable chemical bindings to constrain the search further. From this process emerged one or more alternative structural models for the substance. At this point, DENDRAL used a theory of mass spectrometry to predict a mass spectrogram from each of these models, and compared these predicted graphs with the one actually observed. On the basis of similarities and differences in the peaks of these graphs, the system ranked its models in the order of their ability to account for the observations.

What, then, is the relation between DENDRAL and DALTON? The research goals that motivated the construction of the two systems were quite different. DENDRAL was concerned primarily with imitating twentieth-century organic chemistry, and thus it incorporated several centuries' accumulated knowledge about chemicals, their structures, and their reactions. In contrast, DALTON is concerned with a much earlier stage in the discovery process, in which early chemists were attempting to formulate models on the basis of rather sparse knowledge. Thus, DALTON and DENDRAL lie at two ends of a spectrum. DALTON studies simple discoveries in a knowledge-poor environment; DENDRAL studies more complex discoveries in a knowledge-rich environment. The design of each is appropriate to its task: the reliance on expert knowledge in DENDRAL and the reliance on less constrained search in DALTON.

Although both systems are concerned with chemical models, they differ in regard to the sense of "structure." DALTON seeks to identify the number of particles of each type that occur in a given substance. For instance, it considers structures such as {h h} for hydrogen and {h o} for water. In constrast, DENDRAL accepts models of this form as input (when given a chemical equation like $C_8H_{16}O$), and further specifies this model by determining how the atoms are linked. Thus, the two systems are best viewed as complementing each other, and one obvious direction for further research would be to extend DALTON to form structural models of the kind that DENDRAL produces. Our focus on early chemistry did not lead us down this path, since the very need to specify such linkages did not become acute until the mid 1800s, when chemists began to work extensively with organic compounds.

Conclusion

In this chapter we have examined the task of formulating structural models, using DALTON, an AI system that operates in this domain, as our principal tool. Our primary examples of structural discovery came from the history of chemistry during the period around 1800, when Dalton and Avogadro proposed the first molecular and atomic models of chemical compounds. Because Dalton and Avogadro employed somewhat different criteria in formulating their models, they sometimes arrived at different explanations. In particular, Dalton proposed monatomic models of hydrogen and oxygen and proposed HO as the structure of water. In contrast, Avogadro proposed diatomic models for hydrogen and oxygen and H_2O as the structure of water.

The DALTON system provides a representation of the atomic hypothesis within which both sets of models can be accommodated. By the addition of appropriate search constraints to the basic system, it can be made to arrive at either of the two accounts. Thus, DALTON illustrates processes of discovery in chemistry that are driven jointly by a representation (the atomic hypothesis), by theoretical constraints (Dalton's rule of simplicity, or Gay-Lussac's law), and by the data derived from observed chemical reactions. (It does not, of course, explain where either the representation or the theoretical constraints came from.)

We saw also that DALTON's task was best formulated in terms of constraint satisfaction, with the conservation of particles and the consistency of models across reactions the two main constraints. Although we did not implement John Dalton's rule of greatest simplicity, we saw that it could be viewed as yet another constraint on the search for models.

When we considered two other domains to which DALTON might be extended, we found that they differed somewhat in their constraints, even though both involved the creation of structural models from reactions. In the case of particle physics, we noted that quantitative attributes such as mass, spin, and charge introduced additional constraints that might limit the search for models. In the case of classical genetics, we noted that conservation of "particles" (in this case, genotypes) was not an appropriate assumption, and that search had to be constrained in a different way. Despite the differences among the representations for these diverse domains, we found the approach taken in DALTON to be applicable to them. DALTON's representation of the atomic hypothesis appears to have wide application to physical theories expressed in terms of particles and their interactions.

IV PUTTING THE PICTURE TOGETHER

In this part we show how a more general system might be built by synthesizing BACON, GLAUBER, STAHL, and DALTON. We sketch processes that could account for such other aspects of scientific discovery as the generation of research programs, the invention of instruments, and the formulation of appropriate representations of scientific problems.

9 An Integrated View of Law Discovery

The four artificial-intelligence systems discussed in chapters 3 through 8—
BACON, GLAUBER, STAHL, and DALTON—address different aspects of the law-
discovery process. Our next step toward a more complete treatment is to
undertake the integration of the results of these separate but clearly related
efforts. There are two natural forms that such an integration might take
(Langley et al. 1985).

The first approach involves viewing the different forms of discovery in
terms of a single unifying framework. We have argued throughout the
preceding chapters that the notion of heuristic search provides such a
framework, and below we shall discuss each of our discovery systems in
terms of the problem spaces they explore, the operators they use for moving
through these spaces, and the manner in which they organize search. Since
we have already described each of the systems in this manner, this treatment will serve mainly as a review. However, discussing the systems side by
side will also serve to highlight their similarities and differences.

The second approach involves constructing an integrated AI discovery
system that includes BACON, GLAUBER, STAHL, and DALTON as components.
This is more difficult than the first form of integration, and in this chapter
we can only outline our plans for such a unified model. We believe that this
exercise will ultimately prove much more useful than simply viewing all
the systems within the same framwork. The introduction of constraints on
the discovery process that are not present when each discovery task is
examined in isolation will make an integrated discovery system a stronger
theory than a collection of independent models. However, an examination
of the systems within the framework of heuristic search will lay some of the
necessary groundwork for this effort, so let us begin by reviewing BACON
and its relatives in these terms.

Discovery as Search

Before attempting to describe our discovery systems in terms of heuristic
search, let us review the basic components of this framework. As with the
analog of physical search, there is a space of possible locations called the
problem space. This space is composed of a set of *states* that can be occupied
at any given time; these are analogous to locations in physical search.
Within this set there exists a special state from which one begins the search
process; this is the *initial state*. Also, there may be an explicit *goal state* that
one wants to achieve; this may be very specific or quite abstract. Finally,

there are *operators* that allow one to generate new states from the current state; applying these operators corresponds to taking steps in the physical search process.

Together, an initial state and a set of operators (along with their conditions for application) define a problem space: All the states contained in that space can be generated by applying the operators to the initial state, then applying them to the resulting states, and so forth. Of course, it is inefficient to generate states in this exhaustive fashion, and this is where heuristics come into play. Heuristics provide suggestions for deciding which operators to apply and which states to expand in order to approach the goal state and avoid undesired states. Heuristic knowledge sometimes takes the form of conditions ensuring that the operators are applied only when they are likely to lead in useful directions. In other cases, heuristic information is contained in numerical evaluation functions that indicate which states are closer to the goal or desirable in some other sense. Both forms of heuristics have been employed in our discovery systems.

BACON as Search

As was noted in chapters 3 and 4, BACON.3 and BACON.4 can be viewed as searching two interconnected spaces: a space of data and a space of laws and concepts. Two relations exist between the data space and the law space: that the laws BACON discovers must summarize accurately the data it gathers while searching the first space, and that BACON's search for laws is embedded within the search for data. A brief review of BACON.3's overall strategy will illustrate this.

Given a set of independent variables and their possible values, BACON runs a complete factorial-design experiment to examine all combinations of independent values and to gather the dependent values associated with each combination. It does this in the exhaustive, depth-first manner illustrated in table 9.1. In the process, the system constructs a hierarchical tree in which the lowest nodes are complete experimental combinations and the higher nodes are partial combinations with some independent values unspecified.

The depth-first nature of this process corresponds to the traditional scientific method of varying one term at a time while holding other terms constant. For example, BACON might select the combination $[X = 1, Y = 10, Z = 100]$, followed by $[X = 1\ Y = 10, Z = 200]$, which is followed by $[X = 1, Y = 10, Z = 300]$. For each of these combinations, the system

Table 9.1
BACON viewed in terms of seach concepts.

SPACE OF DATA

Initial state: the null combination [ ].

Goal state: a complete experimental combination of independent values.

Intermediate states: a partial combination of independent values.

Operators:

    Specify-value   specifies the value of an undetermined independent value.

Heuristics and evaluation functions: none; search is exhaustive

Search control: exhaustive depth-first search with backtracking; generates all goal states
   (experimental combinations).

SPACE OF LAWS

Initial state: a set of independent and dependent terms.

Goal state: one or more laws involving constant values or linear relations.

Intermediate states: new terms defined as products, ratios, or intrinsic properties of initial
   terms.

Operators and heuristics:

    Note-constant   Propose a law when a term has a constant value.

    Note-linear   Propose a law when two terms are related linearly.

    Define-product   Define the product of two terms when they are related inversely.

    Define-ratio   Define the ratio of two terms when they are related directly.

    Define-intrinsic-property   Define an intrinsic property and assign it values when
      encountering a nominal variable.

    Note-common-divisor   Replace a set of intrinsic values with integers when they have a
      common divisor.

Search control: depth-first search constrained by heuristic conditions on operators.

would note the associated dependent values (say $W = 200$, 400, and 600, respectively). After considering all the values of Z, BACON would proceed to search for a law that would cover the data. In this case it would define the ratio W/Z, which has the constant value 2 when $X = 1$ and $Y = 10$. This constant value would be stored at the node $[X = 1, Y = 10]$, the parent of the three nodes on which the law was based.

The depth-first search through the data space would next consider the partially specified combination $[X = 1, Y = 20]$, followed by the three complete combinations in which Z is 100, 200, and 300. Suppose that in this case BACON were to find the law $W/Z = 1$, which would be stored at the $[X = 1, Y = 20]$ node. Suppose further that when $X = 1$ and $Y = 40$, BACON were to find that the law $W/Z = 0.5$ best covered the data. Assuming that no additional values of Y remained to be considered, BACON would search for a law relating the values of the independent term Y and the higher-level dependent term W/Z. In this case, it would find the law $YW/Z = 20$, which would be stored at the parent node $[X = 1]$.

The point is that, for each node in the data search tree (except the terminal nodes), BACON carries out a separate search for laws that hold under those conditions. The resulting laws are used as data at the next higher level in the data tree, until ultimately the system arrives (ideally) at a set of laws covering all the data. Thus, in the above example BACON searches for laws that hold when $X = 1$ and $Y = 10$, for others that hold when $X = 1$ and $Y = 20$, and for others that hold when $X = 1$ and $Y = 40$. At the next higher level of description, it looks for laws that hold when $X = 1$, for others that hold when $X = 2$, and for a final set that hold when $X = 3$. This search for laws at different levels of generality is reminiscent of the search for characterizations of classes at different levels of abstraction in the conceptual-clustering task discussed in chapter 6.

BACON's search for laws is interesting in its own right. The system employs a small number of operators, summarized in table 9.1. The first two, NOTE-CONSTANT and NOTE-LINEAR, state laws in terms of constant values and linear relations, respectively. The second two, DEFINE-PRODUCT and DEFINE-RATIO, define new theoretical terms as products or ratios of existing terms. The final two operators, used to postulate intrinsic properties and common divisors, are employed only in BACON.4.

BACON's initial state is a set of data clusters, each specifying the value of the varied independent term and the observed values of one or more dependent terms. The goal is one or more laws that summarize these data in terms of either constant values or linear relations. BACON employs its operators to search the space of laws indirectly, by searching for terms that have constant values or are related linearly. The various operators are used to this end, but the conditions under which these operators are employed are as important as the operators themselves. For instance, DEFINE-PRODUCT is used to generate a new term only when the values of two existing terms are related inversely and DEFINE-RATIO applies only when the values of one term increase as those of another increase. NOTE-CONSTANT and NOTE-LINEAR apply only when BACON observes constant values or linear relations, and DEFINE-INTRINSIC-PROPERTY and NOTE-COMMON-DIVISOR are used only when the numerical methods cannot be applied because the independent variables are nominal rather than numerical.

Table 9.2
GLAUBER viewed in terms of search concepts.

Initial state: a list of facts containing only constant terms.
Goal state: a list of laws rélating classes, along with definitions of those classes.
Intermediate states: a mixed list of facts and laws, with some class definitions.
Operators:
    Form-class   defines a class and substitutes it into facts.
    Determine-quantifier   specifies existential or universal quantifiers.
Heuristics:
    for Form-law   Select the object occurring in the most analogous facts.
    for Determine-quantifier   Quantify universally if the data justify it.
Search control: Best-first search with no backtracking (hill-climbing)

Given these heuristic rules, BACON carries out a depth-first search through a space of concepts and (implicitly) laws. Given a choice, the system focuses on relations between more recently generated terms rather than older ones. Thus, in discovering Kepler's third law BACON first defines D/P as the ratio of D and P, then defines D^2/P as the product of D/P and D, and finally defines D^3/P^2 as the product of D^2/P and D/P. Although BACON does not explicitly include a strategy for backtracking, if it fails to note regularities among recently defined terms it automatically turns its attention back to earlier ones. (This seldom happens during actual runs, since the program's heuristics are usually sufficient to point the way to useful laws directly.)

GLAUBER as Search

Unlike BACON, the GLAUBER system is presented with a set of facts that it must summarize; as a result, it searches only a space of laws and concepts and does not search a space of data. However, the laws and concepts considered by GLAUBER are quite different in nature from those found by BACON. This difference is due largely to the data the two systems have available. BACON considers mainly numerical data and always searches for numerical laws; GLAUBER is given only symbolic (and relational) data and searches for qualitative laws.

Table 9.2 summarizes the system in terms of search concepts. As was stated in chapter 6, GLAUBER employs two distinct operators: FORM-CLASS, which creates an extensionally defined class of substances based on a set of facts in which each occupies a similar role, and DETERMINE-QUANTIFIER, which substitutes the class name into other facts containing these objects and decides on the appropriate quantifier each of the resulting qualitative laws. These operators are always interleaved; FORM-CLASS is applied to define a new class, followed by multiple applications of DETERMINE-QUANTIFIER for various laws, followed by another use of FORM-CLASS, and so forth.

This stylized alternation means that the interesting decisions in GLAUBER revolve not around which operators are applied but around how they are instantiated against the current set of laws and data. For a given set of facts there are many possible classes that GLAUBER could form, and it relies on heuristic knowledge to determine the most appropriate one. This brings to light another difference from BACON: GLAUBER employs a numerical evaluation function to decide which class to form, favoring classes based on the greatest number of analogous facts or laws. GLAUBER also uses a numerical threshold to determine whether to place a universal or an existential quantifier on its laws. These control strategies differ markedly from the symbolic heuristics used in BACON (which, ironically, match against numerical data).

STAHL as Search

Our third discovery system, STAHL, shares BACON's use of symbolic heuristics to direct search through the space of componential models. However, like GLAUBER, it deals with purely qualitative representations and is presented with the data on which it operates, so that it searches only one problem space. The initial state is a set of reactions[1]; the goals are to distinguish elements from compounds and to determine the elemental components of each compound.

STAHL employs the five basic operators presented in table 9.3. The first of these is INFER-COMPONENTS, which generates a componential model directly by specifying the elements that make up a substance. Like all STAHL's operators, this one is strongly linked to a heuristic rule that indicates when it should be applied. In this case, the conditions state that one may invoke INFER-COMPONENTS whenever one has a reaction containing a single substance in either the input or the output. Different conditions constrain the application of REDUCE and SUBSTITUTE. REDUCE, which is called only when the same substance occurs on both

---

1. This is not quite accurate, since STAHL processes and accepts reactions incrementally. However, this seems the best description when one is viewing the system in terms of search.

Table 9.3
STAHL viewed in terms of search concepts.

Initial state: a list of reactions and the substances involved.
Goal state: the components of each compound substance.
Intermediate states: components of some substances, modified reactions.
Operators and Heuristics:
    Infer-components   decides on the components of a substance.
    Reduce   cancels substances occurring on both sides of a reaction.
    Substitute   replaces a substance in a reaction with its components.
    Identify-components   identifies two components as the same.
    Identify-compounds   identifies two compounds as the same.
Search control: depth-first search constrained by heuristic conditions, with intelligent
    backtracking.

---

sides of a reaction, causes both occurrences to be deleted. SUBSTITUTE applies when a substance whose components are known occurs in some reaction; in such cases, SUBSTITUTE may be used to replace the substance with its known components.

These three basic operators are complemented by two actions concerned with determining when two apparently dissimilar substances are actually the same. IDENTIFY-COMPONENTS applies when two componential models that have been inferred for a given substance differ by only one element. In this case, STAHL infers that the differing elements are identical and replaces all occurrences of one by the other. IDENTIFY-COMPOUNDS carries out the same action with regard to compounds, applying when two apparently different compounds have been found to contain exactly the same elements. In fact, one could view these as the same operator applying under slightly different conditions.

Despite the heuristic conditions placed on STAHL's operators, cases still arise in which multiple choices are possible. In such situations, STAHL prefers INFER-COMPONENTS to REDUCT and SUBSTITUTE; however, if the former is not applicable, the system attempts to apply a sequence of operators—either REDUCE followed by INFER-COMPONENTS or SUBSTITUTE followed by REDUCE followed by INFER-COMPONENTS. These sequences can be viewed as macro-operators that are useful in avoiding intermediate states that may lead STAHL down incorrect paths. Even with such cautionary measures, STAHL sometimes arrives at inconsistent conclusions, and then it must determine the source of the problem and remove the inappropriate inferences.

Table 9.4
DALTON viewed in terms of search concepts.

Initial state: a list of reactions and the components of the substances involved.
Goal state: a model of each substance, specifying the number of atoms of each component; a model of each reaction, specifying the number of molecules of each substance.
Intermediate states: partial models of some substances and reactions.
Operators:
  Specify-molecules   specifies the number of times a substance occurs in a reaction.
  Specify-atoms   specifies the number of atoms of a substance in a given molecule.
  Conserve-particles   determines remaining numbers of atoms on the basis of conservation.
Heuristics:
  for Specify-molecules   Consider only multiples of the combining volumes.
  for Specify-atoms   Select simpler models before more complex ones.
Search control: depth-first search with backtracking, constrained by heuristics.

STAHL recognizes two forms of inconsistency, and it responds to them in different ways. The first involves noting that two models have been inferred for the same substance. In such cases, STAHL looks for additional evidence to support one of the models, rejecting the other when it is found. The second type of inconsistency involves circularity in models (e.g., A is composed of B and C, B is composed of A and D). In this situation, STAHL introduces a conceptual distinction, actually rewriting one of the observed "facts" to avoid the recursion. Both types of recovery can be viewed as backtracking, but in each case the system reasons about the source of the problem in such a way that only a few changes need to be made. As a result, the majority of the inferences made up to that point can be left unchanged.

DALTON as Search

Of the four discovery systems we have examined, DALTON is the easiest to cast in terms of heuristic search. In chapter 8 we saw that this system begins with a set of reactions and with knowledge of the components of compounds, and has the goal of formulating molecular models that explain these reactions. Molecular models contain two types of information: the number of molecules each compound contributes to a given reaction and the number of atoms of each element in a molecule of a given compound. The first of these is specific to a particular reaction; the second is required to hold for all instances of the compound in question. As a result, DALTON relies on two basic operators: SPECIFY-MOLECULES, which proposes the number of molecules of a substance in some reaction, and SPECIFY-ATOMS, which proposes the number of atoms of some element in some molecule. DALTON applies the first of these a number of times, until the number of molecules has been specified for each substance, and then applies the second operator until a complete model for each substance has been proposed. However, because each operator can be instantiated in multiple ways, DALTON proposes one, two, three, or even more occurrences of a molecule or atom. The resulting search is organized in a depth-first manner, with DALTON giving preference to simpler models and backtracking if the final model violates the conservation constraint (i.e., if it does not have the same number of particles of each type on both sides of the reaction).

In addition to the simpler-models-first heuristic, DALTON uses two more powerful methods to constrain the search process. First, when the system has generated complete models for the input side of a reaction and has hypothesized the number of molecules in the output side, it can use its knowledge of conservation to determine the number of atoms occurring in the output substance. It is not clear whether this is best viewed as a separate operator CONSERVE-PARTICLES (in chapter 8 we called it SPECIFY-COMPOUND) or as heuristic knowledge used to constrain the application of the SPECIFY-ATOMS operator, but the result is the same regardless of the label. Second, DALTON can employ knowledge of combining volumes to constrain the application of the SPECIFY-MOLECULES operator, so that only models in which multiples of the observed combining volumes occur are considered. Using this heuristic, DALTON arrives at quite a different model of the water reaction than when it relies on the simpler-models-first heuristic.

DALTON's concern with multiple reactions forces it to revise an earlier model in the light of new information. For instance, if DALTON is given only the water reaction, a monatomic model of the hydrogen molecule accounts for the data (including combining volumes) perfectly well. However, to account also for the ammonia reaction one must posit a diatomic hydrogen molecule. If the water reaction has already been handled, then DALTON must backtrack and find a new model of water consistent with the diatomic assumption. This does not require one to discard the ammonia model, even though it is "lower" in the search tree. Thus, DALTON's backtracking is "intelligent" in the sense that only models affected by the revised model need be reexamined.

Toward an Integrated Discovery System

Our review of the four discovery systems in terms of search provides a common language for describing the programs and clarifies the similarities and differences among them. However, it is unsatisfying in that we are still left with four independent models of discovery, each dealing with a different aspect of this complex process. In the current form, each system tells only part of the story; in order to achieve a fuller understanding of the nature of the scientific process, the separate components should be combined into a single, integrated discovery system.

Undertaking this integration will increase our knowledge of the relations among the various forms of discovery. In turn, this understanding will constrain the component systems, since the outputs of one program will have to conform to the inputs of another. This will lead to revisions of the existing systems that will produce more robust and plausible discovery programs. Further, the resulting system will be more nearly self-contained, relying less on the programmer and more on its own devices. To the extent that this can be achieved, an integrated discovery system will be much less susceptible to the criticism that discoveries are being "built in" through the provision of the necessary inputs.

Integration has some implications for the nature of the search that would be carried out by the system. Clearly the operators used by each of the component systems would remain the same, as would the heuristics for applying those operators. The initial states for each component would be largely the same but would no longer be provided by the programmer; instead they would be generated by other components as output. However, in combination with a set of operators and rules for applying them, an initial state effectively defines a problem space. Thus, to the extent that discovery system A's initial state is created by another system B, one could argue that B has defined the problem space that A will search. This may lead A to specify a new initial state for B, thus defining a new space for it to search. The dream of an AI learning system that lifts itself by its own bootstraps is an old one, and we do not expect to achieve it in the near future. However, we do believe that it lies in the direction we propose to explore, in which individual learning systems are combined to form a whole that becomes greater than the sum of its parts.

Below we examine some scenarios in which significant interactions might take place among BACON, GLAUBER, STAHL, and DALTON. In each case, we treat the individual systems as black boxes and focus on the relation between their inputs and outputs. Although we are far from actually combining these programs into a unified system, we hope that these examples will convince the reader that such a system is not only possible but necessary if we ever hope to understand fully the complex process we call scientific discovery. The actual construction of this system lies somewhere in the future.

Designing Experiments and Generalizing Laws

As the history of chemistry demonstrates, the discovery of qualitative laws often precedes the discovery of quantitative relations. Since GLAUBER is concerned with the former and BACON with the latter, it seems natural to consider whether GLAUBER might contribute something to BACON's discovery process. Two connections suggest themselves, one involving BACON's search through the space of data and the other relating to its search through the space of laws. Let us consider these in turn, using examples from chemistry in both cases.

In order to run its factorial-design experiments, BACON relies on the programmer to provide a set of variables and their associated values. For instance, in finding Dalton's law of simple proportions, the system must be told not only to vary the input element and the resulting compound but also what elements and compounds to employ as values. This is an awkward formulation, since the resulting compound is most easily viewed as a dependent term rather than an independent one. However, BACON's approach to intrinsic properties required such an arrangement, and we responded with terms and values like those shown in table 4.22.

However, suppose that an extended version of GLAUBER had determined which elements reacted with one another and what compounds were produced in each case. In an integrated system, GLAUBER could pass this information on to an extended BACON, which could use the knowledge to decide which experimental combinations to examine. Moreover, since the resulting compounds would have already been determined, it seems much more plausible to use them as observationally controlled independent terms. For instance, suppose BACON were to be told by GLAUBER that nitric oxide, nitrous oxide, and nitrogen dioxide were all substances that resulted from reactions between nitrogen and oxygen. Given knowledge of this class of compounds, an extended version of BACON might design an experiment in which the substances entering a reaction (oxygen and nitrogen) were held constant while the output of the reaction was varied. If quantitative variables such as the weights of the substances were to be examined, the resulting experiment would lead BACON to Dalton's law of multiple proporttions, as described in an earlier chapter.

The second interaction involves using GLAUBER's output to bias BACON's generalization process for intrinsic properties. BACON's current strategy is very conservative; initially it associates all potentially relevant symbolic conditions with the intrinsic values it postulates, and it generalizes these (by removing conditions) only when it finds that a set of intrinsic values are useful in a new context. In the example of Ohm's law (table 4.1), the system assumed that conductance values were conditional on both the wire and the battery, and removed the battery constraint only after finding linear relations between sets of intrinsic values. However, the availability of the classes generated by GLAUBER presents an alternative approach to generalizing conditions. Rather than remove conditions entirely, one can produce a more general rule by replacing the symbol in a condition with the name of some class containing that symbol. For instance, suppose BACON has stored a set of intrinsic values in which a condition for retrieval is that one of the substances entering the reaction is HCl. Next, suppose that the system finds the same intrinsic values useful when the substance is HNO_3 instead of HCl (i.e., a linear relation is detected). Also assume that GLAUBER has defined the class of acids, containing the substances HCl and HNO_3 as members. Rather than infer that the HCl condition is irrelevant, BACON might decide that the intrinsic values should be retrieved whenever an acid is involved in the reaction. This more conservative approach to determining the conditions on intrinsic values would allow BACON to express a larger class of hypotheses than it currently can. Of course, the system could eventually decide to remove this condition entirely should the intrinsic values prove useful for nonacids as well.

This approach to generalization suggests that GLAUBER might find a use for BACON's output as well. Imagine an alternative scheme for generalizing intrinsic values in which BACON iterates through all symbolic values of an independent term, collecting those for which a set of intrinsic values is useful. Suppose the connection between symbols and values is stored in propositions such as (intrinsics of {HCl} are {1.23 2.76 4.35}) and (intrinsics of {HNO_3} are {1.23 2.76 4.35}).

Given such a set of propositions, GLAUBER could define a class (say A) on the basis of those substances for which the values were useful, and could formulate a law summarizing this knowledge, such as

∀A (intrinsics of {A} are {1.23 2.76 4.35}).

This class name could then be substituted into other qualitative facts, leading to the formulation of additional laws. Thus, one can imagine GLAUBER aiding BACON's generalization process, or BACON's generalization method providing data for GLAUBER's discoveries, depending on which system is allowed to operate first. In principle, interesting feedback could occur, with GLAUBER enabling BACON to make discoveries that lead to new findings by GLAUBER.

Determining the Components of Acids

Both STAHL and GLAUBER deal with qualitative inputs, and both are capable of dealing with reactions among substances. This suggests that there is considerable opportunity for interaction between the two systems, particularly in the domain of chemistry. As with BACON and GLAUBER, communication can occur in either direction; however, let us first consider how STAHL might take advantage of GLAUBER's output.

GLAUBER is presented with facts such as

(reacts inputs {HCl NaOH} outputs {NaCl}),

and in response it generates abstract laws like

∀ salt ∃ acid ∃ alkali (reacts inputs {acid alkali} outputs {salt}).

Given such laws as its data, a STAHL modified to handle quantifiers would try to determine the components of the "substances" involved. In this case, the system would infer that all salts are composed of an acid and an alkali. Although this conclusion is not very surprising, it is an inference one would like the discovery system to make.

More complex interactions become possible when one realizes that concepts like HCl and NaOH are not actually primitives. Like the higher-level concepts acid and alkali, they were defined in terms of observable characteristics of sample substances. For instance, samples labeled HCl share nearly identical tastes, colors, and other perceptual properties. The fact that members of this class share more features than do members of the more general class of acids does not make HCl any less of a class.

Following this line of reasoning, suppose that GLAUBER were to be given various facts concerning the tastes and colors of a large set of samples (let us call them o1, o2, and so forth). Some of these samples would have very similar tastes and very similar colors. On the basis of such shared properties, these chemicals would be grouped into the classes we know as hydrogen (H), chlorine (Cl), and so on. If the primitive substances had participated in reactions such as (reacts inputs {o1 o2} outputs {o3}), GLAUBER would rewrite these in terms of the new classes, giving reaction laws like

∀H ∀Cl ∃HCl (reacts inputs {H Cl} outputs {HCl}).

GLAUBER would then process such laws to determine still higher-level classes and laws, such as those involving acids and alkalis. However, they could also be passed as inputs to the STAHL system.

Given inputs such as ∀H ∀Cl ∃HCl (reacts inputs {H Cl} outputs {HCl}), our extended STAHL would apply its rules to infer the components of the substances involved. In this case, it would immediately infer that all instances of HCl are composed of hydrogen and chlorine. Although this inference is not very interesting by itself, suppose that STAHL then passes this result back to GLAUBER as additional data. In order to do this, it must represent the inference in GLAUBER's terms; however, the format (components of {HCl} are {H Cl}) would serve quite well. Further, suppose that STAHL has reached analogous conclusions from other reactions, such as ∀H ∀NO$_3$ ∃HNO$_3$ (components of {HNO$_3$} are {H NO$_3$}). Given reactions like those discussed in chapter 6, GLAUBER formulates the classes of acids, alkalis, and salts. In the process, it substitutes these class names into other facts and laws that refer to members of the classes. Given componential models like the ones above, GLAUBER would formulate (through substitution) the laws

∃ acid (components of {acid} are {H Cl})

and

∃ acid (components of {acid} are {H NO$_3$}).

It would then attempt to determine the appropriate quantifier in each case. Since each of these laws covers only half of the "facts" that it might cover, an existential quantifier is used in both cases.

Given the laws

∃ acid (components of {acid} are {H Cl})

and

∃ acid (components of {acid} are {H NO₃}),

GLAUBER might note that these are identical except for the substance classes Cl and NO₃. On the basis of this similarity, the system would define a new class (say acid-components) with the differing substances as members. Along with this, GLAUBER would formulate the law

∀ acid-component ∃ acid (components of {acid} are {H acid-component}).

This law states that there is a class of substances that always form acid when combined with hydrogen. GLAUBER could discover the inverse law (that an acid usually has hydrogen as one of its components) by considering (components of {HCl} are {H Cl}), (components of {HNO₃} are {H NO₃}), and so on. GLAUBER would infer that ∀ acid ∃ acid-component (components of {acid} are {H acid-component}). The point is that, working together, GLAUBER and STAHL could arrive at laws that neither could discover in isolation. In effect, GLAUBER directs STAHL's search through the space of componential models by providing new reactions, and STAHL directs GLAUBER's search through the space of classes and qualitative laws. A similar line of reasoning might lead the GLAUBER-STAHL hybrid to the conclusion that every metal has phlogiston as one of its components.

Building Structural Models

As we have seen, STAHL focuses on determining the components of chemical substances, whereas DALTON is concerned with the number of particles involved in a reaction. Thus, STAHL can be viewed as laying the groundwork for a detailed structural model, and DALTON as responsible for finalizing the model. Moreover, DALTON requires knowledge about the components of a substance in order to test its conservation assumption, and it would seem natural for this information to come from STAHL. In fact, the coupling between these programs is already close enough that they can be viewed as successive stages of a single system, and we expect they could be merged without a major research effort. Let us explore the form such a combined system might take.

Three distinct stages can be identified in the process of building structural models. The first, identifying the components of substances, is the focus of the STAHL system. The potential extensions of this system that have been discussed, such as providing the ability to postulate unobserved components, would not alter the system's basic goal. The second stage, determining the number of times each component occurs in some substance, is the focus of DALTON. Even with the possible extensions we have proposed for this system, such as determining numerical attributes of the components, the basic task remains the same. The final stage, which we have so far ignored, involves specifying the manner in which the various components are connected to each other. The early chemists were able to avoid this issue, but the discovery of organic molecules eventually forced them to deal with it. Kekule's proposal for the structure of the benzene ring was essentially an insight into the connections among the components of that compound. Search in this stage would involve selecting a pair of components to connect and selecting a type of bond to connect them.

We envision a single discovery system that searches the space of structural models, first determining the components involved, then identifying the number of particles taking part, and finally modeling the connections among these particles. Starting with very abstract models, this system would successively instantiate them until their complete structure had been determined. At each stage in this instantiation process, the system would employ constraints such as the conservation assumption to reject some models in favor of others. Although the space of models would be quite large, the use of such constraints would considerably limit the actual search required. Although significant work would be involved in constructing such a program, it would be an important step toward integrating the four discovery systems we have described.

Discovering the Principles of Inheritance

In chapter 6 we outlined an extended version of GLAUBER that would be able to note patterns among conjunctions of facts. We discussed the application of this system to Mendel's data on heredity and showed how it could be used to infer genotypic classes (e.g., pure-breeding green peas G, hybrid green peas G', and pure-breeding yellow peas Y) from observations about phenotypes (e.g., green and yellow peas). In chapter 8 we proposed an extended version of DALTON that, given genotypic descriptions of the offspring of various matings, would be able to infer Mendel's two-trait model to account for those descriptions.[2]

---

2. In fact, this could best be accomplished by the integrated version of STAHL and DALTON described in the preceding subsection.

These extensions suggest one way in which the revised GLAUBER and DALTON could profitably interact. The process would begin with GLAUBER observing a set of reactions and rewriting them, on the basis of regularities among those reactions, at a higher level of description. The results would then be given to DALTON, which would devise structural models to account for the high-level reactions. In this version GLAUBER would serve mainly as a preprocessor for DALTON, transforming direct observations into an initial state that the structural modeler could operate upon. However, information can flow in the opposite direction as well, with DALTON passing its results back to GLAUBER for use in the formulation of new classes and laws.

Consider an example from the domain of classical genetics. We saw in the genetics example in chapter 6 how an extended version of GLAUBER could form classes such as G (pure greens), G' (hybrid greens), and Y (pure yellows). Associated with these classes would be the laws in which they take part, including the following:

$\forall$G (reacts inputs {G G} outputs {G}),
$\forall$Y (reacts inputs {Y Y} outputs {Y}),
$\forall$G $\forall$Y (reacts inputs {G Y} outputs {G'}),
$\forall$G' (reacts inputs {G' G'} outputs {G G' Y}),
$\forall$G (has-property object {G} color {green}),
$\forall$Y (has-property object {Y} color {yellow}),
$\forall$G' (has-property object {G'} color {green}).

In chapter 8 we saw how an extended DALTON could infer "molecular" models for each of the genotypic classes. If the proposed system were to arrive at the same conclusions as Mendel, we would have G = {g g}, Y = {y y}, and G' = {g y}.

Once DALTON had made these structural inferences, it would pass the resulting models back to GLAUBER in some form that GLAUBER could handle, such as

$\forall$G (components of {G} are {g g}),
$\forall$Y (components of {Y} are {y y}),
$\forall$G' (components of {G'} are {g y}).

Given this information and the color information shown above, our extended version of GLAUBER would note that two of the "facts" involve green-colored classes. This would lead it to formulate a new class of green peas, with the classes G and G' as members.[3] As a result, GLAUBER would substitute the new class name (say F) into other laws, for which quantifiers would have to be determined.

In this case, the evidence would not justify universal quantifiers, so the system would produce two existentially quantified laws and a universal law indicating color regularity:

∃F (components of {F} are {g g}),
∃F (components of {F} are {g y}),
∀F (has-property object {F} color {green}).

The first two laws translate as "Some members of the class of green peas (F) are composed of substances g and g" and "Some members of the class of green peas (F) are composed of substances g and y." However, GLAUBER would not be done with these laws. Since the two statements are identical except for the substances g and y, GLAUBER would define a new class (say P) with these substances as members and formulate another, more general, law subsuming the original laws. This law is stated as

∀P ∃F (components of {F} are {g P}).

It can be paraphrased as "Each member of the class P combines with one green substance to form some member of the class of green peas (F)." This example is similar to the earlier one in which GLAUBER noted hydrogen as a component of acids, but it can be interpreted somewhat differently. In the context of genetics, the above law states that g is a *dominant* trait, since it leads to green plants whenever it occurs as a component. Again, we have seen that complex feedback between two discovery methods can lead to laws that could not be discovered by either method alone.

Constraining the Search for Structural Models

We observed in chapter 8 how DALTON's search through the space of structural models can be altered by heuristics, such as the rule of combining volumes that led to Avogadro's model of the water reaction. However, we have not discussed the origin of the information used by such rules. For instance, Avogadro's heuristic must know the combining volumes for a

3. Actually, it is likely that such a class would have been defined much earlier. The exact timing has little relevance as long as GLAUBER is aware that G and G' are related in some manner.

reaction before it can be used to constrain search. Since this information is numerical, it is natural to consider BACON as a possible source. Reviewing BACON's chemical discoveries, we find that the system's common-divisor method generates the combining volumes required by DALTON. Thus, in principle, BACON's output can be used to direct DALTON's search through the space of possible models.

We also discussed in chapter 8 an extended version of DALTON that would be able to determine numerical properties of the components in its models; for example, it might estimate the relative atomic weights of elements taking part in a set of reactions (a major concern of chemists at the beginning of the nineteenth century). One can imagine DALTON, given such estimates, placing additional constraints on its models and using these constraints to reject some models in favor of others. For example, the system might require that the estimated atomic weights be consistent across different reactions.

However, in order to estimate the relative weights of the components in a model, DALTON would have to know the combining weights of the substances involved in a set of reactions. Again, BACON is the obvious source for such knowledge, since it generates combining weights at the same time it produces combining volumes. In summary: BACON has the potential to place significant constraints on DALTON's search process. It is interesting to observe that data-driven methods, such as those used in BACON, can be an aid to theory-driven behavior of the kind found in DALTON.

Structure of the Proposed System

The above scenarios provide some idea of the behavior we expect from the integrated discovery system. However, we have not discussed the structure of the proposed system. In particular, we should consider how closely linked the systems will be to one another. In considering the relation between STAHL and DALTON, we decided that the coupling should be very close, since these systems can actually be viewed as dealing with different stages in the same search process. But it is not clear that the same conclusion holds for the interactions among BACON, GLAUBER, and STAHL-DALTON, since these systems seem to address genuinely different aspects of discovery (the search for quantitative laws, the search for qualitative laws, and the search for structural models). More likely, the systems should be given access to a common memory, and care should be taken to ensure compatible representations.

If we assume that the systems should be loosely coupled, we must still specify whether interaction occurs occasionally or continuously. The first approach assumes that one system would begin, run its course, and then deposit its results in the common memory (usually, in this context, called a *blackboard*). At this point, control would be assumed by another system, which would take advantage of its predecessor's results to define the problem space it would search. This approach fits well with the current version of GLAUBER, which processes information in a non-incremental fashion and thus requires all facts at the outset of a run.

An alternative scheme would have the systems running concurrently, with each depositing results on the blackboard, and with these results dynamically affecting the paths taken by other systems. This approach is well suited to STAHL, which already uses an incremental approach to the formulation of componential models. Although an incremental system such as STAHL (or a somewhat incremental system such as BACON) can be provided with all the data at the outset, a non-incremental system such as GLAUBER cannot be run in the inverse mode. Thus, if we decide to pursue an incremental version of the integrated discovery system, we will have to revise GLAUBER substantially to make it fit into this framework.

Conclusion

In chapters 3 through 8 we examined four aspects of the diverse activity known as scientific discovery: finding quantitative laws, generating qualitative laws, inferring the components of substances, and formulating structural models. Our approach involved constructing AI systems that focused on these different facets of science and then testing their abilities to replicate historical discoveries. We drew many of our examples from the history of chemistry, which provided useful tests for each of the systems and which allowed us to explore potential connections among the discovery programs. We found that each of the systems could be usefully viewed as carrying out search through a space of laws or models, and we examined the operators and heuristics used to direct search through these spaces. We also found that each of the systems has some important limitations, and proposed a number of extensions that should lead to improved future versions.

Although each of the four systems—BACON, GLAUBER, STAHL, and DALTON—has contributed to our understanding of discovery, we believe that an even greater understanding could result from an exploration of the relations among the systems. We envisage an integrated discovery system incorporating the individual systems as components, with each component accepting input from one or more of the other components. Such an integrated system would be much less dependent on its programmer for carefully presented data than are the individual components, and the requirement for meaningful interaction would place additional constraints on the component systems.

As we have remarked several times, scientific discovery is a multifaceted process, and even within such an expanded framework we must omit many of its important aspects. For instance, we have not addressed the mechanisms underlying the planning of experiments, the invention of new instruments of measurement, or the selection of useful representations. In the next chapter we address these issues and related matters. Our discussion will necessarily be a good deal less concrete even than our proposals in this chapter for integrating the four systems. Nevertheless, we believe that enough is known today about the processes of scientific discovery that we can say something relatively definite about these additional topics.

10 Discovering Problems and Representations

In the preceding chapters we have focused mainly on one aspect of scientific discovery: the discovery of laws and concepts concealed in data. Within that domain, we examined primarily data-driven discovery (that is to say, search guided only by quite general nonsubstantive heuristics), although we did extend the analysis to consider the role of general theoretical constructs, such as symmetry and conservation, as search heuristics.

Our theory of discovery is embodied largely in a set of computer programs—BACON, GLAUBER, STAHL, DALTON—that demonstrate the adequacy of particular discovery processes by making actual discoveries. In chapter 1 we noted that scientific discovery embraces a number of activities besides the discovery of laws, including the discovery of research problems, the invention of scientific instruments, and the discovery and application of good problem representations. In the present chapter, we wish to discuss these three facets of scientific discovery, but at a less concrete level than in the preceding chapters. In particular, we shall not be able to provide, in discussing instruments, problem finding, and representation, the sorts of very specific definitions of our concepts and evidence for them that are offered by the hard coin of computer programs that actually run and whose ability to account for the phenomena can be tested in detail. Nevertheless, we will present our ideas in as specific a form as possible. We believe that they go a considerable distance toward providing specifications for such programs. We intend these ideas as something more than promissory notes, if something less than cash.

Processes for Finding Problems

It is easy to imagine a stupid problem generator offering problems that no scientist would put forward. Just as young children can endlessly repeat "Why?" no matter what one says to them, so could a computer. It is more difficult to create a generator that could model the ability of good scientists to (sometimes) create the right problems in the right circumstances. No scientist can do this consistently; anyone engaged in research will agree that most of the many questions that come to mind are sooner or later rejected as unimportant or as having no prospect of solution, or for both of these reasons. To be a reasonable subject of scientific research a question must have two properties: The answer must have significant interest for basic or applied science, and some ideas must be available as to how to begin the process of searching for an answer. A good problem generator should produce a reasonable proportion of reasonable questions, and should be able to filter such questions, keeping the best for further consideration.

It has sometimes been argued that the construction of a clever problem generator of this kind is impossible in principle. For example, suppose we were to try to use Mill's (1843) canon of difference as the basis for such a generator. The canon reads as follows.

The Method of Difference   If an instance in which a phenomenon occurs and one in which it does not differ in only one other circumstance, it is the cause, or effect, or an indispensable part of the cause, of the phenomenon.

Now, for any phenomenon observed to occur from time to time but not universally, we can set the problem of determining its causes and effects by searching for the unique "circumstance" that distinguishes appearance from nonappearance. An immediate objection will be raised: How can we create a complete list of all circumstances that are coexistent with the phenomenon under consideration? Such a list is probably endless, and even if it is finite we can never be sure that ours is complete. Therefore, even if we have a generator of "circumstances," and hence a problem generator, we can never be sure that the premise of Mill's canon is satisfied; there may be another circumstance that distinguishes between appearance and nonappearance, that is a real cause, and that is not on our list. However, the criticism itself rests on the faulty assumption that we are seeking an *infallible* method of scientific discovery. The discovery process solves the problem of infallibility, as it does the problems of the certainty and uniqueness of generalizations, by ignoring it. All we require is a problem generator that will set some problems. We require neither a guarantee that solutions, in the form of laws, can be found, nor a guarantee that the laws can be strongly verified. (The latter point was discussed at length in chapter 2.)

If we drop unnecessary requirements of infallibility, there is still good use for Mill's canon if certain conditions are met. Upon studying a phenomenon, the problem generator must be able to create a list of circumstances that are reasonably likely causes (preferably in order of likelihood), and it must also produce different hypothetical causes for different phenomena. The probable relevance of a cause can be assessed only by the application of knowledge that is already available, so that problem generation and the results of scientific discovery bootstrap each other.

Mill's canon of difference is used here just as any other inference rule is used. The goal of satisfying the conclusion of the rule is replaced by the goal of satisfying its premises. The fallibility of the canon is simply part of a wider (we might even say ubiquitous) fallibility: The requirements of a formal schema of reasoning clash with the richness and elusiveness of the real world. Either we preserve the infallibility at the price of making application of the scheme impossible, or we use the scheme practically at the price of occasional (perhaps frequent) failure.

But instead of continuing with this list of requisites for a problem-generation system, let us try to describe several different feasible problem-generation processes.

Recursive Problem Generation

The method of difference provides a process for recursive problem generation: If causes or effects are found for a phenomenon, the problem can then be posed of finding *their* causes and effects. A similar recursive generation of problems is seen clearly in systems of means-ends analysis, such as the General Problem Solver of Newell and Simon (1972). In attacking the problem of reaching a goal G from a starting point S, means-ends analysis may reach a new state, G_2 or S_2, by applying an operator to G or S. Now the original problem has been replaced by a problem of going from S_2 to G or from S to G_2, as the case may be.

Attempting to solve a problem by applying an operator, O, may also create new problems if certain conditions have to be satisfied before the operator can be applied. For example, the goal of gaining information about elementary particles by causing them to collide sets the problem of devising operations for bringing about such collisions.

Mathematics teems with examples of cases where new problems are posed because it is seen that their solution would contribute to the solution of important problems previously posed. Fermat's Last Theorem, for example, has been a fecund source of significant new mathematical problems.

The AM program of Lenat (1977) can be interpreted as a recursive problem generator. Its goal is to generate "interesting new concepts" using criteria of interestingness that have been provided it and operators for generating new concepts from old. As it adds concepts to its store, it creates the problem of using these concepts to generate still others.

Accidental Discovery

Pasteur said that "accidents favor the prepared mind." What makes a phenomenon so surprising that a scientist such as Fleming, Roentgen, or Becquerel attends to it? Although the details of the process are not fully understood, it is well known that attention is often attracted to phenomena that are familiar to the observer but that turn up in an unusual environment, or to new phenomena in a familiar environment, provided that the phenomena are relevant to the viewer's usual range of interests. Something familiar or understandable must be noticed, but noticed in unexpected surroundings. Such noticings are frequent in everyday perception. One notices a spot on one's shirt. Neither spots (irregular shapes) nor shirts would attract one's attention, for both are familiar objects. It is their concatenation, a spot in a wrong place, that does the trick. The lysis of bacteria was no new phenomenon to Alexander Fleming (1929), nor was the growth of mold; it was, again, their concatenation that attracted his attention.

If unfamiliar juxtapositions of familiar phenomena capture attention, what holds it? In the case of a scientist, it can be conjectured that an "accident" will be dismissed promptly if an explanation of it, in terms of scientific laws already known, readily comes to mind. If one does not, then the accidental phenomenon becomes a likely target for scientific inquiry. Fleming, unable to understand *why* a mold destroyed some bacteria, had found his problem. He pursued it by seeking to determine what species of mold produced this effect, and on what bacteria, whether the effect was produced by the organism itself or by some substances it manufactured, and so on. Without taking into account a factor external to basic science —the prospect of finding a powerful agent for destroying dangerous bacteria—one might find it difficult to explain why Fleming gave this particular research target a high priority. A problem-finding program needs information to allow it to alter its priorities among tasks to reflect external, application-driven objectives as well as internal, science-driven ones.

Accidental discovery requires both prepared minds to notice the phenomena and "prepared" laboratories to originate them. It is not accidental that such discoveries often happen in laboratories equipped with new instruments or concerned with newly discovered substances. There is nothing exceptional or unexplainable in accidental discovery. In the presence of new substances and instruments and new experimental arrangements, the simple goal of exploring a new domain systematically can generate reasonable research problems.

In fact, systematic exploration of new domains has played a large role in the histories of many sciences. Many of the experiments of Oersted, Ampère, Faraday, and their contemporaries on electricity and magnetism fall into this class: What is the action of a magnet on different metals and their compounds? Does a magnet act through air and other gases? What is the action of a magnet on light? Existing knowledge—a taxonomy of substances and their properties and components—is the major prerequisite for the generation of such problems.

A Problem-Generating System

Problem formulation can be said to begin with noticing, and what is noticed can be either a phenomenon presented "accidentally" (as in the examples just recounted) or a signal from previous investigators that something is important, practically or scientifically.[1]

Problems of Determining Scope of Phenomena

Noticing a phenomenon, or having one's attention called to it, does not in itself define a research problem. However, it is possible to sketch a definitional process that could be mechanized in a wide range of situations. A phenomenon can often be represented as an n-term relation among a set of objects. For example, Fleming's observation that a mold lysed some bacteria can be represented by $L(m, b)$, where m is a mold, b a culture of bacteria, and L the relation that m lysed b. From this representation, a series of research problems can be defined: to find the range of molds that can produce these effects, to find the range of bacteria or other organisms that are affected, and to study how the intensity of the effect depends on the pair (m, b). This is, in fact, a part of the research program that Fleming carried out after his accidental discovery of the phenomenon. Of course, to apply this problem-generation strategy one must be able to designate candidates for the sets to which m and b belong. Generally, prior knowledge in the form of classifications (the relation *is a*) will provide candidates. For example, the fact that *Penicillium*, the organism originally observed, *is*

---

1. In awarding the Nobel Prize to the Curies in 1903, the Swedish Academy of Sciences cited "their joint researches on the radiation phenomena discovered by Henri Becquerel."

a mold suggests extending the experiment to other molds. The fact that the target organism *is a* species of bacteria suggests generalization to other bacteria. Every developed field of knowledge has its taxonomies and criteria of similarity that can be used as a basis for generalization and for the consequent generation of candidates.

As we saw in chapter 6, GLAUBER is very congenial to the strategy we are describing. Having identified a class of reactions in terms of the class membership of its inputs and outputs, GLAUBER can explore the range of reactions of this type by varying one of the input or output substances while holding others constant. If we interpret $L(m, b)$ as a reaction whose output is lysed bacteria, then Fleming's program, pursued with GLAUBER's inference rules, produces extensional definitions of the class of lysing agents and the class of lysable organisms.

Problems of Characterizing Phenomena

When we have identified a range of objects that participate in a phenomenon, we can generate another collection of research problems by undertaking to characterize that range. Thus, if we have $R(a, b)$, for some set of *a*'s we can create the problem of finding the properties, P, such that $P(a)$ for these *a*'s. Again, generating this class of research problems requires prior knowledge of candidate properties of the set of *a*'s and its supersets, of methods for determining their presence or absence, and of methods for constructing compound concepts. For example, having isolated a certain substance as a digestive enzyme, a biochemist may proceed to carry out a series of chemical analyses to determine the identity of the substance. Series of standard tests will be used to determine if it is a protein, to measure its molecular weight, and, in recent years, if it is a protein, to establish its amino-acid sequence and its tertiary structure.

The GLAUBER, STAHL, and DALTON programs all respond to problems of characterizing phenomena. We have already seen how GLAUBER does this. STAHL, given a set of reactions, undertakes to describe the substances that take part in these reactions in terms of their constituents. DALTON, given the combining weights and volumes of substances, seeks to build a particulate model of them that accounts for their reactions, assuming conservation of numbers of the particles taken as elementary.

Problems of Purification

A related generator, given $R(a, b)$, would create the problem of determining what aspect or component of *a* produces the effect on *b*. Here, prior knowledge is required of what components *a* has and of the operations that are available for purifying such components (filtering, flushing, evaporating, centrifuging, and so on). For example, when it was discovered that the mottled leaves of tobacco plants with the tobacco mosaic disease were infectious (Stanley 1935), a "natural" next step was to isolate the infectious substance from the leaves, purify it, and identify the purified substance (a virus, in this case).

At the most abstract level, purification consists in dividing a substance into fractions and determining which of the fractions (if any) is capable of producing the originally observed effect. The process is repeated until the intensity of the effect can be enhanced no further or until a "pure" substance is obtained—for instance, when a substance becomes crystalline, or when a liquid is obtained that continues to boil at constant temperature. Fleming extracted penicillin from the *Penicillium* mold, purified it, and then characterized it chemically. Another classic example of such a program of research was the work of the Curies that led to the discovery of radium.

As with all of the problem-generation methods we have mentioned, a purification problem, once defined, is of interest only if there are known methods of pursuing it, or if it is transformed into the subproblem of finding such methods. Subproblem generation of the latter variety can also be formalized: Given a problem whose solution requires techniques *a*, *b*, *c*, ..., discover these techniques in the literature or create the subproblem of developing them.

Problems of Identifying Relevant Variables

The starting point of the explorations for the programs BACON, STAHL, GLAUBER, and DALTON was the data presented to them. These data defined the law-finding problem for the program.

Given data on the weights and temperatures of some substances, BACON finds Black's law, introducing the concept of specific heat along the way; but by what problem-defining process does BACON choose precisely the variables of weight and temperature from the enormously long list of potential candidates? When we take into account the prior knowledge available to experimenters at the moment they undertake a new inquiry, the selection of the "right" variables does not seem mysterious. When Joseph Black undertook his experiments on temperature, the list of parameters that were deemed relevant to the analysis of chemical processes and that could be measured was not long. Moreover, it was a part of everyday knowledge that the more hot water was mixed with a given amount of cold water, the hotter the mixture would be. Long before Black's time, quantity of matter was already associated with either weight or volume. A system to select data for a BACON-like program could arrange concepts in an order of priority that reflected the frequency of their use. With time and progress of discovery, the ordering of variables on the list would change. As new phenomena were discovered and new measuring instruments devised, new variables would be added to the list.

If selecting relevant variables is not a difficult matter, why did thirty years pass after the invention of practical thermometers before Black's law was discovered (Magie 1935, pp. 146–160)? We know that Fahrenheit and Boerhaave had performed almost the same experiments that Black later used as the source of his data. Why did they not find the law? The difficulty certainly did not lie in the problem of identifying relevant variables. Boerhaave employed quantity of matter (measured both by volume and by weight) and temperature as his variables, as Black did. He found, in fact, that 1.5 volumes of mercury produced the same change in temperature as 1 volume of water (which implies a ratio by weight of 21 : 1). We may conjecture (there appears to be no concrete evidence on this point) that, given the uncertainties of measurement at that time, the ratio of 1.5 : 1 was close enough to unity to justify the conclusion that, in terms of volume, the difference in chemical substances (mercury and water) affected their volumes and temperatures but not the heat equilibrium. By the time Black did his work, the accuracy of measurement had presumably improved to the point where a volume ratio of 1.5 : 1 could no longer be ignored, much less a 21 : 1 ratio in the specific heats by weight of his two substances. Of course, if we were to set its error-tolerance parameter sufficiently high, BACON, using data on volume and temperature, would reach exactly the same conclusion that Boerhaave did, and would not discover a need for the new substance-dependent parameter, specific heat. With a stricter error limit, BACON, like Black, introduces the new concept.

Problems Generated from New Laws

The discovery of new laws such as those found by BACON and its sister programs provides a basis for the generation of new problems. After finding a new law, one can explore the effects of varying quantities that were held constant in the original experiment. BACON, in fact, approaches experimentation in just this way; it varies one independent variable at a time, introducing a new one as soon as a regularity has been discovered among those introduced previously.

The things that are varied to create new problems may be qualitative as well as quantitative. One can generate problems by considering how the lawful behavior of a system is changed by the replacement of one or more of its components. For example, a hydrogen atom consists of a positively charged proton associated with a negatively charged electron. After the law determining the radiation emission lines of this structure had been established, it was natural to consider the modified system in which the electron was replaced by some other negative particle. One such particle then known to science was the μ meson. Hence, it became possible to pose the problem of determining the law of emission from a system in which the electron had been replaced by a meson. But this created a new problem: finding a source of meson-containing "atoms." Since they do not exist in nature, they had to be produced in order for the experiment to be carried out.

Prior knowledge suggests a method for creating such a system: Put all its components closely together in space, and let nature do the rest. In the above-mentioned case, this might mean directing a beam of mesons at a sample of hydrogen and slowing down the mesons to increase the chance of their interacting with the hydrogen nuclei. For each of these goals, we can continue to create new subgoals until we reach operations that can be carried out with current equipment (Corben and DeBenedetti 1954).

A different sequence of problems can be generated from the original hydrogen atom by replacing the positive particle (the proton) with another positive particle (say a positron). That research program was also carried out, and it resulted in the production and study of positronium (DeBenedetti 1956).

This process of generating research problems from existing knowledge can be generalized in several ways. Suppose the existing knowledge consists of a large number of schemas, some representing known systems and some representing experimental designs. The schema for an experiment would include information about the components of the experimental system, their arrangement, the measurable properties associated with each, methods for recognizing components and for producing them, and so on. Such schemas define a state space of possible experiments, which may be explored by modifying one or more of its aspects. In the example given just above, the initial state is a partially filled schema for experimenting with the hydrogen atom. The (problem-setting) goal is a new experimental situation, and we have sketched out the way in which that goal can be realized. To have any considerable power, a system of this sort would have to have not only a general schema for experimentation but also specialized schemas for particular domains, such as electrochemistry, hydrostatics, and elementary particles.

The Agenda of Research Problems

As we have just seen, the initial goal of creating an experiment resolves itself into a complex subgoal structure produced by the problem generator. Thus, a whole agenda of new problems can be created in the context of solving other problems. The discovery of a new substance or a new kind of object leads readily to problems of testing, in the new context, known laws that apply to similar substances or objects. The invention of a new instrument leads to problems of search for laws in the domain where the instrument can be used to make measurements.

As an example, if a new elementary particle is discovered, the problem can be considered of which laws applying to other particles (e.g., symmetry or parity laws) apply also to this one. As a quite different example, suppose that in an experiment on heat a mercury thermometer has frozen. Now the problem is posed of creating a new instrument that can measure the temperature below the freezing point of mercury and that will provide measurements agreeing with the mercury thermometer in some range where both are operative. This creates subproblems of creating states of low temperature and seeking parameters that change monotonically with temperature. If such a parameter is found, then a new thermometer based on this parameter must be calibrated in the range of overlap with existing thermometers.

Problems of Interrelating Knowledge

Every scientist, having inherited a large body of knowledge, including theories, searches for additional regularities within that knowledge and confronts the knowledge with new laws that are discovered. This process may yield generalizations. For example, Dalton, in his *New System* (1808), quotes the following regularity:

If a quantity of any elastic fluid be compressed by mechanical force, its temperature is raised, or it parts with a quantity of its heat.

He then confronts this generalization with a well-known phenomenon:

A piece of iron may be hammered till it is red-hot.

Putting generalization and fact together, Dalton proposes the following:

It is an universal law in nature that whenever a body is compressed ... it loses a portion of its heat.

Now whether this is in reality a law of nature is not yet, perhaps, clearly ascertained; but this is certain, that a person apprehending such a law is more likely to have a proper bent given to his investigation than one who makes a number of experiments without any fixed object in view.

Conclusion: Problem Formulation

We have carried these examples far enough to demonstrate that the generation of research problems is a problem-solving process that can be formalized and approached in the same way as other problem-solving processes. We cannot, of course, claim that our proposed formalization would encompass all problem-formulation tasks. We have emphasized that in formulating new problems, the scientist draws upon a wide range of knowledge that is already available. Problem formulation, like problem solving, is an incremental process that again calls for Pasteur's "prepared mind." But it is not a magical or mysterious process.

Our analysis of the problem-generation process should also have made evident that there is no sharp line between problem generation and problem solving. This is already clear from the structure of BACON and the other problem-solving systems discussed above. They operate by generating hypotheses that fit the data they examine. Their many stages of computation can be interpreted as steps of solving different problems that were generated tacitly but never made explicit.

Invention of Scientific Instruments

Data are derived from measurements, and measurements require instruments. Where do instruments come from? To give a complete account of the origins of measurement and instruments, we would have to begin with the human senses. Basic comparative judgments of location, length, size, and color are made with the eyes, unaided by mechanical instruments. Weight is judged by lifting, roughness by touching, sourness or sweetness by taste, sound intensity and pitch by hearing.

Scaling these qualitative measures numerically calls for the definition of standard units with which stimuli can be compared. But, as we have shown in chapter 4, the establishment of fundamental measurements is intimately tied up with the introduction of intrinsic concepts. We have seen how BACON, supplied with data on the mutual accelerations of labeled but otherwise undescribed objects, is able to arrive at the new concept of inertial mass and to assign numerical masses to the objects, using one of them as the standard. In the same way, BACON is able to discover and apply a scale of specific heats and a numerical scale of refractive indexes.

Any intrinsic concept, in association with the experimental arrangement that allows it to be measured, can be employed as a scientific instrument. For example, a spring and a unit mass can be used to measure the relative accelerations of that mass with other objects, and hence to measure the inertial masses of those other objects. In this case, as in many others, the discovery of the instrument for measuring inertial mass is coincident with the discovery of the concept itself and the law of conservation of momentum.

Let us look at the case of temperature, the measurement of which we did not examine in any of the examples in the previous chapters. In our study of Black's Law, using BACON, we assumed that we already had available an appropriate thermometer. We begin now with the simple sensory observation that we can distinguish different degrees of heat (i.e., of temperature) in a substance—that is, that the substance may be of various degrees of coldness and hotness that we can produce and identify.[2] What was required next was the observation, which could be accidental, that various substances expand when heated. Using liquids (which were easier to handle and to measure precisely), early investigators of the phenomena of heat and temperature defined arbitrary scales, taking observable qualitative phenomena such as the freezing and boiling points of water as anchor points for the scale and interpolating linearly between these anchor points. Of course, different scales resulted when different substances and different anchor points were used. The theory-based thermometric scales we now employ

2. In 1701 Newton published anonymously in *Philosophical Transactions* a phenomenological temperature scale using as points along the scale such phenomena as "heat of the air in the middle of the day in the Month of July," "the greatest heat of a bath which one can endure for some time when the hand is dipped in it and is kept still," "the heat at which a mixture of two parts of tin and one part of bismuth is melted," "the heat of coals in a little kitchen fire made from bituminous coal and excited by the use of a bellows," and so on (Magie 1935, pp. 125–126).

required another step—essentially, the introduction of an intrinsic variable. Suppose that, instead of graduating a thermometer directly, we simply mark on it a dense array of points. We now heat some gas at constant volume and, with the thermometer immersed in it, measure the pressure periodically and record the point on the thermometer that has been reached at the same moment. If we now assign to each point a number proportional to the corresponding gas pressure, we have constructed a gas thermometer whose zero will be determinate. Since the constant of proportionality is not fixed, we can assign it any value we please. For example, we can assign it so as to obtain the Kelvin scale, with absolute zero ($0°K$) at approximately $-273°C$ and with the boiling point of water at $373°K$. Our new thermometer will be theory laden in the same way that an instrument for measuring inertial mass is theory laden: The scale is selected in such a way as to simplify the expression of certain laws.[3]

Virtually identical considerations entered into the invention of ammeters, voltmeters, and other electrical instruments. When Ohm found that the deflection of a magnetized needle adjacent to a closed circuit varied inversely with the length of the resistance wire in the circuit, this observation made it natural to define the amount of current as proportional to the deflection of the needle and the resistance as proportional to the length of the wire. (As a matter of historical fact, the use of the swing of the needle to measure the intensity of the current was first proposed by Ampère [see Magie 1935, pp. 450–451], who named the instrument a galvanometer.) Once the magnitudes had been defined in this way, these definitions could be extrapolated to additional measuring instruments, or even modified if recalibration with the new instruments led to simpler forms of the laws.

As the history of the galvanometer illustrates, new instruments most often begin with the discovery of new phenomena. The discovery that the trajectory of an ionized atom or molecule is deflected when the ion passes through an electric or magnetic field was the basis for the mass spectrograph, used to identify molecules by determining the masses of particles derived from them. Mikhail Tswett's observation that his attempts to extract chlorophyll from leaves were sometimes unsuccessful because of the physical adsorption of the pigment on the plant tissues led him to the idea

---

3. It may seem odd that the same measurement operations can simultaeoulsy define an intrinsic concept and test an empirical law. Many authors, for this reason, have argued that $F = ma$ is a definition of force (or mass), and hence not an empirical law. For a solution of this conundrum, showing that there is no contradiction, see Simon 1977, pp. 393–394.

of separating out the various components of chlorophyll by filtering it down a long column, so that different components with different adsorptive strengths would be deposited at different locations; this produced the important instrument we call the chromatograph.

By this account, the invention of instruments is not a wholly separate chapter in scientific discovery, but is part and parcel of the discovery of new phenomena and of the laws governing these phenomena.

The Sources of Representations

If, in this book, we were to pursue theory-driven discovery farther than we have, we would have to address in a more complete manner the topic of representation. In the data-driven discovery of BACON, a single representation, consisting of list structures whose elements can be assigned numerical properties, was sufficient for our purposes. The data provided to BACON were uniformly numerical or nominal, and the laws that BACON discovered could all be expressed in terms of the standard mathematical language of functions of real variables. When we moved on to GLAUBER, STAHL, and DALTON, we had to provide those programs with suitable representations for chemical equations. There had to be a way to represent chemical substances as well as the "before" and "after" states of chemical reactions. In addition, DALTON had to be supplied with representations for particles (atoms) and for parcels of such particles (molecules). In all these cases, the representations were simply made available to the programs; there was no question of their discovering them. Where do such representations originate? What can we say about processes for discovering or acquiring new representations? Before we try to answer these questions, we must undertake to define the concept of representation a little more carefully.

What Is a Representation?

By a representation we mean a scheme for holding information in a memory, combined with processes for operating on that information to access it, alter it, or draw inferences from it. To characterize a representation, it is essential that we describe both the memory organization and the operations that are easily and rapidly performed on it. For example, in BACON and the other programs we have examined, information is stored in memory in lists or structures of lists. If we were talking of a paper-and-pencil representation, it would be easy to say what we meant by "lists." We could arrange items in order down a page, so that sequence in the listing would correspond to the relation of *next* on the list. If our eyes are fixed on any item on the page, it is easy to scan down to the next item. With this representation, however, it is much less easy to insert new items in a list; we are compelled to write them between the lines or, if there is not room for that, to draw arrows from an item to the new item to be inserted immediately after it, and from that item to the next. Thus, paper, pencil, and eyes provide a good medium for representing and extracting information from relatively static lists, but they do not provide convenient machinery for continually and extensively modifying a list.

A list representation can also be used with a computer. Here, adjacent items on a list are not usually stored in adjacent physical locations. Instead, with each item is stored the address of the item that is next on the list. Now a list can be scanned by following these "pointers"—a relatively simple and speedy computer operation. Moreover, a new item can be inserted in a list by storing it in an arbitrary location and changing the pointers appropriately. If we wish to insert *C* between *A* and *B*, we simply change the pointer address stored with *A* from the address of *B* to the address of *C*, and store with *C* the address of *B*.

As we proceed, we will provide examples of a number of other kinds of representations besides lists. In each case, we will describe not only the symbol structures that are stored but also the main operations that can conveniently be performed on them. From a computational standpoint, two representations are equivalent only to the extent that the same information can be stored in them and extracted from them with the same ease. This point—the essential role of the basic operations in defining a representation—will become particularly important when we talk about imaginal representations and mental images. To use the metaphor "mental image" does not imply that there are literally pictures in the head (much less, that there is a little man there to look at them). It simply implies that the information is stored in such a way, and in association with operators of such a nature, that somewhat the same information can be held, and the same inferences drawn, as if there were an actual visual stimulus before the eyes, available for scanning.

Representation by List Structures

Representations undoubtedly develop incrementally, and their origins lie in the architecture of the human brain, which is adapted to capture and record the information with which the senses present it (pace Immanuel Kant). Hence, we begin by postulating the kinds of representation that are "wired in," or, if not wholly innate, develop through common everyday sensory experience, anticipating by many years the representation of anything we would call scientific knowledge.

Thus, we may assume in humans an initial capacity to represent objects, to associate properties with objects and relations with systems of objects, and to represent changes in such structures (e.g., changes in object properties or moves of a subobject from one location in an object to another). How can we represent these capacities in a computer simulation?

From the standpoint of computer simulation (and abstract brain architecture), the symbolic structures we call *list structures* and the *list processes* that operate on such structures provide very powerful and general machinery for representing objects, properties of objects, relations among objects, and changes in relational structures. It is this generic list-structure representation that lies at the foundation of BACON, GLAUBER, STAHL, and DALTON.

Suppose that a system already has some knowledge of a natural language (e.g., English), and that it has processes for extracting meanings from simple prose and representing such meanings by list structures and their associated processes. How would such a system build up a specific representation about a new kind of situation described to it? To make our discussion more concrete, we take as our example of such a system the UNDERSTAND program constructed by Hayes and Simon (1974), which is able to understand the instructions for simple, puzzle-like problems and to construct internal representations for such problems. We describe to this program the missionaries-and-cannibals puzzle mentioned in chapter 1. UNDERSTAND proceeds by noticing that nouns—missionary, cannibal, bank, boat—are used to designate various types of objects. It notices that missionaries, cannibals, and the boat are associated with one or the other bank of the river, and that missionaries and cannibals may be associated (as passengers) with the boat. It notices that certain properties of sets of missionaries and cannibals—their numbers—are important. It notices that associations can be altered by rowing a subset of missionaries and/or cannibals from one bank of the river to the other. Having extracted this information from the English prose, UNDERSTAND then begins to use its generic list-structure representation to build a specific problem representation. Nouns become names of lists; properties are associated with lists as values of attributes (e.g., if a list is stored in memory describing water, then color may be one of its attributes, whose value is blue); relations among objects become relations among lists; actions become processes for altering lists. Thus, a list of river banks is created in memory, its members being "left" and "right." With each bank is associated a list of its missionaries, a list of its cannibals, and its boat (if any). A move operator is created that deletes one or more missionaries and cannibals (but a total of not more than two) and the boat from the lists of one river bank and adds them to the lists of the other bank. A test operator is created that compares the numbers of missionaries and cannibals on each side of the river. All these entities are created by UNDERSTAND in direct response to the language of the problem (more strict, to its understanding of the language), and all make use of the small generic set of abstract representational capabilities that are already available to UNDERSTAND. If we are willing to admit that these generic capabilities are available *ab initio*, the question of where representations come from—at least these simple kinds of representations—is answered.

Now, the representations required for BACON, GLAUBER, and STAHL are no more complex—in fact, are simpler—than the representation required for the missionaries-and-cannibals puzzle. BACON calls for names and numerical values of variables. In the course of search, new variables are created. GLAUBER and STAHL call for names for substances and for patterns of reactions. Each reaction has a list of input substances and output substances. The principal actions are naming classes of substances that play similar roles in reactions (GLAUBER) and replacing substances in reactions (STAHL).

DALTON is slightly more complex. Here, a quantity (volume) is associated with each substance in each reaction. This quantity must correspond formally to the number of packets (molecules) of objects (atoms) also associated with the substance. The main operation is a test of whether the number of atoms of each species is preserved from the input side to the output side of the reaction. When it is not for some species, then the number of atoms per packet of that species is increased.

We can conjecture, although we cannot guarantee, that there would be no great difficulty in constructing a program that, if given a description of the problems with which any one of our four programs is confronted, would construct a specific representation appropriate for the program to act on. All the specific representations it would construct, however, would belong to the general class of list-structure representations. We will soon want to consider how such a representation-constructing program could also accommodate sentential representations (reasoning in terms of natural or formal languages) or geometric and pictorial representations (reasoning in terms of mental images).

What would be the design of a system that could accept inputs in the form of visual or auditory stimuli rather than natural-language text? Consider a system that has the generic capability of noticing objects in a visual scene, noticing properties of those objects and relations among them, and noticing modifications of the structures of objects and their relations. That program could proceed in just the same manner as UNDERSTAND to create an internal representation of the scene and of changes in it. A simple program of this kind named GRANIS (Coles 1972) uses a graphic-display system to analyze and construct an internal representation of geometric figures drawn on a screen with a light pen. The internal representation is a system of list structures of exactly the same kind as those we have been considering. GRANIS, which can accommodate not only simple polygons but also circuit diagrams and diagrams of chemical molecules, constitutes at least a primitive form of pictorial representation or imagery. It understands the pictures drawn for it sufficiently well to construct internal representations and then answer questions about their properties. Because it has a standard, generic representation for lines, and for configurations of lines that represent objects, GRANIS does not have to construct new representations for any of these in order to deal with particular task domains.

Sentential Representations

There is a view, held widely but not universally among researchers in artificial intelligence, that information is represented "in the head" or in the computer in the form of sentences stated in some natural or artificial language, and that inference processes are logical reasoning processes in this language. The first-order predicate calculus is often proposed as an ideal language for such a generic representation. This point of view is one of the bases for so-called logic programming, and for programming languages (e.g. PROLOG) that are used for this purpose.

The idea that scientists "think in words" or use logical formalisms explicitly is hotly contested by other researchers, and by most scientists who have examined and speculated about their own thought processes. For example, Hadamard (1945, pp. 75–76) has written: "I insist that words are totally absent from my mind when I really think and ... even after reading or hearing a question, every word disappears at the very moment I am beginning to think it over.... I think it also essential to emphasize that I behave in this way not only about words, but even about algebraic signs. I use them when dealing with easy calculations; but whenever the matter looks more difficult, they become too heavy a baggage for me. I use concrete representations, but of a quite different nature." The alternative representations to which Hadamard refers he later calls "images," but he describes them as "strange and cloudy" and not pictorial in any concrete or detailed sense.

We will return to the subject of images as generic representations. For the moment, we need only observe that different people may employ different representations in their thought, and that Hadamard's introspections, even if valid, do not foreclose the possibility that others use sentential representations (or that Hadamard himself does at levels not accessible to introspection).

Now, there is no particular incompatibility between sentential representations and list structures. A basic element of a list-structure representation is a relation $P(X, V)$, which may be read as "The value of property P of object X is V." All that needs to be added to attain the full expressiveness of the predicate calculus is some way of representing connectives and quantifiers, and this is easily provided within the list-structure representation. Why, then, do we not regard the latter representation as equivalent to the sentential? We do not because they are not *computationally* equivalent (Simon 1978); the operations that are easily and quickly performed on list structures (for example, moving a symbol from one list to another, or changing the value of a symbol on a list) are not the same as those that are quickly performed in the sentential representation (for example, constructing a new proposition that is a consequence by *modus ponens* of two previous ones). Hence, by experimenting with a person or a computing system to determine what operations can and what operations cannot be performed easily, we should be able to distinguish which of these two representations (if either) is being used to process information held in memory.

Although the representations used in BACON and its companion programs belong to the general class of list-structure representations, they are certainly not sentential; the operations performed by the productions that draw inferences bear little resemblance to the basic deductive operations of the predicate calculus. If there is any doubt of this, it can be settled quickly by undertaking to axiomatize the productions in terms of the predicate calculus. To do this, even the simplest productions—for example, those that exploit correlations between pairs of variables—would have to be replaced by large and complex sets of axioms.

"Pictorial" Representations

What is the relation of list-structure representations to the generic representations that might be regarded as "images" or "pictures"? The question is not easy to answer, partly because images can take on many forms and can exist at many levels of abstraction. For example, the representation of the missionaries-and-cannibals puzzle given earlier in this chapter could be viewed as "pictorial." The geometry of real rivers and the physiognomies of real missionaries and cannibals are not preserved, but the basic spatial topology of the problem is; two river banks are represented as separate symbolic entities, and with these entities are associated symbols representing the objects (people, boats) that are located on those banks. Moreover, the basic operation is a "move" that symbolically takes a boatload of people from one bank to the other. Hence, although the picture is abstract, it has many of the characteristics of a picture, and it provides a model of the situation described.

On the other hand, only by a forced interpretation could this representation be viewed as sentential. We would have to interpret the list of missionaries on the left bank as equivalent to a sentence like "Missionaries A and B are on the left bank." But what is less plausible, we would have to interpret the move operator as an inference rule that allows the new distribution on the two banks to be inferred from the old one. If such an interpretation is allowed, then any representation can be regarded as "sentential," and the whole topic of representation dissolves into fog.

The STRIPS system (Fikes and Nilsson 1971) provides some further insight into the relation between sentential and pictorial representations. STRIPS was initially designed to do sentential reasoning, and it represents the missionaries-and-cannibals puzzle by a set of sentences asserting who is on which side of the river. It also has inferential capabilities for deriving new sentences from the given ones. However, to make *moves* in searching for a solution to the problem, it employs special *move operators* designed to modify a base set of sentences that defines the current state. This base set of sentences is equivalent to the set of list structures we used to describe the problem in our "pictorial" representation. Thus, STRIPS is a mixed representation with both sentential and pictorial capabilities, each of which is used where it is most efficient.

An important characteristic of a pictorial representation is that each component occupies a specific position and holds specific spatial relations with other components. If the representation uses list structures, each component can be labeled with its position. For many problems in physics that can be represented by diagrams, inferences are drawn from the relations among components that occupy the same region of the diagram. The new knowledge derived from these inferences can then be "propagated" to adjacent regions, where they permit new inferences to be drawn, and this process can be repeated until the problem is solved. Larkin and Simon (1985) have shown how the use of diagrams in this way in pendulum problems can greatly reduce the amount of search required to solve the problems. Knowledge of the force on one side of a pulley makes it possible to calculate the force on the other side and the total force supported by the pulley. The newly calculated forces can then be used to calculate the forces on other nearby ropes and pulleys.

It is easy to add directional and distance information, beyond the information literally visible to the eyes, to "pictorial" list-structure representations. GRANIS provides one example of how this can be done. For another example, a representation of a chessboard used by Simon and Barenfeld (1969) for research on chess positions incorporated 64 nodes to represent the 64 squares on the board. Each square was connected to adjacent squares by relations like NW, E, S, and so on, so that from a given square one could readily find the diagonal of squares that lay to its right and below it (i.e., southeast of it). Distance could be measured in terms of numbers of squares traversed.

If by "pictorial" we mean "having the metrical properties and the properties of continuity (or near-continuity) of drawings on paper," then list-structure representations appear to be inadequate. At a later point in this chapter, we will return to the subject of imagery and take a closer look at the nature of imaginal representations.

The Significance of Representation

Our fundamental task in distinguishing among representations is to find in what respects they are not computationally equivalent. Inferences that are drawn easily with the use of the operators associated with one representation may be drawn only with difficulty, or not at all, if the operators associated with another representation are used. We have provided some examples of this nonequivalence in our discussion of three broad genera of representations: list-structure, sentential, and pictorial. However, one can consider a much more elaborate taxonomy of representations than the one we have proposed thus far, for the operators available for use with a given representation are not fixed for all time but may be augmented and developed by learning. Among the operators, we must include all productions whose conditions consist of tests that can be applied to the represented situation and whose actions generate new information (i.e., make inferences) on the basis of the test results. To state the matter more simply: As a person becomes experienced in using the representation of, say, a chessboard, he or she acquires more and more ability to recognize significant features in any chess position that is seen or imaged, and to draw out the implications of these features for evaluating the situation and finding possible moves that would be appropriate. These recognition capabilities must be learned over a long period of interaction with chess positions; there is substantial evidence that a chess grandmaster may be able to recognize 50,000 or more such chess features in different positions.

We can postulate that with every field of expertise is associated one or more specific representations, with which are associated, in turn, numerous operators that permit the expert to extract from situations large amounts of information that is not available to novices (even novices who employ the same generic representation but do not have the same learned store of productions). Consider a simple example of such an elaboration, using as a starting point a very basic graphical or pictorial form of representation:

An automobile, B, moving at the constant speed of 28 feet per second, passes a stationary auto, A. Just at the moment it passes, A begins to move with a constant acceleration of 4 feet per second squared. How long does it take for A to overtake B, and how far have the autos gone at the time of overtaking?

To simplify the discussion of this example, suppose that paper and pencil are provided, so that the representation need not be held in the "mind's eye" but can be scanned visually. One graph we could draw (figure 10.1) would employ time as the abcissa and distance traveled as the ordinate. The trajectory of car B would be a straight line through the origin with a positive slope of 28 ft/sec. The trajectory of car A would be an upwardly curved line (a quadratic) with a positive slope starting at zero and increas-

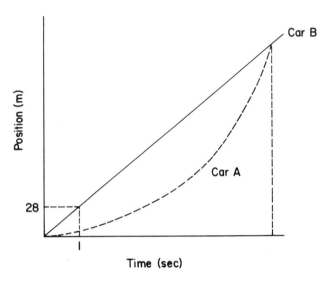

Figure 10.1

ing at 4 ft/sec². The time of overtaking is the time at the intersection of the two lines, and the distance is the ordinate of the intersection; however, visual inspection of the graph does not allow any easy conclusion to be drawn as to what that time and that distance are.

Consider an alternative graph (still a pictorial representation) in which the abscissa again represents time, but the ordinate represents speed (figure 10.2). On this graph, the trajectory of car B is a horizontal line at a height of 28 ft/sec. The trajectory of car A is now a straight line through the origin with a positive slope of 4 ft/sec². The two lines intersect when the cars are going at the same speed, and it is readily inferred that this time is 7 seconds. However, it is the areas under the two lines that represent the distances traversed. At the point of intersection, car A (the triangle) has gone only half as far as car B (the rectangle). If we extend the two lines an equal distance to the right, until $T = 14$ sec, we will notice immediately that the excess distance of car A in the second interval (the triangle above the rectangle in this interval) is exactly equal to the deficiency in the first interval. Hence, car A overtakes car B after 14 seconds. There are other ways in which the same conclusion could be reached by combinations of inspection of the diagram and calculation, but this particular path will serve to illustrate our point. The inference is not "made" by the diagram on

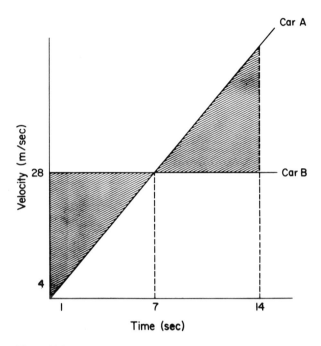

Figure 10.2

paper, but by the viewer (or the interpreter, in the case of the computer). And the viewer will not make it (as many human subjects do not) unless he or she *notices* the relevant features of the diagram—in particular, the areas under the trajectories—and is able to interpret these features in terms of the kinematics of the problem (that is, to interpret the areas as distances traversed). This is a learned ability—a part of the process of acquiring the productions that enable one to recognize and interpret relevant features and thereby to become an expert who is able to use this particular representation effectively.

The dependence of a person's ability to use a representation effectively upon learned capacities for recognition of cues is most simply illustrated by the effects of alphabets on reading skill. The written Serbian and Croatian languages are essentially identical, but the former is written in the Cyrillic alphabet and the latter in the Roman. Serbians can read Croatian newspapers and books only very slowly and with difficulty, and vice versa. Anyone who can read a language normally written in Cyrillic, Greek, Hebrew, Sanskrit, or ideographic Chinese or Japanese notation has encountered this difficulty when confronted with texts in one of these languages written in a Roman phonetization. All the necessary information is present in the representation; what is missing are the productions that recognize elements (words) in the unfamiliar representation and then access their semantic counterparts in memory.

Building Representations

A program worthy of being called COMPLEAT SCIENTIST would have to be capable of creating representations for the scientific problems it encountered. Our discussion thus far suggests that a capability for creating list-structure representations would go a long way toward satisfying this requirement, for, as we have seen, list structures can be used to represent in ways that we ordinarily would call pictorial.

There has been only a modest amount of work with programs capable of creating their own problem representations. The UNDERSTAND program described above characterizes pretty well the present state of knowledge on this subject. There are, of course, numerous programs possessed of a general representational format that can be applied to the representation of specific problems that fall within their domains. There has also been speculation, and a little experimentation (Larkin et al. 1985) on systems that are supplied with several different representations and that can use analogy to select one of these for representing a new problem when it is presented to the system.

Although the answer to the question of where representations come from is far from complete, a significant start has been made toward the design of systems that will be capable of constructing representations for scientific and other problems.

Imagery in Discovery

Even though, in our research on BACON, we have made no direct approach to the phenomena of visual imagery, we cannot conclude our analysis of the processes of scientific discovery without expanding a little further our discussion of that topic. Imagery is prominent in the literature of discovery,[4] and those who have emphasized its role would reject a model of discovery that did not employ imagery extensively in its thought processes.

---

4. For a discussion of imagery, see Miller 1984. A classical contribution to this topic is Hadamard 1945.

As we have seen, visual imagery uses a particular genus of representation, which we earlier called pictorial. We use the terms *pictorial* and *imaginal* to refer to an internal representation when the information it contains appears similar, and similarly organized, to the information in an external picture or diagram, and when the inferences that can be drawn from it rapidly and effortlessly are similar in kind to those that can be drawn immediately from a picture or diagram.

The Study of Visual Imagery

Visual imagery has been a troublesome topic in psychology because of the difficulty in obtaining objective evidence for its existence and character. The layman's source of evidence for imagery is introspection; seeing things in the "mind's eye" is a frequent experience in everyday life. But the evidence of introspection is warrantedly suspect, both for its subjectivity and for its vagueness. What we can mainly report about our mental images is that they are picture-like. To understand the part that visual images play in thinking, we need more information than that.

Contemporary cognitive psychology studies visual imagery by giving subjects tasks that call for such imagery, and ascertaining what kinds of information are available to the subjects from the images and how rapidly the information can be retrieved.[5] From such research we are beginning—but only beginning—to get an understanding of how images are used in thought. It is widely believed, and probable, that there are large differences among individuals in the uses of imagery, but we shall not consider these in the subsequent discussion.

We have argued that representations, including imagery, can be understood only in relation to the processes that operate on them to store, modify, or retrieve information. When we say that information is stored in a memory in lists, we mean that operators exist that, when an item of information is given, will quickly find the next item on the list, insert the item promptly in a list in memory, delete the item from a list, or perform rapidly other simple actions that depend on the associative structure of the memory. The list, or associative representation, involves storage in such a manner as to make these kinds of operations easy and fast.

5. Kosslyn 1981 is a major survey and analysis of research on imagery, containing a concrete and relatively detailed proposal for modeling the imaging mechanisms. The theory of the implementation of visual imagery in the human mind that we set forth in this subsection is generally consistent with Kosslyn's at the level of resolution of our discussion.

What is the corresponding characterization of memory in the form of imagery? We have already suggested the answer. Memory is imaginal when it can be used to extract promptly the same general kinds of information that could be extracted from an actual picture or diagram. For example, if we visualize a rectangle and then add its two diagonals, we can "see" at once that the two diagonals have an intersection at the center of the rectangle. This example is not conclusive, since it is so familiar that the information about the intersection might be remembered and not "seen." However, when more complex and less familiar situations are imaged, experience can hardly account for the rapidity with which inferences can then be made.

In what follows, we shall make much use of the analogy between mental images and drawings on paper, However, mental images, at their most complex, are far simpler than complex diagrams that can be drawn on paper and interpreted. The following example will illustrate the limits of human mental imagery. Consider a square, with sides one foot long and corners A, B, C, D. Around A as center, draw a circle with a radius of one foot; around the diagonally opposite corner, C, draw a circle with radius of $\frac{1}{2}$ foot. Do the two circles intersect? A drawing of the situation will show immediately that they do, and a simple calculation that the combined radii total $1\frac{1}{2}$ feet in length, while the diagonal is only 1.414 feet, will prove that such an intersection must exist. But can one *see* it without first confirming its existence by calculation or drawing? Some subjects say they can; others, probably a majority, say they cannot.

The "Flash of Insight"

In the literature on scientific discovery, mental imagery is frequently mentioned as playing two distinct roles. On the one hand, it is often claimed (by scientists and by historians of science) that scientists do their thinking not in words but in images. On the other hand, the claim is sometimes made that highly creative discoveries (Kekule's discovery of the structure of the benzene molecule is often cited in this connection) are produced through the unexpected and instantaneous experiencing of novel images not consciously constructed or motivated. These two claims are independent, or at least the first is independent of the second. The second has been the unwarranted source of a great deal of mysticism about the discovery process. In particular, the subconscious nature of the process is a red herring. All it actually implies (if it is true) is that this particular aspect of discovery is not available to the awareness of the discoverer, and hence that the discoverer cannot be a source of a reliable description of the process that produced the sudden image. It does not in any way imply that the process is fundamentally different from other processes of discovery—only that we must seek for other sources of evidence about its nature.

Because the evidence of "flash of insight" images is anecdotal and fragmentary, we will not try to explain them here. We will focus instead on the role of imaginal representations in everyday scientific thinking. Even here we will find as many research questions as answers.

Imagery and Inference

Although it is difficult to objectify the evidence, there is no reason to doubt the testimony of the many scientists who assert that they use imagery of some kind as a principal mode of thinking. Let us see how we can accommodate imagery in discovery systems. We have already alluded to this topic in our brief discussion of pictorial representations.

To fix our thoughts, we will begin with two-dimensional and three-dimensional representations with (some) metrical geometric properties. A representation may depict only the geometry of a situation, or this geometric representation may be elaborated to incorporate elements that are present solely in imagination. These elements may be processed by drawing them on paper, or simply by imaging them in the "mind's eye."

The evidence suggests that processing information in a drawing or a chart and processing it in the "mind's eye" have much in common. That is to say, the kinds of inferences that can be made readily in the two cases are highly similar. More information can be retained reliably in the display on paper than in the limited memory capacity of the "mind's eye," but this seems to be the principal difference between the two representations. In other respects they resemble each other closely—perhaps because they use exactly the same physiological mechanism to process the information once it is inside the head. However that may be, we will assume that, at least in first approximation, the processes for extracting information from mental images are much like the processes for extracting information from line drawings on paper. If this assumption is not literally correct, it at least provides a useful and roughly accurate analogy.

An Example from Chess

Let us begin with an example we have already introduced: a chessboard during a game of chess. This example is particularly informative, for it shows how a grandmaster can play chess "blindfolded"—that is, in the mind's eye and without sight of the board—with only a small loss in skill. When experts look at the chessboard or its mental image, they notice not only the configurations of pieces on it but also the important relations between pieces that attack or defend one another. The subjective experience (for the expert) of looking at the board or the image is one of perceiving "lines of force" emanating from and to pieces.

Now, these perceived chess relations are not literally visible, as the pieces are, yet they are almost palpably perceived by experienced players. The processing explanation, in terms of production systems, is straightforward: A familiar visible pattern—the shape of a bishop, say—evokes, as its action, the mental images of relations of attack and defense along the diagonals emanating from the bishop's position. (Bishops move only along diagonals.) These relations are simply adjoined to the image in the same way that we could draw them on a paper-and-pencil representation of the board. We can imagine the expert's perceptual mechanism containing a learned process such as

Bishop on square X → Add lines of attack along diagonals from X.

The expert player's representation of a position is best interpreted as containing these automatically evoked relations as well as the physically visible pieces. And the mechanism that thus enriches the representation can be the same one that operates when a person who has been told to image the diagonals of a quadrilateral "notices" that they have a point of intersection.

Some Examples from Simple Physics

The grandmaster's imagery may seem esoteric, but there are many commonplace parallels. Imagine two interlocking gears, one to the left of the other. Suppose, now, that the gear on the left rotates clockwise. One readily "sees" the gear on the right moving counterclockwise. Focusing on the cogs at the point of contact, one "sees" the cog of the gear on the left pressing downward on the cog that it touches, "forcing" the other gear to turn counterclockwise. Productions very like those postulated for the chessboard can add all this information to the mental picture of the gears.

As a second example (Larkin, personal communication), imagine a sensitive balance, from one arm of which is hung a piece of gold weighing 3 ounces and from the other arm of which is hung a piece of silver of the same weight. The two weights are lowered into a jar of water so that they are immersed without touching the bottom of the jar. Is the balance still in equilibrium? If not, which arm will descend: the one with the gold, or the one with the silver? A person who has well-developed visual imagery will "see" the two weights immersed in the water, and will image the silver weight, being less dense than the gold, as larger in volume. He or she may then "see" that a greater force of water is pushing up on the silver weight than on the gold one (to balance the displaced water), and that the gold weight therefore descends while the silver weight rises. Such a person may even "see" that the system will again be in equilibrium when the silver weight, at the surface, has a portion immersed that is just equal in volume to the total volume of the gold weight. There is a great intermingling here of inference with anything that can truly be called imaging. Since no actual gold and silver weights are present, the viewer must *construct* the latter to be larger than the former, on the basis of knowledge of their densities. Only after that construction step can it be "seen" that they are of different sizes. Similarly, a visualization of the differences in buoyant forces depends on an application of *knowledge* about the laws of buoyancy. The seeing would have to follow the knowing. This being the case, it may well be asked what function in the whole inference process is played by visualization, as distinct from knowing and sentential reasoning. Although no certain answer can be given to this question, a plausible interpretation is that the images serve to sum up and temporarily store the knowledge that is relevant to the problem, thereby reducing the strain on short-term memory. The mental picture of the two weights replaces propositional knowledge of their respective sizes. This picture is replaced, in turn, by the more schematic one of the larger net upward force on the silver weight pushing it toward the surface.

Further support for this interpretation comes from a problem sometimes posed as a challenge to students of physics (J. H. Larkin and C. Fisher, personal communication):

A monkey is trying to climb a rope that runs over a pulley and has a flour sack suspended from its other end. The monkey and the flour sack each weigh exactly 50 pounds. Can the monkey climb the rope?

Visualization provides little help toward answering this question until forces are added to the scene: the monkey's pull on the rope of $(50 + K)$ pounds, which, transmitted through the tension of the rope, creates a $(50 + K)$-pound upward pull on the flour sack. Now, subtracting the

50-pound gravitational pull on each against the $(50 + K)$-pound upward force, we find a net upward force on the monkey and the sack of K pounds each. This will produce an acceleration for each of $(K/50)g$. No matter what the value of K, or how it varies with time, the monkey and the sack will rise or fall together. By giving an initial impulse in excess of 50 pounds and then continuing to pull with a 50-pound force, the monkey can arrive at the pulley at the same time as the sack. Once the forces have been added to the diagram, "seeing" or inferring the consequences is relatively easy. When this step has been taken, even more difficult problems can be solved by most persons: What if the monkey weighs 50 pounds, but the sack only 30? Or, vice versa? The role of the diagram in this problem appears to be both to evoke productions that add essential information about the forces and to store this information.

Imagery in Electromagnetic Theory

Nineteenth-century physics provides a marvelous example of the development of visual imagery associated with the shift from action-at-a-distance models to field-theory representations of electromagnetism and other physical phenomena. Action at a distance, with an inverse-square law, can be envisioned in terms of the geometric relation between two bodies, one acting upon the other (or each exerting force on the other). The force exerted by a body is seen in three dimensions as gradually diffusing with distance, but in such a way as to conserve the total amount projected to the surface of the spherical boundary at each distance from the source.

Siméon Denis Poisson was apparently the first to add a potential function to this representation. This amounts to noting that the force at any point in space can be envisioned as the vector gradient of a scalar function at that point. (The gradient defines the direction and the steepness of the line of steepest descent.) Introducing the scalar potential function makes it possible to "see" the line integral of the force on a path between two points as the net change in potential between the points—the net gain or loss in altitude, so to speak.

Another component was added to the representation by Michael Faraday, who visualized the lines of magnetic and electrical force (made literally visible by iron filings in a magnetic field). William Thomson (Lord Kelvin) and James Clerk Maxwell took the representation further by converting the lines of force into "tubes of force" and showing that these could be viewed as filled with an incompressible liquid, the velocity of which at any point corresponded to the magnitude of the force. Where the tubes were crowded together, they were narrower in cross-section, and hence the liquid flowed more rapidly (for the force was greater); where they were sparse, they expanded to fill the space, and the liquid flowed more slowly (for the force was less). A necessary and sufficient condition that the tubes fill the space was that the force obeyed the inverse-square law. This analogy was developed beautifully by Maxwell, who showed that many of the basic laws of electricity and magnetism, and their consequences, could be imaged directly in this way without resort to equations, thus vindicating Faraday's "intuitive" (pictorial) theorizing.

Parallel to this growth of imagery there developed a calculus representation of the same phenomena, and experts became adept at working back and forth between the visual and the symbolic representation. The principal operators of the vector calculus (gradient, divergence, and curl) were all visualizable, as were the relations among line, surface, and volume integrals symbolized by Gauss's theorem, Green's theorem, Stokes's theorem and other theorems of the same type.

These developments were associated especially with Cambridge University mathematicians during the first half of the nineteenth century. It is interesting to compare the writing of Maxwell and William Thomson, both strong mathematicians who were in full command of the representations. Thomson makes only occasional reference to the geometric picture, preferring to describe the situations with formal mathematical symbols; Maxwell writes with equal fluency in the visual language of Faraday and the symbolic language of the calculus, frequently translating back and forth from the one to the other. A similar story of the interaction between visual images and equations could be told for the theory of relativity and its predecessors in the electron theories of Abraham, Lorentz, and others.

The study of the imaginal and mathematical representations used in these sophisticated domains of physics supports several conclusions about representations. First, there is not a constant stream of wholly novel representations that emerge as knowledge of a subject develops; rather, a very small number of basic representations (most of which have been available since antiquity) are gradually elaborated. Faraday, Maxwell, and their successors all operated with a representation of a three-dimensional Euclidean space and mathematical structures that permitted the description of functions in that space. Second, it follows that the main task of the scientist is not to invent representations to fit his problems, but to evoke, apply, and adapt representations with which he or she is already familiar. The process of adaptation consists primarily in devising new inference operators.

Representation of Motions

The ability to represent motion directly, either on paper or in mental imagery, is severely limited, and the need for it obviated by various devices. In the field theories we have been describing, the surrogate for motion in the representations is the path along which the motion takes place, positions along the path being parameterized by the times at which they are reached. Thus, the force fields of electrodynamics and steady-state currents are represented as the direction fields of systems of differential equations. This technique for representing motion implicitly has much earlier roots— for example, in Newton's *Principia*, where, in the basic development of the laws of the central-force model, time-parameterized paths are depicted in the diagrams. The very term "fluents" seems to derive from this representation.

An alternative way of envisioning time in the behavior of non-steady-state systems is to represent it in a spatial dimension, as in the example of the moving cars given in the preceding section. Time can be represented along the abscissa of the external or internal picture, and some other variable (distance or velocity, for example) along the ordinate. Now the pictorial representation has become a metaphor for relations among variables that are not spatial at all.

Imagery in Chemistry

There are a number of representations in chemistry that illustrate the flexible, almost Protean character of visual imagery. At one extreme is the literal pre-quantum-mechanics picture of the carbon atom, with symmetrical spherical angles of about $108°$ between its pairs of bonds. Similar geometric representations played an important role in the conceptualizing of the phenomena of polarization and stereometry. Nearer to the abstract end of the range are the familiar two-dimensional representations of organic molecules that depict the physical proximities and bondings of the component atoms. Experts who examine such diagrams can immediately "see" the loci of potential fracturing, replacement, and rearrangement. Their experience has provided them with productions that recognize features of the diagrams and augment them with knowledge of possible actions.

Another representation much used in chemistry is the one we have employed in DALTON. This representation accommodates time (as does the missionaries-and-cannibals representation) by dividing it into discrete steps, moves, or reactions. Laws of particle conservation are built into the "moves" that are visualized to carry one state into another.

The representations of chemistry, like the representations of physics, have ancient roots. Their components are more or less abstract representations of particles localized in space, with some of their relations with neighboring particles indicated. As in physics, progress in chemistry has required not the invention of wholly new representations but the modification and development of these basic models of ensembles of particles.

Implementation of Imagery

Earlier, we commented on the apparent inadequacy of list structures for handling complex imagery, especially imagery that involves continuous geometry. A major alternative representation that has been offered is a two-dimensional (or three-dimensional) raster of discrete points, like the array of discrete dots on a television screen. Though such a representation is not continuous, it can be refined to any desired level of resolution. A blackboard, after all, is not continuous either, nor are particles of chalk, yet chalk on a blackboard can be used successfully to represent straight lines and (most important) their intersections.

If each dot (pixel) on a raster is thought of not as a Euclidean point but as covering a small area, it can be guaranteed that line intersections will not be missed. The intersection between two lines will then simply be an area shared by both. Grids of this kind are often used, in combination with appropriate limiting techniques, in topology.

We do not want to insist on this or any other particular representation as a "true" description of human visualization of space. Rather, we wish merely to show that there exist plausible symbolic means for representing continuous geometric figures to a reasonable level of resolution.

Summary: Imagery

We have provided only a small and unsystematic sample of the numerous specific visual representations that are used in science. It is easy to think of counterparts of the ones we have described that are used in biology, geology, sociology, or neurophysiology. Visual images that depict the memories of information-processing systems as boxes and the symbol-transmission paths of the systems as links between the boxes are often employed.

We hope that our examples have shown the following.

• Mental imagery as a mode of thought can be explained in the same terms as any other kind of problem-solving representation: as a set of symbol structures on which certain operations can be performed to make explicit some of the information that is initially implicit. The operations, in the form of productions, constitute a substantial part of what must be learned in order to use a particular representation skillfully.

• It appears that, at most points in the history of science, scientists need not invent new representations to make their discoveries but can employ standard representations that are part of the common pool of knowledge and technique.

• New representations emerge as elaborations and particularizations of a few basic, generic representations, such as the propositional, the list-structure, and the pictorial representations. The elaboration takes the form of new tests for recognizing features, new actions (and especially new inference processes) associated with these tests, and new correlating definitions to specify the correspondence between features of the representation and features of the real world. These new productions are mainly limited to particular task domains.

Much remains to be done in building information-processing systems that are capable of inventing and elaborating representations, but the first steps have been taken in such programs as UNDERSTAND, AM, and EURISKO, and it seems relatively clear in what directions such construction can proceed. Progress in these directions would fill in one of the principal gaps in the theory of scientific discovery.

Conclusion

In this chapter we undertook to explore aspects of scientific discovery other than the extraction of scientific laws from data. We sought to show that the general approach, in terms of information processing, that provides mechanisms for discovering laws also can provide mechanisms for discovering new scientific problems, new instruments for scientific observation, and representations adapted to the inferential tasks that discovery entails.

Converting the mechanisms sketched in this chapter to the concreteness of running computer programs whose veridicality as components of a theory of discovery can be tested empirically and in detail is a beckoning target for continuing research in this area. Some of the scientific problems for such research have been posed. The requisite measuring instruments (including the computer) are available. The principal generic representations are known. All the ingredients are present to allow the work to proceed.

11 Envoi

The hypothesis with which we began our research was that scientific discovery can be explained as a form of problem solving; that its basic processes are "normal" problem-solving processes, adapted to the particular characteristics of the domain of discovery. We have described the evidence we have gathered to test this hypothesis, all of which seems to us to support it strongly. But we are quite aware that the evidence bears selectively on the various processes of discovery; some of them have been examined in detail, while others have only been discussed in a sketchy fashion. That is why, in our preface, we described this book as a progress report.

When we have lectured on some of the findings reported here, we have often been asked questions of the following kind: "You have given an interesting account of certain processes that occur in scientific research, but haven't you missed the real discovery process?" The form of the question is quite standard; only the content of what the questioner goes on to claim is the real discovery process varies. Our answer has two parts. First, the use of the definite article—"*the* real discovery process"—is ill advised. As we have emphasized throughout this book, there is no single unique process that accounts for scientific discovery. Discovery is the result of a complex web of activities. In particular, "the real discovery process" is not problem-finding or the identification of relevant data (the most common nominees). Both of these are important processes, and in chapter 10 we have tried to outline how they can be accomplished within the framework of information processing. However, they are only two among the many important processes involved in scientific discovery, and they are neither less nor more mysterious than the others. Second, we respond to the question of the particular content of the questioner's "real discovery process": Whether or not it is unique, haven't we ignored that process? A comparison of our taxonomy of processes of scientific discovery, set forth in chapter 1, with the topics that have been taken up subsequently will show that we have addressed all the processes contained in that taxonomy. Our analyses of some of the processes have been far less complete than one might desire— we do not pretend to have final answers. We have, however, said enough about each so that readers can judge for themselves the present state of the evidence.

But a lingering doubt may remain. What about the creative spark—the flash of genius, as the U.S. Supreme Court once described it in a patent case? What about those sudden insights—of Kekule, Poincaré, and others—that are so lovingly recounted in the histories of science? Can the processes we have postulated really explain the great discoveries that have produced scientific revolutions through major paradigm shifts? Such doubts will remain in some minds, and legitimately so, until the day when a program embodying normal problem-solving processes produces a major paradigm shift and initiates a scientific revolution. Of course, if the doubters are right, that day will never come. We see no urgency to settle the matter right now, nor do we think we have evidence of the kind just mentioned. However, we should like to make a few comments as to why we believe that no special processes need be postulated in order to account for sudden or major scientific discoveries—that is, why we think the theory we have built and the evidence we have accumulated can be extrapolated to the entire domain of scientific discovery, including the most important and the most impressive discoveries.

In chapter 2 we discussed Planck's discovery of the law of blackbody radiation and the consequent introduction of the quantum of action into the theory. The first part of that discovery—the discovery of the mathematical form of the law itself—was sudden, taking only a few hours at most, but thoroughly BACON-like in its sequence. This was truly data-driven discovery of exactly the kind we have investigated most thoroughly. No "creative spark" need be postulated, or any other processes beyond quite plausible heuristics for search. The second part of the discovery—the rationalization of the law in terms of classical physical mechanisms—also requires no special processes. Planck proceeded, over a period of two months, to work backward from the known result, modifying his previous derivation of Wien's law only at a few points where it had to be modified to "come out right." The modification depended on formulas in combinatorics, a topic with which Planck was already familiar. It is hard to see any sudden illumination in this part of the process, or anything besides extensive but selective heuristic search in spaces of appropriate (and available) representations.

It might be argued, and Kuhn (1978) appears to take a position of this sort, that the quantum was not really discovered in 1900—that until 1905, when Einstein and Ehrenfest pointed to the significance of the quantization that Planck had inadvertently introduced, there was no quantum theory. Even if that view were to be accepted, it would not make the case for sudden discovery via a unique creative process; it would simply add the processes that Einstein and Ehrenfest employed in 1905 to the sequence of events leading up to quantum theory.

Since the discovery of the law of blackbody radiation initiated one of the most fundamental scientific revolutions of all time, the absence of any appearance of abnormality in the processes that produced it provides strong evidence for the generality of our theory, and in particular for its applicability even to paradigm-shifting discoveries.

We would like to imagine that the great discoverers, the scientists whose behavior we are trying to understand, would be pleased with this interpretation of their activity as normal (albeit high-quality) human thinking. We would like to think that they would be happy to consider themselves and their behavior as an integral and lawful part of that great system of nature that they, and we, seek to understand. But science is concerned with the way the world is, not with how we would like it to be. So we must continue to try new experiments, to be guided by new evidence, in a heuristic search that is never finished but is always fascinating.

Bibliography

Amarel, S. 1972. Representation and modeling in problems of program formation. In B. Meltzer and D. Michie (eds.), *Machine Intelligence 6* (New York: Elsevier).

Anderson, J. R. 1976. *Language, Memory and Thought*. Hillsdale, N.J.: Erlbaum.

Anderson, J. R. 1977. Induction of augmented transition networks. *Cognitive Science* 1: 125–157.

Anderson, J. R. 1983. *The Architecture of Cognition*. Cambridge: Harvard University Press.

Anderson, J. R., P. J. Kline, and C. M. Beasley. 1979. A general learning theory and its application to schema abstraction. *Psychology of Learning and Motivation* 13: 277–318.

Anzai, Y., and H. A. Simon. 1979. The theory of learning by doing. *Psychological Review* 36: 124–140.

Arons, A. B. 1965. *Development of Concepts of Physics from the Rationalization of Mechanics to the First Theory of Atomic Structure*. Reading, Mass.: Addison-Wesley.

Avogadro, A. 1811. Essay on a manner of determining the relative masses of the elementary molecules of bodies, and the proportions in which they enter into these compounds. Translated from *Journal de Physique* 73: 58–76. In H. M. Leicester and H. S. Klickstein, *A Source Book in Chemistry, 1400–1900* (New York: McGraw-Hill, 1952).

Bacon, F. 1620. *The New Organon and Related Writings* (F. H. Anderson, ed.). New York: Liberal Arts Press, 1960.

Banet, L. 1966. Evolution of the Balmer Series. *American Journal of Physics* 34: 496–503.

Berthollet, M. 1788. Memoir on dephlogisticated marine acid. In *The Early History of Chlorine* [Alembic Club Reprints, no. 13 (London, 1897), pp. 11–31].

Black, J. 1756. Experiments upon magnesia alba, quicklime, and some other alkaline substances. In *Essays and Observations, Physical and Literary*. Edinburgh.

Boyle, R. 1662. *A Defense of the Doctrine Touching the Spring and Weight of Air*. Excerpts reprinted in W. F. Magie, *A Source Book in Physics* (New York: McGraw-Hill, 1935).

Bradshaw, G. L., P. Langley, and H. A. Simon. 1980. BACON 4: The discovery of intrinsic properties. In Proceedings of the Third National Conference of the Canadian Society for Computational Studies of Intelligence.

Brown, J. S. 1973. Steps toward automatic theory formation. In Proceedings of the Third International Joint Conference on Artificial Intelligence.

Buchanan, B. G. 1966. Logics of Scientific Discovery. AI Memo 47, Computer Science Department, Stanford University.

Buchanan, B. G., and T. M. Mitchell. 1978. Model-directed learning of production rules. In D. A. Waterman and F. Hayes-Roth (eds.), *Pattern-Directed Inference Systems* (New York: Academic).

Buchanan, B. G., G. L. Sutherland, and E. A. Feigenbaum. 1969. Heuristic DENDRAL: A program for generating explanatory processes in organic chemistry. In B. Meltzer and D. Michie (eds.), *Machine Intelligence 4* (New York: Elsevier).

Carnap, R. 1952. *The Continuum of Inductive Methods*. University of Chicago Press.

Cavendish, H. 1766. Three papers. *Philosophical Transactions* 56: 141–184.

Cavendish, H. 1784. Experiments on air. *Philosophical Transactions* 74: 119–153.

Cavendish, H. 1785. Experiments on air. *Philosophical Transactions* 74: 372–384.

Chase, W. G., and H. A. Simon. 1973. Perception in chess. *Cognitive Psychology* 4: 55–81. Reprinted in H. A. Simon, *Models of Thought* (New Haven: Yale University Press, 1979).

Chi, M. T., P. J. Feltovich, and R. Glaser. 1981. Categorization and representation of physics problems by experts and novices. *Cognitive Science* 5: 121–152.

Coles, L. S. 1972. Syntax directed interpretation of natural language. In H. A. Simon and L. Siklossy (eds.), *Representation and Meaning* (Englewood Cliffs: Prentice-Hall).

Corben, H. C., and S. DeBenedetti. 1954. The ultimate atom. *Scientific American* 191, no. 6: 88–92.

Dalton, J. 1808. *A New System of Chemical Philosophy*. London: Bickerstaff.

DeBenedetti, S. 1956. Mesonic atoms. *Scientific American* 195, no. 4: 93–102.

Doyle, J. 1979. A truth maintenance system. *Artificial Intelligence* 12: 231–272.

Earman, J. (ed.) 1983. *Testing Scientific Theories*. Minneapolis: University of Minnesota Press.

Emde, W., C. U. Habel, and C.-R. Rollinger. 1983. Discovery of the equator, or concept driven learning. In Proceedings of the Eighth International Joint Conference on Artificial Intelligence.

Everitt, B. 1980. *Cluster Analysis*. New York: Halsted.

Feigenbaum, E. A., and H. A. Simon. 1984. EPAM-like models of recognition and learning. *Cognitive Science* 8: 305–336.

Feigenbaum, E. A., B. Buchanan, and J. Lederberg. 1971. On generality and problem solving: A case study using the DENDRAL program. In B. Meltzer and D. Michie (eds.), *Machine Intelligence 6* (New York: Elsevier).

Feyerabend, P. K. 1970. Consolations for the specialist. In I. Lakatos and A. Musgrave (eds.), *Criticism and the Growth of Knowledge* (Cambridge University Press).

Fikes, R. E., and N. J. Nilsson. 1971. STRIPS: A new approach to the application of theorem proving to problem solving. *Artificial Intelligence* 2: 189–208.

Fisher, D. 1984. A Hierarchical Conceptual Clustering Algorithm. Technical report, Department of Information and Computer Science, University of California, Irvine.

Fleming, A. 1929. On the antibacterial action to cultures of a penicillium, with special reference to their use in the isolation of *B. influenzae*. *British Journal of Experimental Pathology* 10: 226–236.

Forgy, C. L., and J. McDermott. 1977. OPS, a domain independent production system language. In Proceedings of the Fifth International Joint Conference on Artificial Intelligence.

Gardner, M. 1969. Mathematical games. *Scientific American* 221, no. 5: 140–146.

Gay-Lussac, L. P. 1809. Memoir on the combination of gaseous substances with each other. English translation in H. M. Leicester and H. S. Klickstein, *A Source Book in Chemistry, 1400–1900* (New York: McGraw-Hill, 1952). Originally published in *Mémoires de la Societé d'Arcueil* 2: 207–234.

Gay-Lussac, L. P., and L. J. Thenard. 1808. Sur les metaux de la potasse et de la soude. *Annales de chimie* 66: 205–217.

Gay-Lussac, L. P., and L. J. Thenard. 1810. Observations. *Annales de chimie* 75: 290–316.

Gelernter, H. 1959. A note on syntactic symetry and the manipulation of formal systems by machine. *Information and Control* 2: 80–89.

Gerwin, D. G. 1974. Information processing, data inferences, and scientific generalization. *Behavioral Science* 19: 314–325.

Gingerich, O. 1975. The origins of Kepler's Third Law. In A. Beer and P. Beer (eds.), *Kepler: Four Hundred Years*. Oxford: Pergamon.

Glymour, C. 1980. *Theory and Evidence*. Princeton University Press.

Hadamard, J. 1945. *The Psychology of Invention in the Mathematical Field.* Princeton University Press.

Hanson, N. R. 1958. *Patterns of Discovery.* Cambridge University Press.

Hayes, J. R., and H. A. Simon. 1974. Understanding written problem instructions. In L. W. Gregg (ed.), *Knowledge and Cognition* (Potomac, Md.: Erlbaum).

Hayes-Roth, F., and J. McDermott. 1978. An interference matching technique for inducing abstractions. *Communications of the ACM* 21: 401–410.

Hempel, C. G. 1965. *Aspects of Scientific Explanation and Other Essays.* New York: Free Press.

Holmes, F. L. 1980. Hans Krebs and the discovery of the ornithine cycle. *Federation Proceedings* 39: 216–225. (Federation of American Societies for Experimental Biology)

Huesmann, L. R., and C. M. Cheng. 1973. A theory of mathematical functions. *Psychological Review* 80: 125–138.

Kahneman, D., P. Slovic, and A. Tversky (eds.). 1982. *Judgment under Uncertainty: Heuristics and Biases.* Cambridge University Press.

Kangro, H. (ed). 1972. *Planck's Original Papers in Quantum Physics.* New York: Wiley.

Kedrov, B. M. 1966–67. On the question of the psychology of scientific creativity. *Soviet Psychology* 5: 18–37.

Kirwin, R. 1789. *An Essay on Phlogiston and the Constitution of Acids.* London: J. Johnson.

Klahr, D., and I. Wallace. 1976. *Cognitive Development: An Information Processing View.* Hillsdale, N.J.: Erlbaum.

Klein, M. J. 1962. Max Planck and the beginnings of quantum theory. *Archive for History of Exact Sciences* 1: 459–479.

Koertge, N. A. 1969. A Study of Relations between Scientific Theories: A Test of the General Correspondence Principle. Doctoral dissertation, University of London.

Kosslyn, S. M. 1981. *Image and Mind.* Cambridge: Harvard University Press.

Kotovsky, K., and H. A. Simon. 1973. Empirical tests of a theory of human acquisition of concepts for sequential patterns. *Cognitive Psychology* 4: 339–424. Reprinted in H. A. Simon, *Models of Thought* (New Haven: Yale University Press, 1979).

Krajewski, W. 1977. *Correspondence Principle and Growth of Science.* Dordrecht: Reidel.

Kuhn, T. S. 1970a. Logic of discovery or psychology of research? In I. Lakatos and A. Musgrave (eds.), *Criticism and the Growth of Knowledge* (Cambridge University Press).

Kuhn, T. S. 1970b. *The Structure of Scientific Revolutions,* second edition. University of Chicago Press.

Kuhn, T. S. 1978. *Black-body Theory and the Quantum Discontinuity.* Oxford University Press.

Lakatos, I. 1970. Falsification and the methodology of scientific research programmes. In I. Lakatos and A. Musgrave (eds.), *Criticism and the Growth of Knowledge* (Cambridge University Press).

Langley, P. 1978. Bacon 1: A general discovery system. In Proceedings of the Second National Conference of the Canadian Society for Computational Studies.

Langley, P. 1979a. A production system model for the induction of mathematical functions. *Behavioral Science* 24: 121–139.

Langley, P. 1979b. Descriptive Discovery Processes: Experiments in Baconian Science. Doctoral dissertation, Carnegie-Mellon University.

Langley, P. 1979c. Rediscovering physics with BACON 3. In Proceedings of the International Joint Conference on Artificial Intelligence.

Langley, P. 1981. Data-driven discovery of physical laws. *Cognitive Science* 5: 31–54.

Langley, P. 1982. A model of early syntactic development. In Proceedings of the Twentieth Annual Conference of the Society for Computational Linguistics.

Langley, P., and J. G. Carbonell. 1984. Approaches to machine Learning. *Journal of the American Society for Information Science* 35: 306–316.

Langley, P., and R. Neches. 1981. R. PRISM User's Manual. Technical report, Department of Psychology, Carnegie-Mellon University.

Langley, P., and S. Ohlsson. 1984. Automated cognitive modeling. In Proceedings of the National Conference on Artificial Intelligence.

Langley, P., and S. R. Sage. 1984. Conceptual clustering as discrimination learning. In Proceedings of the Fifth Biennial Conference of the Canadian Society for Conceptual Studies of Intelligence.

Langley, P., G. L. Bradshaw, and H. A. Simon. 1981. BACON 5: The discovery of conservation laws. In Proceedings of the Seventh International Joint Conference on Artificial Intelligence.

Langley, P., J. Zytkow, H. A. Simon, and G. L. Bradshaw. 1983. Mechanisms for qualitative and quantitative discovery. In Proceedings of the International Machine Learning Workshop.

Langley, P., J. M. Zytkow, H. A. Simon, and G. L. Bradshaw. 1985. The search for regularity: Four aspects of scientific discovery. In R. D. Michalski et al. (eds.), *Machine Learning*, vol. 2 (Palo Alto: Tioga).

Larkin, J. H. 1983. Mechanisms of Effective Problem Presentation in Physics. Complex Information Processing Paper 434, Department of Psychology, Carnegie-Mellon University.

Larkin, J. H., and H. A. Simon. 1985. Why a Picture is Worth Ten Thousand Words. Technical report, Department of Psychology, Carnegie-Mellon University.

Larkin, J., J. McDermott, D. P. Simon, and H. A. Simon. 1980. Expert and novice performance in solving physics problems. *Science* 208: 1335–1342.

Larkin, J. H., F. Reif, J. Carbonell, and A. Gugliotta. 1985. FERMI: A Flexible Expert Reasoner with Multi-Domain Interfacing. Technical report, Department of Psychology, Carnegie-Mellon University.

Lavoisier, A. 1789. *Traite elementaire de chimie*. Paris: Chez Cuchet.

Laymon, R. 1983. Newton's demonstration of universal gravitation and philosophical theories of confirmation. In J. Earman (ed.), *Testing Scientific Theories* (Minneapolis: University of Minnesota Press).

Leicester, H. M., and H. S. Klickstein. 1952. *A Source Book in Chemistry, 1400–1900*. New York: McGraw-Hill.

Lenat, D. B. 1977. Automated theory formation in mathematics. In Proceedings of the Fifth International Joint Conference on Artificial Intelligence.

Lenat, D. B. 1983. EURISKO: A program that learns new heuristics and domain concepts. *Artificial Intelligence* 21: 61–98.

Lindsay, R., B. G. Buchanan, E. A. Feigenbaum, and J. Lederberg. 1980. DENDRAL. New York: McGraw-Hill.

McDermott, J. 1982. R1: A rule-based configurer of computer systems. *Artificial Intelligence* 19: 39–88.

Magie, W. F. 1935. *A Source Book in Physics*. New York: McGraw-Hill.

Mendel, G. 1865. Experiments in plant-hybridization (translation). In J. A. Peters (ed.), *Classic Papers in Genetics* (Englewood Cliffs, N.J.: Prentice-Hall).

Michalski, R. S., and R. E. Stepp. 1983. Learning from observation: Conceptual clustering. In R. S. Michalski et al. (eds.), *Machine Learning* (Palo Alto: Tioga).

Mill, J. S. 1843. *A System of Logic*. In *Collected Works*, vols. VII and VIII (University of Toronto Press and Routledge & Kegan Paul, 1963).

Miller, A. I. 1984. *Imagery in Scientific Thought*. Cambridge, Mass.: Birkhauser.

Mitchell, T. M. 1977. Version spaces: A candidate elimination approach to rule learning. In Proceedings of the Fifth International Joint Conference on Artificial Intelligence.

Mitchell, T. M. 1979. An analysis of generalization as a search problem. In Proceedings of the Sixth International Joint Conference on Artificial Intelligence.

Mitchell, T. M. 1982. Generalization as search. *Artificial Intelligence* 18: 203–226.

Musgrave, A. 1976. Why did oxygen supplant phlogiston? Research programmes in the chemical revolution. In C. Howson (ed.), *Method and Appraisal in the Physical Sciences* (Cambridge University Press).

Newell, A., and H. A. Simon. 1963. GPS, a program that simulates human thought. In E. A. Feigenbaum and J. Feldman (eds.), *Computers and Thought* (New York: McGraw-Hill).

Newell, A., and H. A. Simon. 1972. *Human Problem Solving*. Englewood Cliffs, N.J.: Prentice-Hall.

Newell, A., and H. A. Simon. 1976. Computer science as empirical inquiry: Symbols and search. *Communications of the ACM* 19: 113–126.

Newell, A., J. C. Shaw, and H. A. Simon. 1962. The processes of creative thinking. In H. E. Gruber et al. (eds.), *Contemporary Approaches to Creative Thinking* (New York: Atherton). Reprinted in H. A. Simon, *Models of Thought* (New Haven: Yale University Press, 1979).

Newton, I. 1686. *Sir Isaac Newton's Mathematical Principles of Natural Philosophy and His System of the World*. Berkeley: University of California Press, 1934.

Nickles, T. (ed.). 1978a. *Scientific Discovery, Logic, and Rationality*. Dordrecht: Reidel.

Nickles, T. (ed.). 1978b. *Scientific Discovery: Case Studies*. Dordrecht: Reidel.

Nilsson, N. 1980. *Principles of Artificial Intelligence*. Palo Alto: Tioga.

Partington, J. R. 1961–62. *A History of Chemistry*. London: Macmillan.

Popper, K. R. 1961. *The Logic of Scientific Discovery*. New York: Science Editions.

Priestly, J. 1774. *Experiments and Observations on Different Kinds of Air*. London: J. Johnson.

Scheele, C. W. 1786. On manganese, magnesium, or magnesia vitrariorum. In *The Chemical Essays of Charles-William Scheele* (London).

Siklossy, L. 1968. Natural Language Learning by Computer. Doctoral dissertation, Carnegie-Mellon University.

Simon, H. A. 1955. Prediction and hindsight as confirmatory evidence. *Philosophy of Science* 22: 227–230. Reprinted in H. A. Simon, *Models of Thought* (New Haven: Yale University Press, 1979).

Simon, H. A. 1966. Scientific discovery and the psychology of problem solving. In R. Colodny (ed.), *Mind and Cosmos* (University of Pittsburgh Press).

Simon, H. A. 1972. The heuristic compiler. In H. A. Simon and L. Silkossy, *Representation and Meaning* (Englewood Cliffs, N.J.: Prentice-Hall).

Simon, H. A. 1973a. Does scientific discovery have a logic? *Philosophy of Science* 40: 471–480. Reprinted in H. A. Simon, *Models of Discovery* (Dordrecht: Reidel, 1977).

Simon, H. A. 1973b. The structure of ill-structured problems. *Artificial Intelligence* 4: 181–201. Reprinted in H. A. Simon, *Models of Discovery* (Dordrecht: Reidel, 1977).

Simon, H. A. 1977. *Models of Discovery*. Dordrecht: Reidel.

Simon, H. A. 1978. On the forms of mental representation. In C. W. Savage (ed.), *Perception and Cognition: Issues in the Foundations of Psychology* (Minneapolis: University of Minnesota Press).

Simon, H. A. 1979. *Models of Thought*. New Haven: Yale University Press.

Simon, H. A. 1983. Fitness requirements for scientific theories. *British Journal for the Philosophy of Science* 34: 355–365.

Simon, H. A. 1985. Quantification of theoretical terms and the falsifiability of theories. *British Journal for the Philosophy of Science* 34: 291–298.

Simon, H. A., and M. Barenfeld. 1969. Information-processing analysis of perceptual processes in problem solving. *Psychological Review* 76: 473–483.

Simon, H. A., and G. J. Groen. 1973. Ramsey eliminability and the testability of scientific theories. *British Journal for the Philosophy of Science* 24: 367–380. Reprinted in H. A. Simon, *Models of Discovery* (Dordrecht: Reidel, 1977).

Simon, H. A., and K. Kotovsky. 1963. Human acquisition of concepts for sequential patterns. *Psychological Review* 70: 534–546. Reprinted in H. A. Simon, *Models of Thought* (New Haven: Yale University Press, 1979).

Simon, H. A., and G. Lea. 1974. Problem solving and rule induction: A unified view. In L. W. Gregg (ed.), *Knowledge and Cognition* (Potomac, Md.: Erlbaum). Reprinted in H. A. Simon, *Models of Thought* (New Haven: Yale University Press, 1979).

Stahl, G. E. 1730. *Philosophical Principles of Universal Chemistry*. London: Osborn & Longman.

Stallman, R. M., and G. J. Sussman. 1977. Forward reasoning and dependency-directed backtracking in the system for computer-aided circuits analysis. *Artificial Intelligence* 9: 135–196.

Stanley, W. M. 1935. Isolation of a crystalline protein possessing the properties of tobacco-mosaic virus. *Science* 81: 644–645.

Stefik, M. J. 1979. An examination of a frame-structured representation system. In Proceedings of the Sixth International Joint Conference on Artificial Intelligence.

Tuomela, R. 1973. *Theoretical Concepts*. New York: Springer-Verlag.

Waltz, D. 1975. Understanding line drawings of scenes with shadows. In P. H. Winston (ed.), *The Psychology of Computer Vision* (New York: McGraw-Hill).

Westfall, R. S. 1980. *Never at Rest: A Biography of Isaac Newton*. Cambridge University Press.

Whewell, W. 1847. *The Philosophy of Inductive Sciences*, second edition. London: John W. Parker.

Winston, P. H. 1975. Learning structural descriptions from examples. In P. H. Winston (ed.), *The Psychology of Computer Vision* (New York: McGraw-Hill).

Wolff, J. G. 1978. Grammar discovery as data compression. In Proceedings of the AISB/GB Conference on Artificial Intelligence.

Zytkow, J. M., and A. Lewenstam. 1982. Czy tlenowa teoria Lavoisiera byla lepsza od teorii flogistonowej? Przycznek do analizy rewolucji naukowej. [Was the Oxygen Theory of Lavoisier better than the Phlogiston Theory? A contribution to the analysis of the scientific revolution.] *Studia Filozoficzne* 9–10: 39–65.

Name Index

Subject Index